DATE DUE		
SEP 0 9 2004		
NOV 19 2004		

LAS POSITAS COLLEGE
LEARNING RESOURCE CENTER

3033 Collier Canyon Road
Livermore, CA   94550

JAPAN: Who Governs?

ALSO BY CHALMERS JOHNSON

BOOKS:

Peasant Nationalism and Communist Power: The Emergence of Revolutionary China, 1937–1945 (Stanford University Press, 1962)

An Instance of Treason: Ozaki Hotsumi and the Sorge Spy Ring (Stanford University Press, 1964; expanded ed., 1990)

Revolutionary Change (Little Brown, 1966; rev. ed., Stanford University Press, 1982)

Conspiracy at Matsukawa (University of California Press, 1972)

Autopsy on People's War (University of California Press, 1973)

Japan's Public Policy Companies (American Enterprise Institute, 1978)

MITI and the Japanese Miracle (Stanford University Press, 1982)

EDITOR AND CONTRIBUTOR:

Change in Communist Systems (Stanford University Press, 1970)

Ideology and Politics in Contemporary China (University of Washington Press, 1973)

The Industrial Policy Debate (Institute for Contemporary Studies, 1984)

Politics and Productivity: How Japan's Development Strategy Works (with Laura Tyson and John Zysman; Ballinger, 1989)

JAPAN: Who Governs?

The Rise of the Developmental State

CHALMERS JOHNSON

 W · W · Norton & Company · New York · London

The text of this book is composed in Sabon with the display set in Bernhard Bold
Condensed and Optima
Composition and manufacturing by the Haddon Craftsmen, Inc.
Book design by Jack Meserole.

Library of Congress Cataloging-in-Publication Data
Johnson, Chalmers A.
    Japan, who governs? : controversial issues in Japanese government
and foreign policy / by Chalmers Johnson.
        p.   cm.
    Includes index.
        1. Japan—Economic policy—1945–   2. Japan—Politics and
    government.   3. Japan—Foreign relations.   I. Title.
    HC462.9.J63   1995
    338.952—dc20   94-21477

ISBN 0-393-03739-8

W. W. Norton & Company, Inc., 500 Fifth Avenue, New York, N.Y. 10110
W. W. Norton & Company Ltd., 10 Coptic Street, London WC1A 1PU

1 2 3 4 5 6 7 8 9 0

Contents

Introduction

Americans are wary of state officials, or bureaucrats. Even when their own bureaucrats perform in an extraordinary way, as for example in the Manhattan Project during World War II or in maintaining a half-million troops in the Saudi Arabian desert during the Persian Gulf War, they seem to pick out and praise, primarily, an exemplary individual—a J. Robert Oppenheimer or a "Stormin' Norman" Schwarzkopf.

There are good reasons for these attitudes. The history and nature of federalism and structurally divided sovereignty in the United States have caused Americans to disregard the state. Most do not even understand the concept of the state, since the word is most commonly used to refer to something that in other countries would be called a province. I use the term "state" as a political scientist to refer to an institution of public power distinct from both ruler and ruled that performs functions such as defense, communications, lawmaking and law enforcement, and sometimes economic development that individuals, families, villages, or enterprises cannot perform for themselves but on which their continuing existence depends.

Even when the state's duties and services are unavoidable, Americans are distrustful and tend to view them as exceptional, referring, for example, to the dangers of the "military-industrial complex." Public service, including that in the armed forces, is highly valued only when it takes the form of heroism or personal sacrifice, not as a vocation. American elites normally circulate from the private sector into government, not the other way around. In part, these attitudes also reflect the legacies of democratic revolutions in England, the United States, and France against monarchical absolutism and the adversarial cultures these revolutions produced.

Japan, quite differently, has a non-adversarial political culture, and its state has for more than a century attracted the best, most highly educated talent available in the society. Since the so-called Meiji Restoration of 1868, which was actually the beginning of a state-led campaign of modernization from above, the Japanese state has always taken precedence over interests based on the economy, the society, or other private concerns. Japan's postwar achievement of national wealth second only to that of the United States (and in a much smaller territory, without natural resources, and with only half the population) is the result of state-society relations that are utterly different from what Anglo-American democracies think of as the norm.

Nonetheless, economic determinists of every stripe, from the prewar Marxists to contemporary American rational choice theorists, continue to try to force Japan into their particular frameworks, be it "bourgeois society" or the idea that all states are captured by the interests they are supposed to regulate. I argue that Japan is what I have called a "capitalist developmental state," and that it is distinct from either a socialist developmental state, of the sort seen in the formerly Leninist countries, or a capitalist regulatory state, as typified by the United States.

These issues remain intensely controversial, particularly among those who do not know much Japanese history and who have powerful interests at stake in maintaining that Japan is just another "free-enterprise" system. To argue, as I have done, that "the Cold War is over and Japan won," is dismaying to Americans who still enjoy thinking of themselves as a unipolar superpower, even if they have to borrow their money and technology from the Japanese. As I write these words, the Japanese economy is undergoing a persistent recession, primarily caused by public policies undertaken to discipline speculators and free riders, and also by the beginnings of a *planned* transition from a producer-oriented, high-growth economy to a consumer-oriented, headquarters economy for all of East Asia. Even in the depths of this recession, the Japanese have a government whose accounts are in the black, households that save close to one-fifth of their disposable income, schools that provide the labor force with skills that come only with a college degree in the United States, relatively inexpensive but adequate pension and health delivery systems, an unemployment rate half that of the United States or Germany, and high-tech industries that do not face conversion to non-military purposes. And yet, American commentary about this Japanese recession reveals a stridency and a paranoia that says more about the United States than about Japan. "Sayonara, Japan Inc." proclaims *Foreign Policy;* "Japan Hits the Wall" predicts *Fortune;* "Whatever Happened to Japan Inc.?" ask the editors of the *Wall Street Journal.*

None of the writers of these articles reads Japanese or has any long-term knowledge or experience of Japan. Each also tries to protect him- or herself by noting that nothing fatal has happened to the Japanese economy; Japan has merely reached a point where it is, at last, as comfortably and unthreateningly mismanaged as the United States. The writer for *Fortune* (November 1, 1993) refers to the Japanese "federal bureaucracy," and puts a reference to "federal agencies" in a quotation from a Japanese professor, thereby revealing that he does not know that Japan does not have a federal system, any more than France does.

All of these writers are projecting onto Japan what they have been taught in English-language economics textbooks. They select data from Japan (say, from the Tokyo Stock Exchange) and analyze what these would mean if they occurred in the context of American economic institutions. They are also keen to find signs that Japan is losing its competitive edge because of the "laws of economics"—meaning Western economic theory—since Japan is assuredly not losing its competitiveness because of anything its competitors are doing.

My own perspective on Japan is very different from that commonly found in the English-language economic press. Even though I first went to Japan and started studying the Japanese language in 1953 (as a U.S. Navy officer), for approximately the next twenty years after that I specialized in the study of Communist China and the Chinese language. From 1967 to 1972, during the height of the Vietnam War and the Chinese Cultural Revolution, I was chairman of the Center for Chinese Studies at the University of California, Berkeley. This is important because when, in the mid-1970s, I shifted to full-time professional research on the Japanese political economy, I approached Japan not from the point of view of American economic orthodoxy (although I also have a degree in economics) but from the perspective of Chinese economic development.

From the disasters of the commune movement and the Great Leap Forward of the late 1950s to the totalitarian nightmare of the Cultural Revolution, I concluded that no matter how insistent the need for social goal setting in a late-developing country, displacement of the market by a Leninist party simply did not work. From this perspective, the high-speed economic growth of postwar Japan offered major insights. There was no question that Japan's development was "plan-rational," that it was guided by the state in directions that the state wanted it to go. It was not purely "market-rational," as American ideology maintained it should be. At the same time it was outperforming both the plan-ideological economies of the Leninist world and the market-rational economies of the English-language textbooks. The Japanese capitalist developmental state seemed to have squared the socialist circle: it involved very high levels of social goal setting without the known consequences of communism. I thus turned to the study of Japan's economic guidance mechanism—its state economic officialdom—with genuine admiration for its achievements and a desire to uncover its secrets.

When I first arrived in Japan at the end of the Korean War, it was impossible to imagine that in only a few decades, half a lifetime, Japan would emerge as the world's richest big country in terms of per capita income. What I saw then as a naive American language student was poverty, labor strife, and incredibly hard work. In 1953, it never crossed my mind to study Japan for insights into new forms of capitalism. Like other foreigners I was drawn to aspects of Japanese aesthetics and philosophy, not to its political economy. It was only much later, in light of the Chinese revolution's going so wildly off the tracks during Mao's Cultural Revolution, that I turned to the study of the Japanese political economy. The results were two books, *Japan's Public Policy Companies* (1978) and MITI *and the Japanese Miracle: The Growth of Industrial Policy, 1925–1975* (1982), and many of the essays collected here.

In the late 1980s, as Japan's wealth and potential power began to influence the global balance of power, some officials of Japan's Ministry of Foreign Affairs concluded that their immediate interests would be better served if my writings were not taken seriously among my fellow countrymen. They therefore began a campaign to label me a "Japan-basher," and this campaign was enthusiastically taken up by some of their supporters in the United States. But this view was never uniform throughout the Japanese government, since my history of the Ministry of International Trade and Industry was translated by MITI itself and is still assigned to new officials to read. MITI remains understandably proud of its role in the Japanese economy, even if its bureaucrats, in dealing with English-speaking foreigners, have more or less gone silent on the history of industrial policy. Interestingly enough, they are not so bashful these days when they are invited to Moscow and other ex-Marxist capitals and asked to explain how Japan succeeded.

I am sometimes still labeled a "Japan-basher," but I do not regard this characterization as accurate. The intent of all my work, including the essays collected here, has been to display and analyze the different assumptions and intentions the Japanese bring to public life, compared to the Americans, and to uncover the likely consequences of these Japanese orientations.

The five essays grouped in Part I under Economics attempt to elucidate the role of the Japanese state in the economic life of Japan. *"La Serenissima* of the East" compares Japan to medieval Venice as an example of a "trading state," one that uses economic policies to achieve what other nations attempt to achieve through military means. This essay was written in 1984 for a conference convened by the Hebrew University of Jerusalem and was published in the journal of the Israel Oriental Society. It anticipates the seminal work of Richard Rosecrance, *The Rise of the Trading State* (1986).

The second essay, on "Social Values and the Theory of Late Economic Development in East Asia," was written in 1990 for a conference called by El Colegio de Mexico in Mexico City. It considers the nexus, if any, between religion and capitalism as propounded by many Western theorists; and it rejects a putative "creative Confucianism" as the East Asian equivalent of Weber's version of protestantism. Instead, this essay credits Japan's industrialization to a dictatorship of development, but one that utilizes market mechanisms to achieve its goals rather than displacing them, as in Leninist mobilization regimes.[1] I present a model of the Japanese developmental state under the rubric of the Meiji-Bismarckian pattern of development. The comparison with Venice and this essay leads logically to the third—the inescapability of the idea of comparative capitalism, just as the once-monolithic conception of communism broke down into different versions associated above all with Soviet and Chinese practices.

The fourth essay in the Economics section is the only one devoted to the trade deficits the United States has had with Japan since the late 1960s. This and the essay that follows it both raise the issue of "revisionism" and its influence on the Japanese-American bilateral relationship. "Revisionism" refers to my (as well as others') observation that Japan has a political economy different from that of the Anglo-American countries in terms of institutions, the role of the state, and the weight of economic nationalism. Most American academic economists maintain that the Anglo-American pattern is the orthodox norm that defines capitalism; hence Japan differs from this alleged norm, and those who point this out are said to be "revisionists."

These essays attempt to show why a policy of pressuring Japan to alter its economic system to make it look like the American system is doomed to fail. They also throw light on the intellectual and practical muddle identified by Robert Kuttner, who wrote that

> Orthodox trade theorists insist laissez-faire is the best route to economic growth. Confronted with the success of non-laissez-faire nations such as Japan and South Korea, they conclude that the resulting trade imbalance must reflect some U.S. failure, such as the budget deficit or not working hard enough. And if laissez-faire is the optimum, the only remedy for America is to keep setting a good example by not fighting back. Thus do our trading partners keep taking U.S. industry to the cleaners, with the complicity of our economic theorists.[2]

Part II addresses Japanese politics and bureaucratic government. The title essay, "Japan: Who Governs?", was published in 1975 in *The Journal of Japanese Studies*. It reflects my growing understanding that the American-written Japanese Constitution of 1947 does not describe the way the Japanese political system actually works and is, in fact, misleading as a guide to that subject. Article 41 says that "The Diet shall be the highest organ of state power, and shall be the sole law-making organ of the state"; but this stipulation is not only untrue, it also conflicts with the Japanese political culture inherited from Japan's century of defensive modernization. There is of course nothing very surprising about this. Japan has a history some 1,500 years older than that of its mentor during the Allied Occupation, and its state played an utterly different role in its initial industrialization than the state did in the United States. The postwar constitution brought about only a reform of Japanese government, not a revolution. My essay was designed to contribute to the empirical and inductive study of the Japanese political system, rather than the formal and deductive approach favored by much of the American Cold War establishment.

Who governs is Japan's elite state bureaucracy. It is recruited from the top ranks of the best law schools in the country; appointment is made on the basis of legally binding national examinations—the prime minister can appoint only about twenty ministers and agency chiefs—and is unaffected by election results. The bureaucracy drafts virtually all laws, ordinances, orders, regulations, and licenses that govern society. It also has extensive extra-legal powers of "administrative guidance" and is comparatively unrestrained in any way, both in theory and in practice, by the judicial system. To find a comparable official elite in the United States, one would have to turn to those who staffed the E-Ring of the Pentagon or the Central Intelligence Agency at the height of the Cold War.

As expected, such an elite has a major influence in society going well beyond its official functions. My essay on what these officials do when they leave office, that is, when they *amakudari* (descend from heaven), was the first in English to detail a pattern of circulation of elites that is the direct opposite from that of the United States. This pattern continues to the present day, as other essays in this collection document. The essay on the language of Japanese government and politics—*omote/ura*—further explores the pervasive influence of state officials in Japanese society. Again, this is what one would expect in light of the aristocratic and Confucian origins of the Japanese state, as distinct from the social and revolutionary origins of the American state.

Even though I documented the role that the Japanese state played in postwar economic development, I remained, like a good American civics student, certain that at some point the constitutional political system would come to life and begin to bring the state apparatus under its control. I thus joined, at least temporarily, the majority of American political scientists and journalists who work on Japan. They spend their time not studying the Japanese state itself but looking for candidates within the Japanese political system who, they hope, might one day assume political direction over the activities of the state. If they could find such a person or group, this would help confirm the American proposition that democratic politics inevitably conforms to the pluralist paradigm. In such a political system, as Philip Cerny points out, "a stable and efficient state consists of little more than a consensus on the rules of the game, a relatively neutral field in which a large universe of diverse and overlapping groups with different interests compete relatively peacefully for shares of power. In this context, the conception of the state as an autonomous structure or independent actor is essentially pathological—a distorting mirror at best, an authoritarian or even totalitarian aberration at worst."[3]

Some of the Japanese candidates proposed for the role of authorized political actor who "delegates" power to the state but also supervises its activities are the deliberation councils *(shingikai)*, organized by each ministry for public outreach purposes; the *zoku* Diet members (captive parliamentarians who work for both themselves and a ministry in the Diet); and the blue-ribbon "administrative reform" commissions that are created approximately every decade to check allegedly excessive bureaucratic power. Needless to say, while all this searching for democratic accountability is going on, the study of the Japanese state as it actually exists is neglected and even an elementary mapping does not exist in English.

My candidate for the democratic surrogate who would breathe life into the constitutional political system was former Prime Minister Tanaka Kakuei (in office as prime minister from July 1972 to December 1974). As the creator of a powerful political machine with at least the potential of dictating to the state, I expected Tanaka to lead Japan into a kind of Huey Long version of democracy. The essay included here on Tanaka deals with the basis of his power and his ultimate failure in one of the massive corruption scandals that have punctuated the Japanese parliamentary system since it was created in the 1890s.

I saw Tanaka as a tragic figure brought down by ex-bureaucrats in powerful political positions, and I intended to write a full-length political biography of him. I still intend to write something further about Tanaka, but I now see his career as exemplifying what I call the "structural corruption" of Japan's bureaucratic state rather than that of a lone ranger attempting to fight it.

The final essay in the section on Politics concerns the collapse of the Liberal Democratic Party (LDP) in the summer of 1993, after the end of the Cold War undermined its continued existence. Equally important to the general theme of this book is how the coalition regime that succeeded the LDP opened the way for an even greater dominance by the bureaucracy of Japanese politics than had existed under the LDP. Despite foreign hopes and expectations about post-LDP politics, the idea that Japan is about to become politically "more like us" remains misguided. Foreign nations that must deal with Japan still do not have an accurate and realistic understanding of how the Japanese government works.

The final part deals with Japan's international relations—with China, with its defense dilemma (it is damned if it defends itself and damned if it does not), and with the other nations of the Asia-Pacific region. These essays all concern the implications of Japan's having achieved great economic power combined with its comparative reluctance to assume commensurate political responsibilities—how this configuration arose and why it persists. The Japanese state was quite creative in living within the Cold War's constraints while also meeting external challenges such as those posed by the People's Republic of China, but great strains are now building up within the Asia-Pacific region as the old balance of power erodes.

One of my main purposes here is to refute the view that the Japanese state is incapable of grand strategy because it is not under the kind of democratic guidance prevalent in the West. It seems to me that in responding to the hegemonic actions and pretensions of the United States, to mainland China's success in consolidating its political revolution and becoming a nuclear power, and to the emergence of a class of emulators of its own economic achievements in Asia, Japan has displayed adept, undoctrinaire diplomacy. It has preserved the country's independence of action and vital national interests while also accommodating its American allies and communist adversaries. This is a squaring of the circle comparable to MITI's use of the market for high-speed economic growth. In this area, as in the area of economics, Japan remains an excellent place to study the overt and subtle functions of the state in open, democratic market societies.

In these essays, as in all my work on Japan, I have incurred many intellectual debts as well as receiving sometimes vital assistance. I would also like to note that the Japanese professors and institutions here acknowledged have remained positive centers of encouragement and support even after the attacks on me as a "Japan-basher" began. I am eternally grateful not just for the friendship of these scholars but also for their professional integrity in times of political and economic change.

My main thanks go to Professor Masumi Junnosuke, the leading chronicler of Japan's political system from the Restoration to the present, who has for more than thirty years aided me in innumerable ways in my research. Professor Akagi Suruki has also made a major contribution to my thinking through his works on the wartime organization of the Japanese state—the *Konoe shintaisei*—and its influence on its postwar successor. Two of Japan's most prominent China specialists, Nakajima Mineo and Tokuda Noriyuki, have been indispensable in drawing my attention to what was *tatemae* (pretense) and *honne* (reality) in Japanese politics, and also by their examples as writers on Asian affairs who do not bend their conclusions to fit the trends of the times. Two former students of both Professor Nakajima and me, Ijiri Hidenori and Nakamoto Yoshihiko, have helped by translating my works into Japanese and by persisting in their own research on the international relations of post–Cold War Asia. Mitsuta Akimasa, himself a former high-ranking official of the Ministry of Education, has been unerring as a guide to the norms of Japanese state officialdom and has helped me avoid some serious blunders.

The director and staff of the International House of Japan and its superb library, where several of these articles were written, have always been supportive of my research. Its leaders include Nagai Michio, Katō Mikio, Matsumoto Hiroshi, Tanami Tatsuya, and Koide Izumi. My most important helper over the years at both Berkeley and San Diego has been Yutani Eiji, whose skill in obtaining the important research materials on the Japanese political economy remains the best in the business. My indispensable intellectual companion in all these endeavors is Sheila K. Johnson, who is both a creative editor and a formidable social scientist in her own right.

All Japanese names in this book are given in the Japanese manner, surname followed by given name. Thus, to give one example, for Tanaka Kakuei, Tanaka is his family name and Kakuei is the name chosen by his parents. Errors of fact or translation and vagaries of interpretation are all to be charged to my account. The articles that were previously published have not been changed except to correct errors, to bring some series of data up to date, and to standardize usage of Japanese names.

C.J.
Cardiff, California
January 1995

I

ECONOMICS

1

La Serenissima of the East

Japan has probably been the focus of more comparative studies than any other contemporary major nation. It has been likened to Germany, Turkey, Russia, the United States and England, and its people seen as or contrasted with the Jews, the Chinese, the Koreans and "Westerners" in general. It is understood to be a conservative society, but its norms violate some of the most basic tenets of Western conservatism. It is a capitalist society in which private property rights are real, defensible in law and inheritable, but one that prefers much higher degrees of plan rationality in its economic policies than almost any other capitalist system. I myself have argued that Japan has come closer to squaring the circle—to achieving social goal setting while avoiding the main unintended consequences of socialism—than any other industrial economy among the historical cases.[1] It operates one of the most successful commercial systems on earth, but does so without the aid of, and often directly contrary to, what the Nobel Prize committee calls "economic science." It is a "modernized" society, but one that offers a challenge to modernization theory at almost every turn. It is today the most conceptually interesting and difficult case for students of comparative political economy, not least because of the fog that surrounds it generated by pundits, journalists, competitors and the Japanese themselves with their persistent attraction to the self-regarding ideology of *Ni-honjinron* (the science of the Japanese).

Let me try to penetrate this fog with a new comparison. The following comments refer not to Japan but to the Most Serene Venetian Republic, which was founded in A.D. 421 and whose constitution persisted unchanged for almost five centuries (from 1310 to 1796):

> For more than a thousand years Venice was something unique among the nations, half eastern, half western, half land, half sea, poised between Rome and Byzantium, between Christianity and Islam, one foot in Europe, the other paddling in the pearls of Asia. . . . Her vocation was commerce; her countryside was the sea; her tastes were voluptuous; her function was that of a bridge between east and west; her obsession was political stability; her consolation, when she needed it, was self-indulgence; and it is remarkable how closely her talents fitted her needs. . . . Venice was a sort of police state, except that instead of worshipping power, she was terrified of it, and refused it to any single one of her citizens; and by these means, at once fair and ferocious, she outlived her rivals, and preserved her republican independence until the very end of the eighteenth century. . . . [She existed] on the edge of the Pax Romana [but displayed a] sense of strange isolation, of separateness, which had made her for so many centuries unique in Europe. . . . She was the most expert and unscrupulous of money-makers, frankly dedicated to profit, even treating the Holy Wars as promising investments. . . . Venice in her hey-day has been described as "one vast joint-stock company for the exploitation of the east." . . . No enemy has ever succeeded in taking Venice by storm. . . . She was never loved. She was always the outsider, always envied, always suspected, always feared.[2]

It seems that there may have been another Japan in medieval Europe, one that only China can rival in longevity, one in which political and economic power were combined, one governed by an oligarchy, one in which the family took precedence over the individual, a republic but not a democracy, and one in which the informal rules of the game were more important than the constitution—a good translation of *condottiere* would be *kuromaku*.

There are many striking similarities between old Venice and contemporary Japan. Venice was surrounded by larger, more powerful states that often used Italy as a battlefield, but it survived and preserved its independence by successfully combining a preference for peaceful trade with a willingness to fight with all its resources to preserve its independence. Modern Japan has likewise normally preferred commerce and its wars have all had a commercial basis. Although the Japan of today has abandoned the second half of the goal from the Meiji era of *fukoku kyōhei* (rich country, strong military), no one who knows Japan well doubts that its leaders intend to secure its survival by whatever means necessary. During March 1982 Wakasugi Kazuo, director of the Trade Policy Bureau of Japan's Ministry of International Trade and Industry (MITI), stated to the press that if the United States and Western Europe resorted to anti-Japanese protectionist measures, Japan might be forced to join the communist bloc. A few days later the Ministry of Foreign Affairs attempted to soften this remark and took the unusual step of declaring that Wakasugi had spoken "imprudently," but it hardly needed to have bothered since no one in the West was surprised by or doubted the truth of Wakasugi's comment.[3] "The Venetians," writes Benjamin Ward, "with their unequalled economic intelligence system based on traders' and consuls' reports, were able to take advantage of the wide variation in grain prices in various parts of the Mediterranean as a normal part of their trading activity."[4] The modern equivalents of these reports are, of course, the telex systems of Mitsui Bussan, Mitsubishi Shōji and the Japan External Trade Organization (JETRO).

On an entirely different line of comparison, though the Venetians were religious, Venice's "political structure was never amenable to clerical intimidation."[5] *Veneziani, poi Cristiani* (Venetians first, then Christians) was the famous rallying cry. One of the leading Western scholars of Japanese religion is at pains to demonstrate the lively religious life of contemporary Japan, but he also adds that whereas 56 percent of Americans answered a 1976 Gallup poll question, "How important to you are your religious beliefs?" by saying, "Very important," only 12 percent of Japanese said so, the lowest percentage giving this response among all the nations surveyed.[6] Keeping ideology at arm's length is, of course, one of the secrets of the Venetian commercial state and of the Japanese developmental one, both of them placing nationalistic goals well ahead of spiritual ones, while tolerating a domestic ideology that stresses the greater spirituality of their people when compared with others.

Venice's ruling class and its "decision-making" processes are famous. (Not making decisions that do not have a commercial rationale is, of course, central to the longevity of such regimes.) Ward writes:

> During its half millennium and more of social stability, Venice was ruled by an oligarchy of some 200 families. The chief executive, the doge, was elected for life, but his children had no right to succession. . . . The great families were mostly engaged in trade. A typical successful career pattern would have a son engage in a number of trading voyages and then settle down in Venice to help run the family business from there. He would begin to serve on some of the less powerful governmental committees and gradually move into more serious involvement in affairs of state, perhaps leaving business affairs largely to other close relatives. When he reached the pinnacle, becoming either doge or member of the Council of Ten, he was a rich man in knowledge of both Venetian and world affairs. He was already an experienced executive, and he would have no doubt at least some experience of war, the times being what they were. And basic decisions would be taken on the basis of the collective judgment of at least a dozen men as worldly as himself. No other state could match this skill and judgment, and Venice reproduced it generation after generation for centuries.[7]

The parallels here are endless. Japan, like Venice, has few class divisions, so much so that Murakami has observed the relative inutility of the concept of class in Japan and the emergence of what he calls a "new middle mass" *(shin chūkan taishū).*[8] At the same time Japan has been ruled in modern times by an oligarchy, explicitly if not constitutionally in the Meiji era (the *genrō* plus the bureaucracy), implicitly in the late Shōwa era (LDP, bureaucracy and *zaikai,* sometimes joined by the press); and the possibilities of Caesarism or demagoguery have been heavily restricted by indirect election (perhaps four or five hundred electors for the party presidency—i.e., the prime ministership—until Ōhira's "reforms" expanded the number to a few million). Collective decision making by seasoned and commercially experienced hands is legendary: Japan's institutions for this purpose include the seniority ranking system (gerontocracy), a circulation of elites from government to business *(amakudari), keiretsu* (lineages) of businesses meeting together at Keidanren headquarters, official public-private deliberation councils *(shingikai),* and the high value put on the norms of consensus *(nemawashi)*.[9]

On the cultivation of successors Morris writes that, even today, "many Venetians seem to work their children very hard, loading them with homework, foreign languages, and mathematics, to sustain the family honor, or get them into universities."[10] The Japanologist need reply with only one word: *Tōdai* (Tokyo University), and all it signifies. Nearly 87,000 engineers graduated from Japanese universities in 1980, 46 percent of them electrical engineers, whereas the total figure for the United States, with twice its population, was 63,000.[11] The contemporary Japanese equivalent of the Venetian trading voyage is the posting abroad for two or three years of new members of the meritocracy in a branch office, university, JETRO office or legation.

There is no need to continue in this vein, and I do not want to overdraw the comparison. Venice and Japan are, of course, different: Venice was a city-state, Japan is a nation-state; Venice was much more open to minorities than Japan (the term as well as the first "ghetto" were both Venetian); Venice never experienced feudalism, Japan certainly did; Venice eventually declined because it allowed a separation of political and economic power (Napoleon's troops were transported into the city on Venetian boats), Japan did the same during the Pacific War but learned from the experience and recovered. There are two main lessons to be derived from the Venetian comparison: First, the Japanese case is neither unique, exceptional, purely culturally based, irrational, nor inherently unstable (the longevity of Venice demonstrates the last point). Second, policies that continuously urge the Japanese to do or be something that they are not are misconceived. If Japan poses problems for Western theory, then so much the worse for Western theory, particularly since Venice was indubitably a part of the Western heritage.

There is actually a good deal of debate about what kind of theory should be applied in trying to understand modern Japan and about the role of theory itself in the operations of the Japanese system. This is particularly true in discussions of the economy. Namiki Nobuyoshi, writer for the *Nihon Keizai* and former MITI official, opens his latest book with the comment that all contemporary economic thought leads up a blind alley when used as the basis of national policy and ends it with a list of "seven grave sins of modern economics" that have allegedly misled economic planners.[12] Namiki believes that the Japanese economy cannot be understood in economic terms.

Even more startling, one of Japan's leading academic economists, Komiya Ryūtarō, argues that "professional economists [are] almost non-existent in Japan" and that "the Japanese government does not hire professional economists."[13] He is referring to anyone who has acquired an advanced research degree in economics and is employed as an expert in economic analysis. Komiya sees nothing in Japan comparable to the Council of Economic Advisers attached to the American president's staff, and no Japanese officials equivalent to the Otto Ecksteins and Murray Weidenbaums who purvey econometric wisdom to the government of the United States. While he acknowledges the existence of *"kanchō* economists" in the Japanese government, he points out that most are not professionals: Kanamori Hisao (formerly of the Economic Planning Agency [EPA]) and Yoshino Toshihiko (formerly of the Bank of Japan) have law degrees; Ōkita Saburō (ex-EPA) had an engineering degree; Yoshitomi Masaru (EPA) has a liberal arts degree; and Shimomura Osamu (Ministry of Finance), Miyazaki Isamu (EPA), and Suzuki Yoshio (Bank of Japan) have undergraduate economics degrees. Only Yoshitomi received a formal education in economics at the graduate level. Komiya believes that the real influence of such men in Japan stems not from their technical expertise but from their good judgment, their ability to mobilize the staffs they supervise and their ties to political leaders.

Komiya deplores this situation, but it may in fact offer a clue to Japan's economic prowess. Ward is in Namiki's camp: "Much of the trouble that the American economy has been in for almost a decade now has been a consequence of excessive confidence in the products of the economist's art."[14] It is undeniable that since 1969, when the Riksbank of Sweden began to award Nobel prizes in economics, there has been a close correlation between the number of Americans receiving the award and the decline of the American economy. At the same time, no Nobel prize in economic science has ever been given to an economist working in a high-growth economy.[15]

What do these random observations on the influence of academic economics in various countries signify? First, modern

Japan's economic policy has certainly been constructed in accordance with and influenced by sound economic principles but these come from the industrial-policy, plan-rational, developmental school of economics and not from the economic-policy, market-rational, regulatory school that prevails in English-speaking countries. Second, the developmental imperatives of modern Japan, dictated by foreign imperialism, late development, a shortage of natural resources, a large population, the need to trade and balance-of-payments constraints, cannot be understood in purely economic terms but rather require a political-economy perspective. Third, the mystifications of the *Nihonjinron* school do not offer an effective alternative to the political-economy approach.

Let me consider the last point first. Despite Namiki's objections to modern economic theory, his substitution of *Nihonjinron* for it merely leads to the old cultural determinism: the Japanese behave like Japanese because they are Japanese. According to Namiki, Japan's superior economic performance is a direct result of the society's "flexible structure" *(jūkōzō)*, which in turn is a product of (1) Japan's special "intergroup dynamics," (2) middle-management control of enterprises, and (3) Confucian ethics.[16] By intergroup dynamics he means the intense competition within and among large Japanese organizations. He sees this as arising from the *iemoto* system and the process of individuation of samurai households away from the older *uji* (lineages), which date from the Kamakura *bakufu*. This is, of course, in accordance with (and probably derived from) the provocative book by Professors Murakami, Kumon and Satō, *Bunmei to shite no ie-shakai (The Ie-type Family Society as a Civilization)*.[17] Unquestionably, the emergence of more dynamic families from the older castes and clans was important for the appearance of entrepreneurship in Japan, but these factors can hardly be related to the system of high-speed economic growth that emerged after the war. Meanwhile, the *jūkōzō* may have contributed just as much to Japan's economic and political disasters over the past century as to its successes. Its only real analytical significance is to argue for the uniqueness and therefore incomparability of Japan, which is the central premise of *Nihonjinron*.

A political-economy approach leads us back to the study of

the history of economic institutions, to the role of contingency in their development and to the explicit influence of political goals on economic processes. One useful way to describe the interaction between politics and economics in modern Japan is in terms of the famous two tendencies that older Japanese Marxists perceived as deriving from the Meiji settlement, one absolutist and the other bourgeois. However, their belief that one tendency was dominant and the other subordinate is erroneous; they coexisted and interacted with each other to produce the high-growth system of the postwar world. Absolutism here refers to the "strong state" of modern Japan in terms of its meritocratic bureaucracy, its fostering of a weak parliament and its monopoly on priority setting. Bourgeois refers to the family-based commercial and industrial initiatives of Japan's modernizers and to the political culture they fostered (*zaibatsu-* and landlord-based political parties, urbanization and "enlightenment"). Both tendencies had their roots in the Tokugawa period and both were powerfully advanced by the Restoration.

W. G. Beasley has usefully summarized this line of analysis:

> It is tempting to [say] that conditions since 1945 have been such as to encourage the resumption of the country's progress towards a characteristically bourgeois society, that is, the course which was set by the Meiji reforms, but diverted in the 1930's by the moves towards war. This would be to designate the period from 1930 to 1945 as a kind of blind alley, leading off at a tangent from the main path of modern Japanese history, which was subsequently resumed. Clearly, the factors making for war before 1941 were as much the product of the Meiji settlement as bourgeois society itself has been. What we have in actuality to consider are variant paths of development from Meiji, which are not necessarily "main" and "subsidiary" ones. We must re-word the proposition so as to ascribe changes of direction to differences of emphasis within a complex continuity, not to intermittent acceptance or rejection of conflicting wholes.[18]

To take this argument one step further, the period of occupation was characterized not by the resumption of the bourgeois path but by the fusion of the two tendencies into one successful system: the state-guided capitalist developmental system, or, to put it in different terms, a plan-rational economy with market-rational political institutions. The genius of modern Japan, much like that of medieval Venice, has been the ability to fuse in an ad hoc manner the effectiveness of the absolutist state with the efficiency of the bourgeois market.

The apparatus of plan rationality, chiefly the economic bureaucracy, was greatly if unwittingly strengthened by the occupation reforms. The allied reformers destroyed the civilian bureaucracy's chief rival, the military; they transferred most of the control powers that had been shared with the *zaibatsu* to the state; they broke up the economic bureaucracy's chief civilian rival, the Ministry of Home Affairs; and, midway through the occupation, they made economic recovery rather than "democratization" their main goal as part of the West's renewed struggle against totalitarianism. At the same time they also created a hospitable political environment for the economic bureaucracy's activities. They rationalized the *zaibatsu* by centering them on banks and trading companies rather than on family holding companies, replaced the imperial institution with the Diet as the supreme ratifier of bureaucratic decisions, allowed Yoshida virtually to fuse the executive and legislative branches by making a bureaucratic career the most direct route to political power, and rectified through land reform the grievances of the farmers under the prewar system. The result was a much more effective developmental state than the early Shōwa version. At its heart was a covert separation between reigning and ruling—the politicians reign while the bureaucrats rule—and a method of stabilizing this division of labor through conservative political dominance, an elaborate circulation of elites and "old boy" networks within the oligarchy, and a relatively equitable distribution of the fruits of high-speed growth throughout the society. The old Venetians would have been impressed.

Notwithstanding the above, there is clearly a considerable degree of continuity between the earlier and later years of the Shōwa era. The year 1945 is not as great a watershed in Japanese institutional history as is sometimes supposed. More than anything else, the occupation provided the opportunity and means for the Japanese themselves to make some changes that were long overdue. When the allied reformers did innovate, the Japanese bureaucrats (through whom the reformers chose to work) subtly modified the new institutions in order to make them compatible with their own objectives (e.g., anti-monopoly legislation, disarmament.).

In my own work on MITI and the history of industrial policy, I have summarized the ingredients of the postwar high-growth system as follows: a combination of the early Shōwa legacy of cartellization and state control, the economic bureaucracy's rise to dominate policymaking, the emergence of a "pilot agency" or "economic general staff," the "Yoshida school" in politics, the open commercial system of the non-communist world contributed by the United States, and domestic popular mobilization in favor of economic growth (the "consumer revolution"). Rather than repeat the elaboration of that scheme here, I would like to explore another compatible formulation by one of Japan's leading economic historians, Nakamura Takafusa.

Nakamura sees two complex sets of causes—war and occupation—as having led to the merger during the early 1950s of what I have called the absolutist and bourgeois streams of development. In his view mobilization for and the actual fighting of a war contributed at least seven different Japanese institutional innovations that were salvaged after the defeat and then harnessed to the goal of *fukoku* (rich country), *kyōhei* (strong military) having proven to be a national dead end. The first of these institutional innovations was heavy and chemical industrialization—i.e., the shift from the first-stage, labor-intensive industrialization of the Meiji and Taishō eras to the greater value-added, second-stage, capital-intensive industrialization of high-growth Japan. Second, the wartime government successfully linked the two halves of the "dual economy" through the subcontracting system. Third, it rationalized the financial system by its authoritative designation of banks that were to serve particular munitions companies. Nakamura writes: "In the postwar reconstruction these [authoritative wartime] relationships were to appear and become entrenched in the form of the powerful financial groupings known as *keiretsu*."[19] Fourth, the wartime Bank of Japan's experience with economic controls "set the stage for such direct controls as Bank of Japan window guidance [i.e., capital rationing] in the postwar economy."[20]

Fifth, and of crucial importance even if scarcely understood outside of Japan, the war contributed the form that the postwar trade union movement would take. Nakamura observes,

The rapidity with which it was possible to form a large number of unions when the Occupation Army ordered their establishment is attributable to the fact that these organizations already existed. Japan's labor unions were formed and have continued up to the present as company, rather than trade, unions largely because these associations of the war years simply shed their old skins and continued their existence after the war ended.[21]

He is, of course, referring to the Patriotic Labor Associations *(Sangyō Hōkoku Kai* or *Sampō)* that the government inaugurated in 1938. The resulting enterprise unions gave Japan the tremendous competitive advantage of a labor force with no incentives to oppose technological innovation, even of a labor-saving type. This is clearly illustrated today by labor's toleration of industrial robots in many industries.

Sixth, in addition to enterprise unionism, the war also strengthened and entrenched the other two legs of the Japanese labor-relations tripod: the seniority wage system and the lifetime employment system. These institutions "first took shape during the depression following World War I, primarily in the heavy and chemical industries; but their expansion into a nationwide system was due to the implementation of wage controls in 1940–41."[22] The "three sacred treasures" (enterprise unionism, seniority wages and lifetime employment), as they have come to be known to Japanese managers, inhibited the development of a horizontal trade union movement by fragmenting workers into labor aristocrats with lifetime security, non-unionized temporaries (including women), and "frame-oriented" (Nakane's term) members of large enterprises in which seniority wages guarantee their loyalty. As a result, during the entire postwar period there were only four years (1946, 1948, 1951, 1952) in which the number of workdays lost to strikes per union member exceeded one day. These figures are much lower than those for the United States and Great Britain during the same period.

The three sacred treasures provide strong incentives for an enterprise to operate at close to full capacity (labor being a fixed cost, it should not be allowed to sit idle) and to innovate in order not to be left uncompetitive while still carrying the costs of its workers. More important, instead of the contractual relationships between management and labor that exist in the West, Japan has a *Gemeinschaft*-like situation in which both management and labor feel they have powerful stakes in the success of a business. Professor Minabe Shigeo, an academic economist, notes:

> Since Japanese workers enjoy lifetime employment, an in-house union, and other company benefits, they have special ties to the company. Thus, the worker often arrives a half hour before worktime, cleans up his workplace, and examines and lubricates his machines and tools. Occasionally workers take part in a general clean-up of the plant and yard. They plant trees and flowers and try to find other ways to make their working environment more pleasant. If an accident, such as a fire, occurs on the assembly line, the worker becomes a fireman or repairman. No matter what happens, the worker feels that it is *his* responsibility—*his* privilege—to take care of *his* workplace and *his* company. In a situation such as this, the question of extra pay never enters the worker's mind. This is *his* responsibility. Hence, these free labor services will add up to the profit margin of the company. In other countries where industry or craft unions are in control, the concept of free labor [i.e., unpaid overtime] is unthinkable. This is what makes Japan tick.[23]

According to Professor Minabe, such free labor can be rationalized as an insurance premium paid by the worker for his lifetime employment, but, belonging to the Nimiki school, he attributes its origin to childhood socialization practices. "Economists should note that there is no Phillips-curve relation in Japan [i.e., the allegedly inevitable trade-off between employment and inflation]. Too much time and effort has been wasted trying to apply Western academic techniques to the Japanese situation."[24]

Nakamura's historical/rationalist explanation seems to come closer to the truth. Yet, ironically, many Americans believe that it was *their* policies during the occupation that created the postwar Japanese labor movement. They explain its differences from the American labor movement by referring to *Nihonjinron;* for example, they read Musashi Miyamoto's 1645 classic, *Gorin-no-sho (The Book of the Five Rings),* for insights into Japanese management. Someone should tell them that in 1645 samurai did not engage in business of any kind and those who abandoned their swords for commerce usually went bankrupt.

Nakamura lists, as his seventh and last contribution of the war to the postwar economic effort, the food administration system of 1941. He contends that it reduced the old tenant farmer system to a shell well before the occupation's land reform and that "this was half the reason that the postwar land reform was able to progress so smoothly."[25]

Turning to the occupation, Nakamura has little to add to the standard list of reforms. He is most impressed by the reinvigoration of competition, which he attributes to the attempted breakup of the *zaibatsu*. In my view the sources of "excess competition" in postwar Japan are to be found in government policies that virtually eliminate the risks of business for *keiretsu* so long as they concentrate on the "strategic industries" designated by the government.[26] Nakamura seems to agree when he argues that MITI's policies during the 1950s and 1960s of restricting competition through cartels

> did not necessarily permit the immediate control of industries by oligopolistic firms. It meant no more than that firms were able to find some shelter during economic downturns; it never acted as a general restriction on competitive conditions in the markets formed after the war. On the contrary, secure in the knowledge that relief was available, firms adopted bold strategies and competition became all the more vigorous.[27]

In fact, so long as the risks of failure were reduced, a company had to compete fiercely for a market share, since that was the basis on which relief would be distributed in hard times. I agree with Nakamura that one result of rationalizing the *zaibatsu* was that aggressive competition tended to replace the standards of reliability and soundness as a major criterion of good management, since the interests of family ownership no longer prevailed. But the tremendous strengthening of competition in the postwar era was primarily a result of the convergence of interests between managers and the bureaucracy rather than the separation of management from ownership.

Nakamura divides the components of the high-growth system into those contributed by the international environment and those by domestic conditions. The former comprises, of course, the GATT-IMF fixed-exchange-rates system, together with the "alliance" with the United States. On the domestic side he lists as key elements government finance, special tax measures, the foreign exchange budgeting system and the importation of foreign technology. I prefer my own, more concrete listing: the two-tiered industrial finance system (government-guaranteed city bank overloaning and government-owned banks of last resort), the *keiretsuka* (grouping) of big business, the Fiscal Investment and Loan Plan *(zaisei tōyūshi)*, "industrial rationalization" (including industrial location policy), indicative planning (actually, government goal setting, in which the Economic Planning Agency functioned in essence as a propaganda organ), the creation of a global commercial intelligence service (JETRO), and the pro-growth, depoliticized tax system (including subsidization through non-standard "reserve funds," rapid amortization and targeted excises to help commercialize new products). The singlemindedness, ingenuity and undoctrinaire quality of this system must be recorded as perhaps Japan's greatest contribution to modern economics.

Although plan rationality and many of the institutions of the high-growth system still exist today, most have been "liberalized" or "internationalized." There is one major exception: the industrial finance component. This is, of course, not a single variable but a very complex "system" in its own right. The core elements include Bank of Japan guarantees to the privileged city banks, city bank overloans, investment-led growth, the maintenance of artificially low interest rates, overbalance in the General Account Budget until 1965 and a business cycle keyed to fluctuations in the international balance of payments.[28] One element that is usually omitted but that became crucially important during the 1970s was an undervalued yen. This was an important policy instrument of the Japanese government, since it made the price of Japanese goods competitive in world markets and made imports correspondingly more expensive and less attractive in the Japanese market. Nonetheless, this instrument was overused and got the Japanese into serious trouble.

During the late 1960s the Japanese government refused to raise the exchange rate of the yen (U.S. $ 1 = ¥ 360), which had been set back during the occupation to help Japan launch its recovery. This refusal was a mistake, perhaps the greatest policy error of the economic bureaucracy during high-speed growth. Japan's failure to revalue led to the second Nixon shock (on the 26th anniversary of Japan's surrender) and to the collapse of the Bretton Woods system that had supported Japanese exports for so long. The two main features of this system, which was conceived as a global currency mechanism to replace the international gold standard, were the substitution of the U.S. dollar for gold and fixed exchange rates. The system depended on the maintained economic vitality of the United States and on its willingness to have its currency used as the basis of global exchange. The system might have collapsed anyway as a result of America's simultaneous wars against poverty and the Vietnamese Communists, but the refusal of the Japanese to revalue their currency when the Germans had already done so twice—in 1961 and 1969—secured its demise. Had the Japanese revalued voluntarily, they probably could have done so for a lesser amount than was eventually forced on them, and they certainly could have avoided the severe inflation of 1973. Moreover, they lost the great advantage in planning and administration that fixed exchange rates afford.

The problem still exists today, when Japan is under attack for maintaining large trade surpluses with *all* its non-OPEC trading partners, even though the yen has allegedly been free to float since February 1973. Why? The answer must be found in Japan's relatively closed capital market and in another component of its financial system: artificially low interest rates. If the market were as open as the Ministry of Finance claims, there should be a rush to borrow from Japanese banks (given the cost of capital elsewhere), an outflow of funds, a rise in interest rates and a rise in the value of the yen. The fact that the Ministry of Finance has not allowed this to occur (through administrative guidance rather than its statutory powers) is not so much a matter of policy as the influence of vested interests created by the high-growth system. The ministry needs low interest rates in order to lower its costs in redeeming the deficits of Tanaka Kakuei's era and it needs a closed capital market in order to keep the funds of its record-breaking domestic savers from flowing abroad.[29] How the Japanese solve this problem will be of intense interest to the rest of the world, but one can be fairly certain that the *Serenissima* of the East does not intend wholly to open up this last bastion of protectionism. To do so would mean ending the structure of high household savings, tax incentives to save and the high-debt-versus-equity financing of industry that has made Japan comparatively rich.

This is only one of many problems that the Venice of the East faces today. Others include a pronounced weakness in the political system of the developmental state (too many party leaders are coming from non-mainstream backgrounds rather than from the Yoshida school of elite bureaucrats); a loss of credibility among its trading partners (prior to February 1982 there were officially no non-tariff barriers to trade with Japan, but then 67 of them were discovered and allegedly rectified); and serious delays in deciding what parts of the privileged agricultural sector can no longer be protected, an uncertainty that threatens the foundations of the political system.

More serious are the strident demands from those economies wounded by Japan that it share the military burdens of the informal trilateral alliance and that it share its wealth in order to help the development of other, poorer countries. Responding sincerely to such demands is no more in Japan's character than it was in medieval Venice's. It is easy to imagine that Japan will be forced to take some action in its own defense and that, as Kataoka Tetsuya has put it, it is merely "waiting for a Pearl Harbor" to convince its domestic public that such action is needed.[30] But it is highly unlikely that this development, when it comes, will be as pleasing to American leaders as they now seem to think. Venice used its arms in its own defense and only rented them to others who claimed to need them. Japan might supply some of its state-of-the-art technology to the United States in the interests of "common" defense (e.g., TDK's high-performance ferrite paint that absorbs radio waves and is crucial to the so-called Stealth aircraft, an airplane that can fly through radar waves undetected), but the price is likely to be high and the bargaining fierce. And Japan might simply decide to sell its military innovations to the highest bidder.

From a longer range perspective, I see no end to the kinds of complaints made by the president of the Canadian Chamber of Commerce in Japan:

> Too many Japanese see trade as a form of nationalistic competition—exports are a victory for Japanese ingenuity and diligence. Imports of manufactured products are too often seen as a defeat caused by some Japanese deficiency or disadvantage. The view of trade as a means of improving living standards through the international division of labor is far less prevalent in Japan than in the West. . . . Those trading company representatives who secure the supply of raw mate-

rials are "heroes." Those people who import finished products in competition with Japanese industry are practically traitors.[31]

The reasons for these attitudes are historical and "Venetian." Many Japanese remember the exploitative *shōkan* trade of the Meiji era when foreigners tried to keep them in line, and some think that the West tried to reestablish this trade in 1947.[32] There is an inherently nationalistic side to Japanese economic activities because of Japan's special history as the only Asian nation to avoid victimization by Western imperialism. Even as these memories fade, the Venetian imperative, the situational nationalism of Japan comes to the fore. Just as it found its own ecological niche on the edge of the Pax Americana after the Pacific War, it must find a new niche now that this dispensation has begun noticeably to wane. The possibilities of cooperation between the Western nations and Japan remain, but the ideology of trilateralism is probably self-deluding, and the new relationships will provide ample work for "special trade negotiators." Such a conclusion is not pessimistic, but merely what historical and comparative study suggests.

Venice has often been described as the "Shakespeare of cities," but Shakespeare himself contributed to the reputation of the city with his most disturbing play, *The Merchant of Venice*. The idea of Japan as the Venice of Asia is logical, historically plausible and ultimately attractive. It would be better to prize Japan for what it is than to continue to pressure it to be something else. At the same time it is in everybody's interest that Japan avoid acquiring a reputation, no matter how undeserved, as the Shylock of the East.

2

Social Values and the Theory of Late
Economic Development in East Asia

One of the critical requirements in the study of late twentieth-century political economy is to understand the sociopolitical forces that have fostered Japan's high-speed economic growth—and by extension that of its emulators in East Asia, the newly industrializing economies (NIES) of South Korea, Taiwan, Hong Kong, and Singapore. Since these forces are not obvious but are highly controversial, the analytical task is one of determining which theories apply to the Asian experience and which ones offer misleading comparisons. Many analysts, following a well-established school of English-language social thought, believe that the key to Asia's economic growth lies in the various societies' "traditional cultural values." In accordance with Western sociological theories that posit a connection between capitalism and religious values, they want to find a link between Asian religion and Asian capitalism. For example, Umehara Takeshi, director of the International Research Center for Japanese Studies in Kyoto, writes, "All the countries now making rapid economic progress, such as Korea, Taiwan, Singapore, and Japan, are countries which have been profoundly influenced by Confucian ideas. There is no doubt that the Confucian thought that exists, consciously or unconsciously, in the countries of East Asia, has had a helpful influence on their economic development."[1]

Here I believe Umehara and others of his persuasion go off the tracks. In my opinion they are trying to interpret the Asian cases using an inappropriate (and perhaps discredited) Western theory; and because of this theoretical inadequacy, they fail to identify the major political drawbacks and dilemmas that these societies face today. Umehara is, of course, in good company. Many others, including Kent Calder, Roderick McFarquhar, and Ronald Dore, follow him to one degree or another down the path first pioneered by Weber. They accept as fact Weber's theory that a link existed between Protestant religious values and the emergence of capitalism in the West, and hence they seek to find a similar link between the spirit of Asian capitalism and Asian religious values. I believe that such an approach is intellectually misguided and will generate wrong answers to questions concerning current economic and political problems that confront these societies. Before introducing the theory that I believe actually applies to the Asian cases, let me explain why I think the Weberian approach is a dead end.

There are problems with Weber's theory of the Protestant ethic and the spirit of capitalism both on its own terms and in light of high-speed economic growth in Asia under capitalist auspices but without Protestantism—a development that Weber did not foresee and explicitly predicted could not occur. The most logical response to Weber's theory and the contra-indicated developments in Asia would therefore be to reject the theory—to question whether there ever was any genuine connection between Protestantism and capitalism in the West since there assuredly was none in Asia. But the power of Weber's method and the influence he has had on English-language social science is such that this course is usually not followed. Instead it is argued that Asian capitalism differs because it rests on different religious values, or that Confucianism is the functional equivalent of Protestantism in providing the worldly but ascetic values that are alleged to be indispensable to capitalism. Dr. Kim Yoon Hyung of Korea, for example, adopts the first stratagem. "Because of this fundamental difference between Puritan and Confucian rationalism," he writes, "the state-guided capitalist economy, which was managed in an absolutely different spirit from Western capitalism (the free-enterprise system—that is, the competitive market economy founded on rational individualism and civil society), became well established in Japan, Korea, and Taiwan."[2] While I agree that the state-guided capitalist economies of Japan, Korea, and Taiwan differ in fundamental ways from the Anglo-American model, I see no reason at all to suppose that such differences are caused by religion.[3]

The likelihood that religion has nothing to do with economic development—in either the West or Asia—is reinforced by attempts to explain Asian economic dynamism in terms of "Confucian capitalism." Weber himself thought of Confucianism as an impassable obstacle to economic development and blamed China's economic backwardness on the influence of Confucianism.[4] Similarly, the Western quest to find an equivalent of Protestantism in Japan in order to accommodate the Meiji achievements to Western theory produced some interesting speculation on Tokugawa religion. But no one has even come close to finding in nineteenth-century Japanese the "mighty enthusiasm" that Weber posited.[5] One of the biggest problems of conceiving Confucius as the god of wealth is timing. In the West, the Protestant Reformation occurred about a century before the appearance of capitalism, thereby suggesting at least the possibility of a superficial correlation. In East Asia, Confucianism developed in the fifth century B.C.; thus it took two and a half millennia before it supposedly fostered any local capitalism. Even then one wonders what the role of Confucianism was, since it is opposed to and explicitly condemns all forms of mercantile activity.

I believe that Weber's contribution to social science theory has been seriously misunderstood. His theory is actually a philosophically idealistic reaction to Marx's materialism. He and Marx were arguing about whether values are independent or dependent variables in the explanation of social phenomena. To divorce Weber's position from this intellectual context tends to trivialize it and make it overly mechanical. Today very few serious historians hold the view that Protestantism had much to do with the emergence of Western capitalism. They are more interested in developments such as the forces that promoted investment in things other than land by the upper classes and vigorous investment by the other classes; the appearance of social mobility, national transportation networks, information flows, and the ending of social barriers to entrepreneurship; and checks on the arbitrary power of rulers and institutions, thus providing predictability and accountability in government.[6] Religion may promote or inhibit these developments, but many other factors are just as important, including scientific breakthroughs, discoveries of new territories, and innovations in military organization. Weber was concerned above all to show that values and similar forms of belief influence these kinds of developments as powerfully as material forces, and that, contrary to Marx, intellectual constructs could not be reduced to materialistic dynamics. Capitalism is not possible without the appropriate values, but there are many other sources of these values than religion. For example, in the Korean case some supporters of Weber nonetheless argue that "nationalism has become the prime motive propelling economic modernization since the 1960s."[7]

Most of the theorists who allege a link between Asian economic dynamism and "creative Confucianism" are actually not interested in Weber but have nationalistic, ideological, or journalistic motives. They want to explain Asia's competitiveness as due to primordial characteristics in order to get their own governments to protect them from it, or to cause the working people in Asian capitalist countries not to compare themselves with workers in other capitalist countries, or to find some new rallying cry for nationalism, or just to popularize very complex socioeconomic developments for readers of their newspapers. Influential examples of this type of writing include Herman Kahn, *World Economic Development* (Westview, 1979); Kim Il-gon, *Jukyo bunka-ken no chitsujo to keizai (Order and Economy in the Confucian Culture Area)* (Nagoya University, 1986); Roy Hofheinz and Kent Calder, *The Eastasia Edge* (Basic Books, 1982); Morishima Michio, *Why Has Japan "Succeeded"?* (Cambridge University, 1982); and Ronald Dore, *Taking Japan Seriously: A Confucian Perspective on Leading Economic Issues* (Stanford University, 1987).

In addition to these writers, there are others who have tried seriously to address the relationship between social values and economic activity. Winston Davis, for example, argues that virtually all applications of Weberian thought to Asian capitalism cannot get around the fallacy of post hoc ergo propter hoc: because industry in modern Asia developed after particular systems of religious values were in place, it developed because of them. "Unless the connection between values and development can be made explicit," Davis writes, "there seems to be no way to turn

Weberian speculation into defensible, testable, or falsifiable hypotheses. I would suggest that more attention be paid to the religious attitudes which appear while development is taking place." Davis is, in fact, the leading writer in English on the growth of new religions in Japan that help people manage the tensions of high-speed economic growth, and on the Japanese ideological use of religion to justify some of the inequities that economic development fosters.[8]

Albert Hirschman has also written a famous essay exploring the relationship between capitalism and social values and how theories of this relationship have changed over the course of capitalism's three centuries. He begins with the eighteenth-century thesis that capitalist relations of production civilized human society because they taught mutual benefit, the need to be prudent and reserved in order to obtain credit, and the virtues of frugality, punctuality, and probity. By the nineteenth century this view was replaced with a vision of capitalism as destructive of truly human values, leading not to civilization but to overindulgence, the cash nexus in all relationships, and alienation. The nineteenth century also inaugurated a new debate over whether capitalism had sufficiently penetrated society in order genuinely to supplant feudal values with bourgeois values. Many English-speaking observers concluded that what was wrong with Germany and Japan was that capitalism had not fully developed there and that these "late-developing" societies suffered from feudal survivals. At the same time in America, many social critics concluded that American bourgeois society was puerile and crass because it had no legacy of feudalism—as in Germany and Japan.

Perhaps Hirschman's most valuable insight in this essay is that neoclassical economic theory taken seriously leads to sociological nonsense. "Economists who wish the market well," writes Hirschman,

> have been *unable*, or rather have tied their own hands and denied themselves the opportunity, to exploit the argument about the integrative effects of markets [for society as a whole]. This is so because the argument cannot be made for the ideal market with perfect competition. The economists' claims of allocative efficiency and all-round welfare maximization are strictly valid only for this market. Involving large numbers of price-taking anonymous buyers and sell-

ers supplied with perfect information, such markets function without any prolonged human or social contact among the parties. Under perfect competition there is no room for bargaining, negotiation, remonstration or mutual adjustment, and the various operators that contract together need not enter into recurrent or continuing relationships as a result of which they would get to know each other well. . . . In this manner, [economists] have endeavored to endow the market with *economic* legitimacy. But, by the same token, they have sacrificed the *sociological* legitimacy that could rightfully have been claimed for the way, so unlike the perfect-competition model, most markets function in the real world.[9]

A sociologically valid theory of the market must therefore incorporate not just market principles and forces but also institutions, rules, histories, legal judgments, and cultural norms concerned with such things as gender, age, inheritance, and family obligations. This is the realm not of economic theory but of political economy.

In one sense the Japanese have built their economic system on a sociological rather than an economic theory of the market— one that recognizes the links and connections between manufacturers and consumers and tries to make the most of them. Thus, the Japanese system is filled with such institutions as *keiretsu* (developmental conglomerates), cross shareholding, cartels of all kinds, insider trading, bid rigging *(dangō),* linkages between banks and borrowers, and officially created trade associations. In short, the Japanese theory of the market rests on an assumption of the naturalness of oligopoly. By contrast the American theory of the market is to regard all contacts among buyers and sellers as forms of collusion and to promote a huge, often parasitic apparatus of anti-trust law and litigation.

Robert Bellah is another thoughtful writer on social values and economic activity. He is concerned with what happens to society when people actually attempt to create an approximation of the "ideal market with perfect competition." Following Tocqueville more than Weber, Bellah wants to identify as precisely as possible a "noneconomic normative order capable of supporting the extensive development of economic rationality."[10] Genuine economic rationality, Bellah holds, is relatively rare in human history because it is so destructive of all other forms of human relationships. It means subjecting all relationships to the test of efficiency—for example, if the shortest distance between two points happens to pass through a cemetery, economic rationality would dictate that society build its road through the cemetery. For people actually to tolerate periods of genuine economic rationality, they need some inner gyroscope that gives them a sense of orientation amidst continuous upheaval. Something like this developed in mid-nineteenth-century America, and *Democracy in America* was Tocqueville's analysis of the gyroscope that made it tolerable to Americans.

The Liberal Democratic Party in Japan has arguably been more of an economically rational party than a conservative one—the true conservatives were the progressive coalitions that ruled postwar Kyoto—but the nature of the Japanese gyroscope is not fully understood. It may be religion, but it may also be based on group loyalties, nationalism, the bonding effects of international competition for market share, such Japanese values as *gaman* (uncomplaining perseverance) so long as all do their share, and ideologies of physical and ethnic distinctiveness. Such popular Japanese fetishes as *Nihonjinron* (the theory of Japanese uniqueness) and racism may contribute to economic growth by persuading Japanese citizens to accept the personal, environmental, and political costs of their mercantilist industrial and trade policies. In other words, traditional social values can provide the raw materials for ideologists, whose intent is to keep the society docile and hardworking.

I hope that the discussion thus far has suggested that explanations of high-speed economic growth in East Asia cannot be reduced to religious values but that, at the same time, an effective managerial strategy for dealing with the societal consequences of economic growth is likely to be more political and social than economic. The theory that I contend more accurately addresses Asia's economic problems than Weberian sociology can best be introduced by another quotation of Albert Hirschman: the "underdeveloped countries as a group are set apart, through a number of economic characteristics common to them, from the advanced industrial countries and . . . traditional economic analysis, which has concentrated on the industrial countries, must therefore be recast in significant respects when dealing with underdeveloped countries."[11] What Hirschman has in mind is the theory of late economic development pioneered by writers such as Thorstein Veblen, Joseph Schumpeter, and Alexander Gerschenkron, a theory that is perhaps best represented today in the books of Alice Amsden and Jung-en Woo on Korea and Robert Wade on Taiwan.[12]

By "late development" all of these writers mean economic development following on and in response to the original beneficiaries of the industrial revolution—or, in the cases of Korea and Taiwan, late late development in response to the industrialization of Japan. Late developers—and the late late developers even more so—differ from the original developers in that socioeconomic factors such as the rise of a bourgeoisie, private investment, entrepreneurship, and even perhaps Protestantism were not as important as the conscious political decision to industrialize. Gerschenkron generalizes that the later the timing of development, other things being equal, the greater the importance of the state in economic affairs. While this point is obvious with regard to the Leninist cases, classical economists have tended not to recognize its applicability to the other successful late developers because they have overgeneralized the Anglo-American experience and because they know too little about Germany and Japan. The theory of late development referred to by Hirschman is addressed above all to the two great non-Leninist late developers—Germany after 1870 and Japan after 1868.

In second-round late development, such as occurred in Germany and Japan, a mobilization regime forces its economic priorities on a society that may not necessarily be recalcitrant but that, in any case, has not evolved the bourgeois mores that press for industrialization from below. The two fundamental types of such mobilization regimes are the Leninist-Stalinist totalitarian model and the Bismarckian-Meiji authoritarian one. Both involve social goal setting, forced saving, mercantilism, and bureaucratism. They differ in that the Leninist-Stalinist strategy relies on a socialist displacement of the market in order to establish its goals whereas the Bismarckian-Meiji pattern is based on market-conforming methods of social goal setting and utilizes the market to implement its goals. The communist-type command economy characteristically retains all ownership and control in the hands of the state, whereas the capitalist developmental state (CDS) rests on genuine private ownership of property but indirect state control of economic decisions. The CDS is infinitely more efficient than its communist rival but not as efficient as the ideal market economy with perfect competition. At the same time it is much more effective in achieving its societal goals than its purely market competitor.

The major sociopolitical problem of all high-speed economic growth is that it generates acute social and political instability. This is doubly so for the late developers because industrialization is occurring in advance of and not in response to social evolution. But even for the original beneficiaries of the industrial revolution, where it occurred at a slower pace and was welcomed by some important elements of society, industrialization led to serious instability, as described and analyzed by Marx and Engels. In these early cases the state became the institution not for leading industrialization itself but for intervening to alleviate the tensions and inequities that industrialization caused. Where it intervened successfully, the state thus headed off the revolutions that Marx and Engels predicted. And in the process these governments became "capitalist regulatory states."

Leninist and CDS regimes deal with the forced sacrifices and political instability caused by industrialization in characteristically different ways. The Leninist approach is cruder and simpler—and, as the events of 1989 and after throughout the communist world showed, less effective. The Leninists rely on a penetrative, totalitarian organizational weapon, the Communist Party, to preempt, channel, or suppress unwanted developments in the society. The elites of the CDS have a quite different problem. They must reconcile their state goals with the mass politics inherent in modernized, mobilized non-traditional societies with highly developed markets, private ownership of property, and large cities—i.e., sectors and locales in which a large measure of self-government and autonomy is the only feasible form of social organization. These regimes set the goals of the society in their elite state bureaucracies. But in order to implement these goals, they must enter the market and manipulate and structure it so that private citizens responding to incentives and disincentives make the market work for the state. I have coined the term "soft authoritarianism" to refer to the political arrangements through which the elites of the CDS attempt to implement their goals.[13]

The political solutions that late nineteenth-century German and Japanese elites came up with can be approximated in the following four-part model. First, at the center is a covert establishment that perpetuates itself through a conservative alliance among the minimally necessary interest groups. Second, the elite takes preemptive measures to forestall formation of mass movements that could interfere with its goals, above all the emergence of a unified labor movement. Third, the elite develops and propagates ideologies to convince the public that the social conditions in their country are the result of anything—culture, history, feudalism, national character, climate, and so forth—other than political decisions. Fourth, the elite undertakes diversionary activities that promote national pride but that also deflect attention from constitutional development. The most common such diversion, learned from Bismarck and the Meiji oligarchs, has been imperialism, but in the atomic age Olympic Games, imperial weddings, anti-Americanism, and revanchist movements (for Japan, the northern islands; for South Korea, North Korea; and for Taiwan, the Chinese mainland) may serve as substitutes. By far the most important substitute for imperialism in the postwar era has been export promotion and competition for market share.

At the heart of this model is the covert conservative alliance that keeps the elite establishment in power. In Bismarckian and Wilhelmine Germany, this included the two strongest economic interests in the country, the grain producers and heavy industry. The German alliance, like the creation of Japan's Liberal Democratic Party in 1955, was intended to wage an all-out attack on organized socialism and was underwritten by state subventions, tariffs, and protectionism. The chief unintended consequence of this arrangement was to stunt democratic development, which in turn provided fertile soil for the later development of fascism and militarism. Economic development in Germany and Japan produced economically capable but politically castrated bourgeoisies, which left the societies vulnerable to reactionary political movements. In the German case, Gordon Craig refers to "the whole miserable history of the German bourgeoisie, which had acquiesced in the powerlessness to which it had been reduced by its defeats in 1848 and 1866 and had compensated for its loss by combining an uncritical nationalism . . . with an idealization of private and cultural values *(Innerlichkeit)* which it used as an excuse for its lack of any sense of political responsibility."[14] The important pre-Nazi German historian Eckart Kehr labeled the resultant system "bourgeois-aristocratic neofeudalism," a term which could apply equally well to prewar Japan.[15]

In late Meiji Japan, after the promulgation of the Meiji Constitution, the conservative allies were the imperial household, the Meiji oligarchs, landowners, and the original *zaibatsu*. In the militarist era, after the seizure of Manchuria, the conservative allies were the imperial household, military leaders, the economic bureaucracy, and the new *zaibatsu*. In the era of high-speed growth, the conservative allies were the economic bureaucracy, the Liberal Democratic Party, and the leaders of big business. Since elections were now unavoidable, this last elite made the narrow interests of farmers and small retailers sacrosanct so long as they voted for the Liberal Democratic Party. Just as in Bismarck's famous alliance of "iron and rye," postwar Japan has rested on an alliance of rice and automobiles—or, in institutional terms, Nōkyō (the agricultural cooperatives), who voted for the LDP, and Keidanren (big business), who paid for it.

The key point here is the distinction between formal sovereignty—what the Japanese call *tatemae*—and concrete hegemony—what the Japanese call *honne*. The heart of soft authoritarianism is the concrete hegemony of a covert elite working within a formal system of legality and popular sovereignty. Such an elite can be extremely effective—as the modern histories of Germany, Japan, Korea, and Taiwan attest—but the attendant political underdevelopment can also be very costly in times of crisis.

It is obviously not my place to recommend either continued soft authoritarianism or further progress toward democracy for contemporary East Asia.[16] But I can perhaps outline the dangers inherent in either course. The danger of full democracy at this point is that it will not lead to political stability but merely reveal the great instability already created by industrialization thus far. Full democracy at this point in such countries as Korea and Taiwan might lead them simply to spin out of control. On the other hand, further democratization could improve the endemic corruption in such societies, their inability to change basic policies because of the resistance of entrenched interests, and their vulnerability to violent groups.

The liabilities of soft authoritarianism have already been made clear. Its strengths are that long-term developmental goals for the economy can be set; serious investment in education and research can be depoliticized; and people can come to see their government as legitimate for what it has accomplished rather than because of the formal political philosophy it expresses. If such countries as Taiwan and Korea choose to continue on this route, then they may want to take the postwar Japanese political system as a model but also as a guide to what to avoid. Following the Japanese course would involve expanding and consolidating the elites beyond the narrow confines of mainlanders, ex-military officers, and corporate directors, certainly to include the incipient bourgeoisie of the cities. It would also mean reinforcing the integrity of the elite through the circulation of its members much as Japan does with bureaucratic *amakudari* ("descent from heaven," i.e., early retirement and posting to the private sector). Overt repression, such as Korea perpetrated in May 1980 at Kwangju, must obviously be avoided.

The most important issue for the elites is to depoliticize the labor movements. One of Japan's major postwar achievements was, after 1960, meeting labor's demand for job security in return for labor's giving up any role in politics. Japan enjoys an unequaled comparative advantage in a labor force that is well educated, not exploited, and organized into company unions. Developmental elites elsewhere in Asia or in Latin America must decide what they want from labor—and then be willing to pay for it.

To take the case of South Korea, its elites are well positioned to employ the politics of diversion. The instability in the North and the possible collapse of communist legitimacy following the death of Kim Il-sung means that Korea's *Nordpolitik* is likely to be as diverting and as profitable as (former West) Germany's *Ostpolitik*. Further justification for elite guidance of Korea's development can be found in the need for very large financial reserves to pay for unification whenever it comes.

A compromise between democracy and soft authoritarianism might be found in a slow process of democratization using the Scandinavian countries as models. This would emphasize the further legal institutionalization of civil and property rights, a court system oriented toward administrative supervision of the bureaucracy and the enforcement of contracts, an up-to-date commercial code specifying the rights and obligations of buyers and sellers, and an accounting system that properly records and taxes values, gains, and losses. Such a course would be compatible with further economic development but would sacrifice a certain amount of direction over it and risk, as noted above, serious political instability.

However, in the long run, greater political instability may result from trying to maintain the current political status quo. The early industrializing states evolved—albeit painfully—in order to avoid the fate predicted for them by Marx and Engels (and many others). The capitalist developmental states may soon face similar internal challenges to their political and social norms. The maintenance of agricultural protection in Japan, for example, is increasingly opposed by many groups in the country as well as by its trading partners. How well the capitalist developmental states adapt to these and other international pressures will depend on the wisdom of their leaders and the degree to which ideological and other distractions lose their effectiveness with the people. Successful economic development from above does impart a degree of political legitimacy, but ultimately such legitimacy can only come from the consent of the governed. Delaying democratization is feasible for a while but not indefinitely. The underdevelopment of democracy in modern Germany and Japan provoked two world wars against one and one world war against the other. Both world wars were aimed at least in part in eradicating the still potent heritages of feudalism in each society. Such an outcome is the ultimate danger in the soft authoritarianism that is inherent in the CDS strategy. At the same time it is much more successful in actually delivering on economic development than its chief rival, Leninism.

3

Comparative Capitalism: The Japanese Difference

Apparently minor incidents or developments sometimes have a much greater impact than their own significance seems to warrant. For example, in revolutionary situations, such incidents sometimes make explicit conditions that have been ripening for a long time, and they appear to bring on the revolution itself. A small occurrence, of no great importance in itself, can serve to reveal the corruption or incapacity of an *ancien régime*. Something like this appears to have happened when President Clinton appointed Laura D'Andrea Tyson as head of the Council of Economic Advisers and the economics profession exploded into a fit of backbiting and ideological hysteria.

Paul Krugman of MIT, himself often touted as the leader of a new wave of economic theorists not mired in the rigidities of the past, spluttered that the Tyson appointment ignored the established "pecking order" in the profession. Robert Lawrence of Harvard commented that the choice must mean that Clinton intended to be his own economic adviser. After several of the profession's Nobel laureates complained that Tyson's appointment had been made without their approval, a standard, mainstream economist, Alan Blinder of Princeton, was named as her deputy.[1]

Laura Tyson is a well-known economist at the University of California, Berkeley, and was then the research director of its Berkeley Roundtable on the International Economy (BRIE). She,

John Zysman, and I jointly edited and contributed to a volume on the Japanese economy.[2] That the uproar over her appointment to chair the Council of Economic Advisers reflects resentment and fear over what she stands for became clear from a speech Paul Krugman made to the 1993 annual meeting of the American Economics Association, held during the period of the presidential transition in January 1993.

Krugman entitled his remarks "What Do Undergrads Need to Know About Trade?" a question that I agree is of central importance to the United States in a post–Cold War world. As a teacher of undergraduates, many of whom will not go on to study advanced economics, Krugman urged that they be given "a solid grounding in the principles of international trade." This is necessary not only because "international trade is now more important to the U.S. economy than it used to be," but also because students are independently reading such books as Lester Thurow's *Head to Head* and Michael Crichton's *Rising Sun* and "live in a time in which Americans are obsessed with international competition." According to Krugman, "The problem is that most of what a student is likely to read or hear about international economics is nonsense." "Our primary mission," he continues, "should be to vaccinate the minds of our undergraduates against the misconceptions that are so predominant in what passes for educated discussion about international trade."[3]

Among the nonsense that Krugman wants to extirpate are such ideas as the need to "forge a new partnership between government and business." He argues that "the ground-level view of businessmen is deeply uninformative," and their experiences in trade should therefore be discounted. Similarly, "students should learn that high productivity is beneficial, not because it helps a country to compete with other countries, but because it lets a country produce more and therefore consume more."

Unfortunately, although high domestic consumption may be considered desirable and the locomotive of economic growth in the United States, it is not universally so regarded. Like most other mainstream American economists, Krugman seems to be annoyed that the world is still organized into self-absorbed nation-states rather than constituting a single, equilibrated, economic system. Instead of approaching the world as it is, however, Krugman would like to define international competition out of existence. As I hope to make clear, the study of comparative capitalism indicates that several capitalist countries want to produce more not in order to consume more but to obtain leverage over other countries and to bolster their own national security and autonomy. From the point of view of international politics, this is as good a reason to increase productivity as for more consumption.

Krugman is equally opposed to the idea that it matters whether or not a particular economy generates high-value-added and therefore highly rewarded, interesting jobs. "Pop internationalists believe that international competition is a struggle over who gets the 'high value' sectors. . . . I think it should be possible to teach students why this is a silly concept." Fearful of letting the issue of jobs enter the discussion, Krugman lays down as a general rule, "Trade policy should be debated in terms of its impact on efficiency, not in terms of phony numbers about jobs created or lost."

Perhaps most important, Krugman wants to vaccinate young Americans against the idea that international trade competition involves winning and losing. "One of the most popular, enduring misconceptions of practical men," he writes, "is that countries are in competition with each other in the same way that companies in the same business are in competition. . . . An introductory economics course should drive home to students the point that international trade is not about competition, it is about mutually beneficial exchange."

It would be pleasant if this were true—if trade were indeed a "mutually beneficial exchange"—but in the real world it is more commonly about a lot of other things, such as the exchange of economic advantages for political favors, the open reaping of rewards for technological innovation, pay-offs to nations where vital resources are at stake and might be controlled by a Saddam Hussein or an Ayatollah Khomeini, and the creation of surpluses that can be used to pay for such things as scientific research, U.N. peacekeeping forces, and developmental assistance. Even the phrase "mutually beneficial exchange" needs to be deconstructed, since it often boils down to an ideological justification for the wealth of manufacturing nations and the poverty of resource-producing and agricultural nations. It is close to scholarly malpractice to say to students that trade is about mutually beneficial exchange without also telling them that it is rules and regimes negotiated by diplomats and lawyers that make it mutually beneficial—and then only some of the time. Most examples of trade that is mutually beneficial belong to the category of managed trade, including trade managed to control for environmental damage.

Japan and its emulators in East Asia, today including mainland China, are never mentioned by Krugman as being worth the attention of undergraduate economics students. To consider them would be to undercut his entire position and expose the fallacies in the economics that he advocates be taught. This is the reason why the economics profession opposes Laura Tyson. She happens to be interested in the economic successes of Japanese corporations that are not disciplined by either capital or labor markets. She believes in studying rather than denouncing Japanese industrial policy. And she is concerned about the challenge posed by systems that compete for market share rather than profitability, by what Thurow calls "producer economics," and by the strong state and what it can contribute to a market economy.

I, too, have been profoundly interested in these subjects and am concerned about what we shall be teaching the undergraduates of the future. I believe that the current debate within the English-speaking economics profession is one of the less anticipated developments caused by the end of the Cold War. Just as during the 1960s the Sino-Soviet dispute spawned the study of comparative communism, so the end of the Cold War has put comparative capitalism on the intellectual agenda. Well before the Berlin Wall came down and the former Soviet Union imploded, the Europeans had agreed to create a single market and the Americans and Canadians had formed a free trade area. These were early signs of things to come. The timing of both of these developments reflected the emergence of the Asia-Pacific region as the main center of global manufacturing, and the European and American responses were in an important sense initiatives to maintain or regain competitiveness for their areas.

This is not to say that the economic performances of Japan and its emulators went unnoticed earlier. Small libraries grew up devoted to "the art of Japanese management" and how "the Japanese company" worked, as well as identifying a "Pacific century" that was about to begin.[4] But until the end of the Cold War this kind of writing was not allowed to contaminate the mono-theistic pretensions of Anglo-American capitalism. During the Cold War, there was only one capitalist god and He lived in the United States, even though there was growing awareness of very promising national churches in Germany and Japan. Nonethe-less, German and Japanese economic achievements were said to be of interest only to area studies, and not proper subjects for the theorists of capitalism (or for the Nobel prizes awarded in "eco-nomic science").

Almost as soon as the Cold War came to its abrupt and unex-pected end, all this changed. There were now discovered to be at least two capitalist gods, one American and one Japanese; and writing about them took on major theoretical significance. Ger-many did not ascend to this level of debate because even though its capitalist institutions diverge from Anglo-American or-thodoxy—its labor unions are corporatist, its banks are more important than its capital markets, and it provides incentives for producers as well as consumers—it is less disruptive of the global capitalist system than Japan. German patterns of intraindustry trade are on a par with other industrialized countries; foreign investors own some 17 percent of German assets compared with 1 percent of Japan's; Germany has real political parties and a highly transparent political process; Germany has sought to come to grips with the nations it once victimized and today is deeply embedded in a multinational environment; Germany ab-sorbs refugees; and Germany is actively engaged in foreign aid to the former command economies of Eastern Europe. Germany is structurally different from American capitalism but it is not (yet) seen as threatening to the vested interests built up around the American model. Japan is another matter.

Throughout the long period of Cold War ideology, Japanese and American leaders scrupulously maintained that there was only one kind of capitalism and that they were both party to it. In this view, whatever differences may have existed between the two, the logic of the market was forcing convergence on both of them, as it was on all capitalist economies. The result of such a convergence would be an emphasis on consumer preferences, price competitiveness, and borderless economies. The obvious differences between Japan and the United States were explained away as either unimportant, temporary (for decades foreigners have been predicting imminent changes in Japan), or a matter of Japanese culture (the Japanese behave like Japanese because they are Japanese). This was the treatment accorded such important aspects of Japan's economic structure as *keiretsu,* unenforced antitrust laws, administratively guided banks, company unions, virtually nonexistent dividends for shareholders, and closed markets. Other aspects, such as Japan's record-setting trade surpluses, its zero-sum struggle to capture market share, and its seeming invulnerability to such events as a doubling of the value of its currency or a 60 percent slide in its stock exchange were explained away as due to macroeconomic imbalances, lazy workers in foreign economies, the lags of the so-called J-curve, Japan's need to pay for imported resources, and many, many other factors.

The reasons for this long obfuscation are not hard to find. American economic theory and Cold War strategy interacted to produce an environment of condescension toward and self-delusion about the Japanese economy. As Kenneth Pyle has written, "More than any other country, Japan was the beneficiary of the postwar international order. For more than a quarter of a century after the end of World War II, Japan operated in extraordinary and uniquely favorable political-economic circumstances."[5] As part of its competition with the Soviet Union, the United States traded economic concessions and access to its own markets for overseas basing rights, votes in the United Nations, and passive support of its war in Southeast Asia.

More important, the United States developed a radical version of the laissez-faire doctrine to oppose to Marxism-Leninism in the ideological dimension of the Cold War. This laissez-faire doctrine, of which Paul Krugman's presentation is standard, led many Americans to believe that it did not really matter whether some products were produced in the United States so long as they were produced somewhere in the capitalist camp—except, of course, for the products of the military industrial complex. The American military industrial complex was exempt from laissez-faire theory, so that by the end of the Cold War weaponry had become the most advanced industrial sector of the American economy, just as it was in the former Soviet Union.

The prominent economist C. Fred Bergsten acknowledges the

existence of comparative capitalism and then dismisses it. He writes, "We have three major economic powers that are much more alike than different—the United States, Europe, and Japan."[6] Some Western businessmen, fearing that their own inept management was about to be exposed, breathed a sigh of relief when during 1992 Japan's artificially inflated equities and real estate markets collapsed. One of Morgan Stanley's "global investment stategists" intoned, "The Japanese will now be more like us. . . . This is the end of an era in Japan—it is no longer a super country with a super economy. It is now another mature, developed industrial country, just like the United States, Germany, and France."[7] One might have thought that an investment strategist would have been interested in a system where stock dividends are less than 1 percent, compared to 3 to 4 percent on average in the West, and where the price of a company's shares relative to its earnings are several orders of magnitude higher than on any other stock exchange. These differences are indicators of major structural variations. Similarly, between 1986 and 1990 Japan's capital stock—plants, equipment, and office buildings—increased some 42 percent, compared with the 22 percent increase in the United States over the same period.[8] No other capitalist system made investments of that size during the late 1980s; Japan's ability to do so cries out for explanation.

It was not the neoclassical economists or the Japan-specializing social scientists of North America who brought this charade to an end. They were too busy defending their theories. Comparative capitalism is getting on the intellectual agenda because some Japanese economists have decided to come out of the closet, because the Japanese dispensers of foreign aid have begun to worry that their money will be wasted if it is turned over to institutions dominated by American economic doctrine, and because one very prominent Japanese industrialist noticed that Japan and the West were on a collision course.

Among the prominent Japanese economists who began to speak candidly about the Japanese economy is Hoshino Shinyasu, former vice minister of the Economic Planning Agency and currently president of the National Institute for Research Advancement (NIRA). In the spring of 1992, Hoshino was invited to Moscow to explain the postwar Japanese economic experience to the Russian Federation's Ministry of Economics. His distillation of the Japanese model included the following points: "The postwar Japanese approach was something close to a planned economy, not true capitalism but capitalism under strict control. . . . In this type of society [Japan, with only one ethnic group] non-transparent rules are accepted in the belief that their purport is understood implicitly. Non-transparent methods such as the Japanese government's administrative guidance would have been regarded as 'unfair' outside of Japan . . . and most likely could not function in the United States. . . . In the American model, emphasis is placed on the method of competition among equally powerful industries, while Japan has been emphasizing an industrial policy of shifting comparative advantage."[9]

An equally prominent academic economist, Professor Shimada Haruo of Keio University, writing in Japanese, argues that MITI's industrial policy "does not take the form of pure government control nor does it function as pure industry self-adjustment. . . . In a sense, it is similar to what takes place in a planned economy of a socialist country. . . . Japanese-type capitalist systems of this nature have heretofore never been subjected to a discussion involving a thorough identification and analysis of advantages and disadvantages."[10] Shimada is rather critical of the treatment of workers in the Japanese system, a view that he tends to moderate when writing in English.[11] On American capitalism, however, he is scathing, "It's been six years since the United States became a net debtor nation. The Americans seem to think that the problem is like a simple 'temporary virus,' but it may be a case of AIDS."[12] So much for Krugman's "mutually beneficial exchange."

The first complaints by the Japanese aid-giving authorities were so subtle that few Westerners noticed. At the 1991 Annual Meeting of the Board of Governors of the World Bank and the IMF, Mieno Yasushi, head of the Bank of Japan, said, "Experience in Asia has shown that although development strategies require a healthy respect for market mechanisms, the role of the government cannot be forgotten. I would like to see the World Bank and the IMF take the lead in a wide-ranging study that would define the theoretical underpinnings of this approach and clarify the areas in which it can be successfully applied to other parts of the globe."[13] Six months later the Japanese had become much more explicit. Kubota Isao, managing director of the Overseas Economic Cooperation Fund, the main foreign aid lending arm of the Japanese government, said of the World Bank's economists, "It's really incredible. They think their economic framework is perfect. I think they're wrong." Japan now favors giving governments a bigger role in developing their economies, on the postwar Japanese model, and dumping the laissez-faire approach championed by Washington.[14]

By far the most important confirmation of these structural differences came in an article in the February 1992 *Bungei shunju* by Morita Akio, chairman of Sony Corporation, vice-president of Keidanren, and co-author of *The Japan that Can Say "No."* It had a sensational impact in Japan, setting off a major controversy that continued the rest of the year. In response to complaints about Japan's adversarial trade by European friends of his, Morita wrote, "We are approaching a point where continued competition by Japanese companies operating under a management philosophy alien to that of Europeans and Americans can no longer be tolerated. . . . These differences of management philosophy are responsible for . . . creating a pricing structure that is impossible for Western companies to beat."[15] In a subsequent Keidanren forum on the furor he had set off, Morita added, "Western business managements typically sell their products at a price that will enable them to pay adequate dividends to their stockholders and good wages and holidays to their employees, and still retain a reasonable level of corporate earnings. With these generous policies, European and American companies, then, cannot compete with the low-profit, mass sales approach of Japanese companies. They claim that it is unfair for Japanese companies to enter their business domain with prices that are determined according to the market principles of Japan."[16]

I shall return to the "market principles of Japan" and detail some ways in which they differ from those of other capitalist economies. But let me begin by looking at Morita's suggestion that Western capitalists are more "generous" than their Japanese counterparts. In his original article, Morita advocated reform of the Japanese system by:

- supplying more vacations and shorter working hours to the labor force;

- paying salaries in accordance with people's work rather than seniority;
- paying dividends equal to those in Europe and America;
- improving relations with suppliers;
- making positive contributions to the community; and
- devoting more attention to environmental protection.

Morita is wrong in thinking that Western corporations do these things merely out of generosity. They are compelled to do them by the structure of incentives they face. Nonetheless, Morita's proposals so alarmed some Japanese, and struck others as so long overdue, that the ensuing debate produced real insights into the Japanese system.

During the spring and summer of 1992, all the major magazines in Japan ran reports of businessmen's symposia on Morita's charges and remedies. The magazine *Voice* published in Kyoto began its report with the comment, "The nations of Europe and the United States are becoming increasingly irritated because their trade deficits with Japan show no sign of improvement; they have begun to question whether it is because, basically, capitalism in Japan is not true capitalism."[17] Saji Keizo, chairman of Suntory, agreed with Morita: "In [our] postwar corporate society, it is unclear who owns a company and where responsibilities lie. . . . Because the starting point of capitalism is to treat capital with importance, a system that does not consider a fair return on capital to be important is wrong somewhere." On this same point, Ushio Jiro, chairman of Ushio, Inc., added, "In Japan's case the company belongs formally to the stockholders but in reality there is a strong sense in which it belongs to the employees." He thought that Japanese corporations were "employee syndicates." Even so, Japanese managers were not constrained in their policies by the interests or demands of either stockholders or employees.

The resultant autonomy of managers gives them the ability to concentrate on gaining market share in both domestic and international competition. Their tactic, repeatedly noted by Morita, is a deluge of high-quality, low-priced products intended to drive competitors out of business. The Japanese government has a term for this: "concentrated, torrential rain-type exports" *(shu-chu gou-teki yushutsu)*.[18] In the *Voice* symposium, Komatsu chairman Katada Tetsuya acknowledged that his company had used this strategy against Caterpillar but that it had had to pull back and let Caterpillar live because Komatsu is no longer welcome in foreign markets "regardless of how high our local procurement rate rises." What these businessmen did not discuss was why concentrated, torrential rain-type exports were a tactic open only to Japanese corporations and not to foreign ones.

In *Bungei shunju*'s symposium, Kawake Jiro, chairman of Oji Paper, defended Japan's low-profit orientation. "Japanese firms' profits are one-third to one-half those of U.S. firms . . . and dividend payout ratios are low. But this only means that Japanese managers take a long-term view of business growth and place emphasis on capital investment and retained earnings to preserve the interests of stockholders."[19] Whether this refusal to pursue short-term profits actually serves the interests of stockholders or not, it does undeniably result in "quality goods at low cost and in volume." Hashimoto Toru, president of the Fuji Bank, was less enthusiastic: "Fattening the company's profits at the expense of employees, clients, stockholders, and society is economic efficiency for its own sake. Only the company profits from it. . . . The Japanese company emphasizes only internal reserves and new investment in plant and equipment."[20]

When asked why these practices existed, many businessmen seemed baffled and fell back on cultural explanations. Asked why companies could not cut the long hours of employees and quit working them to death (so-called *karoshi*), Higuchi Kotaro, president of Asahi Breweries, replied, "We are troubled by the fact that we have many so-called company loyalists who won't go home at the prescribed time. . . . We hope to bring the hours down somehow to a prescribed level of less than 1,800 hours [per year]." All of this talk about company loyalists, torrential exports, and low profits greatly alarmed Kuroda Makoto, MITI's best known hard-line negotiator with the United States. "We must not provide a dangerous basis for the argument that says Japan conducts itself by a different set of rules and must be treated differently. . . . For some time I have repeatedly stated that we should avoid expressions such as 'Japanese-style practices.' "[21] Kuroda did not dispute anything Morita had said, but he did consider it deeply imprudent to discuss these matters in the public press.

Morita did not actually say anything new. Japan's restrictions on the rights of corporate owners and its transformation of workers into company nationalists have long been well-known to industrial sociologists specializing in the Japanese economy. Even former Singapore prime minister Lee Kuan Yew said in a summer 1992 interview that he welcomed "Akio Morita's thoughts on how Japan should do business" as a breath of fresh air, not as something he had never heard of before.[22] Morita's contributions were to draw attention to Japan's structural differences and to publicize them.

Some nine years earlier Matsumoto Koji, then an official of the Business Behavior Section of MITI's Industrial Policy Bureau, wrote one of Japan's most important analyses of these issues in a book entitled *Kigyo-shugi no koryu (The Rise of the Japanese Corporate System).*[23] Matsumoto begins his book with the premise that "Japan's economy has greatly outclassed that of every other nation," a view that few serious observers would any longer dispute. But what is Japan's secret? Not culture, groupism, feudal survivals, or Japan's absorption and emulation of Western-style capitalism. Matsumoto argues that according to Western definitions, Japan's corporations are not of the capitalist variety; or, conversely, according to a new definition of capitalism, which Matsumoto dubs *kigyoism,* they are ultracapitalist.

Is the Japanese economy capitalist? Matsumoto comes at this question from several interesting points of view. Just as a monarchy can have a democratic government, a country can have a formally capitalist system—private property, joint stock companies, markets—and yet not be capitalist. "The contemporary Japanese situation," he writes, "can be viewed as a noteworthy example of such a case. . . . A new economic system has developed and been nurtured in Japan inside a shell of capitalism." On the other hand, if one "understands the essence of capitalism to reside in control by those bearing the risk, which leads to managerial autonomy, rather than in private ownership . . . one can call the Japanese system a restructured form of capitalism that emerged in response to new conditions in a new age."

In Matsumoto's analysis, Japan's key restructurings were

- "de facto total separation of management from the wishes of the owners" and

- a shift of "the burden of corporate risk to the side of labor" by restricting the ability of workers to move from one company to another, thereby achieving
- "the autonomy of management."

Japan is dynamic because its managers devote themselves to competing with other companies at home and abroad, without having to serve the parasitic interests of shareholders or the passive interests of workers who have no stake in the viability of the company. "Free economic principles alone do not guarantee the growth of productive capacity," Matsumoto writes. "Managerial autonomy is necessary. . . . The superiority of the Japanese corporate system is that it keeps managerial autonomy, once the core of capitalism, intact." American managers are at the mercy of the American capital markets, where investors can dump their shares if performance lags, and the American labor markets, where workers can quit or strike if their pay and benefits are poor. Matsumoto contends that Japanese managers are free from these restraints.

On shareholding, he writes, "Ordinarily, it is the shareholder who selects a company whose shares he wants to acquire, but in Japan it is the reverse, and the company selects shareholders it wants to have acquire its shares." These chosen shareholders are a firm's domestic competitors, intermediated by its financial partners; together they hold approximately 70 percent of the shares of each other's firms thereby preventing takeovers by keeping the numbers of tradable shares below a controlling interest. The shares that a company holds in its competitors' firms are never sold, regardless of price.

On workers, Matsumoto does not go beyond familiar interpretations of Japan's major innovations—enterprise unionism, seniority wages, career job security in upper-tier exporting companies for male heads of households, and the lack of a serious political role for labor in Japan. He compares the loyalty that Japanese workers feel toward their companies to nationalism in places such as the United States, France, or China. Nationalism is fostered because people are normally not able to choose whatever country they want and freely move from one to the other. Just as the inability to country-hop produces nationalism, so the relative inability to job-hop in Japan produces labor commitment to the firm. Japan's elimination of an efficient labor market thus contributes to the autonomy of its managers. It also greatly increases the interest of managers in the quality of the educational system, since once they employ a man straight from school they are obliged to keep him for most of his working life.

The question is where did these Japanese practices originate and how have they been maintained over long periods of time? Why don't workers and investors rebel against practices that discriminate against them? What is Japan's secret? Most serious Japanese researchers into these questions, including Matsumoto and Shimada Haruo, hold that such things as cross shareholding, the fight for job security, an emphasis on producers' interests, and the search for national political and economic independence got started during the bitter struggle for survival during and in the decade following the Allied Occupation. Matsumoto argues that *zaibatsu* dissolution eliminated capitalist control from the corporation and put managers in charge. Shimada concludes, "The postwar reforms implemented by the occupation forces can be credited with providing the framework for today's Japanese capitalism." The reforms were the work of "New Dealers and were more thorough and idealistic than any implemented in the United States."[24] This is undoubtedly true as far as it goes, but it fails to take into account the Japanese government's prewar and postwar industrial policy and how it built on and shaped the heritage of the occupation. A lot more happened in the forty years since the end of the occupation than Japan's passive acceptance of the work of some New Dealers.

Industrial policy means the government's "development, guidance, and supervision of industry."[25] It explicitly does not mean the tired old cliché about the state's picking winners, nor does it mean the state's displacement of the market. Economic competitiveness does not result from picking winners but from a long-term strategy aimed at learning to win. The logic of industrial policy springs from the realization that what is problematic in economic activity is the organization of production, not consumption by households and individuals. As Thomas McCraw explains, *"Investment* by the producers, because it is so far removed in time from ultimate consumption, must be attended to in careful, deliberate fashion. It cannot be left to the whims of individuals, who will usually act in their own short-term self-interest, as [Adam] Smith correctly argued. It must be done through organizations; and it is best done with the positive assistance of wise public policy. . . . The German and Japanese economic systems today are just as market-oriented, just as 'capitalistic,' as is the American. But they are far less centered on the individual."[26] McCraw faults Adam Smith for his "obliviousness to the industrial revolution" and above all for his "hostile attitude toward organizations."

Serious industrial policy means modifying the old-fashioned concept of comparative advantage to concentrate on industries with a high human-capital content such as steel, machine tools, and semiconductors. This is what the postwar Japanese state taught its managers and industrialists. When Amaya Naohiro of MITI says that Japan broke all the rules, he does not mean that it broke the rules of producer economics, only those of consumer economics.[27] The basic measure of performance in producer economics is savings and investment; the goals of such an economy are market share and ever higher value added products, not short-term profitability. The postwar Japanese state took over the structures that the occupation left behind and oriented them toward producer economics.

In concrete terms, this meant, for example, creating a financial structure that encourages managers to compete for market share. In an analysis of Japan's financial system four decades after the occupation, Zielinsky and Holloway observe that "Markets are a means to an end for Japan and not, as they are in the United States, an end in themselves. The stock market, like other markets, is made to work for the benefit of Japan and its goal of national security through economic strength. Over the years, the government has intervened in almost every market. . . . Since shares are owned by corporations, the bureaucrats need not compete with shareholders in determining whether companies should focus on profits or market share. Market share is the predetermined goal of Japan's managers, and they are thus more receptive to industrial policy than would otherwise be the case."[28] Under conditions like these it is sheer nonsense for the *Harvard Business Review* during 1992 to argue that "In the new global economy, all companies—Japanese, American, European, and others—must compete for the same capital."[29] The function of Japan's state financial authorities is precisely to ensure that

that is not true. Their role, as Eamonn Fingleton puts it, is "to channel the nation's enormous pool of savings into the right industries and to ensure that corporate clients stay in line with industrial policy (by, for instance, encouraging buy-Japanese sourcing policies)."[30] Officials of Japan's Ministry of Finance like to compare their relationship to the banking community to that of "the escort of a convoy of ships by a warship."[31]

As we have seen, what Morita called the "market principles of Japan" depend on the structure of the Japanese corporation, which in turn depends on the institutions of capitalism inherited from the occupation, which in turn were modified by the government's industrial policy. Lying behind industrial policy is the strong Japanese state itself. It is the *sine qua non* of Japan's economic achievements. But to raise the state is to become instantly embroiled in controversy. The very concept "state" is very poorly understood in contemporary American social science since the Anglo-American political tradition is built on the triumph of society over the state. In American usage even the term "state" is reserved for what in other social systems would be called a province or a prefecture.

Hostility to the state and an emphasis on the individual and his or her rights against the state is very old in Western political thought. This tradition was strongly reinforced by the Cold War, which was conceived as a contest between a state-led command economy and a state-as-referee laissez-faire economy. The seeming victory of the state-as-referee conception has given American social science, in particular, an ethnocentrism and an ideological quality that seems to have erased all Western memory of the state from Plato's *Republic* to Hobbes' *Leviathan*. Thus, for example, even when the idea of a strong state is recognized, it is still thought of as something derived from an analytically prior society. One standard work of American political economy argues that "the strong state is one with the political support to be strong, a state with the compliance or enthusiasm of at least some societal actors that support the actions of strength. When that support disappears, so does state strength."[32] And yet, in the twentieth century alone, we have seen strong states in Russia, Germany, China, and Japan that substituted nationalistic projects for societal support and that mobilized and transformed their civil societies in order to support these projects.

The key to the relationship between a state and its society is the source of the legitimacy that exists between them. When a state's existence is predicated on its submission to the representatives of the society, we have a weak state and a strong society, such as in the United States. When a state substitutes itself for society and legitimates itself through some political project such as social revolution or economic development, we have a strong state and a weak society, as in Japan after the Meiji era. Asian economic success, pioneered in Japan but duplicated in various different ways in South Korea, Taiwan, Hong Kong, and Singapore, is based on the activities of what I have called the "capitalist developmental state." Manuel Castells has defined the capitalist developmental state and explained its legitimacy as follows:

> A state is developmental when it establishes as its principle of legitimacy its ability to promote and sustain development, understanding by development the combination of steady high rates of economic growth and structural change in the productive system, both domestically and in relationship to the international economy.[33]

A developmental state is like a revolutionary state, although at a less sweeping level. "They [revolutionary states] never pretended to be legitimate in terms of the acquiescence of their subjects, but in terms of the historical project they embodied."[34] Contrary to American political science theory, the power of the Japanese state has not been delegated to it by the elected representatives of the people; the state has instead imposed its economic achievements on the people and won their allegiance in doing so. The American state is legitimated by its processes, whereas the Japanese state is legitimated by its achievements.

When talking about a strong state, people in the West usually think in terms of the totalitarian state of Nazi or Stalinist practice, or perhaps of the "tax-and-spend" Moloch of American campaign rhetoric. As McCraw observes, "Contempt for bureaucracies runs so deep in the popular consciousness that denouncing them is like shooting fish in a barrel."[35] But this is not necessarily the case in East Asia. There we have what has been described by Michael Lind as the "catalytic state." "A catalytic state," he writes, "is one that seeks its goals less by relying on its own resources than by acting as a dominant element . . . while retaining its distinct identity and its own goals. As a catalyst, this kind of state is one that seeks to be *indispensable* to the success or direction of particular strategic coalitions while remaining substantially *independent* from the other elements of the coalition."[36] The neoliberal thesis that "the state is withering away in the face of a resurgence of society, both from below in the form of popular movements, and from outside in the form of global finance and global corporations" Lind finds to be more apparent than real, particularly in light of the power and influence of Germany and Japan.

This catalytic apparatus, which I have referred to in the Japanese context as the "economic general staff," is itself legitimated by its meritocratic character. It attracts the best talent in the country and continuously seeks new information from all possible sources. It is insulated from the corruption that strong-state systems normally generate. Japan displays the usual qualities of an Asian kleptocracy only in its ruling party, but the party's functions in the Japanese system are to reign, not to rule. The latter is entrusted to the elite officialdom. Japan pioneered the capitalist developmental, or catalytic, state and illustrated to the rest of the world that the state can play an important role in market economies well beyond the roles envisioned in laissez-faire economics.

The collapse of communism discredited the attempt to implement social goals through the socialist displacement of the market. But that failure does not necessarily support the abandonment of social goals entirely or a reliance only on laissez faire. As James Kurth argues, "The next stage of history will not be dominated by state-communism, but it probably won't be dominated by liberal-capitalism either. It is more likely that it will be shaped in major ways by states practicing the social market and organized capitalism."[37] Thus, Asian capitalism, understood as a version of Japan's combination of a strong state, industrial policy, producer economics, and managerial autonomy, seems destined to lie at the center rather than the periphery of what economists will teach their students in the next century.

4

Trade, Revisionism, and the Future of Japanese-American Relations

A goal intended through the implementation of the [Action] Program is that Japan's market will achieve an openness exceeding the international standard. . . . On the basic standpoint of "freedom in principle, restrictions only as exceptions," government intervention shall be reduced to a minimum so as to leave the choice and responsibility to consumers.

—Nakasone Cabinet, *Outline of the Action Program for Improved Market Access,* July 30, 1985

With respect to Japan, the President announced today a separate Administration initiative. He has directed the Secretaries of State and Treasury to join me in forming a high level committee, which will include Commerce, Labor and other interested agencies, to propose negotiations with Japan on structural adjustment matters. These matters include structural impediments to trade, balance-of-payments adjustment, and such anticompetitive practices as bid-rigging, market allocation, and group boycotts. These negotiations would initially focus on major structural barriers to imports such as rigidity in the distribution system and pricing mechanism. The negotiations sought by the United States in this Structural Impediments Initiative will address broader issues and will take place outside of section 301.

—Statement of Ambassador Carla A. Hills, the U.S. Trade Representative, May 25, 1989

What unites the revisionists is their view that Japan's economy and society are not organized around classical notions of free markets, in which the direction of the economy is determined by the independent actions of consumers and corporations, all operating to maximize their profits and incomes. This challenges the conventional wisdom (hence "revisionism") among American policymakers that Japan is fundamentally similar to the United States and other Western capitalist democracies.

—Peter Ennis, *Tokyo Business Today,* January 1990

The learned give up the evidence of their senses to preserve the coherence of the ideas of their imagination.

—Adam Smith

I believe that these four statements and observations are interrelated and that the interconnections among them go a long way toward explaining why during 1989 Japanese-American relations began markedly to worsen. These quotations illustrate at least four aspects of the growing tendency of Japanese and Americans to see each other as adversaries. First, Japan seems unable to alter its economic behavior despite the objections of other nations and its own proclaiming of some nine different economic reform programs since 1981. Throughout this period Japan nonetheless maintained a trade surplus in manufactured goods with *all* its trading partners. No version of the theory of comparative advantage can account for such a result. Second, despite the Americans' deep confusion about what they want from the international economy—success of the Uruguay Round of GATT negotiations, forcing their executive branch to begin to act in the national interest, or ending America's role as "liberal dupe in a world that does not operate according to neoclassical economic principles"—the Structural Impediments Initiative is addressed to Japan alone.[1] It thus reflects the influence of revisionism.

Third, so-called revisionism vis-à-vis Japan is merely the intellectual recognition that Japan's alleged fundamental similarity to the Western capitalist democracies was always based on ignorance of Japan itself. The idea of Japanese-American convergence is a Western intellectual conceit with roots in the Allied Occupation of Japan after World War II and in the United States' shift from an alliance with China to an alliance with Japan as the basis of its Cold War strategy in East Asia. Revisionism is thus also concerned with the ideological redefinition of

Japan during the Cold War era in accordance with the interests of the Western alliance and with the role Japan will play now that the Cold War is ending. Fourth, and finally, is the influence of a set of theological principles—the doctrine of free trade—serviced by an entrenched priesthood—the professional economists—that is much more interested in defending its articles of faith than in understanding what is going on in international economic relations. Along with other creators of smokescreens, some of whom I will also discuss below, the economists contribute to the debate about Japan by hurling epithets of heresy, apostasy, and "anecdotal reasoning" at anyone who disagrees with them.

Japan's peculiar patterns of trade, American policy, revisionism, and doctrinaire economists constitute a complex whole that I shall disaggregate and analyze below. First, however, I propose to put some data on the table: nine aspects of recent Japanese economic behavior that I contend support the view that Japan is a mercantile power, not a free trader. By mercantile power I mean a nation that uses state action to export the utmost possible quantity of a nation's own manufactures and to import as little as possible of those made in other countries. By free trader I mean a nation that uses state action to promote a trading system in which the lowest-cost producer always gets the order. The nine things I shall discuss are (1) the difference between foreign and domestic prices of Japanese products; (2) why it took Japan 29 years to give Texas Instruments its patent on the integrated circuit; (3) the influence of Japan's land-use laws on domestic demand; (4) why it is that collusion *(dangō)* among several thousand Japanese construction companies in their bids on Japanese construction projects can go on indefinitely; (5) the economic and regulatory effects of the lack of a code of administrative procedure for Japan's state bureaucracy; (6) the significance of predatory pricing by Fujitsu and NEC in bidding on public purchases of electronic equipment; (7) what "ownership" might mean in Japan in light of recent merger and acquisition activity; (8) the effects of Japanese industrial groups *(keiretsu)* on free competition in high technology industries; and (9) the influence of Japan's distribution system on the "preferences" of Japanese consumers.

There are many other aspects of the Japanese capitalist developmental state that distinguish it from the capitalist regulatory states of the English-speaking world. Some of these include its insistence on Japanese-produced or Japanese-owned cement, paper, aluminum, and other basic materials despite equal quality and lower price being readily available on the international market; its pretense of "opening" its markets or "liberalizing" its financial services only after all possibilities of foreign competition have been eliminated; and its elaborate industrial policies for fostering higher value-added industries of the future. These nine were chosen because they were all highly salient in Japanese practice as recently as the winter of 1989–90 and because they help explain why simultaneously a revisionist approach to relations with Japan became popular among many different foreign groups and leaders.[2]

PRICES

Any consumer doing a little comparison shopping in Japan and abroad at the end of 1989 discovered one of the most obvious features of the Japanese economy: Japanese prices for both Japanese and imported goods are much higher than in foreign markets. Take the Macintosh computer, for example. It is popular among researchers because it is easy to use and has many functions. During the summer of 1989 it cost $4,000 (¥540,000 at U.S. $1 = ¥135) in the United States and ¥868,000 ($6,430) in Japan. The *Nihon keizai shimbun* reported that "hand-carry the Mac on the trip back" was commonly heard at Japanese universities among technicians going abroad; and it told of a University of Tokyo scientist who in September 1989 spotted three other Apple computers, in addition to the one he was carrying, in the arrival area at Narita airport.[3]

During 1988 the Economic Planning Agency reported that the cost of living in Tokyo was 97 percent higher than in New York. It also contended that some 30 percent of the savings theoretically achievable because of the upward valuation of the yen against the dollar had been absorbed by the Japanese distribution system.[4] Persistent reports of this kind led the Japanese Ministry of International Trade and Industry (MITI) and the U.S. Department of Commerce to make a joint, controlled survey between October 18 and 28, 1989. Sixty percent of the goods on the two ministries' list could be bought for less overseas, while 90 percent of the foreign-made items cost the same or more in Japan than in their home countries. A Japanese-made car, for example, that sold for $16,800 in Tokyo could be bought for $14,042 in Chicago, whereas a U.S.-made sedan selling for $13,-507 in Chicago cost about $25,613 in Tokyo.[5]

MITI officials immediately began to distance themselves from their own figures with the usual mutterings about "special factors" and "cultural differences." It was nonetheless hard to see why someone in Tokyo, regardless of cultural background, would prefer to pay $55.63 for a pair of American blue jeans that an American consumer could buy for $32.[6] After the joint report was issued, Prime Minister Kaifu created a task force to examine ways of narrowing the gap between domestic and foreign prices; but the Economic Planning Agency declined to participate, and MITI said it was dissatisfied with the prime minister's effort. MITI also went on to say, in a disingenuous argument, that some foreigners who had been making large profits selling such products as chocolates at Japan's inflated prices would not be pleased if these prices came down.[7]

Separate foreign and domestic prices for the same goods are classic signs of mercantilist trade policies. They allow Japanese exporters to use high domestic prices to subsidize exports and to resort to predatory pricing when necessary to hold on to or expand foreign markets. As the Joint Economic Committee of the U.S. Congress put it, "The response of Japanese exporters to the rapid yen appreciation since 1985 provides further indication of the closed nature of the Japanese market. Japanese export prices have fallen sharply relative to domestic wholesale prices. This implies a kind of price discrimination by Japanese producers, with export prices bearing little relationship to domestic prices. . . . Since price discrimination can persist only if the two markets are kept separate, Japanese exporters appear able to keep their exports from reentering the domestic market to undercut domestic prices."[8] Keeping the two markets separate is one consequence of Japanese governmental policies, as we shall see in the discussions of *dangō,* the distribution system, nonenforcement of the Antimonopoly Law, and several other structural features of the Japanese economy.

PATENTS

According to former U.S. Trade Representative Clayton Yeutter, piracy of American intellectual properties costs the entertainment industry annually some $2 billion and the computer and software industries an estimated $4 billion.[9] During the mid-1980s, when IBM charged Fujitsu with illegally copying its operating software, alleged inadequate protection of intellectual property rights became a major issue in Japanese-American economic relations. In November 1988 the American Arbitration Association ordered Fujitsu to pay IBM $400 million compensation, and this is just one of many cases in which Americans claim to have been victimized.[10]

There are many different issues in this field. One of them is Japan's practice of automatically making patent applications public 18 months after they have been filed regardless of whether a patent is ultimately granted. This means that an inventor cannot even exploit his invention as a trade secret in Japan if he or she fails to receive a patent. Another issue is the United States' enactment of Section 337 of its Tariff Law, which empowers the American government to ban imports that infringe on U.S. intellectual property rights. In 1989 a GATT dispute panel found that Section 337 violates the GATT treaty, but the U.S. Congress did not repeal the legislation—and probably will not until it sees the results of the Uruguay Round of GATT negotiations. Still a third issue is the fact that the United States gives patents to the first to invent whereas Japan gives patents to the first to file; Japan's practice is closer to the international norm than that of the United States. However, the most contentious issue is the extreme delays in Japan in the issuing of patents.[11]

On February 6, 1960, Texas Instruments filed an application for a Japanese patent protecting Jack Kilby and Robert Noyce's invention in 1959 of the integrated circuit. Some 29 years later, on October 30, 1989, the Japanese Patent Office, which is an integral part of MITI, granted the patent. It will run through November 27, 2001. Texas Instruments stands to make significant royalties during the 1990s from Japanese semiconductor manufacturers but, needless to say, the company was unable to protect its property in Japan during the almost 30 years when its Japanese competitors took over 90 percent of the Japanese market and 80 percent of the American market for computer semiconductors.[12] Some American officials believe that Japan is engaged in a similar kind of delay in granting a patent to Corning Glass to cover its fiber optics technology.[13] Japan responds that its Patent Office is understaffed.

Major issues for the future are Japan's direct purchase of foreign companies that own intellectual properties rather than negotiating licensing agreements—e.g., Sony's purchase of CBS Records and Columbia Pictures—and the tendency of Japanese firms to file floods of frivolous patent applications. In her speech to the Japanese National Press Club on October 13, 1989, Ambassador Hills cited a case in which Mitsubishi Electric filed 300 patents that compete with the core technology of an American electric lamp maker. For these reasons the United States has made protection of intellectual property rights a major element in the Uruguay Round of GATT negotiations.

LAND

According to former British Prime Minister Margaret Thatcher, 75 percent of the income of Japanese farmers comes from state subsidies.[14] The main beneficiaries are not, however, farmers, who are rapidly declining in numbers, but rather a politically potent network of agricultural cooperatives that control supplies of fertilizer, feed, seed, credit, and insurance to rural areas and that also purchase, process, and distribute farm products. The agricultural cooperatives, combined with a massive gerrymander that makes a rural vote many times more valuable than an urban vote, constitute one of the bases on which the long-term reign of the Liberal Democratic Party (LDP) has rested.[15]

The foundations of Japanese politics are similar to Bismarck's alliance of iron and rye, which supported the German capitalist developmental state before World War I. As Charles Maier writes in his introduction to the reissue of Gerschenkron's *Bread and Democracy in Germany*, "Gerschenkron identified the Junkers' persistent political influence as a major impediment to liberal democracy in Germany. . . . German East Elbian producers were extensively subsidized by the remainder of the country to continue production of expensive wheat and of a rye crop that was less preferred for domestic consumption but was exported as animal fodder." Like Veblen and Schumpeter before him, Gerschenkron identified and analyzed the link between "agricultural protection . . . and its role in preserving Junker influence."[16]

The linkage in Japan is similar. Instead of iron and rye, the alliance is more one of automobiles and rice—or, institutionally, of Keidanren (big business) and Nōkyō (the federation of agricultural cooperatives). These organizations respectively pay for and vote for the LDP, which in turn maintains to the outside world a facade *(tatemae)* of parliamentary democracy while in practice it leaves actual policymaking to a Bismarckian-style elite state bureaucracy. Just as in pre–World War I Germany, there has also developed in Japan an elaborate ideology that removes this conservative alliance from the realm of politics by claiming that it merely reflects Japanese culture. Thus, for example, Hayashi Yoshiro, a former minister of welfare and during 1989 a candidate for prime minister, defended Japan's protection of agriculture by saying, "Rice is a religious issue in Japan."[17]

No one is advocating that Japan change its culture in any sense of the term. If the Japanese want to subsidize their farmers, that is their business. But it is important to ensure that the Japanese, and not their trading partners, pay for these preferences. This is where land utilization in Japan enters the international economic equation. Per capita imports of finished goods into Japan in 1988 were only $750, compared to $1,500 for the United States, $2,700 for Britain, and $3,000 for West Germany.[18] Among the reasons for this discrepancy is Japan's forcing its households to spend more than a third of their income on food. Moreover, the tremendous pent-up demand within Japan for better housing is frustrated by a land-use law that encourages using land for inefficient agriculture or financial speculation.[19]

To take only one of the most obvious examples, Tokyo's 23 wards have a total of 25,000 hectares of housing land on which 8.35 million people live. There are available, however, some 36,000 hectares of urban farmland in Greater Tokyo, which includes the 23 wards and the surrounding suburban areas.[20] The tax system discourages the sale of land because annual property taxes are low compared to sales and inheritance taxes. This greatly restricts the supply of land available for development while encouraging the use of land as collateral for speculative borrowing and investment. It is also undeniable that Japan's cramped housing makes it impossible for many Japanese to buy, use, store, or park many of the goods they sell to the rest of the world. Again, it is Japan's own business how it wants to organize its own society, but it is the United States' business whether it is worth it to continue to buy Japanese manufactured goods when the Japanese do not or cannot buy farm products or manufactured goods from abroad.

DANGŌ

On November 23, 1989, some 98 Japanese construction companies admitted that they had overcharged the U.S. Navy for work done at the Yokosuka naval base, and they agreed to return ¥4.7 billion (c. $32.6 million) to the U.S. government.[21] The Americans had charged that the excessive payments resulted from prior consultations *(dangō)* in which the Japanese contractors set the prices they would charge for the work. The United States got some of its money back because it threatened to sue the firms and seize their assets in American courts. According to the *Nihon keizai shimbun,* "The Japanese government maintains that it does not permit practices that violate the Antimonopoly Law, and it refuses to admit that the *dangō* collusion system in bidding exists."[22] One probable reason why the government refuses to admit that *dangō* exists is that it could not exist without the cooperation of the government. I shall explain this point below.

According to one careful estimate, excess profits from collusion in Japan's construction industry alone amount to between 16 percent and 33 percent of the industry's revenues.[23] Since the Japanese government awards between $100 billion and $300 billion in construction contracts annually, this amounts to somewhere between $16 billion and $99 billion. This is close to or more than the entire revenue raised annually by Japan's highly controversial consumption tax *(shōhizei),* which is estimated to be $31 billion (the 1989 tax cut was only $18.6 billion).[24] In other words, if the Japanese government would enforce the Antimonopoly Law against the construction industry, it could abolish the consumption tax and still enhance revenues.

The odd thing about Japan is not that this type of corruption exists but that it is dealt with so lightly. The United States files about 80 criminal indictments in antitrust cases per annum, and convictions sometimes result in prison sentences (about 20 in the period 1985 to 1988 in the United States versus none in Japan). According to the Japanese press, *dangō* is rampant. It flourishes virtually unchecked because it is a source of huge payoffs to the ruling party and because innumerable officials of the Ministry of Construction take up lucrative positions in private construction firms when they retire. Despite American protests, the Japanese have done nothing more than promise to reform and offered a few "sweetheart" deals to some American firms in order to prevent a foreign united front. For example, Bechtel has been included in a joint venture for a new terminal building at Haneda airport, and Schal Associates received a contract for 6 percent of a new Yokohama conference hall. According to *Zaikai tembō,* "It may be premature to say so but it is not an understatement that the industry's so-called self-examination [*hansei*] in light of the Yokosuka *dangō* case was a clever pose adopted toward the foreigners and their pressure."[25] And it worked. On the day the Japanese firms agreed to return some of their illegal profits, U.S. Trade Representative Hills decided not to apply section 301 of the Trade Act of 1988 to the Japanese construction industry.[26]

As John McMillan has shown, collusive agreements such as the 1973 OPEC cartel are quite unstable and normally break down for internal reasons: it is hard to divide the spoils, the agreement—being illegal—must be self-enforcing, and the excessive profits invite in outsiders.[27] In Japan, the government solves most of these problems for the conspirators. It establishes a ceiling price on all projects, thereby making it easy for construction firms to agree on their illegal bid, and it only invites certain companies actually to make bids. This last requirement totally shuts out foreigners except as members of a joint venture with a Japanese partner. In order for the Ministry of Construction to put a firm on its lists of qualified bidders, it considers only the quality of work done previously in Japan. Thus, for a foreign firm to win a contract it must make a bid, but it is not allowed to make a bid unless it has won a previous contract. Obviously, these rules could be changed, but the obstacles to doing so are political.

REGULATION

Japan is the only major democratic nation without a code of administrative procedure.[28] This means that so-called administrative guidance by Japan's powerful state bureaucracy can often result in rampant lawlessness in favor of those enterprises and interests that enjoy privileged access to the bureaucracy. A foreigner, or for that matter a Japanese who is not part of the establishment (the Recruit corruption case of 1988–90 concerned the attempt by one Japanese outsider to buy his way in), cannot hope to know how to conform to this regulatory environment since it changes as the bureaucrats involved change. There is no system of laws that establishes explicit, transparent rules governing Japan's administrative procedure. In this respect Japan is closer to the former centrally planned economies than to those that are judicially accountable. Some aspects of regulation in Japan show brilliant work by devoted officials—Taggart Murphy believes this is true of the Ministry of Finance's guidance of overseas investment during the 1980s—but other aspects display what Frank Upham has called "regulatory anarchy."[29] Whichever it is, regulation in Japan is not based on any set of laws that an outsider can learn and conform to.

PREDATORY PRICING

In November 1989 Fujitsu, Ltd., Japan's leading computer company with annual sales in the $18 billion range, bid ¥1 (0.7¢) to win a public contract for computers for the city of Hiroshima. City authorities estimated that the contract was worth more than $70,000. This was Fujitsu's third successful ¥1 bid in two years (it lost out to NEC's ¥1 bid for a computer system for a library in Nagano Prefecture when the two companies ended up drawing straws). The American press made much of MITI's ordering Fujitsu President Yamamoto Tokuma to apologize publicly for his ¥1 bid, which he did. This was seen as evidence that MITI is still a potent agent of industrial policy, even though MITI sources have been saying for years that MITI has lost its influence.[30] Much more significant, however, was the fact that Japan's Fair Trade Commission issued only a "stern warning" to both Fujitsu and NEC. In any other capitalist country the two companies would have been fined severely and Yamamoto most likely would have gone to jail, apology or no.

This form of dumping, or "pricing under cost of production," is actually part of a strategy to drive competitors out of business in order to enlarge market share. For the same reasons, Japanese computer companies try to place their equipment in key locations, such as banks, government offices, and universities, so that other organizations that must interact with these agencies will have an incentive to buy the same equipment in order to be compatible. In the case of the Hiroshima contract, Fujitsu was willing to lose up to ¥3 million in order to get a foot in the door, but it planned to make up to ¥500 million in hardware and peripherals for the system it would install.[31] In its penetration of the South Korean market, Fujitsu used *amakudari* bureaucrats from MITI to place its machines, at fire-sale prices, in all the banks and government offices. Similarly, Japan's global dumping of DRAMS (dynamic random access memory chips) during 1985 led to the 1986 Japan-U.S. semiconductor agreement and, in April 1987, to the United States' levying of $300 million in sanctions because of Japan's noncompliance. Seen strategically, dumping and predatory pricing both aim at eliminating competitors so that a monopoly position can be achieved. Dumping overseas is usually financed by high domestic prices for the same products.

OWNERSHIP

In the earliest forms of capitalism, at least in theory, ownership and control were not distinguishable because they meant the same thing: owners also controlled their businesses. With the rise of capital markets and professional managers, however, the two concepts have diverged. Today ownership in a joint stock company depends upon the number of voting shares owned by an individual or organization, whereas control is exercised by a professional managerial class employed by the owners to run the corporation for their benefit. In Japan, however, this distinction has once again become blurred. Here the managers are ascendant and the owners have become invisible to the point that the concept of ownership no longer means much of anything. This was brought home to T. Boone Pickens, the American capitalist, when he acquired 26 percent (the largest single amount) of the shares of a Japanese auto headlight manufacturer, Koito Seisakusho, but was denied either a seat on the board of directors or so much as a look at its books. Koito is actually part of the Toyota *keiretsu,* with Toyota holding 19 percent of its shares. Toyota is Koito's prime customer, occupies three seats on the board of directors, and appoints key managers. Thus, while it is not the owner, Toyota does have control. Given that a majority of Koito's shares are never traded regardless of price, Pickens is Koito's owner but he has no control whatsoever. Moreover, the Japanese legal system is uninterested in Pickens' putative rights as an owner.[32]

In a 1989 *Nihon keizai shimbun* poll, an overwhelming 83.5 percent of the 182 corporations that responded acknowledged that "stable shareholders" controlled over half of their outstanding equity shares and never trade them.[33] This suggests that ownership is no longer an issue in Japan and that the economic system is something other than "capitalist." It may even be a better one. There is, of course, no obligation for Japan to conform to the capitalist pattern, and given the abuses during the 1980s of the leveraged buyout of American firms, it is probably wise not to. But Japan's structure also blocks foreign acquisitions of Japanese firms as a way of entering the Japanese market. Acquisition of an existing firm is often a better marketing strategy than a joint venture, licensing agreement, or greenfield start-up. Japan's blocking of acquisitions is not only an anticompetitive practice but also a nontariff barrier to trade. The appropriate foreign response might be to block Japanese acquisitions in foreign markets.[34]

KEIRETSU

One of Japan's major contributions to modern industrial organization is the "industrial group" or "developmental conglomerate"—known in Japanese as *zaibatsu, kōgyō shūdan,* or *keiretsu.* These terms refer to slightly different configurations, but they all share the integration of functionally diffuse enterprises into a single cooperative unit, huge concentrations of capital, and the financing of risky ventures and R&D on the basis of profitable, secure businesses. Examples include the cooperation among different firms, banks, and trading companies in the Mitsubishi or Sumitomo groups and the integration of heavy electrical machinery with advanced electronics and telecommunications in the Hitachi, NEC, and Toshiba *keiretsu*. These organizations came into being during Japan's industrialization as innovative institutions for financing and exploiting imported technology. Today they are superbly adapted to the huge R&D costs and short product life cycles of high-technology industries.

There is no such thing as pure competition in any high-technology industry, and the use of such phrases as "market failure" to explain the role of government and public policy in these industries is highly misleading. Small, undercapitalized companies cannot hope to compete with coordinated industry/government efforts by foreign countries, as American firms demonstrably have not competed. Much of the world is shifting to Japanese rules in order to compete with the Japanese *keiretsu*, regardless of economic ideology. Such experimental American organizations as the Semiconductor Research Corporation, SEMATECH, MCC Corporation, and the failed U.S. Memories are evidence of this trend. "Like it or not," writes the Semiconductor Industry Association, "America, the European Community, and other nations are being forced to conduct global business using some of the same practices as the Japanese in order to remain competitive."[35]

A global shift to Japanese rules would interfere with free trade but would not necessarily be anticompetitive. Managed trade is already a fact of life. As Lawrence Krause has argued, "We do not now have an open trade system of the kind hypothesized by GATT, and [as the 1980s have shown] such a system is not necessary to have expanding trade and a healthy world economy."[36] Managed trade exists in such sectors as fuels, food, automotive products, steel, textiles, clothing, and consumer electronics. And Japan, as the world's largest importer of raw materials, obtains monopsonist advantages by importing primarily through its trading companies. Under these conditions the issue is not whether managed trade is desirable but the failure of the United States to manage its trade as effectively as Japan does. In order to meet the competition of Japan, other countries must copy or match Japan's *keiretsu*-type company structures, its mercantilist industrial and trade policies, its ability to make capital available on a preferred basis to strategic industries, and its managerial incentives that impose long-term perspectives on company operations. Neoclassical economic theory is not only irrelevant to this challenge, it is downright misleading.[37]

DISTRIBUTION

The Japanese government has tightly controlled retailing since 1937 in order to serve the interests of small retailers—defined as outlets with four or fewer employees—and, in postwar Japan, to ensure that they vote for the LDP. The results are that the number of retail stores per capita is 75 percent higher in Japan than in the United States, the next highest country, but the value added per employee is 28 percent less. The Economic Planning Agency acknowledges that this system produces a 50 percent higher markup on imported goods over domestic goods. What it does not say is price is actually irrelevant because foreign goods are normally not allowed in the distribution system. As the *Japan Economic Journal* (November 25, 1989) reported, there are some 70,000 Japanese stores in electrical appliances alone that are vertically organized distribution channels from manufacturers to retailers. These channels restrict competition in terms of price and "close the distribution system to newcomers and outsiders."

The answer to such distribution *keiretsu* would appear to be opening new outlets that compete on price—something like the K-Marts, Targets, Mervyns, Cost Pluses, and Sears that populate every American shopping mall. But the Large-scale Retail Stores Law of October 1973 stands in the way. As modified in 1982, it requires that the proprietor of a prospective new store obtain the prior approval of all local shopkeepers before MITI, which administers this law, will permit the store to open. This law, and the political interests that stand behind it (primarily the LDP), have halted modernization of Japan's distribution system. The law also explains why the largest-scale retail outlets in Japan are located in the countryside, as far as possible from their privileged competitors and from their customers. Many Japanese leaders, including Prime Minister Takeshita at the 1988 summit meeting, have promised reform, but nothing will happen until reciprocity is forced on Japan—until, for example, Japanese auto parts manufacturers or hotel buyers are required to get the permission of local competitors to open businesses in America.

When confronted with the evidence that Japanese customers' preferences no more dictate what is on the shelves than they do in Havana, Japanese spokesmen usually retreat to the argument that foreign salesmen do not try hard enough in Japan. This implies that Japanese salesmen did and do work hard in making their products available to American consumers. This is not true. The people who worked hard in postwar American retailing were the American buyers who went abroad to find low-cost suppliers and spent time in places such as Taiwan, Hong Kong, and Singapore instructing local manufacturers in the patterns and standards they required. In Japan, by contrast, wholesalers and manufacturers use their leverage to prevent their customers from changing to cheaper sources, and they are undeterred by the courts or the so-called antitrust authorities.[38] Even the biggest of the Japanese supermarket chains, Daiei, does not want international competition. In 1988 Daiei's president remarked, "I approve [retail liberalization] in both general theory and in the particulars. It is, however, not necessary to repeal the Large-scale Retail Stores Law. That would be unacceptable—before you know it, there would be a Sears opening next door!"[39]

JAPANESE RESPONSES

When confronted with the thought that the nine problem areas listed here might not be occurring randomly and might constitute mercantilism, Japanese trade spokesmen and their foreign representatives respond in several characteristic ways. My list is not exhaustive—and it can never be, given the exceptional creativity of the Japanese economic bureaucracy in nullifying the concessions Japan has made in the successive rounds of multilateral trade negotiations. As James Fallows has put it, "In 1985, with the dollar worth 250 yen, the American trade deficit with Japan was about a billion dollars a week. In 1989, with the dollar worth 125 to 135 yen, the American trade deficit is a billion dollars a week. . . . Classical free-trade analysis has proved virtually useless in predicting how Japan's trade balances would respond to a rising yen. . . . By continuing to launch new industrial assaults rather than simply buying better, cheaper products from abroad, Japan suggests that it does not accept the basic reciprocal logic of world trade."[40]

The normal Japanese response usually involves one or more of the following stratagems: first, the allegation that communication difficulties exist between Japan and its trading partners or that Japan has been misunderstood. Thus, for example, both Ishihara and Morita in *The Japan That Can Say "No,"* Watanabe Taizō of the Foreign Ministry, and Prime Minister Kaifu responded to the Structural Impediments Initiative with warnings against "emotionalism," "emotional arguments," "hysteria," and pleas for "calmer attitudes."[41] The former EC High Commissioner in Japan, Andreas van Agt, learned in Japan that his difficulties were due to a "communications gap."[42] Ivan Hall was among the first to note the esoteric language of the Japanese-American "mutual understanding industry."[43] A frequently encountered example of this language is the use of the term "confusion" as a euphemism for genuine competition, as in "Allowing Americans to bid on government contracts will create confusion in the Japanese construction industry." Semantic problems and alleged misunderstandings are substituted for substantive attempts to resolve problems.

A second stratagem is to foster the illusion of change. This was also an old favorite among Communist fellow travelers in the West, who often acknowledged that problems used to exist but were now irrelevant because of sweeping changes that were occurring. Many foreign commentators on Japan make the same claim. Thus, for example, George Russell, a senior editor of *Time,* in a review of Karel van Wolferen's *The Enigma of Japanese Power,* speaks of "The deep changes that are now sweeping through Japan as a result of its growing wealth" and of how "a deeply conservative, inward-looking society is undergoing a significant and quite rapid change of character." Usually, no evidence is offered to substantiate these claims.[44] Gerald Curtis told a New York audience in September 1989 that "Japan is going through a profound transition, coming to the end of an era that represents more than half of its entire modern history." What he actually seems to have meant was that in January 1989 Hirohito died. But what sort of changes, if any, this might produce he did not say.[45]

These ideas are fostered by Japanese officials. For example, Kuroda Makoto, a former senior trade negotiator for MITI, holds that "The rate of change in the Japanese economic structure is very high." Interestingly enough, Ishihara Shintarō has identified Kuroda as his ideal kind of trade negotiator because he really knows how to say "no" to Americans.[46] Americans seem to be particularly susceptible to wishful thinking about change in Japan. For example, one U.S. Department of Commerce official, following a negotiating session in Tokyo, concluded. "There's a new breeze blowing at MITI."[47]

In promoting the illusion of change, some Japanese spokesmen also tend to misuse statistics. Thus, Wada Mitsuo, a professor of business administration at Keio University, reported in a lecture on "Retailing in Tokyo: The Distribution System in Transition" for the Japan Society of New York, that "the number of small 'mom and pop' stores is declining as a portion of all retail outlets from 70 percent in 1964 to 57 percent in 1985 . . . in the process creating a distribution system more closely resembling that of the U.S. and Europe."[48] What Wada did not say is that mom and pop stores in 1985 were only 5 percent of all retail outlets in Europe and 3 percent in the United States.

One of the most notable examples of the Japanese reliance on the illusion of change was the coordinated bureaucratic and press campaign that led up to Japan's agreement, on April 5, 1990, to an "interim report" in the Structural Impediments Initiative. Although these negotiations were virtually identical to those that accompanied the telecommunications and semiconductor talks, the Action Program, first and second Maekawa reports, Ron-Yasu summits, and the MOSS talks of the early and mid-1980s, Japan's last-minute agreement that it was time to correct its "import-discouraging business practices" was hailed as the functional equivalent of V-J Day. The *New York Times* reported "A Shift in Basic Policies" (April 6, 1990), the *Los Angeles Times* a "Landmark Trade Accord" (April 7, 1990), and the Foreign Ministry's Watanabe Taizō emphasized Japan's "sensitive political leadership." A *Los Angeles Times* editorial, entitled "Japan's Kaifu Blinks (Thankfully)," saluted Japan's eleventh-hour agreement as a "breakthrough." None of these journalistic agencies noted that the agreement was virtually unimplementable because the opposition parties controlled the upper house of the Diet and could block implementing legislation, that Prime Minister Kaifu was the same leader who appointed two women to his cabinet after losing the 1989 upper house election on issues of importance to women and then fired them both as soon as the LDP won the general election of February 1990 (precisely what the LDP intended to do with its agreement with the United States as soon as the heat was off), and that during the Reagan era Prime Minister Nakasone had infinitely greater political clout and authority than Kaifu but was unable to deliver on any of the promises he made.

Fallows' conclusion is unavoidable: "the constant expectation that Japan is about to change is the central intellectual flaw in our trading policy. . . . It is foolish for America to adopt a policy that will fail unless [basic social changes in Japan] occur—which is what all our market-opening strategies boil down to. . . . We should base our plans on the assumption that Japan's internal order is not going to change."[49] Even with the end of the 40-year reign of the LDP, Japan's trade surpluses regardless of international economic conditions and the continuities in the Japanese state bureaucracy mean that those who expect change bear the burden of proof.

A third stratagem is to charge that critics of Japan are racists. This is, of course, at the heart of the Morita-Ishihara tract, but it also occurs in many other places. During the summer of 1989 the so-called intellectual magazines of Japan were filled with articles about how America was reviving the threat of the "yellow peril."[50] Even if it were true, such writers still never explain the seeming discrepancy that it is the foreign racists who possess an "excess demand" for Japanese goods, while the Japanese eschew foreign products. In his advice to Americans, Morita Akio unwittingly lays bare this anomaly: "Instead of seeking to buy key components from Japan, American industries should produce those components by themselves. The strength of my company is that we have a policy of producing all key components ourselves."[51]

A fourth stratagem is to arrange "sweetheart" deals in Japan for a few influential foreign firms, thereby dividing the foreigners and setting them to argue among themselves about whether Japan's market is open. For example, Japan gave Texas Instruments 10 percent of its domestic semiconductor market between

1960 and 1970 while entirely excluding Motorola and other U.S. firms, and it recently included Bechtel and Schal in some construction projects.[52] This strategem is successful because the United States has no overall trade policy toward Japan and it therefore mistakes token gestures for genuinely open markets.

A fifth stratagem is to explain foreign complaints about Japan as stemming from cultural differences. Thus Nukazawa Kazuo, Keidanren's chief *"gaijin* handler," pleads for "cultural relativism" in America's and Europe's understanding of why Japan cannot live up to GATT rules. And the Japanese government refused to consider the small number of foreign lawyers practicing in Japan as an issue of "unequal market access" but explained it instead as the result of "a clash of legal cultures."[53]

The sixth stratagem I have encountered is a new one, shifting the argument from issues of trade to ineluctable processes such as the decline of the West and the rise of Japan as a new, intrinsic "hegemonic power." According to this argument, talk about Japanese barriers to beef, lumber, rice, and most manufactured goods is mere haggling over details when what is at issue is the equivalent of the decline of the Roman Empire. Faced with the inevitable, the United States is unreasonable to ask the Japanese government to end its discrimination against foreign goods and services. A new world is coming into being, and a Pax Nipponica may be in the offing. Needless to say, the intellectual godfather of this line of reasoning is Paul Kennedy and his unexpected bestseller *The Rise and Fall of the Great Powers*.[54] A variant of this stratagem is Japanese breast-beating about their technological prowess combined with threats to cut off American access to Japanese technology. Ishihara Shintarō and the technonationalist Karatsu Hajime particularly like to use this gambit.[55]

The seventh and final Japanese response is to reverse the charges made against them and to claim that America is worse. Throughout the 1980s, as Japan's trade surpluses with the United States mounted, the Japanese press launched a steady drumbeat against the United States, portraying American workers and managers as lazy, American products as shoddy, American society as torn by racial conflict, and any foreigner critical of Japan as a racist "Japan-basher."[56] American society does have problems, and pointing them out often does cause Americans to lose sight of foreign problems. This stratagem thus often works but it also promotes arrogance and complacency in Japan and removes incentives to negotiate.

AMERICAN RESPONSES

The American responses to the economic challenge of Japan are inconsistent and torn by a series of contradictions. They also reflect the changing nature and distribution of power in the world—not just the rise of Japan and its emulators in the Asia/ Pacific region but also the collapse of bipolarity. In one sense, the late 1980s responses—the Omnibus Trade and Competitiveness Act of 1988, Super and Special 301s, Section 337 of the Tariff Act, and the Structural Impediments Initiative (SII)—were a "demonstrable act of frustration," as former Prime Minister Thatcher put it. On the one hand, the trading relationship between the United States and Japan has contributed to their being the two richest big nations on earth. On the other hand, as James Fallows observes, "Japan's inability or unwillingness to restrain the one-sided and destructive expansion of its economic power" threatens to make them both much poorer.[57]

The United States needs to figure out why, in the words of former Under Secretary of State for Economic Affairs Richard McCormack, Japan is "immune to our currency realignment measures and other efforts to be more competitive."[58] Is it because the Japanese political system has rigidified and vested interests are frustrating all efforts at reform? In that case, *gaiatsu* (foreign pressure) like Super 301 and SII might be appropriate. The United States has long played a role comparable to that of an unrecognized opposition party in the Japanese political system and has probably been more effective in causing change than the opposition parties themselves. The heightened "trade friction" of recent years might therefore best be seen as simply a new episode in an old game. On the other hand, if Japan is immune to changes in its economic environment because it is a different kind of system from that imagined by American economic theorists, then something more than 301 and SII will be required. If, for example, Japan's foreign economic policy reflects genuine mercantilism—protecting its domestic market, overcharging domestic consumers, using the overcharges to subsidize exports, and predatory pricing abroad to destroy competitors—then

GATT rules are irrelevant and policies tailor-made for Japan will be required.

The American responses, like the global effort to adjust not simply to Japan's economic power but particularly to its methods of acquiring it, are confused and contradictory because the Americans do not have a clear idea of what they are dealing with in Japan and much of their social science is parochial, acontextual, and ideologically biased. From one perspective the American trade deficit with Japan cannot be caused by Japanese trade barriers since these barriers were the same or worse when the United States was running big trade surpluses. At the same time, during the period of American surpluses, no one imagined that Japan was abiding by the rules of free trade. The international trading system is supposed to be self-correcting: current account surpluses lead to capital flows and currency realignments that either alter consumers' purchasing decisions or lower their levels of living. Why are these mechanisms not working? This is the realm of the so-called macroeconomic imbalances that some analysts think are the true cause of the American trade deficit.

After the Reagan administration cut American taxes in the hope (or under the cover) of supply-side predictions that this would enhance government revenues, something like the so-called Stockman catastrophe, named after President Reagan's budget director, should have occurred. There should either have been sky high interest rates in order to finance the resultant government deficit or, what the Reaganites hoped for, drastic cuts in government spending. Neither occurred because of the influx of Japanese capital. As the Joint Economic Committee of the U.S. Congress acknowledges, "Between 1982 and 1987, $465 billion in long-term capital flowed out of Japan, while only $49 billion flowed in. A substantial portion of this capital outflow went into U.S. bonds and permitted the U.S. budget deficit to be financed with less pressure on U.S. interest rates."[59]

Why did Japan send its excess savings to the United States, particularly when it was exposed to enormous risks of loss as the dollar declined in value against the yen? Was it because the Japanese system could not find ways to invest it domestically and had to go abroad? Neoclassical economists answer these questions one way and adherents of Lenin's theory of imperialism offer another explanation. But in either case, to say that "market forces" were responsible is to trivialize the discussion. Perhaps the Ministry of Finance was pursuing its own foreign policy, building leverage over the United States as a form of *zaiteku* mercantilism. Omae Ken'ichi, one of the most popular Japanese spokesmen on economic policy, seems to imply as much: "It is better that the yen remain high until Japan can buy up more American resources and it is better that the U.S. budget deficit continue a bit longer. . . . Japan's prosperity is built on the U.S. budget deficit."[60] One should add of course that the prosperity Omae is talking about is that of an abstract entity, not the Japanese people. "Rich Japan, poor Japanese" *(tomeru Nihon mazushii Nihonjin)* is merely another one of the contradictions that currency realignments exposed—the Japanese have become the world's richest people in per capita terms, but they only have evidence of it when they go abroad on vacations. The domestic prices of imports did not fall.

The actual results of the currency realignments following the Plaza Accord suggest that macroeconomic problems are not the main cause of the Japanese-American trade imbalance. The system worked—except in the case of Japan. American exports did grow on a global basis as their prices declined, and higher domestic prices for imports did begin to cut American consumption of them. Three years after the Plaza Accord, Senator John Heinz complained that Japan accounted for only 14 percent of U.S. trade but for 40 percent of the U.S. trade deficit and that despite its position as the economic superpower of the Pacific, Japan still imported less than one-third as much from the Asian newly industrializing economies as the United States did.[61]

The United States could end the trade deficit tomorrow if it followed the advice of many Japanese pundits (Morita Akio is a prime example) and cut American demand for Japanese goods. This could be easily done by reimplementing the Nixon surcharge of 1971, this time directed solely at Japanese products wherever they might be manufactured outside the United States, or by following Fallows' proposal for an across-the-board tariff on Japanese goods.[62] The United States has not done this because it wants to avoid too great a contraction of domestic American demand, which might lead to global recession and disaster for the high-debt developing countries. As Geza Feketekuty of the USTR's office notes, "Unless both surplus and deficit countries take steps to correct a major trade imbalance, any [single country's] effort to correct such an imbalance will have a deflationary bias."[63]

Up to the winter of 1989–90 American policy was not aimed at causing Americans to buy fewer goods from Japan but at trying to get the Japanese to buy more from America. This policy is to be preferred because it maintains a trading relationship that has enriched both sides and because it does not destroy economies of the Third World. But attempts to lower trade barriers in Japan have become hopelessly intertwined with multilateral negotiations aimed at improving the GATT system. The resultant contradictions stand a good chance of frustrating improvements on both fronts.

In September 1986, the United States took the lead in starting the Uruguay Round of multilateral trade negotiations. Scheduled to last four years, this round aims at modernizing the GATT rules to make them mutually beneficial for all participating nations in the 1990s. The issues this round addresses are long-term reform of agricultural trade, obligations governing trade in services, adequate standards and effective enforcement of intellectual property rights, and GATT dispute settlement procedures. On some of its issues with Japan, such as the protection of rice, the United States eschewed a bilateral approach and left the matter to the Uruguay Round.

Midway through the round, however, the United States became alarmed by the size of its bilateral trade deficit with Japan and by the fact that devaluation of the dollar was correcting its deficit with Europe but having no effect on Japan. The U.S. Congress therefore passed the Trade Act of 1988 with its Super 301 procedures that are formally aimed at all nations but that actually target only Japan.[64] The new Section 301 requires the executive branch to investigate foreign barriers to trade, establishes a procedure for selecting priority targets and demanding their removal, and requires or authorizes economic retaliation if such demands are not met.[65] Inheriting both the Uruguay Round and the Trade Act, the Bush administration, to the extent that it had a trade policy at all, seemed to want to succeed with GATT more than it wanted to implement Super 301 vis-à-vis Japan. Therefore, it chose to implement Section 301 in a way that would make it easy for Japan to respond—three of the four products

Japan is accused of barring are items of government procurement—and it launched SII as what Edward Lincoln called a "learning process."[66] Japan unfortunately claimed not to understand this "deft political orchestration" and reacted with its usual charges of being victimized.[67] Japan is also tempted to see whether other U.S.-EC disputes will allow its own agricultural protection to go on unpunished.

These various issues must be separated. The Uruguay Round is needed to provide new rules for trade among nations that are not capitalist developmental states. Nonetheless, GATT rules will not correct Europe's or America's economic problems with Japan. In my opinion Japan requires narrowly focused, tailor-made, closely monitored, and minutely verified policies—i.e., those based on specific reciprocity rather than the unconditional most-favored-nation status (extending the same rights to all) enjoyed by members of GATT. All of the current policy instruments in existence or being negotiated are inadequate for the problem of Japan. The Uruguay Round, even if it succeeds in keeping GATT alive, does not address the United States' $60 billion trade deficit with Japan. The Trade Act of 1988 itself is fatally flawed because it addresses unilaterally all nations whereas the only unilateral problem that really needs to be addressed outside of GATT is Japan. SII is premised on the theory of Japanese-American convergence and is merely a rerun of the failed negotiations of the Reagan years.[68] What is missing are overall American policies toward Japan and toward making the American economy competitive with Japan's.

A major cause of this persistent confusion is the intellectual vested interests of the economics profession in upholding a doctrine that is increasingly without empirical foundations. A University of Wisconsin economist, Theodore Morgan, has compared the use of data in articles published in American economics, political science, sociology, chemistry, and physics journals from 1982 to 1986. His analysis showed that 42 percent of the articles in the *American Economic Review* developed mathematical models without any data, compared to 18 percent for the *American Political Science Review,* less than 1 percent for the *American Sociological Review,* zero for the *Journal of the American Chemical Society,* and about 12 percent for the *Physical Review.* Morgan also found that another 39 percent of the articles published in the *American Economic Review* were based on data previously published or generated by others rather than having been done by the authors themselves.[69]

This information helps to explain why economists who do not read a single character of Japanese and have made no empirical investigation of the Japanese economy nonetheless make pronouncements on the Japanese economy as if they knew what they were talking about. Thus, for example, Jagdish Bhagwati, in an excoriation of the U.S. Congress and the Trade Act of 1988, claims that Japanese consumers' preferences are dictated by "American cultural hegemony," that "America's greater openness vis-a-vis Japan is open to doubt," and that "there is enough evidence to show that Japan's imports respond to price changes, such as the rise of the yen and the fall of the dollar, much the way other nations' imports do."[70] Since neither the Japanese government nor private Japanese economists agree to the latter point, it seems to be rather an article of faith with economists—a variation on the syllogism that a necessary condition for superior economic performance is free or almost free trade: since Japan has demonstrated very superior economic performance, it must have had free or almost free trade. This same kind of dogmatic thought has long stood in the way of an objective appraisal of Japan's industrial policy. All the English-speaking economists have been able to contribute is the obligatory tone of mocking derision that accompanies use of the phrase "picking winners."[71]

If the United States cannot correct the U.S.-Japan trade imbalance, then the larger partnership between the two countries cannot survive. These issues of trade are not isolable from the broader context of change that is transforming the most basic structures of international relations.[72] In the first two postwar decades, American policy toward Japan was based on the proposition that Japan had great strategic significance but only minor economic significance. This has not been true at least since the end of the Vietnam War, but the events of 1989 threw into dramatic relief just how anachronistic the Japanese-American relationship had become. The collapse of the legitimacy of communism almost everywhere signaled that economic power has come to prevail over military power and that pragmatic institutional innovation has come to prevail over ideological pretensions (not least of these pretensions being the unseemly and unwarranted celebrations of the "victory of capitalism").[73]

A review of the more than two decades' old American trade deficit with Japan suggests two things about the future of Japanese-American relations. First, the United States must either begin to compete with Japan or go the way of the USSR. This means that it must emulate or match Japan's accomplishments in government-business relationships, industrial policy, and industrial organization. Even if they must ignore or fire some academic economists, Americans can no longer avoid the truth that "countries that try to promote higher-value, higher-tech industries will eventually have more of them than countries that don't."[74] Concretely, Americans must undertake a massive analysis of the Japanese political economy in order to establish what it is that the Japanese have done that should be emulated—their saving rate, industrial policy, mode of transferring savings to industry, labor-management relations, leveraging the costs of new industries on the profits of old ones *(keiretsu)*, and quality-controlled manufacturing systems—and what the Japanese do that reflects mercantilism and for which they should be required to pay fines. This program implies not Japan-bashing but learning from Japan, in all senses of the term.

Second, the Japanese-American relationship is too important to be left to lobbyists, *gaijin*-handlers, and professional "friends" of either Japan or the United States. The two countries are quite dissimilar. They have utterly different social histories, resource endowments, processes of industrialization, experiences of international relations, political philosophies, and outlooks on life. Americans are more likely to be individualistic and optimistic even when it makes no sense to be so, whereas the Japanese are commonly preoccupied with *jimae-shugi*, meaning the desire to be self-sufficient and independent as a people. In order to work together, they must know as much as they can about the other, read the other's books, and pay attention to their differences. If such an effort is to be called "revisionism"— and its antonym would appear to be "ignorance"—then let us make the most of it.

5

The Foundations of Japan's Wealth and Power and Why They Baffle the United States

In a 1993 review essay, Karel van Wolferen likens an invitation from one of Washington's neoconservative think tanks to debate the true secrets of Japan's economic success to what it would be like if the editor of *Nature* proposed a discussion on whether the earth is round or flat.[1] The endless MacNeil Lehrerism that afflicts American public policy discussions—meaning the inclination to pair nonsensical views with those of people who have done their homework and to believe that the search for elementary understanding of an issue is comparable to a sporting event—is one of the most frustrating aspects of current Japanese-American relations. One is forever debating the basic details of modern Japanese history with people who are nearly innocent of the subject but who nonetheless have quite fixed opinions about the nature of the Japanese political economy. Even though knowledge of the facts is the basis for all intelligent discussion, there is one area of policymaking in which this rule is normally suspended—namely, policy toward Japan.

Why is this? There are many complex reasons, but three in particular are, I believe, worth stressing at this time. First are the ideological blinders that prevent Americans from looking squarely at Japan. These are caused in part by the ideological dimensions of the Cold War, including the United States's and Japan's attempts to fit Japan ideologically into the "Western" camp in that struggle. The end of the Cold War is bringing this ideological dimension into clearer focus, including the vested interests that have built up in both the United States and Japan in the Cold War relationships.

Second is the unusual—from an American point of view—situation in which Japanese nationalism is expressed almost entirely through economic claims and achievements. Observers who do not understand this linkage consistently misinterpret data from the Japanese economy because they assign it to the wrong people for analysis—namely, to economists. By training and orientation such people are both blind to and ignorant of nationalism. It is like asking a retriever to do the work of a bloodhound.

The third reason why Americans are baffled by the Japanese economic and technological challenge is because the Japanese economy is guided by a state strategy. This is hard for Americans in particular to fathom since the guidance of their own economy is so obviously left in the hands of those who inherited their wealth, those who represent institutional investors and who face narrowly defined fiduciary responsibilities, those who seek private interests without any regard for the public consequences, and those who through lobbying or trust violation can obtain insider or political advantages. Japanese economic strategy requires that the public interest be elevated over private interests, and it delegitimizes the pursuit of private motives openly acknowledged.

The Japanese economic strategy is comparable to the American pursuit of a military strategy; and many norms of Japanese economic life—long hours, service to the group, wearing uniforms, equitable pay, and long-term goals—are perfectly familiar to the American military.[2] Interestingly enough, the proposal during August 1993 of the U.S. Marine Corps that it recruit only single men and women because "the weight of family-related problems can disrupt the individual's concentration level [and] result in decreased performance" would be perfectly familiar to a Japanese salaryman, except that Japan's solution is different. It relies on a rigid, gender-based division of labor within the family which, in effect, frees the father to devote his life to the company.[3] Also like a military strategy, Japan's economic strategy implies indirection, disinformation, and deception in order to defeat the nation's economic competitors. *Ceteris paribus*—other things being equal—as the economists would say, the adversary, firm, or nation with a strategy will defeat the one without a strategy.

In this essay I propose trying to put some flesh on each of these three skeletons. At the end I shall return to that famous question, What is to be done?

I

What is the present-day "Japan problem" of the United States? It is many things. It is trade friction. It is learning to live with a super-rich but politically cautious and sometimes seemingly irresponsible Japan. It is trying to convince Japanese investors in the United States that they must obey American laws.[4] It is the attempt to come to grips with Japan's exploitation of the easily lobbied government of the United States, which also means coming to grips with influence peddling by corrupt lawyers and other Americans. And it means trying to mitigate the influence of cultural, ethnic, and even racist stereotypes by both countries.

But these aspects of the Japan problem are not conceptually difficult. Japan and the United States are at present the world's two richest nations, and they achieved that status at least in part because of the economic interdependence they developed with each other. The prosperity they both enjoy should be sufficient incentive to cause them to work hard at finding compromises in the practical and mundane aspects of their problems in living together.

The more serious Japan problem in the United States is theoretical and intellectual. In the United States, it reflects above all the overly elevated position of economists as ideologists and justifiers of the United States during the Cold War and on into a post–Cold War world in which the United States flatters itself it is the pivot of a unipolar world. Economists enjoy their positions as priestly defenders of laissez faire, and they therefore have vested interests in perpetuating their ideological influence as long as possible. Unfortunately for them, they did not anticipate that Japan would become very wealthy, they still cannot explain how it happened in terms that are consistent with their own doctrines, and they are deeply threatened by this development and by the emulation of the Japanese model elsewhere in Asia, including China. They pretend that no one knows or understands why Japan developed as fast as it did and that great controversy surrounds alternative explanations. They are in the dark partly because they do not read Japanese and have made no empirical investigation of Japanese economic history.[5]

Just as during the Cold War the former Soviet Union gave its chief ideological roles to Marxist-Leninists, the United States gave those same roles to economists. In its main ideological dimension, the Cold War was portrayed as a contest between a socialist state that displaced the market in order to achieve its goals and a state-as-referee that allegedly let its goals be set and achieved by private actors seeking private interests. The seeming victory of the American conception has tended to entrench economists as the high priests of American-style capitalism. Even so, these are worried priests. They vaguely suspect that their own position is as extreme as that of the former Leninists, and they look desperately for evidence that the doctrine they espouse is valid. For if Japan's economic success reflects the effectiveness of its state policies for development, then the English-speaking economists are in danger soon of becoming as little in demand as Marxist-Leninists.

The economists are unable to analyze the Japan problem because at root it is actually not an economic problem, but a matter of differing political systems. The key variable and the great asymmetry between Japan and the United States is the state. Japan has a strong state and a long history of its society passively accepting leadership from the state. In this respect, Japan is much closer to the history of modern Germany than it is to any English-speaking country. It is important to understand that Americans who are confused by contemporary Japan are also people who know very little about modern Germany. By contrast, the United States has a relatively weak state, except for its military-industrial complex, which American political and economic theory considers exceptional and does not allow to contaminate sociopolitical orthodoxy. Equally important, the historical legacy of the United States is hostile to the concept of the state for two particular reasons: the federal structure of its government, and its not wholly successful attempt to divide sovereignty among three allegedly co-equal branches of government.

As Andrew Vincent writes, "Federalism encourages centrifugal forces, distinct legal structures and a general mistrust of centralism. The State, in its historical development, has been a centripetal force; the balance of forces rests at the centre, even though a State may *tolerate* or even encourage some local autonomy." Similarly, the separation of powers tends to raise questions about where sovereignty lies and whether it even exists. This can give rise to the legitimation crisis that Jurgen Habermas alleges afflicts the modern capitalist state, torn between maintaining the conditions of free enterprise and the need to intervene in the economy to avoid the social crises that capitalism causes.[6] Japan thus far has been immune to this type of legitimacy crisis for its state.

Needless to say, there is a great deal of self-deception and ideology in the American lack of attention to the nature and power of the state. This is most apparent in what the rest of the world is least able to avoid about the United States—its role as a global military hegemon. But this lack of explicit theorizing about the state and the desire to subsume the state in almost anything else—theories of the "capture" of the state by private interests, calling state officials "civil servants," insisting that the state is concerned only with "administration" of a separate political will—means that analysts from an American background are particularly likely to misunderstand strong states, such as those that have derived from the Confucian tradition in East Asia.

This tendency is exaggerated by an American academic political science that, like economics, has become a handmaiden of American power, that seeks to emulate the scientific pretensions of mathematized economics, and that is afraid of empirical research outside its own Anglo-American confines. Not all American academic economics and political science is ideological, but the stress on theory rather than induction tends to give preference to ideology masquerading as theory. A good example is the fad in political science called "rational choice" theory. Its roots are economic determinism, a belief in the withering away of the state, and other recently refurbished neo-Marxist propositions. Its popularity reflects the desire to see an idealized conception of the United States as a universal model for other countries—an aspect of American hegemonism—and to ward off the challenge of Japan and its emulators as different and perhaps more effective forms of political economy. Enormous efforts have been made to try to force Japan to fit the categories of rational choice theory and to define the Japanese state out of existence.[7]

Japan's economic success is significant; it was not based on transitory or negligible Japanese advantages; and it constitutes the greatest anomaly in the prevailing paradigm of American political and economic thought. Which brings me to my own work, *MITI and the Japanese Miracle: The Growth of Industrial Policy, 1925–1975,* published in 1982, which led to the controversy about so-called revisionism. My history of Japan's industrial policy and the various bureaucracies that formulated and implemented it caused me to identify Japan as a "capitalist developmental state," as distinct from a "capitalist regulatory state" such as the United States. The idea that the Japanese state had played primarily a developmental role in its economy, rather than the regulatory role prescribed by Anglo-American theory, produced the international discussion of revisionism, meaning that the theory of the capitalist developmental state forced a revision of English-language orthodoxy on the role of the state in the economy. Because of my book, some Japanese and American commentators dubbed me the "godfather of revisionism," and took it upon themselves to discredit revisionism—not by addressing the evidence in both the Japanese and American cases but by alleging that the revisionists were "Japan-bashers," which turned out to be a code word for racists.

The whole contretemps over revisionism appears embarrassing in light of the collapse of the LDP and the positions taken by the leaders of the coalition government that followed it. From the highest reaches of the most popular government in postwar Japan we learned that Japan's markets actually are closed, that results-oriented trade would be a good idea and in conformity with the normal working procedures of the Japanese economic bureaucracy, that for the past thirty years the Japanese construction industry has paid off favored politicians in order to keep all forms of competition under control, that the condition of "rich Japan, poor Japanese" was caused primarily by the hyperconservative monetary policy of the Ministry of Finance during the same period that the Reagan administration in the United States was pursuing a hyperliberal fiscal policy, that during World War

II the Japanese government was responsible for aggression in Asia and for conscripting non-Japanese women in occupied countries into front-line army brothels, and that the primary institution of governmental policymaking has been not the ruling party or private interest groups but the central state bureaucracy.[8]

These views are not particularly those of the revisionists; in most cases they amount to nothing more than common knowledge among reasonably well-educated people who live and work in the Asia-Pacific region. The role of the revisionists was to insist that such realistic propositions about the Japanese government needed to be incorporated into the foreign policies of both governments. It turns out that it was not revisionism that misled Japanese and American citizens concerned about the future of their relations but the platitudinous propaganda of the Japanese Gaimusho (Ministry of Foreign Affairs), the U.S. Department of State, and the teachings of their numerous minions and flatterers around the world.

In retrospect, I believe that the work of the revisionists—the books and articles by Karel van Wolferen, Glen Fukushima, James Fallows, Pat Choate, Marie Anchordoguy, Michael Crichton, Clyde Prestowitz, and me, among others—was important in accelerating a shift in U.S. attention to the problems of the Pacific.[9] But the long-range success of this effort, particularly at the American official level, remains in doubt. The U.S. government is virtually flying blind in terms of the competence of its diplomatic, trade, and military officials to deal with Japan.

It is perplexing that the American government pays so little attention to a nation the size of two Germanies and with the potential to become a superpower in every sense of the term, while it lavishes its resources on such places as Kuwait, Somalia, and Russia. It is hard to imagine any serious reason other than intellectual hegemonism and vested interest why Americans should want to think of Japan as their clone, emulator, or follower. Japan is some 1,500 years older than the United States, and the idea that Japan is like or converging with the United States is on the surface of it silly and implausible. With the end of the Cold War and the widespread recognition that the global economic center of gravity has shifted to East Asia, the idea that Japan is different from the United States and the United Kingdom is hardly worth noting. That ought to be the starting point for serious social science and serious policymaking today.

II

In his study of postwar Japanese grand strategy, Kenneth Pyle stresses that economic nationalism was not just something the Japanese fell back on because political nationalism had been discredited by the war. It was the basis of all their plans and actions. Japan's "primary commitment to economic nationalism," he writes, "also produced a determination to avoid any collective security commitments and any involvement with security affairs beyond the home islands."[10] The author of the strategy, former Prime Minister Yoshida Shigeru, once remarked to his subordinate (later prime minister) Miyazawa Kiichi, "The day [for rearmament] will come naturally when our livelihood recovers. It may sound devious [*zurui*], but let the Americans handle [our security] until then."[11]

Almost fifty years after the end of the war, Japan's livelihood had more than recovered, but its government was still being *zurui* about giving up economic nationalism and the Americans were still handling its security. Ozawa Ichirō, the political strategist behind the Hosokawa government of 1993, deplores this situation, and in his best-selling plan for the reform of the country calls on Japan to become an "ordinary country" *(futsū no kuni).*[12] "There are problems that cannot be settled merely by paying money," he writes. "We are not entitled to criticize the United States with our [import] controls being left untouched."[13]

I think it is fair to say that in the postwar world Japan's basic stance toward other countries and in organizing its domestic economy was one of economic nationalism. But it is necessary to explain what this means. Economic nationalism is not necessarily the same things as mercantilism, adversarial trade, or protectionism, although it certainly can on occasion include those tactics.

"Nationalism" itself is a very broad concept, and it has been used to refer to many different types of political movements. These include state building via warmaking in the emergence of modern Britain; reform nationalism of the sort seen in Meiji Japan and in Prussia after its wars with Napoleon; socially conservative nationalist revolutions such as those in nineteenth-century Latin America; liberal nationalism (the Risorgimento, J. S. Mill, etc.); and thinking "with one's blood," which can turn "nationalist quarrels into Darwinian zero-sum affairs."[14]

But this is not what is meant by economic nationalism. The Meiji reforms imply nationalism, in that industrialization in order to defend the country against Western imperialism dictated an entirely different role for the state in economic affairs than in the Anglo-American "West." The successes of the movement also helped to legitimate this different role for the state. But economic nationalism means both more and less than forced development from above.

Liah Greenfeld's understanding of nationalism in terms of self-respect, of overcoming a sense of national inferiority, and her stress on the uses of nationalism to paper over status inconsistencies relates to how I conceive Japanese economic nationalism. She writes, "The worth of the nation—the psychological gratification afforded by national identity and therefore its importance—is related to the experience of dignity by wide and ever widening sectors of humanity. Nationalism originated as a reaction—one of many possible reactions—to the structural contradictions of the society of orders. It was a response of individuals in elite sectors of society, who were personally affected by these contradictions and were placed by them in a state of status-inconsistency."[15]

Japan certainly experienced the contradictions of the society of orders and their transcendence through the redefinition of the society in nationalist terms. The reaction of the great nineteenth-century modernizer and educator Fukuzawa Yukichi to the inconsistencies in his and others' statuses—they were lower-ranking members of the ruling samurai class but increasingly unable to meet their debts to the lowest class, the merchants—is a good example.[16] Over time what began in Japan as an elite protest against various status inconsistencies spread and was spread by mass education, the reforms of the occupation, and the rise of new reference groups to all classes and genders within the society and in comparison with other societies.

The status inconsistencies that Greenfeld mentions need not occur only within a society. They also can occur among societies: the phrases "economic superpower" and "political pygmy" often used about Japan today are an obvious example. Ozawa Ichirō in his best-selling *Nihon Kaizō Keikaku* compares Japan to a "dinosaur with a huge body but a tiny brain."[17] Nationalism may be equally effective in resolving or transcending such invidious national comparisons. As Greenfeld observes, "Economic globalization is entirely consistent with nationalism. The belief that it spells the end of nationalism is based on the mistaken assumption of the primacy of economics in social life, the idea of economic determinism."[18]

According to Greenfeld, twentieth-century nations seeking to overcome their feelings of national inferiority have turned most commonly to Leninism. This is certainly true of mainland China and Vietnam, where communism supplied the organizational weapons and the anti-Western vehemence for powerful movements of national liberation and regeneration. China's achievement of thermonuclear status and Vietnam's driving the United States from its territory validated both nations as truly sovereign, and as major players on the international stage. With their successful assertions of national sovereignty behind them, China and Vietnam today are trying to extricate themselves from the dead ends of Leninist economics, but that is another story, and one that also has delicate nationalist implications.

The Sino–Vietnamese–Leninist route was blocked for Japan, even though there were powerful forces within Japan that wanted to pursue it for at least the first fifteen years after 1945. As Ellis Krauss puts it, because of the pacifism of the Japanese public and the war-renouncing clause of the Japanese Constitution, "national security could no longer be gained through military means. Economic growth was the only way Japan could once again catch up with the West and assert itself as a major nation again."[19] Under the capable leadership of Yoshida Shigeru and his intrusion of high-ranking state officials into positions of political leadership, Japan chose to regain its national self-respect through economic achievements and economic leadership.

By economic nationalism, then, I mean that the Japanese pursue economic activities primarily in order to achieve independence from and leverage over potential adversaries rather than to achieve consumer utility, private wealth, mutually beneficial exchange, or any other objective posited by economic determinists. *Raison d'état* prevails over the economic interests of individuals in Japan. Historically speaking, this is a much more common motive of organized economic activities than the economic rationality that forms the basis of many academic theories. True economic rationality is relatively rare in human history. In any case, economic nationalism continues to be the fundamental principle of Japan's government-guided capitalism even though Japan has caught up with and surpassed its former external reference economies.

The results of this effort are there for all to see. It is why at the end of Japanese fiscal year 1992 Japanese direct foreign investment totaled $246 billion, while net foreign investment in Japan was just $15.5 billion. It is also why an old-fashioned nationalist like Ishihara Shintarō goes around talking about the "technology card" and saying that "If Japan told Washington it would no longer sell computer chips to the United States, the Pentagon would be totally helpless. . . . Japan now has a decisive technological advantage."[20]

Japan has been able successfully to pursue a strategy of economic nationalism for at least two reasons. One is that the strategy is compatible with the institutions and values Japan inherited and/or salvaged from its century and a half of defensive modernization. The other reason is that Japan's wartime conqueror and chief peacetime competitor, the United States, continues to cling tenaciously to nineteenth-century English economic doctrine in the face of the Japanese challenge. The result has been much like the Austrians and Prussians clinging to obsolete military doctrines in the face of Napoleon's innovations: they were defeated until they began to work on their own counterstrategies.

Japan's most important institutional and value difference from the United States relates to the scope and domain of government. As Krauss puts it, "The size, scope, and domain of government is the most controversial and conflictual value question in American history and politics." It was the root cause of the American Civil War. By contrast, in Japan, "It is freedom from foreign control that is emphasized . . . not the freedom of society from one's own government, and especially not freedom from economic intervention." In Japanese discussions of industrial policy, "Government's role is not subject to public conflict or controversy as it is in the United States."[21] This gives Japan a formidable comparative advantage, one that it has pursued relentlessly, and one that it continuously renews by close study of and attempts to manipulate the American political process.

III

There are many different strategies that arise out of Japan's economic nationalism, including industrial policy, economic intelligence collecting both domestically and internationally, foreign aid tied to sales by Japanese companies, concessionary sales of technology to key agencies in order to secure foreign markets (e.g., Fujitsu's virtual gifts of computers to South Korean banks and government agencies), promotion and protection of general trading companies that have the capacity to tie together many companies into package deals (e.g., the Baoshan steelworks deal in China), the strategic use of joint ventures and co-production schemes to extract proprietary technology from foreign enterprises, the rigging of stockholders' rights to prevent foreign takeovers of domestic companies, and so forth. None of these devices is hard to understand once their strategic intent is taken into account. To illustrate this point, let me discuss two elements of Japanese strategy: the strategic use of the distinction between the public and the private, and the strategic use of the distinction between the formal and the covert. These are two aspects of Japanese economic nationalism that are commonly overlooked by foreigners.

It is simply astonishing how many foreign scholars of Japan, including those who read Japanese, continue to use the concept "private sector" in its parochial Anglo-American sense in writing about Japan. It is not that they do not know about *amakudari* (the circulation of elites from government ministries to non-governmental posts in the society), or about "the overwhelming respect Japanese have for public authority" (as noted by the political theorist Patricia Boling),[22] or about the neither-fish-nor-fowl status of national policy companies such as the Kansai International Airport Company. It is, rather, that they refuse to think about the implications of such common features for Japanese society.

Let me offer some examples. In October 1993, the *Nihon kei-*

zai shimbun noted that "Currently 39 presidents, or 26% of the presidents of Japan's 150 *private banks* [emphasis added]—city banks, long-term credit banks, and regional banks—have come from the two powerful financial bureaucracies [the Ministry of Finance and the Bank of Japan]."[23]

In August 1993, the *Shūkan tōyō keizai* detailed how every major company in the Japanese construction industry—including Obayashi, Kajima, Shimizu, Taisei, and Takenaka—had at least two directors from the Ministry of Construction and innumerable *komon* (advisers), *san'yo* (counselors), deputy department chiefs, and branch office advisers who had completed full careers as officials in the state bureaucracy before joining a firm.[24]

In the bribery arrests that started to sweep Japan during the second half of 1993, most of the allegedly civilian politicians whom the police pulled from their offices—mayors of major cities (e.g., Sendai) or governors of major prefectures (e.g., Ibaraki, Tokushima)—were also former high-ranking officials of the state bureaucracy.

In the Kansai airport project, even though the Japanese had agreed to let American construction firms bid for some parts of major "public works" projects, they are now denying that it is a public work. Diet-enacted national legislation created the Kansai Airport Company (law number 53 of June 30, 1984), the Aviation Bureau of the Ministry of Transportation directly supervises it, the government put up ¥85.4 billion of its initial capital of ¥128.1 billion, and the company is listed in the official *Tokushu hōjin sōran (Directory of Special Legal Entities).*[25] And yet the Japanese government maintains that it is a private enterprise since there has been more private participation in it than in virtually all other previous projects of its type.

As a matter of economic nationalism, Japan has a long record of enlisting private activities for public and national purposes, while delegitimizing private activities pursued for private ends. The *locus classicus* on this subject for prewar Japan is Byron Marshall. He writes that Japanese business men "denounced the philosophy of economic individualism for its stress on the pursuit of personal gain, and claimed that Japanese businessmen were motivated by patriotic devotion and a willingness to sacrifice for the common good."[26]

In the contemporary period, Boling draws some of the consequences from her study of the meanings of "public" and "private" in the West and *kō* and *shi* in Japan:

> While both Japan and the West may regard private interest as particular, narrow and selfish, many Western theorists also see private interest as an essential building block of the public or common good. Japanese thinking, however, posits a public good or interest (i.e., that of the emperor or the state) which is universal and all-encompassing, and always opposed and superior to private perspectives. The notion of the public good as a paramount value and private perspectives or interests as selfish and dishonorable continues to affect Japanese social and political life. . . . The bureaucracy is presumed to be impartial and immune to special pleading, and therefore able to "correctly pursue the best interests of the whole according to the supreme principles of justice and public interests" [quoting Matsumoto Sannosuke]. It is interesting to contrast the Japanese faith in the expertise and impartiality of bureaucrats to the work done on the "capture" of government agencies by special interests in the United States.[27]

My purpose in quoting these materials is not to applaud either the Western formulation or the Japanese one but, rather, to stress that serious differences exist on so basic an issue as the nature and limits of the public sphere.

Japanese, in their economic activities and elsewhere, also continue to make a distinction between *tatemae*—principle, formality, face, pretense—and *honne*—reality, actual practice, the face without makeup, the way we do things. This distinction became politically important in Japan during the period when it was victimized by the unequal treaties imposed on it by the Western imperialist powers, starting with the United States. Among the terms of these treaties, particularly the Harris Treaty of 1858, was extraterritoriality for Americans in Japan. This meant that they were not subject to Japanese criminal laws. The unequal treaties also severely limited Japan's tariff autonomy. The Western powers made clear that they imposed these terms because Japan was, in their eyes, uncivilized and needed to reform itself to look more or less like a Western country. Japan thus had a practical interest in causing Westerners to see in Japan Western-type legal codes, parliamentary bodies, and commercial practices, regardless of how Japanese actually did things.

In the broader sense of political culture, the distinction between *tatemae* and *honne* reflects and parallels the Japanese fascination with the formally powerful but covertly weak and the formally ordinary but covertly powerful. Almost surely derived from the country's long experience of feudalism, Japanese love to dwell on the differences between emperor and shōgun, those who are carried and those who carry *(katsugareru ō* vs. *katsugu mono), seiron seiji* (public opinion politics) and *ura seiji* (unseen politics), a *kagemusha* (dummy general) and a *kuromaku* (wirepuller), or, in short, puppets and puppeteers.[28] These distinctions refer to actual events in Japanese politics that are as old as the Heian era and as contemporary as the eight-party coalition of former Prime Minister Hosokawa that was actually put together by former LDP secretary general Ozawa Ichirō.[29]

It should of course be understood that the Japanese are fully aware that most foreigners take a *kagemusha* for the real thing; they thus use *tatemae* politics in their strategies of indirection and disinformation. One of their best stratagems to gain more time in negotiations is to cause Westerners to think that the Japanese government has lost control of a situation and needs time to recover. A good example of this ploy at work occurred during the G-7 summit in Tokyo in July 1993.[30]

IV

My reasons for raising these problems—America's preoccupation with "classical" economic theory and its failure to understand Japan's economic nationalism and its economic strategies—is to ask, finally, What is to be done? We must recognize that in dealing with Japan the United States is virtually flying blind. There is no apparatus in place to provide middle managers throughout the American government with the kind of information they need on Japan—certainly nothing even slightly comparable to the quality of information that was available on the former USSR and China during the Cold War. Throughout the U.S. government, expertise on Japan is conspicuous by its absence. Neither the Bush nor the Clinton administration appointed a single cabinet-level official with substantial knowledge and experience of Japan and who could read the Japanese language. This was apparent during the last two presidential trips to Tokyo by Bush and Clinton.

Equally important, if the U.S. government ever does wake up and wants to staff its departments and agencies with knowledgeable personnel, it will discover that recruits are few and far between. This is because of the failure of American universities to internationalize and to begin to respond to the new agenda after the Cold War. As Eugene Skolnikoff of MIT writes, "The disciplinary structure of universities creates another difficulty with a long history: the inconvenient fact that the world's problems do not conform to that structure. The need for multidisciplinary approaches to public issues is well understood, but the record of research universities in attempting to apply their knowledge to understanding those issues and recommending policy alternatives has been decidedly mixed."[31]

There is today no single American university with a fully adequate program in Japanese studies backed by a library oriented toward contemporary affairs. Many young Americans are gaining some first-hand experience of Japan, often as teachers of English in Japanese high schools under an excellent program operated by the Japanese Ministry of Education. But when they return to American universities to follow up on their experiences, what they typically encounter is a brew of French literary theory, obsolescent English economic doctrine, rational choice theory, and gender studies. What they actually need are courses in the Japanese economy and finance, history, language study, and empirical political science and sociology. What they need are programs similar to those developed on the USSR during the 1950s or on China during the 1960s.

The first thing to be done, then, is to strengthen and reorient our national analytical capacity to understand and react to Japanese achievements. This includes recognition that the world's center of gravity in manufacturing has migrated to East Asia, where learning from Japan and competition with Japan are simultaneously being pursued.

Second, we must adopt our own industrial policy. Japan and the other high-growth economies of East Asia have demonstrated that the state can be a critically important contributor to the success of market economies. These contributions include the things that Adam Smith specified—education, investment in infrastructure, incentives to save—but also public measures to provide one's own citizens with good jobs in high-tech industries.

Finally, I believe, we must adopt results-oriented trade. This is the logical conclusion from our recognition of the differences we have vis-à-vis Japan and from our record of failure to negotiate acceptable trade rules with Japan. Neither of these tasks should overtax the abilities of Americans, once they get beyond the stale verities of the Cold War and the self-congratulatory image of being a lone superpower.

POLITICS

6

Japan: Who Governs?
An Essay on Official Bureaucracy

In a famous essay, Maruyama Masao tried "to give a rough sketch of the massive 'system of irresponsibilities' that constituted Japan's fascist rule. Three basic types of political personality can be abstracted from this sketch: the Portable Shrine, the Official, and the Outlaw (or *rōnin*). The Shrine represents authority; the Official, power; and the Outlaw, violence."[1] Although Maruyama was addressing himself to the essence of late military-era politics, his "rough sketch" still contains most of the essential insights that scholars have advanced to account for the nature of modern Japanese politics, either before or after the war: the marked separation between power and authority, the movement of policy initiative from lower statuses upward toward higher statuses (for example, the *ringisei*), and the alleged system of irresponsibilities that comes to the fore whenever policy goes awry (as, for example, over pollution, land prices, or yen revaluation).

Maruyama's tripod also seems to live on into the present, judging from the number of three-fold analytical schemes that students of Japanese politics have advanced. Nagai Yōnosuke endorses it explicitly. He suggests that in the 1970s the portable shrine is the Liberal Democratic Party (LDP) faction leader, held aloft by the bureaucracy, and prodded by the new *rōnin*—the press, and, he might have added, the emerging forces of consumer protest, residents' committees, and "reform" *(kakushin)* mayors.[2] In a different formulation, Taguchi Fukuji refers to "the quasi-monopolistic usurpation of the decision-making function by the 'Triangular League' made up of the top leaders of the ruling party, the senior officers of the government, and the financial tycoons."[3] In Taguchi's view, the financiers *(zaikai)* are not, of course, *rōnin* but have in fact gained status, as Maruyama said they would if they played the game. But the entrance of the *zaikai* into a structured relationship with power and authority seems itself to be a prime cause of the creation of new *rōnin*. Even the phrase "Japan, Inc.," although derided by American specialists because of its crudity and lack of nuance, appears to owe something to Maruyama's conception. Like a physical tripod, each leg is indispensable for the stability of the structure. It is an endlessly fascinating process to study how each focus of political force interlocks and interpenetrates with the others, but in the end they still must be seen as somehow "incorporated," as Maruyama thought they were, if one is really going to try to answer the question of who governs in Japan.

Two-thirds of the tripod has been reasonably well documented. Good studies exist of both the ruling and opposition parties, and, to a lesser extent, of the interest and pressure groups, including big business, professionals, labor, and a few others. Books on the historical and social background of contemporary politics, as well as on the American occupation, elections, the constitution, local government, and foreign and defense policy, provide much important information for any understanding of the structure. Only the official, the power-holding bureaucrat, remains relatively unscrutinized. In a valuable introductory survey, J. A. A. Stockwin notes, "There is no comprehensive study in English of the national bureaucracy," a circumstance that may help to explain why the triangular formulations of Maruyama and others do not today elicit universal acceptance.[4]

This lacuna is not one that can be filled in a short essay. My own research commitment is to the study of a single element of the official bureaucracy—the trade and industry officials of the Tsūsanshō (Ministry of International Trade and Industry, or MITI) and its predecessors.[5] I believe that we shall reach an adequate understanding of the official in Japanese politics only when we have studies of the vicissitudes and accomplishments of most of the ministries, agencies, and public enterprises that make up the Japanese government. Research of this sort is possible and is underway. Here I wish to signal the significance of the topic by exploring in various dimensions the controversy that has surrounded the role of the official in Japan from the occupation to the present day. My purpose is neither to support nor to challenge Maruyama's idea of the powerful but unsanctioned official and his vital but ostensibly invisible activities; it is rather to follow up on his and others' efforts, the most provocative and courageous we have, to explain bureaucratic power in Japan. Leaving aside constitutional clichés, Marxist substitutes for thought, and the tautologies of national character studies, practicing political scientists, myself included, are not yet prepared to answer who governs in Japan, although we have mountains of evidence, much of it contradictory, to sift on the subject.

I

Two significant books illustrate the controversial nature of available work on Japan's governmental bureaucracy. One is by a group of American and Japanese scholars—Ezra Vogel, editor, *Modern Japanese Organization and Decision-Making*—and the other is by a group of Japanese scholars—Ari Bakuji, Ide Yoshinori, et al., *Gendai gyōsei to kanryōsei (Modern Administration and the Bureaucratic System)*.[6] In the first, some of the American scholars approach the subject of officialdom in much the same way that an anthropologist comes to the study of an utterly strange civilization—open-minded, ready to find the secrets of success, and impatient with the premature carpings of the hypercritical or ideological. Albert Craig, in the leading article of the Vogel volume, explicitly adopts the language of functionalism and is properly and insightfully determined to show that the Japanese bureaucracy "works." At times he seems to veer toward normative functionalism—the belief that because a practice occurs it must be functional for something—and to quibble with the facts, but his article is a deliberately administered antidote to the "large literature written by ex-bureaucrats and newspaper reporters to expose the foibles, failings, formalism, and frustrations of bureaucratic life in Japan."[7]

By contrast, Ari, Ide, and their colleagues are neither ex-bureaucrats nor newspaper reporters, but their essays are centrally in the stream of critical, reform-minded literature in Japan on the bureaucracy. In the lead-off essay, Kawanaka Nikō deplores the exclusivity and divergence from constitutional stipulations of the bureaucracy's monopoly of policy planning and observes that "In Japan, the idea that policy is formulated through discussion with the people is not developed." Kojima Akira challenges the view of foreigners that interministerial agreement is reached on the basis of consensus, and he is alarmed by the fact that it is more efficacious for citizens to approach officialdom through "appeals" *(chinjō)* than through openly political processes.[8]

What does this divergence of orientations between two scholarly symposia on more or less the same subject signify? Craig is of course right that too much of Japan's journalism on its bureaucracy is facile and insensitive to its accomplishments. When an English commentator on Japan's economy, asked to account for its performance, responds, "Certainly, the very high standard of the civil servants and the fact that they all want Japan to grow," one can only agree.[9] It is for the same reason that the Organization for Economic Cooperation and Development singled out "the efficiency of the administration" in making an optimistic forecast for the Japanese economy just at the time that most other open economies were staggering under the impact of OPEC price hikes and inflation.[10] The writings of Matsumoto Seichō, Fukumoto Kunio, and others, including some Westerners, while often suggestive, will not help us to understand why the Japanese governmental bureaucracy is as comparatively small, inexpensive, and effective as it is.[11] At the same time, it cannot be overlooked that while many foreigners study Japanese bureaucracy functionally, the most serious Japanese scholars approach the problem as one of *gyōsei kaikaku,* or reform of administration. After all the qualifications have been made, there remains a hard core of serious domestic criticism of Japanese officialdom that foreigners are in danger of ignoring—for one way to find out what powers and attributes the bureaucracy possesses is to find out what the Japanese want to reform in their bureaucracy.

From at least February 6, 1948, when the Katayama cabinet set up the Temporary Administrative Structure Reform Deliberation Council (Rinji Gyōsei Kikō Kaikaku Shingikai), to the present, the Japanese government has not been without at least one, and usually several, high-level commissions devoted to reform of the bureaucracy. It is true that most of these bodies have ended up merely trying to check or reduce the inexorable growth of the bureaucracy or to cut through red tape. However, the most important of them did reflect a real sense of crisis and was charged to deal with Maruyama-type issues: how to make the bureaucracy accountable to the groups that the constitution said were authorized to govern. This was the Temporary Administrative Investigation Council (TAIC) (Rinji Gyōsei Chōsa Kai), established February 15, 1962, and made up of the president of the Mitsui Bank, Satō Kiichirō, as chairman, and a Yomiuri vice-president, the chairman of the public employees union, a former procurator general, the president of the Shōwa Denkō corporation, the chairman of Sōhyō, and a distinguished academic specialist—Rōyama Masamichi—as members. Most important, both houses of the Diet authorized the creation of the TAIC and provided it with its own staff of some 21 specialists and 70 researchers. The council presented its report directly to the prime minister on September 29, 1964.[12]

Since that time at least four successor organizations have been created to implement its findings. The most important of these is the Administrative Supervision Committee (Gyōsei Kanri Iinkai), established by law on July 1, 1965, under the chairmanship of the director general of the Administrative Management Agency and known to the officials it was supposed to watch as the *"Ometsukeyaku"*—an ironic reference to the shogunal watchdogs of the feudal age. This committee publishes annually the authoritative so-called *Administrative Reform White Paper (Gyōsei kaikaku no genjō to kadai).*

What have been the results? Not many, according to most Japanese observers, except perhaps the dropping of the word "temporary" *(rinji)* from the titles of the most recent reform committees. Some simplification of administration has been carried out: the government readjusted and consolidated some 1,641 permissions, approvals, licenses, and so forth *(kyoninkaken)* that the public previously had to obtain from bureaucratic offices (about 15 percent of the total of 11,088 statutory permissions identified by the TAIC) and did the same for some 1,636 reports that citizens had to make to ministries and agencies (about 22 percent of the total of 7,449 such reports). The government also cut the number of deliberation councils *(shingikai)* from 277 in 1965 to 236 in 1972. But on the main objectives of the TAIC, the *Japan Times,* not known as a purveyor of leftist exposés, wrote editorially: "No progress whatsoever has been made by the Government in its administrative reform efforts, with the sole exception of a hold down on Government personnel increases." It added, "Japan's bureaucratic structure was one aspect of Japanese life which General Douglas MacArthur failed to reform. Instead of chopping away at the base of the bureaucratic pyramid, he simply chopped off the apex, by purging key wartime Government officials. In due course, the pyramid grew a new apex, much like a starfish renewing a dismembered limb and the bureaucracy continued unchanged from the prewar days."[13]

The most devastating critic of the results of *gyōsei kaikaku* was himself a member of both the TAIC and the Administrative Supervision Committee—Ōta Kaoru, the former secretary general of Sōhyō. In his book, he deplores the fact that the main Sōhyō unions, which are made up of government employees, together with the Socialist Party, have done as much to frustrate administrative reform in order to keep their jobs as has the Liberal Democratic Party, with its cadres of former elite bureaucrats.[14] He further suggests that a first measure of reform would be to abolish the Administrative Management Agency attached to the prime minister's office and says that all members of the Administrative Supervision Committee agreed with this view. He explains that because the officials of the Administrative Management Agency have no power over private businesses and control no public enterprises like those under the supervision of other ministries, they depend, upon recommendations from the influential ministries when it comes time for them to retire and descend from heaven *(amakudari).*[15] Thus, their official functions of supervising the bureaucracy are contradicted by their need to cultivate the bureaucracy.

Ōta supplies innumerable examples of the notorious territorial consciousness *(nawabari ishiki)*—also known, in some of the Japanese language's better metaphors, as *kakkyo-shugi* (hold-one's-ground-ism), *takotsubo-shiki gyōsei* (the foxhole method of administration), and simply *sekushonarizumu*—of the various elements of the bureaucracy and of some of its costs to the citizenry. One example must suffice. For the past ten years governmental committees have been trying to find solutions to the problems of traffic jams and smog in the big cities and of high fares of taxis and the indifferent manners of their drivers. At one time the Ministry of Transportation (which controls the taxi business) and the Police Agency (which controls traffic) had agreed to restrict the number of private cars entering cities, and the MITI (which supervises the automobile manufacturing industry) and the Ministry of Construction (which builds and manages freeways) had dropped their opposition. It failed to come about, however, because the Public Safety Commissions, which had been penetrated by the automotive industry, intervened with the Police Agency, which is under the commissions' influence, and caused it to change its position. As for taxis, the proposed solution was to allow personally managed taxis to operate, but this ran into the *nawabari* (territory) of the Land Transportation Bureau (Rikuun Kyoku) of the Ministry of Transportation. It could not give up its powers of central government control of large taxi companies to local governments, as was suggested, anymore than it could relinquish its powers to approve the location of every bus stop in the country. To do so would mean diminishing the ministry's jurisdiction, the cardinal taboo governing the lives of all active-duty officials.[16]

With regard to the question of who governs, Ōta records that the TAIC's key proposals for bringing the main ministries under the control of at least the cabinet were defeated by ex-bureaucrat politicians. The TAIC recommended that there be established "cabinet assistants" *(naikaku hosakan)* with powers of general coordination over the ministries, giving the prime minister greater ability to exercise leadership, and a "cabinet members' budget conference" *(yosan kakuryō kaigi),* which would remove some of the budgeting powers held exclusively by the Ministry of Finance and place them in the cabinet. The fact that these reforms were defeated is not of as great concern to us here as is the fact that their espousal by the TAIC is good evidence that the Japanese themselves recognize where power really lies.

Many non-Japanese seem to believe that coordination and supervision over the bureaucracy are carried out within the LDP's Political Affairs Research Council, or in one of the blue-ribbon deliberation councils *(shingikai)* attached to the cabinet and the various ministries, or through some even less formal channels.[17] The evidence to support such a view is quite thin. It is true that the Political Affairs Research Council significantly increased its intervention into bureaucratic affairs, including the budget, during the early 1970s and particularly under the Tanaka cabinet.[18] Yet this council has also long been known as the exclusive preserve within the ruling party of former bureaucrats.[19] Even under the Tanaka cabinet, the prime minister's alleged strong political leadership over the bureaucracy was ambiguous, particularly given the widely acknowledged fact that his ambitious plan for renovating the Japanese islands was drafted by MITI officials.[20]

The disarray within the LDP following Tanaka's resignation seems unlikely to have strengthened party supervision of the bureaucracy. Instead it brought to the fore—although behind the scenes—the most powerful former bureaucrats in the party: Shiina Etsusaburō, former vice-minister of Commerce and Industry and former vice-minister of Munitions; Fukuda Takeo, who became famous for his performance as Budget Bureau director in the Ministry of Finance, September 1947–September 1948, when he helped bring down the (socialist) Katayama cabinet by refusing to supply funds for a pay increase unless the government raised railroad fares, and then found the funds after the Ashida cabinet had been installed; and Ōhira Masayoshi, Ministry of Finance, 1936–52.[21] These men were the real political leaders of Japan following Tanaka's downfall and the ones who created the Miki cabinet. There can be no doubt whatsoever about their high capabilities and their devotion to the welfare of Japan, but there can also be no doubt that they are former officials and that they represent both the strengths and dangers of bureaucratic preeminence in the Japanese government.

As for the possibility that *shingikai* play an important role in controlling the bureaucracy or in policy planning, the opposite is more commonly the case. To take only one example, former MITI vice-minister Sahashi in an interview with this author described MITI's prestigious Industrial Structure Council as a *kakuremino,* a fairy's cape for creating the semblance of official-civilian collaboration.[22] While *shingikai* undoubtedly perform important communications functions—both from the bureaucracy to civilian groups and vice versa—they would require a much greater degree of independence, including a separate budget and secretariat, to hold their own against their sponsoring ministries.[23] In general, all authorities agree that the most difficult coordinating task in the Japanese policy-making process is among the ministries and agencies themselves; once an interministerial agreement has been reached, the chores of taking the proposal or the bill through the party, cabinet, and Diet stages are relatively less onerous.[24] The overwhelming weight of cases deemed worth recording in the various collections devoted to postwar policy making concern intra- and inter-ministerial bargaining, particularly with the Ministry of Finance.[25]

Turning from coordination among rival ministries and the budget to lawmaking itself, we come to the heart of the matter. John Locke's definition of political power is worth recalling: "Political power, then, I take to be a right of making laws with penalties of death and, consequently, all less penalties for the regulating and preserving of property, and of employing the force of the community in the execution of such laws, and in the commonwealth from foreign injury, and all this only for the common good."[26] Dahrendorf agrees: the truly powerful elites are "those who are able, by virtue of their positions, to make laws."[27] In Japan, despite the fact that the constitution gives this power exclusively to the elected members of the Diet, it is the bureaucrats who actually initiate and draft virtually all important legislation. They also contribute significantly to the passage of bills within the Diet and possess extralegislative ordinance powers that are almost on a par with the statutes themselves.[28]

Two leading independent scholars begin their text on Japanese administration with an account of the postwar attempts at bureaucratic reform; they then append their own list of what they regard as indicators of genuine reform. The first is "establishment of the independence of the Diet in the enactment of legislation."[29] They write: "Because the Liberal Democratic Party is actually composed to a large extent of former bureaucrats, the policy formulation and enactment of legislation powers, particularly that of initiative, are largely located within the bureaucracy." They add that the two greatest powers of the bureaucracy are the initiating of legislation and the compilation of the budget. In addition, since the bureaucracy drafts the legislation, it always includes within each bill delegations of ordinance powers to particular agencies; these powers include cabinet orders *(seirei)*, urban prefectural ordinances *(furei)*, ministerial ordinances *(shōrei)*, and rules and regulations *(kisoku)*. Instead of the rule of law *(hōchi-shugi)*, the two authors conclude that Japan employs "administration through law" *(hōritsu ni yoru gyōsei)*.[30]

Looked at from the opposite point of view—that of the practicing bureaucrat—precisely the same opinion emerges. Former MITI vice-minister Sahashi characterizes the Diet as merely an "extension of the bureaucracy" and agrees that Japan has a "government of administration" rather than a government of laws. He contends that it is absurd to think of Japanese officials as merely the "administrative technicians" of a supreme legislative branch. "The bureaucracy drafts all the laws," he writes. "All the legislature does is to use its powers of investigation, which for about half the year keeps most of the senior officials cooped up in the Diet."[31]

Even the investigatory powers of Diet members are used only spasmodically. In his full autobiography, Sahashi notes that members of the ruling party generally do not, as a matter of principle, query bureaucratically sponsored legislation, and that opposition members can often be brought around or, at least, be persuaded to temper their opposition by supplying them with special information or playing up to their known enthusiasms.[32] Twenty years ago, Ōta Kaoru complained about what he called these "put-up jobs" *(yaochō)* in the Diet: opposition Diet members, the largest number of whom his labor federation had elected, would obtain documents from officials in order to question the government in the house, but then the same bureaucrats who had supplied the documents would come forward to answer the questions.[33] There seems no doubt from many accounts that the power of the bureaucracy with regard to legislation goes well beyond the initiation of legislative proposals and includes a degree of managing the bills within the Diet itself.

II

How has this concentration of power in the civil service come about? Did the bureaucracy really manage to circumvent the reforms of the occupation? Is there true continuity between the imperial officials *(tennō no kanri)* of the prewar period and the national bureaucrats *(kokka kōmuin)* of today? Opinion is by no means unanimous on these questions. Sahashi Shigeru, a former bureaucrat who reached the highest non-political position in his service, believes that the answer to the last question is yes. He writes that "despite fundamental changes in the society a century after the Meiji Restoration, we still have a Meiji era bureaucratic structure."[34] A scholar, Misonō Hitoshi, disagrees. He finds key differences between the "spirit" of the prewar and postwar officials, and argues that whereas imperial bureaucrats were motivated by a sense of loyalty and diligence to the emperor and his government, national officials only work with an eye toward their early retirement and reemployment in a public or civilian enterprise.[35] Such contradictory opinions could be repeated endlessly.

Certain obvious similarities do exist between the status and powers of the contemporary bureaucracy and those of late Meiji, Taishō, and early Shōwa officials. In prewar Japan, "government service was the career of greatest prestige," and it still is.[36] The imperial universities, particularly Tokyo University, were training schools for bureaucrats *(kanryō yōseijo),* and they still are. Bureaucrats used to enter politics after retirement, and they still do, although they no longer enjoy the privilege of imperial appointment to the House of Peers and must be elected. "Out of more than forty prime ministers in modern history, roughly one-third were recruited from high-ranking civil bureaucrats," note Ide and Ishida, although the ratio in the postwar world from Higashikuni to Miki is closer to half than to a third (Shidehara, Ashida, Yoshida, Kishi, Ikeda, and Satō were all former bureaucrats).[37]

There is still a marked separation between the higher-level career service—the equivalent of commissioned officers—and those ineligible for promotion to senior, policy-making posts. Isomura and Kuronuma comment that we still see old terms in use, such as *"kōtōkan* (high officials) dining room" or *"kōtōkan* bathroom"; it may even be that today's "consciousness of power" *(kenryoku ishiki)* is greater than the status consciousness of the feudal period. Moreover, although all *kanryō* (officials, in the sense of both high status and role) were supposed to have been changed into *yakunin* (officials, in the sense of role only), the separation between national and local officials not only persists but was exacerbated by the policies of the occupation.[38]

However, there are also key differences. Postwar officials are paid less, must retire earlier, and probably work harder. Until the war, summer half-day work schedules had been traditional for all but essential services. The former vice-minister and then minister of the old Ministry of Commerce and Industry and the great postwar "senior" *(senpai)* of all MITI officials, Yoshino Shinji (the brother of Yoshino Sakuzō), records that the current practice of all equals and seniors retiring when one person advances to the vice-minister's chair did not exist before the war; there were officials of longer service working in the ministry when he was vice-minister. It was also unthinkable in the days of his active service for politicians to interfere with the budgets of the bureaucrats, as they attempt to do today.[39]

The key difference is that the postwar bureaucracy, at least for the greater part of the postwar period, has had fewer rivals for power than did the prewar bureaucracy. Paradoxically, Maruyama's tripod may be of greater relevance to contemporary Japan than to the period which directly concerned him. John Maki, in one of the earliest articles to draw attention to the problem of the bureaucracy after the war, generalized: "Modern Japan—until the surrender in 1945—was ruled by a combination of three power groups, the militarists (army and navy men and chauvinistic individuals and organizations), the monopoly capitalists *(zaibatsu),* and the bureaucrats."[40] He might have added that the three groups' share of power was roughly reflected by the order in which he named them.

Before the war national power was divided between the *tōsuiken* (prerogative of supreme command), which was exercised by the army and navy, and the *kokumuken* (in essence, the power to pass, promulgate and execute laws), which was exercised by the civilian ministers of state and the bureaucracy. In the course of constitutional development, the former came to take precedence over the latter and, in the minds of many Japanese political scientists, led to the fatal contradictions in the Japanese government that were displayed during the Pacific war. General Tōjō attempted to overcome the contradictions by holding simultaneously the offices of prime minister and minister of war, but he still never gained control over some segments of the bureaucracy nor over the navy. "The causes of Japan's defeat in the Pacific war," writes Shinobu, "are many, but one of the basic causes was the Emperor System state order, which stood in the way of a centrally-controlled direction of the 'total war.' "[41] Today the *tōsuiken* is no more, and the military rivals to bureaucratic power have passed from the scene.

As for political rivals to bureaucratic power, they existed both before and after the war, but it would require detailed ministry-by-ministry analyses to determine which power was ascendant where in either the prewar or postwar periods. After 1932, with the assassination of Inukai, the political parties began to lose influence and in 1940 were merged and dissolved into the Imperial Rule Assistance Association. This movement promoted the rise of bureaucratic power but it also promoted the rise of military power. The bureaucracy did not really come into its own until defeat and occupation destroyed the military.

From approximately 1948, with the beginning of the occupation's "reverse course," until the conservative merger in 1955, the answer to who governs in Japan is clearly the bureaucracy. After 1955 political party influence grew, but Itō Daiichi believes that the bureaucracy adjusted to the rise of the LDP and continued its by then accustomed role. He notes that there was a marked strenghtening of the various ministerial secretariats around the time of the conservative merger and interprets this as a sign that the bureaucrats were adding the capability to contribute to political policy formulation for the LDP.[42] During the 1960s the so-called politicians' factions within the LDP *(tōjinha)* tried to bring the bureaucracy under party control; probably their most significant action was the creation of the TAIC itself.[43] However, these efforts did not really alter the relations between the party and the bureaucracy, and the creation of the Tanaka cabinet in 1972 owed less to the actions of the politicians' factions than to the weakening of the ex-bureaucrats' factions as a result of domestic and international policy failures. The LDP's persistent internal factionalism is also significant in causing the LDP to devote more attention to internal political competition than to political leadership, thereby leaving the field open for and making the party dependent upon the bureaucracy for policy leadership.[44] For all of these reasons, the alleged ascendancy of party over bureaucracy during the early 1970s has probably been exaggerated by commentators.

The case of the economic rivals to bureaucratic power is more clear-cut. Before the war the bureaucrats failed to bring the zaibatsu under control, and the so-called reform bureaucrats *(kakushin kanryō)*, who allied themselves with the military in order to try to nationalize the zaibatsu, succeeded only in alienating themselves from their anti-militarist colleagues and concentrating the Japanese economy further into zaibatsu hands. We can recognize, today, in the wartime efforts of reform or control bureaucrats such as Kishi Nobusuke (Tōjō's Minister of Commerce and Industry and the first Vice-minister of Munitions) a movement toward the rationalization of Japan's industrial structure. For example, between 1939 and 1945, as a result of the government's amalgamation programs, the number of ordinary banks declined from 338 to 61. Nonetheless, Byron Marshall's conclusion is supported by all analysts of the pre-1945 "controlled economy":

> The "new economic structure" established by the promulgation of the Major Industries Association Ordinance in the autumn of 1941 merely extended and tightened the system of cartel control that had been created in the early 1930s at the request of the business community itself. True, the control associations were now brought under the direct supervision of government bureaucrats, but the real power remained in the hands of the directors of the respective control organizations, who were for the most part executives of the leading private companies in each field. . . . Despite the elaborate administrative structure that existed on paper during the war years, neither effective centralization nor bureaucratic control was ever fully implemented.[45]

Ironically, it was during the occupation that the fondest dreams of the wartime "control bureaucrats" *(tōsei kanryō)* were finally realized. With the militarists gone, the zaibatsu facing dissolution, and SCAP's (Supreme Commander for the Allied Powers) decision to try to get the economy back on its feet, the bureaucracy finally found itself working for a *tennō* who really possessed the attributes of "absolutism" *(zettai-shugi)*. In one area after another, SCAP brought about the conditions of control that had eluded Tōjō and Kishi during the war. On November

19, 1946, for example, the Economic Stabilization Board, following SCAP's wishes, shifted responsibility for rationing and allocations from the wartime, zaibatsu-dominated control companies to the ministries having jurisdiction over particular industries.

Similarly, during 1947 SCAP encouraged the creation of some fifteen *kōdan* (public corporations), four in the foreign trade sector, eight in the domestic distribution sector, one price adjustment *kōdan*, and two in the economic rehabilitation sector. One vignette from the *kōdan* era is revealing. On August 10, 1947, representatives of the match industry petitioned SCAP against establishing a *kōdan* for their industry. They feared the creation of onerous controls. "The petitioners further contended," reads a SCAP report, "that the kōdans were being established not so much to help industry as to provide jobs for the bureaucrats at the sacrifice of industries. The petition was denied by SCAP on the assumption that the petitioners probably wanted to retain the controls in their own hands."[46]

Some SCAP officials were aware that in reducing the power of the zaibatsu they were increasing the power of the bureaucracy. A SCAP history records the dilemma posed for the Japanese government by SCAP policy and how the government resolved it: "At this juncture the [Japanese] Government was faced with two conflicting policies. On the one hand, SCAP had ordered the Government to maintain economic controls [SCAPIN 47, September 22, 1945]. On the other hand, the abrogation of wartime economic control legislation was required. A decision was not made until September 1946, when the Diet passed the Temporary Demand and Supply Adjustment Law [Law No. 32, September 30, 1946]."[47] This law gave to the Ministry of Commerce and Industry and, in 1949, to its successor, MITI, the kind of hard economic control powers that throughout the war the government had had to share with the zaibatsu.

Regarding the *kōdan*, SCAP later reflected, "It was evident that kōdans in themselves were dangerous as outcroppings of a wartime Japanese system and disclosed an urge on the part of the Japanese to return to undemocratic governmental operations after the Occupation had ended."[48] Undemocratic or not, the occupation allowed the Japanese bureaucracy to assume powers that it had not been able to exercise in earlier periods. During the

1950s, the bureaucracy used these powers to guide the economy toward its heavy industrialization and unprecedented growth. Satō Kiichirō, the head of the Mitsui Bank and in 1962 the chairman of the TAIC, recalls, "During and after the war . . . Japan's economy was controlled until it has become second nature with us to uphold a planned, controlled economy."[49]

Effective direct control always requires a closed economy, which existed in Japan more or less throughout the decade of the 1940s. During the 1950s, the linkages to the rest of the world through foreign trade loosened the controls, and during the 1960s, trade and capital liberalization drastically reduced them. But this did not mean the subordination of the bureaucracy to the *zaikai*. During the early 1970s the *zaikai* sometimes acted and more often spoke against official policies, but this trend came to a halt during the pollution, energy, and monetary crises of 1973–75. Japanese industry and commerce are no longer under the direct control of the economic bureaucracy, and the bureaucracy will undoubtedly play a different role in the Japanese economy of the future than it did during the period of high-speed growth. That it has a role to play, however, no one doubts.

As this discussion has sought to show, the key to unravelling the secrets of the bureaucracy's rise to power in Japan lies in further research on the militarist, wartime, and occupation eras. Gary Allinson's comment is certainly warranted:

> Far more than historians have yet demonstrated, key aspects of postwar Japanese society took shape during the 1930s. Perhaps the most fundamental change to emerge out of that period was a strong emphasis on rational, comprehensive planning at the national level. The central government had played the major role in determining national policies since the Meiji Restoration, of course, but in the war period central planning assumed a new level of intensity. After 1937 officials formalized central planning by establishing agencies which systematically controlled and distributed the nation's resources. Postwar bodies, such as the Economic Planning Agency and the Ministry of International Trade and Industry, carry on the practices implemented during the war years. They symbolize a legacy of planning which stems directly from the 1930s. In the absence of that legacy, Japan's postwar economic history would certainly have followed a different path.[50]

The most influential article on the subject of the official bureaucracy differs only slightly from Allinson in pointing to the occupation as the period in which the legacy of the thirties came to fruition. In 1958 Tsuji Kiyoaki listed three reasons why the bureaucracy turned out to be the primary political beneficiary of the settlement imposed on Japanese society by the Allied occupation. These were, first, the decision by the Allies to carry out the occupation through indirect government; second, the belief of the Japanese people that their bureaucracy was politically neutral (a belief, we might add, that is held even more strongly by Americans, as a result of the influence of Max Weber and the ubiquitous doctrine of "scientific management" taught in most schools of public or business administration); and third, the absence of experienced politicians in the postwar political parties, a result of the long period of military suppression of party life, which caused the parties to welcome former bureaucratic policy makers into their ranks.[51] Tsuji's first reason has long seemed the most compelling. As early as 1947, Maki warned that "the decision taken . . . to retain a Japanese government in power after the surrender, although it was to be completely under the control of the Supreme Commander for the Allied Powers, meant, in effect, that the bureaucracy would escape the fate to be dealt out to the militarists and the zaibatsu."[52]

SCAP was not unaware of the implications of indirect rule. In its history of the "Reorganization of Civil Service," occupation officials wrote, "The utilization of the Japanese governmental machinery, as desired, was not possible without the existing organization but, while the decision insured effective administration, it entailed the longterm problems of achieving reforms within the bureaucratic system through the bureaucrats themselves."[53] SCAP chose to attempt to reform the bureaucracy nonetheless.

Occupation officials were suspicious of the widespread destruction of personnel records of civil officials and the dissolution of the ministries of Greater East Asia and of Munitions on August 26, 1945, the day before the first occupation soldier arrived in Japan. SCAP therefore included the bureaucracy in the purge directives from the beginning. The directors of the purge removed from office some 11.92 percent of *shinnin* and *choku-*

nin ranks, with the Ministry of Home Affairs being the hardest hit (slightly more than 60 percent of its highest officials were purged and the ministry itself was broken up into the present ministries òf Home Affairs, Construction, Labor, Health and Welfare, and the Police Agency). SCAP also brought to Japan an advisory commission on the civil service, which drafted the National Public Service Law of 1947. There is no doubt that this law proved ineffective in terms of the aims of the occupation, but this was the result more of bureaucratic subterfuge than of indirect rule. In 1950, a member of the commission commented, "The proposed civil service law was submitted to the Diet in the fall of 1947. Unfortunately, the nucleus of feudalistic, bureaucratic thinking gentlemen within the core of the Japanese Government were [sic] astute enough to see the dangers of any such modern public administration law to their tenure and the subsequent loss of their power. The law which was finally passed by the Diet was a thoroughly and completely emasculated instrument compared with that which had been recommended by the Mission."[54]

Despite this setback, SCAP went ahead with the reexamination of all the members of the civil service who had not been purged. This process led to the famous "paradise examination" of January 15, 1950, so named because the bureaucrats could take as much time as they wanted, drink tea, eat, and smoke. A few stayed for fifteen hours. However, some 7,432 civil officials were reexamined, and about 30 percent failed to be reemployed as a result.

The problem was not, it seems to me, with indirect rule or the size of the purges; it was rather the way in which the positive reforms got lost or modified in the context of SCAP's attempts to solve the serious labor problems of 1948 and 1949. The dictates of American national policy and the Japanese economic situation ultimately forced SCAP to abandon its efforts to democratize the bureaucracy in favor of efforts to raise its efficiency.

In order to end the strikes of government railroad workers that plagued the economy throughout 1948, MacArthur personally ordered the government to pass laws banning strikes among civil servants and to separate railroad and a few other categories of workers into public corporations *(kōsha)*. As a result public employees in Japan became divided into three different categories. At the center of the bureaucracy are those officials covered by the National Public Service Law; they have the right to organize (itself a major difference between the prewar and postwar bureaucracies) but not the rights to collective bargaining or to strike. Segregated from them are the public employees covered by the Public Corporations and National Enterprises Labor Relations Law—five government departments and three public corporations—who have the rights to organize and to collective bargaining but not the right to strike (they do so anyway with great frequency). Finally, for no very clear reason, the employees of *kōdan* and of mixed public-private enterprises, such as Japan Air Lines, are covered by the Trade Union Law, in which all three rights prevail.[55]

The upshot of these late occupation developments was to break up the solidarity—as well as the communist dominance of public workers' unions—that had developed in the civil service and to reconstitute the higher bureaucracy as an elite service. By mid-1949, SCAP and the Japanese government had taken the decisive measures that would ultimately lead to the rebuilding of the Japanese economy.[56] Economic growth became a vastly higher priority of the occupation than civil service reform, and the bureaucrats regained their morale and ceased to worry about preserving their positions in the society. This was not necessarily a bad thing, but certainly John Maki's prediction of 1947 was borne out: "So long as the bureaucrats are not balanced by another strong political group, they will continue to govern Japan as they see fit—not as they did before the surrender, perhaps, but nevertheless as the sole group directing the government."[57]

III

One legacy from early Shōwa politics that contemporary officials have inherited is the whole complex world of public enterprises—what Isomura and Kuronuma call the problem of "quasi-administration" *(ese-gyōsei)* and what others deride as the privileged sanctuaries of the "migratory birds" of the bureaucracy, i.e., "retired" officials who join and retire, with a large retirement bonus at each stage, from one or more of the 113 "special status companies" that the bureaucrats themselves have created, funded, and supervise.[58] Even though non-Japanese scholars have hardly touched this subject in their research, no appreciation of the full extent of the bureaucracy's powers is complete without mention of it. Prewar Japan had many "mixed enterprises"—corporations in which the government owned a large part of the equity and participated extensively in the management—but there was simply nothing comparable to the contemporary maze of *kōsha, kōdan, jigyōdan, kōko, kinko,* and *eidan.*[59] Undoubtedly the traditions of governmental initiative from the Meiji era, combined with the precedents of wartime and occupied Japan, condition the Japanese people to accept these forms. It is also true that the largest of them (the Japanese National Railways, the Nippon Telegraph and Telephone Corporation, and the Japan Monopoly Corporation—that is, the three *kōsha*) comprise natural or public monopolies (although there are also private rail lines) and are therefore comparable to public enterprises found in all open, mixed economies.

Nonetheless, some aspects of the proliferation of such entities in Japan are not normally encountered in other countries and greatly disturb Japanese specialists on national and local government. One aspect is the degree to which public corporations have become prime landing spots for *amakudari* (descended from heaven) bureaucrats, particularly from the Ministry of Finance. Former MITI vice-minister Sahashi has charged that the ministries have deliberately established many special status companies for no other reasons than to expand their jurisdictions and to provide employment for their retired officials.[60] Another cause of concern is the tendency for public corporations to preempt the functions of local governments in many areas. More and more aspects of daily life have been drawn back under the control of the central government, which has given rise to the cynical remark *sanwari jichi*—local government is only 30 percent independent of the national government.

A third problem concerns the extent to which Japan's *kōdan, kōko,* and so forth are free from political or ministerial interference. Such independence is supposed to be one of the main strengths of the public corporate form. Some Japanese writers fear that the public corporations are actually extensions of bureaucratic power but with little or no bureaucratic responsibility. A fourth concern is the way the enterprises are financed. The Ministry of Finance's Fiscal Investment and Loan Plan (Zaisei Tōyūshi Keikaku)—the so-called second budget—is the actual basis for allocating to the corporations the large funds available from postal savings, compulsory old-age pension funds, appropriations, and other sources. This "plan," drawn up by officials of the Ministry of Finance in consultation with other ministries, the staffs of the public corporations, local authorities, interest groups, and other bodies with access to this most powerful of Japanese ministries, is the only part of the national budget that does *not* require Diet approval.[61]

Japanese law recognizes many different kinds of "juridical persons," such as joint stock companies, limited joint stock companies, limited partnerships, unlimited partnerships, private limited companies, mutual companies, incorporated foundations and associations, and juridical persons established under special laws *(tokushu hōjin).* The last category, itself very broad and including banks, religious and educational corporations, is the one of immediate concern here. Within the classification of *tokushu hōjin,* we find *kōsha,* which are primarily wholly publicly owned utilities. Private utility enterprises subject to government regulation, such as the electric companies and private railroads, are not *kōsha,* although they too maintain close relationships with their supervisory ministries and accept *amakudari* bureaucrats into the ranks of their executives.

Differing from *kōsha* in slight ways, including the laws that regulate their labor relations, *kōdan* are government corporations engaged primarily in construction work. *Jigyōdan* differ from *kōdan* only in that they seem to engage in everything except construction and are smaller. *Kōko* are public finance corporations in which all the capital is supplied by the government, whereas *kinko* are public finance corporations in which the capital for their loans is supplied cooperatively. A *kikin* seems to be the same thing as a *kōko,* only smaller. There is only one *eidan* (although there were many during the war): the Teito Rapid Transit Authority (that is, the subway) in the Tokyo metropolitan region. Still in the category of *tokushu hōjin* but differing from all the above public entities are the special companies *(tokushu kaisha),* which are genuine mixed public-private joint stock companies. There are over ten of them, including the Electric Power Development Company, Japan Air Lines, the Tohoku District Development Company, the Kokusai Denshin Denwa

Company (KDD—literally international telegraph and telephone company but known officially by its Japanese name in order to avoid confusion with ITT—and an obvious exception to the generalization that all public utilities are *kōsha*), and many others.[62]

Except for one or two *kinko,* all of the above were established after the war (between 1906 and 1949 the Japanese National Railways were managed as a government department). Some were spun off from ministries under SCAP pressure; others were established to increase efficiency or to assist in a particular activity (for example, the Kaigai Keizai Kyōryoku Kikin, Overseas Economic Cooperation Fund, or the Kaigai Ijū Jigyōdan, Overseas Immigration Service). Some public enterprises have been set up by the Diet as a way of getting around the bureaucrats' resistance to administrative reform, since they are allegedly more efficient than the ministries. Others were created to overcome problems of ministerial jurisdictional competition, although the experience during 1974 of the Nihon Genshisen Kaihatsu Jigyōdan (Japan Nuclear Ship Development Agency), which the Science and Technology Agency, MITI, and the Ministry of Transportation all disowned when its ship Mutsu broke down at sea, suggests that the stratagem does not always work. Best known are the big construction *kōdan*—Japan Housing Corporation, Japan Highway Public Corporation, Forest Development Corporation, New Tokyo International Airport Corporation, Honshu-Shikoku Bridge Authority—that spend huge sums of public trust funds and affect the lives of most citizens.

The numbers of governmental special corporations have expanded continuously since independence, except for 1968 after the Satō government applied the brakes to their creation (see Table 6-1). One widely acknowledged reason for this growth is the need to provide employment for retired bureaucrats, although the Council of Governmental Special Corporation Employees denounces the practice and many retired officials themselves are distressed by the need to *amakudari.*[63] Nonetheless, active-duty officials are often praised for creating them, and there is considerable evidence that Ministry of Finance, MITI, Ministry of Construction, and Ministry of Agriculture and Forestry bureaucrats devote a good deal of time to thinking of new ones and of ways to generate Diet support for them. Hiramatsu Morihiko, while on active duty with MITI in the late 1960s, gained the reputation of being a politically astute official for having created three public corporations: the Japan Electronic Computer Corporation (Nihon Denshi Keisan K.K.), the Pollution Prevention Corporation (Kōgai Bōshi Jigyōdan), and the Overseas Petroleum Development Corporation (Kaigai Sekiyu Kaihatsu Kōdan).[64] The senior officials of virtually all public enterprises are former bureaucrats.[65]

Most of the public corporations provide important services and would exist even if the problems of the early retirement of civil servants were solved. Many operate in sectors where the capital requirements or risks are so high that no group other than the government could think of entering. Beyond organizational feather-bedding, the main complaint against them is that they are too tightly controlled by the central government and that the central government is unresponsive to the real needs of citizens. For example, it is charged that the Ministry of Construction (one of the few ministries in which technical officials rise to the highest non-political post in the service) is indifferent to the problems of urban housing and river pollution, and devotes most of the funds of its corporations to highway construction, regional development, and industrial support facilities. At the same time, the central government will not release public funds directly to local entities to build what they need. Control over the corporations is clearly in the hands of the ministries: even mixed enterprises cannot issue bonds, dispose of

TABLE 6-1   Changes in the Numbers of Special Legal Entities, 1946–72

1946	6	1959	61 (+8)	1966	108 (+3)
1953	22	1960	65 (+4)	1967	113 (+8 −3)
1954	25 (+3)	1961	71 (+6)	1968	109 (+1 −5)
1955	33 (+8)	1962	81 (+10)	1969	110 (+2 −1)
1956	39 (+6)	1963	94 (+14 −1)	1970	112 (+5 −3)
1957	44 (+5)	1964	99 (+5)	1971	112 (0)
1958	53 (+9)	1965	105 (+8 −2)	1972	113 (+4 −3)

Source: Isomura Eiichi and Kuronuma Minoru, *Gendai Nihon no gyōsei* (Tokyo: Teikoku Chihō Gyōsei Gakkai, 1974), p. 345.

profits, or change rates without the approval of the minister concerned. Many Japanese see this as preferable, however, to political supervision: the budgets of *kōsha* and *kōko* must be approved by the Diet, which is one reason why the Japanese National Railways do not operate profitably, since politicians do not like to raise fares. In a relatively rare example of successful reform, in 1987 the Nakasone cabinet broke up and privatized both the Japanese National Railways and the Nippon Telephone and Telegraph Company.

Public corporations constitute only a segment of the total power position of the Japanese bureaucracy. As in many other areas of Japanese government, these organizations reveal a discrepancy between the authority under which they operate—Diet-enacted legislation—and the actual locus of power which guides them—the bureaucracy. In addition, critics charge that the bureaucracy is most responsive to interests with special access to it or to its own organizational imperatives. It is these conditions, which are comparable in form if not in seriousness to those identified by Maruyama for the prewar period, not the functions that the bureaucracy and the corporations perform comparatively well, that continue to generate controversy in Japan today.

IV

In a 1973 nationwide public opinion poll on the bureaucracy, conducted by the secretariat of the prime minister's office, members of the public were asked whether over the previous two years any of them had had some contact with an office of a city, prefectural, or the national government. Out of a sample 2,445 people, some 67.9 percent had had such contact—60.6 percent with a local organ, 6.1 percent with a regional organ, and 1.3 percent with a national organ. Some 32.1 percent had no such contact. When asked to state what image they held of the bureaucracy, in which no preset choice was offered but all answers were recorded, some 20.2 percent replied that the bureaucracy was "serious" *(majime),* 20.5 percent used the word "hard" *(katai),* 9.2 percent said "arrogant" *(ōhei),* 12.7 percent said "inefficient" *(nōritsu ga warui),* 16.4 percent included the phrase "unadaptable" *(yūzū ga kikanai),* 14.4 percent thought the bureaucracy "lacked a feeling of service" *(sabisu kokoro ga nai)*, and 12.5 percent thought bureaucrats were "friendly" *(shinsetsu)*. Only 2.7 percent used the term "elite" *(kanryō erīto)*, and only 2.9 percent mentioned *amakudari* (although 5.4 percent of the respondents who were residents of Tokyo raised this). Some 24.3 percent had no thoughts at all on the subject. By a ratio of 35.2 percent to 19.0 percent more people thought the bureaucrats' abilities were on balance superior rather than inferior (6.5 percent thought they were clearly superior, 3.2 percent thought they were clearly inferior, and 36.1 percent did not know).[66]

None of this is very surprising. Japan is an open, democratic society, although it has a long authoritarian past. Bureaucracy is a permanent part of the Japanese scene, and the poll does not record any citizen mentioning the need for administrative reform *(gyōsei kaikaku)*. Some knowledgeable people believe that reform is necessary, as we have sought to show, but no one suggests that bureaucracy can or should be eliminated. What this suggests to me is the need to conceptualize bureaucracy in Japan (and in many other societies as well) as a constant contender for political power and to eschew further speculation on whether a reform of the Diet, the LDP, or the opposition parties is the "answer" to bureaucratic preeminence.

One conceptualization proposed by Randall Bartlett argues that today's open societies have four main protagonists in the "market" instead of the classical two: consumers seeking utility maximization, producers seeking profit maximization, politicians seeking vote maximization, and bureaucrats seeking security maximization. Whether this formulation is adequate, it does point to the reality of "bureaucratic interests" and moves away from the excessive concern of public administration specialists with the rationality or functions of bureaucracy. For example, it allows Bartlett to contend that "it is only when the recommendations of the bureaucracy present an *obvious* possibility of damaging vote positions that they will be rigorously checked by government."[67]

Official bureaucracy was not established in Japan for scientific reasons but by the Meiji oligarchs to prevent the nascent political parties from placing their supporters in the administration. There are grounds for criticizing the bureaucracy's performance over the past 75 years, but it has certainly been equal or superior to that of such groups as the military, the politicians, and the economic leaders. With regard to the future, all of the envisaged solutions to the problems facing Japan and comparable societies are likely to entail an enlargement of official bureaucracy. Given its experience with bureaucracy and its alertness to the political problems of bureaucracy, Japan may adjust to the consequences of such an enlargement better than some other open societies. The bureaucracy does not rule in a vacuum in Japan, but it does hold an ascendant position and is likely to continue to do so. Political scientists or political reformers who ignore the bureaucratic dimension are likely to misconceive the true capabilities and limitations of the Japanese government.

7

The Reemployment of Retired Government Bureaucrats in Japanese Big Business

In foreign discussions of the connections between government and business in Japan, it is sometimes supposed that government and business are two distinct entities and that the close cooperation between them reflects a pervasive "consensus" in Japanese society. This view overlooks the fact that in many critical industries the businessmen who have dealings with government officials are themselves retired government officials, and that in industries where there are large numbers of retired bureaucrats—such as steel, petroleum, electric power, and banking—there is much more "government-business consensus" than in industries where such relations do not exist. Moreover, among firms within a particular industry, those with former officials on their boards of directors have more intimate ties with the government than those that do not have such directors. As the *Japan Economic Journal* noted on April 23, 1974, "It is not coincidental that administrative guidance can produce best effects on the premise of such government-business relationships [as the] hiring of retired government officials by business firms." In this essay, we explore the extent, causes, and effects of the movement of personnel from bureau office to board room, and the attitudes of bureaucrats, businessmen, and the public toward such activity.

LIFE BEGINS AT FIFTY

Government officials retire early in Japan, virtually without exception in their early or mid-fifties, for reasons that will be explained later. Upon retirement they then obtain new employment of three general types. (1) In a private, profit-making enterprise. The movement from ministry or agency to a private business is known as "descent from heaven" *(amakudari)* and is subject to minor legal restrictions. (2) In a public corporation or "special legal entity," i.e., an enterprise established by law and financed in part from public funds, such as the Japan Housing Corporation, the New Tokyo International Airport Corporation, and the Tokyo Expressway Public Corporation. Reemployment by such an organization is called "sideslip" *(yoko-suberi)* and is not subject to legal restrictions. It has been charged that the bureaucracy has set up or expanded such public corporations, whose large numbers are a conspicuous feature of Japanese public administration, partly with an eye to its own reemployment in them. (3) In the political world, chiefly by becoming a candidate for election to the Diet, most commonly as a member of the House of Councillors in the national constituency. This post-retirement career is called "position exploitation" *(chii riyō)*, referring to the fact that it is usually open only to bureaucrats who served in choice national or regional posts that are particularly suitable for building general political support. Good posts from which to launch a political career include: chief, Forestry Agency or Food Agency, Ministry of Agriculture and Forestry; chief, Ports Bureau, Ministry of Construction; chief, Medium and Small Enterprises Agency, Ministry of International Trade and Industry (MITI); chief, regional bureau of MITI; chief, Banking Bureau or National Tax Agency, Ministry of Finance; Vice-Minister of Education; and chief, Juvenile Homes Bureau, Ministry of Health and Welfare.

One other source of post-retirement employment that has not been given a specific name by the Japanese is the numerous trade associations that represent various industries, such as the Petroleum League of Japan or the Iron and Steel Federation. Although grouped generally under *amakudari,* this form of work differs in that the trade associations are not profit-making enterprises and employment by them is not subject to the legal restrictions that apply to private businesses. Bureaucrats will often spend a few years immediately following retirement as officials of a trade association and then go on to make a true descent to a private business. According to information reported to the Upper House Budget Committee of the Diet on March 15, 1974, some 143 different trade associations employed 214 former government officials, primarily from MITI. In the same Diet session, in reply to a direct question from a Councillor concerning the Petroleum League of Japan, Director General Yamagata Eiji of MITI's National Resources and Energy Agency said that the League's executive director, one of its managing directors, and one member of its board were former MITI officials.[1]

The legal restrictions on *amakudari* are dominated by one huge loophole: very lax enforcement. According to article 103 of the National Public Service Law (Law No. 120 of 1947, amended by Law No. 222 of 1948), "Personnel are hereby prohibited for a period of two years after leaving the public service from accepting or serving in a position with a profit making enterprise which involves *a close connection* [*missetsu na;* italics added] with any agency of the state . . . with which such persons were formerly employed within five years prior to separation from the service." This law also establishes a National Personnel Authority which has among its various duties the power to grant exceptions to article 103 when it finds that "a close connection" between a retired official's former work and his proposed new employment does not exist. After repeated protests from the press, public, and employees of firms receiving "descended from heaven" bureaucrats that the Personnel Authority was giving out exemptions too freely, the Authority began in 1965 to supply annual reports to the Diet on its activities for the previous year. The report lists and describes the numbers of bureaucrats at the level of section chief and above retiring each year, and reports on the exemptions to article 103 it has granted. This reporting has not, however, stilled the public criticism of *amakudari* since it shows that the Authority's investigations are limited to asking the minister of the bureau from which an official retired whether there was a close connection between the man's previous and proposed work. As we shall see, the minister has every incentive to deny that any connection existed.

The Personnel Authority's report to the Diet for 1973—

known to the press as the "Amakudari White Paper"—was released on March 26, 1974.[2] It revealed that there were 180 descents from bureaucracy to business during 1973 and only one refusal by the Personnel Authority, making 1973 the second highest year during the high-growth decade 1963–73.[3] The 1973 report provoked particularly bitter comments in the press and in Diet speeches because of the widespread criticism of administrative guidance and alleged government inaction in the face of serious inflation. The report at least raised suspicions that bureaucrats on active duty but looking ahead to retirement, as well as those already retired, might be more interested in protecting the interests of businesses than of the public.

1963	1964	1965	1966	1967	1968	1969	1970	1971	1972
165	133	128	147	123	136	174	193	167	176

The report also revealed that MITI had risen from fifth in 1972 to second in 1973 as a jumping off spot for *amakudari,* although the Ministry of Finance retained its usual leading position. The following ministries and agencies were the "ten best" contributors to *amakudari* during 1973:

Ministry of Finance	33
Ministry of International Trade and Industry	32
Ministry of Construction	24
Ministry of Agriculture and Forestry	20
National Tax Agency	18
Ministry of Transportation	18
Hokkaido Development Agency	9
Ministry of Posts and Telecommunications	6
Food Agency	4
Ministry of Health and Welfare	3

MITI's great leap from 14 in 1972 to 32 in 1973 is partly explained by the reorganization of the ministry that took place in July 1973 and that necessitated the retirement of several bureau chiefs and other top officials.

The most spectacular and widely noted descent in 1973 was that of Yano Tomoo, former vice-minister of the Economic Planning Agency. Yano retired July 1, 1973, at the age of 53. Six days after his retirement, on July 6, 1973, the Diet passed the "Market Cornering and Hoarding Prevention Law," which his agency had drafted and sponsored in the Diet. This law was intended to restrict the activities of the big trading firms, which had been accused of controlling markets for various commodities and of manipulating real estate prices. In October, Yano was employed as an adviser *(komon)* to Mitsui Bussan (Mitsui Trading Co.), precisely one of the firms that the law his agency drafted was supposed to control. The National Personnel Authority explained its approval of Yano's employment by Mitsui Trading by noting that he had retired before the law had been enacted (six days before).[4]

Other major descents of 1973 were Akazawa Shōichi, former director of MITI's Heavy Industries Bureau, to become an adviser to Fujitsū Computers, a major recipient of MITI subsidies for the development of domestic computers; and Sakano Tsunekazu, former chief of the Securities Bureau, Ministry of Finance, who joined Nippon Kayaku (chemicals) as a member of the board of directors.

The most important instances of *amakudari* are those of the retired administrative vice-ministers of each ministry, the highest career officials (non-political) of the government. Among the vice-ministers, those from the Ministries of Finance and International Trade and Industry, the two most powerful bureaucracies, are always watched closely by the press and public. In general, vice-ministerial *amakudari* from Finance has been to the banking world and into politics, while MITI leaders have gone to the steel, electric power, petroleum, and automobile industries. An unusually vivid example from the financial world involves two former vice-ministers: Kōno Kazuyuki, vice-minister of finance from August 1953 to July 1955, who then retired at the age of 48 after 25 years in the ministry and rose to become president of the Taiyō Bank; and Ishino Shinichi, vice-minister of finance from April 1963 to April 1965, who then retired at age 53 after 30 years in the ministry and rose to become president of the Kobe Bank. On October 1, 1973, these two banks merged to become the Taiyō Kobe Bank, Japan's seventh largest and with the largest number of branch offices (302) of any bank. The press noted that the earlier careers of the two presidents smoothed the way for Ministry of Finance and Bank of Japan approval of the merger, and in financial circles the new Taiyō Kobe Bank is commonly referred to as the "Finance Ministry Bank" *(Okura Ginkō).*[5]

The most remarkable stories of post-bureaucratic business success are found among the former MITI vice-ministers. Two absolute top leaders of Japanese industry are Hirai Tomisaburō, president of the New Japan Steel Corporation, and Tamaki Keizō, president of the Tōshiba Electric Corporation. Hirai entered MITI's predecessor, the Ministry of Commerce and Industry, in 1931 and retired as MITI vice-minister in 1955, while Tamaki served from 1930 to 1953, when he retired as vice-minister. The fact that they have risen to the presidencies of Japan's largest (New Japan Steel) and ninth largest (Tōshiba) firms in terms of sales is exceptional, as we shall discuss later, even in the exceptional world of Japanese business practices.

On the opposite page is a list of all of the vice-ministers of MITI and their post-retirement positions since the establishment of the ministry in 1949, up to 1973.

There are a few points to be made about this list. Five former vice-ministers held prominent posts in the petroleum industry (Imai, Ishihara, Matsuo, Ojimi, and Ueno), about which more is said below. Kumagai, as executive director of Sumitomo Metals, is noteworthy in that his appointment followed the bitter clash between MITI and Sumitomo Metals in 1965 over administrative guidance; the press regarded his position as both a sign of MITI's determination to bring Sumitomo under control and of Sumitomo's willingness to back down after the confrontation.[7] Sahashi, easily the most colorful and controversial of the MITI vice-ministers, became famous in Japan for his refusal to accept a post in private industry after he retired.[8]

THE CAUSES OF *Amakudari*

"Descent from heaven" is primarily a postwar development. The prewar civilian bureaucracy did not retire as early as contemporary officials do, was better paid, was not so large in numbers, and its most senior members (vice-ministers, directors gen-

NAME	VICE-MINISTER DATES	AMAKUDARI POSITION(S)
(1) Yamamoto Takayuki	5/49– 3/52	Vice-pres., Fuji Iron and Steel. Died May 17, 1961.
(2) Tamaki Keizō	3/52–11/53	Pres., Tōshiba Electric.
(3) Hirai Tomisaburō	11/53–11/55	Pres., New Japan Steel.
(4) Ishihara Takeo	11/55– 6/57	Executive Director, Tokyo Electric Power Co.; Dir., Overseas Petroleum Development Co.
(5) Ueno Kōshichi	6/57– 5/60	Executive Director, Kansai Electric Power Co.; Dir., Kansai Oil Co.
(6) Tokunaga Hizatsugu	5/60– 7/61	Executive Director, New Japan Steel.
(7) Matsuo Kinzō	7/61– 7/63	Executive Director, Nippon Kōkan; Pres., Fuyō Petroleum Development Co.
(8) Imai Zenei	7/63–10/64	President, Japan Petrochemical Co.
(9) Sahashi Shigeru	10/64– 4/66	Refused to *amakudari*. Economic consultant.
(10) Yamamoto Shigenobu	4/66– 5/68	Executive Director, Toyota Motor Co.
(11) Kumagai Yoshifumi	5/68–11/69	Executive Director, Sumitomo Metals Co.
(12) Ojimi Yoshihisa	11/69– 6/71	Vice-President, Arabian Oil Co.
(13) Morozumi Yoshihiko	6/71– 7/73	Adviser to Prime Minister Tanaka.[6]

eral, and bureau chiefs) commonly received Imperial nominations to the old House of Peers upon retirement. Perhaps most important, prewar officials regarded it as an affront to their pride and contrary to their responsibilities as officials of the Emperor—they were most definitely not "servants of the public"—for them to join a civilian, profit-making enterprise. There were instances of private firms employing former state officials, but these were more often retired army or navy officers than civilian bureaucrats.[9]

The lower purchasing power of postwar pay scales is one of the causes of *amakudari,* although it is very difficult to compare prewar and postwar salary levels because of the extreme complexity of the Japanese civil service and because of the change in the ranking system that occurred during the Allied Occupation. Prewar pay scales also differed from ministry to ministry. One calculation for the civil service as a whole in 1938 estimates that the monthly salary for the two highest levels of officials was slightly less than U.S.$100 at the then prevailing exchange rate (¥100 = U.S.$28.50), plus about U.S.$700–800 additional salary annually in the form of bonuses.[10] In 1965, the salary of a vice-minister was ¥210,000 per month (c. U.S.$585 at then prevailing exchange rate of ¥100 = U.S.$.28), plus bonuses worth 4.3 months salary per year and a high allowance for expenses. Bureau chiefs' salaries were slightly more than half that amount.[11] Writers on the Japanese civil service conclude that the purchasing power of the 1938 salary was greater than that of the 1965 salary, but they do not believe that postwar officials have been poorly paid by civilian standards. The problem arises when the salary level is considered in conjunction with relatively poor retirement benefits and the practice of early retirement. An official has his income cut in half on retirement, which comes at the time when he must meet heavy expenses for his children's university education. He therefore must obtain further employment.

Why has the practice of early retirement developed in the bureaucracy—and in Japanese civilian enterprise as well? There are many reasons. An overall conditioning factor for the whole economy is the relatively recent development of guaranteed "lifetime" employment after acceptance into an agency or firm. Since an employer generally cannot dismiss his employees in times of economic downturn—labor becomes a fixed cost under lifetime employment—he finds it advantageous to keep his work force as young as possible, the more senior employees being also the most expensive. Thus he will retire senior employees as rapidly as possible. In the most enlightened firms such early retirees may be reemployed on an annual basis and without the guarantee of permanent employment, or they may be reemployed by a subsidiary or subcontracting firm at a lesser salary and also without the guarantees that apply to regular employees. The bureaucratic equivalent of this practice is the occasional reemployment of a retired official as an adviser to a ministry.

Within the world of officialdom, early retirement results from the workings of two basic norms in the context of the overall forces of supply and demand for labor and the general expansion of the bureaucracy that occurred during and after World War II. These two practices are the *nenkō* system, or rewards and ranking on the basis of strict seniority, and the influence of so-called academic cliques *(gakubatsu),* which refers to the fact that over 70 percent of all senior officials in 1965 were graduates of Tokyo University and their internal rivalries establish the rules for the bureaucracy as a whole. Graduates of one particular year's graduating class from Tokyo University are regarded as absolutely senior in rank to graduates of a later year, and competition for advancement goes on among those of the same year of graduation (the bureaucracy in general hires new employees only immediately following graduation).

To take the Ministry of Finance as an example, every year about 30 or 40 recent university graduates who have passed the Higher Level Public Officials Examination enter the ministry. After about 14 years, this group will have advanced to the section chief level (before the war it took only about 11–12 years to make section chief). After about 25 years (16 years before the war), some of them will have achieved the bureau chief level. Not all the members of one class will pass through the various sieves that exist beyond the section chief level. These sieves, progressively narrower, are chief of the General Affairs Section of each bureau, deputy bureau chief, bureau chief, director general of adjunct agencies, and finally one administrative vice-minister. Those who do not make it beyond section chief will begin to think about outside work, although they will not be obliged to retire until someone from their entering class or from a junior class becomes vice-minister. Because of the extreme age grading and sensitivity to seniority, officials throughout their careers are identified with their university graduating class, a principle that derives from both the general *nenkō* system and the need to differentiate internally the large body of Tokyo University alumni. When one man from a class becomes vice-minister, all others from the same class are under a heavy obligation to retire so that he will have absolute seniority within the ministry. Conversely, the new vice-minister is under an equally compelling obligation to find suitable positions for his equals or juniors who are retiring.

The key man in each ministry charged with the smooth operation of this retirement and reemployment process is the chief of the secretariat, a position equivalent in rank with that of the most senior bureau chief. Chief secretary is the most common stepping stone to the vice-ministership, and it is assigned to only the most promising officials. The chief secretary's main task is to identify those officials who are likely to be promoted to bureau chief, and for the remainder, as it is said in Japan, "to stimulate retirement" *(kanshō taishoku)*. His main means of stimulation is to find the retirees new jobs—to cause those who retire to "grow young again." One aspect of this problem that will concern him most is the number of available public companies *(kōsha)* and public corporations *(kōdan)* controlled by his ministry to which he can recommend transfers for those who do not *amakudari*. As the National Personnel Authority acknowledges, some public corporations have been created by ministries primarily as a form of self-defense against possible unemployment. The problem of the numbers of *amakudari* and *yokosuberi* landing spots became increasingly critical as of the late 1960s. The bureaucracy expanded greatly during and after World War II, and the largest numbers of officials in the bureaucracy in 1966 were from the classes of 1939–41. There is very great pressure from the classes below on a particular official for him to retire and thereby allow for further promotions. In order to make it easy for him to do so, the chief secretary, the vice-minister, and the minister with his political connections will be constantly on the look out for a new civilian job for him.

In sum, early retirement and subsequent "descent from heaven" derive from a combination of the necessity of finding employment after retirement, the guarantee of career employment after initial acceptance, strict seniority by university graduating class, the predominance of Tokyo University graduates in all ministries, and the pressure of junior grades moving up the seniority ladder.

There are three general observations to be made about this

system. First, the causes and consequences of *amakudari* are well recognized in Japan, and they are considered to be serious problems, not normal or desirable operating procedures. Seniority, large numbers, the influence of Tokyo University—all have been exposed and heavily criticized in Japanese media. There have been several proposals to overcome these problems through political action, particularly by improving retirement benefits.[12] Second, some of the causes are probably temporary, particularly the large numbers that resulted from the expansion of the bureaucracy in the 1940s. Japan has entered a period of labor shortage, which as it becomes more widely felt will remove one major incentive to early retirement. Third, the system does not produce flagrant corruption because the individual official does not normally seek his own post-retirement job; it is found for him by the political and administrative leadership of his ministry. Many officials have testified that they had no knowledge of a possible open position until their minister recommended them for it or until they were contacted by the employing firm after they had retired. Thus, there is some credibility to the National Personnel Authority's findings that a direct connection does not usually exist between the official's former duties and new employment. Nevertheless, there can be no doubt that the need for post-retirement *amakudari* has weakened the overall independence of the Japanese civil service. There can also be no doubt that, over time, the continued practice of *amakudari* contributed to serious corruption, as was revealed in 1993, in the bribery and bid-rigging scandals throughout the construction industry. Virtually every general contractor and local government employed a former official of the Ministry of Construction in order to participate in the bidding on public works projects.

BUSINESS ATTITUDES TOWARD *Amakudari*

During the 1950s, when the Japanese economy was still subject to strict governmental controls, many firms sought out and welcomed retired bureaucrats as a means of improving their access to official agencies where critical approvals, import and export licenses, and investment funds were obtained. In industries such as steel, every major firm acquired a former vice-minister or at least a Heavy Industries Bureau chief, with impressive results.

"It is said that any major MITI decision," wrote two *Asahi* reporters, "is known within the hour in the offices of Nippon Steel Corporation, Nippon Kōkan, and Kawasaki Steel Corporation."[13] The same relationship existed in electric power generation, long a major area of MITI responsibility prior to the Allied Occupation and a leading recipient of retired bureaucrats after independence. Generally speaking, the 1950s offered a seller's market to the retired official seeking employment. It was also the heyday for bureaucrats who chose to go into politics after retirement.

The situation changed during the 1960s. As the number of retirees increased and governmental controls declined, the market for the skills of ex-bureaucrats noticeably weakened. Long-service employees of firms or organizations receiving retired officials began to identify themselves as "native-born" *(haenuki)* members of a firm and to express their growing resentment over newcomers entering at the top. Banners hanging on the office buildings of public corporations protesting the announcement of new *yokosuberi* appointments appeared with increasing frequency in the late 1960s and early 1970s. Private firms continued to hire ex-bureaucrats, but less for their connections than for their special expertise or professional knowledge—particularly in the areas of international trade, high finance, and new technology. The 1973 report of the National Personnel Authority noted that of the 180 retired officials receiving exemptions from the law, 83 were administrative officials and 97 were technical officials, which was regarded as an unusual rise in technicians. Interestingly enough, technicians were generally five or six years younger than administrators at the time of retirement.

During 1973, private businessmen's alarm over the role of ex-bureaucrats in their midst came into the open with the increasingly frequent announcements that former officials were being named to the presidencies of corporations. Not all firms accept ex-bureaucrats—Idemitsu Petroleum, for example, has a company policy against employing them—but in those that do, an informal rule had developed that no matter how good the ex-official might be, the top post—the presidency of the firm—would be reserved for a "civilian." But then on May 30, 1973, Hirai was named president of Japan's biggest firm, New Japan Steel, which followed by only a year Inoue Yoshimi's achievement of the presidency of Kobe Steel. Inoue had served in the Ministry of Finance from 1934 to 1956, retiring as director of the Printing Bureau. Another startling development was the choice of Tamaki in the summer of 1972 to succeed Dokō Toshio as president of Tōshiba. Tamaki was the fifth-ranked vice-president within the Tōshiba hierarchy, and Dokō himself had not been a Tōshiba native son, having come to the firm from the presidency of Ishikawajima-Harima Heavy Industries. Tō-shiba old-timers were reportedly dismayed by having another outsider as president and by Tamaki's leap over four of his seniors. Two other rapidly advancing ex-bureaucrats looked like they might soon become presidents: Kashiwagi Yūsuke (Ministry of Finance, 1941–71), vice-president of the Bank of Tokyo; and Murai Shichirō (Ministry of Finance, 1942–69), executive director of the Sanwa Bank (Kashiwagi made it, Murai did not). One of the most exceptional developments was the advancement of Murata Hisashi to the vice-presidency of Mitsui Trading Company, given Mitsui's strong internal loyalties. Murata's attractiveness to a big trading company was, however, obvious. He worked for MITI from 1936 to 1958, during which time he served as deputy chief of the International Trade Bureau and saw overseas service in the New York consulate, as well as extensive travel in South America, the USSR, Southeast Asia, and Europe. He was chief of the Coal Bureau when he retired.

What lies behind this advancement during the early 1970s of retired bureaucrats to the top echelons of Japanese commerce and industry? Two general reasons have been advanced by Japanese business analysts. First, retired bureaucrats do not belong to the major internal factions that influence all large Japanese organizations, including big businesses. While this would normally be a disadvantage in terms of their advancement, it was a strong point in the early 1970s because they were seen to be neutrals. The large number of mergers in the late 1960s tended to exacerbate factional rivalries, and neutrals were in demand. This was clearly a factor in Hirai's promotion to the presidency of New Japan Steel, where the old Yawata and Fuji factions continued to compete despite the merger. Second, many "godfathers" of Japanese industry, as they are styled in 1974 parlance, decided that they needed the "defensive type" of chief executive rather than the 1960s' "attack type" for the period after the yen revaluation and the alleged "confusion" of the Japanese economy. The organizational specialists from the bureaucracy are said to be of the defensive type. This was clearly a major factor in the choice of Tamaki as president of Tōshiba.[14]

Most analysts do not expect to see continued advancement of ex-bureaucrats to the top posts, except in banking where Ministry of Finance connections are invaluable. (This has proven to be accurate, especially for regional banks, where *amakudari* officials increased their dominance.) Of the 500 companies listed on the first division of the Tokyo Stock Exchange, some 350 made personnel changes in March 1973 at the level of managing director and above. About 50 replaced the top man. Until 1973, ex-bureaucrats had not figured prominently in this list, and even in 1973 their numbers were small. Many more directors of firms come from banks that have made loans to the firm than from officialdom. Still, the achievements of the bureaucratic contingent were real and marked a new development in the structure of the Japanese economy.

One additional aspect of the role and reception of ex-bureaucrats in big business is their special positions in industries and firms subject to "administrative guidance" by the government. From the point of view of the individual firm in such an industry, the chief merit to the enterprise in accepting an *amakudari* official is his familiarity with the "license approval authority" *(kyoninkaken)* of the government. If an industry is receiving "administrative guidance," executives of the firms involved will normally conclude that it is convenient to accept a few ex-bureaucrats into their ranks. From the point of view of the government, it seems clear, although it is impossible to prove, that placement of *amakudari* officials has been motivated not only by a desire to secure post-retirement employment for them but also as a matter of positive policy to enhance the effectiveness of administrative guidance. This is apparent from the large numbers of ex-bureaucrats in firms that are specially favored by the government for development or in firms that receive substantial subsidies.

In the petroleum industry, for example, the *Asahi* newspaper (April 16, 1974) reported the results of its own investigation, which showed that there were about 50 former senior officials from MITI at the level of director and above serving in every petroleum importing and refining firm except Nippon Oil, Idemitsu, Esso, and General Oil. This number included five former vice-ministers of MITI. The petroleum industry is subject to close and, from the standpoint of the public, extremely controversial "administrative guidance" from MITI under the provisions of the Petroleum Industry Law of 1962. An assistant section chief in the Petroleum Department of MITI's Resources and Energy Agency who was fired and indicted in the autumn of 1973 for allegedly having accepted bribes from the industry, defended himself in his first trial session by characterizing the relations between MITI and the industry as like "relations between relatives" *(shinrui-zukiai)*.[15]

Among the various petroleum firms, the *Asahi* identified Kyōdō Sekiyu (Kyōdō Oil Co.) as an *"amakudari* company." This firm was originally set up in 1965 under the strong guidance of MITI through the merger of several medium and small petroleum enterprises. Its competitors, particularly its foreign competitors, referred to it as a "MITI dummy." According to the *Japan Times* (May 2, 1974), the government would like to see Kyōdō develop into a Japanese "major" which would free Japan from its heavy dependence on the international, chiefly American, petroleum firms. Until May 1, 1974, the president of Kyōdō Oil was Mori Chikao, who served in MITI from 1934 to 1959 as Mine Safety Bureau chief, and Light Industries Bureau chief. Mori, who resigned the Kyōdō presidency to become president of the Oil Resources Development Company, was replaced at his old post by Koide Eiichi, who served in MITI from 1935 to 1962 as chief of the Public Utilities Bureau and of the Heavy Industries Bureau, retiring as administrative vice-minister of the Economic Planning Agency on loan from MITI. Between 1962 and 1974 he was a senior official (vice-president in 1974) of the Kyushu Electric Power Company, the firm that supplies electricity to Hirai Tomisaburō's steel works at Yawata and like all electric power companies of major concern to MITI. Below Koide at Kyōdō, the executive director and two managing directors were also from MITI.[16]

There seems no doubt that the pattern in the petroleum industry reflects a close connection between *amakudari* policy and the larger economic objectives of MITI. While Kyōdō appears to be a special project of MITI's, other petroleum firms have taken on ex-bureaucrats as a matter of both the government's administrative guidance and self-defense. Nagayama Tokio, a former chief secretary of MITI and chief of the Textiles Bureau, became president of Shōwa Petroleum, and Itō Shigeki, president of Maruzen Petroleum, was a former MITI Mining Bureau chief and director general of the Patent Agency. Even Shell and Mobil have accepted personnel from MITI. This pattern, which has long existed in the iron and steel and electric power industries, has also emerged in the domestic computer industry, a major focus of MITI's "fostering" activities as part of its plan to change Japan's industrial structure toward information-intensive, non-polluting, tertiary industries.[17]

CONCLUSION

The reemployment of retired government officials by private enterprise in Japan began as a largely *ad hoc* process in response to very real needs of businesses and bureaucrats. Over time, it came to be semi-regularized and used for larger purposes of governmental policies, most of which had been identified and justified in terms of the national interest by the administrative and elected leadership of Japan. *Amakudari* does not appear to reflect some kind of plot or stratagem to circumvent laws or to obtain unfair advantages. Its rationale is a reflection of circumstances that have confronted the nation in the past and that persist in lessened form to the present time. This is not to say that *amakudari* is the only or the best means to deal with these problems, or that the side effects of *amakudari* do not create different but equally serious problems. Nonetheless, it is the way that the Japanese have actually dealt with some of the personnel problems of their civil service and is one aspect of their implementation of so-called administrative guidance. It seems proper to end on this factual note and thereby perhaps avoid the common foreign pitfalls of confusing Japanese ideals of consensus and harmony with the realities of Japanese practice or of projecting Western norms onto a society that does not necessarily share them.

8

Omote (Explicit) and *Ura* (Implicit): Translating Japanese Political Terms

Judging from their extensive commentary on the subject, one would have to say that the Japanese believe they have a problem with their language in international negotiating situations. Writers on international politics regularly point to failures in translation, or to misunderstandings derived from the language, as major contributing factors to international disputes involving Japan, even when Japanese spokesmen have been more or less accurately translated. The frequent recurrence of this theme in discussions of Japan's international relations would itself seem to justify a discussion of the problems encountered by a translator of Japanese in the political and economic fields.

Thus, for example, in his press conference of July 27, 1945, Prime Minister Suzuki Kantarō, responding to the terms of the Potsdam Declaration which had just been received in Tokyo, said that the government's attitude was one of *mokusatsu suru*. This was taken by the Allies to mean "treat with silent contempt" and a rejection of their terms, when in fact the *Mainichi Daily News* has argued that Suzuki's intended meaning was "no comment" (today, he could make himself clear simply by saying *nō komento*, a long-accepted form of Japanized English). According to the *Mainichi*, the government had in fact already decided to accept the Potsdam Declaration. The result of this con-

157

fusion was the prolongation of the war and the atomic bombing of two Japanese cities.[1]

A more recent and much more extensively discussed example is what Prime Minister Satō said to President Nixon when they met alone, except for their interpreters, in the White House on November 19–20, 1969. The issue was Nixon's request for a limitation on Japanese textile exports to the United States (which concerned a political promise Nixon had made to American textile industry operators and unions during the 1968 election campaign) in return for having already agreed to the reversion of Okinawa to Japan on the terms that Satō desired. Nobody knows what Satō actually said, but everyone interested at all has speculated on it. Professor Nagai Yōnosuke guesses that Satō said something like *Jibun mo seijika dakara, sono kimochi wa yoku wakaru. Sakkyū ni kaiketsu suru yō zensho suru,* which Akatani Gen'ichi, Satō's translator, probably rendered as, "I'm a politician too, so I know how you feel. I will immediately move forward on the matter with a view to bringing about a solution."[2] The leading American commentators, Destler, Fukui, and Sato, disagree. They doubt that Satō said, *zensho suru* (I will do my best) but something more like *mondai ga areba nantoka suru* (If you have a problem, I will do something about it).[3] One of Japan's best informed journalists, Nawa Tarō, comes to the heart of the matter. He states unambiguously that Satō said, *saizen no doryoku o suru* (do my very best to . . .) but that this has a *Nihon-teki imi* (Japanese meaning), namely, *doryoku shita ga dame datta* (I've done my best but it's useless). He believes that Satō was misinterpreted, as if he had said, *maemuki ni doryoku suru* (I shall endeavor to do it in a positive manner).[4] Perhaps one day we will learn the definitive answer from Nixon's famous tapes. In any case, Satō did not do anything, and Nixon thought Satō had reneged on a promise, which led Japan and the United States to the damaging confrontation over textiles in 1970 and ultimately to the "Nixon shocks" of 1971.

My interest here is only in the controversy that has surrounded Satō's language and in the Japanese belief that there is a *Nihon-teki imi* (Japanese cultural meaning) to Satō's words that was improperly translated. As a matter of fact, Destler, Fukui, and Sato are convinced that Satō was neither mistranslated nor misunderstood, but that he was unable for political reasons to deliver on the promise he had made to Nixon and that he therefore denied he had made a promise.

Suzuki Takao contends that "When we read a foreign language, we are really thinking in our native language most of the time."[5] This may well be true, but the challenge for the translator of political and economic language (perhaps in other areas, too) is to break this habit. It is necessary to do so because while a reader may be thinking in his native language, he must avoid thinking in terms of his native political institutions, values, and concepts if he is going to understand the foreign institutions that the foreign language describes and interprets. This problem is acute in the Japanese case.

Obviously such basic political concepts as authority, power, bureaucracy, oligarchy, and so forth are supranational and supracultural, and they may be rendered in both Japanese and English. Nonetheless, their use in the analysis of Japanese politics and government is always complicated by the unusually bifurcated or split-level quality of the Japanese polity. All politically organized societies reveal a discrepancy between the formal and the actual, between the ideal and the normative functioning of their political institutions, and it is precisely the existence of this discrepancy that gives rise to political science, as distinct from political philosophy, political education, or political advocacy. In the Japanese case, however, for well-known ancient, medieval, and quite modern historical reasons, the expected discrepancy is not merely a feature of interest to political scientists and a source of active politics and political change; it is rather a structural feature around which the polity has been organized and evolved. Thus, the discrepancy between *omote* and *ura* (front and back, visible and invisible), which is found in all societies, is more pronounced in Japan and perhaps the single most important datum for the political analyst. There is indeed a *Nihon-teki imi* to the most ordinary Japanese political words, depending on whether they are being used to refer to the *omote* or *ura* level of politics. The translator must bring this structural feature to light, or at least avoid confusing the reader who thinks about politics in a frame of reference that ignores or is insensitive to a broad separation between *tatemae* (principle) and *honne* (actuality).

Diet proceedings, for example, are the *omote* or visible side of the political process; they are constitutionally the most important events of Japanese politics because the Diet is the "highest organ of state power" (art. 41). But the invisible political process, the *ura,* is much more important for actual decision-making, and it takes place in "private" if nonetheless institutionalized meetings among bureaucrats, Liberal Democratic Party (LDP) members, Cabinet officials, and *zaikai* (big business) leaders. This extra-constitutional process is not illegal, since it is legitimized by the *omote* process. Everyone knows of its existence, even if he or she never knows exactly who participates or how decisions are made. The budget, for example, is created by the bureaucrats, who also initiate most other legislation, even though the LDP, the *zaikai,* and other groups also have inputs into the budgetary process. Only the results are *omote;* the actual bargaining is *ura.* Equally important, the *ura* level of politics is entwined with and sometimes tainted by the political financing of the LDP. This is the world of the *kuromaku* (literally "black curtain," meaning, behind-the-scenes leadership), the *ura* of the *ura* (as in *uragane,* invisible money), that has influenced so much of Japanese politics in the LDP era (1955–93).

This split-level political process is a rich source of language, and its translation involves not only understanding and a good ear but also analysis and insight into a complex, highly rational political system. Japanese politicians are not great orators, since oratory is inappropriate in an *ura* meeting where their skill is really tested. Instead the most capable of them communicate through *haragei* (non-verbal communication, literally "belly art," which means something close to an adult version of "good vibes"). It is interesting to recall that Satō reportedly said before departing for his controversial summit meeting, "Since Mr. Nixon and I are old friends, the negotiations will be three parts talk and seven parts *haragei.*"[6] Nixon may or may not have understood Satō's *haragei,* but it seems certain that Satō did not catch Nixon's, which is unusual for so accomplished a practitioner of the art.

Sometimes real politics erupt in the *omote* world, even though they are not supposed to; *omote* is an arena where surprises should not occur. The occasion for such an eruption is usually a *hōgen* (irresponsible utterance) or a *shitsugen* (slip of the tongue), slight terms for what are actually very big events in Japanese politics. Minister of Finance Kataoka Naoharu literally set off the financial crisis of 1927 with what was probably a genuine *shitsugen* about the bankruptcy of the Watanabe Bank. On November 27, 1952, MITI Minister Ikeda had to resign after remarking much too clearly, "It is unavoidable that [the government's policies of priority to heavy industry] will probably drive a few small businessmen to bankruptcy and suicide."[7] This *hōgen* was followed three months later by the equally famous "*bakayarō* election," after Prime Minister Yoshida called a Socialist questioner in the Diet a "damn fool." Some *hōgen* are certainly intentional, a device for mobilizing media attention and launching a *būmu* among the people. Prime Minister Satō's comment of August 15, 1965, that "So long as Okinawa has not been returned to Japan, the postwar era will not come to an end for our country" was probably such a case.

One frequently discussed characteristic of Japanese politics is the marked separation between authority and power in politics, and in many other areas of organized life, which gives rise to such phenomena as *gekokujō* (juniors making policy for seniors) and Maruyama's famous distinctions among the authority-laden but powerless *mikoshi* (portable shrines), the powerful but unauthorized *kanri* (state officials), and the outlaw *rōnin* (masterless samurai).[8] Authority appears mostly at the *omote* level, power at the *ura*. Within the *ura*, the power-holding group of greatest interest to the Japanese public, and to political scientists, is Japan's talented corps of *kōkyū kanryō* (higher-level bureaucrats), the top graduates of Tokyo University's Law School who have made it on the *erīto kōsu* to power and who later *amakudaru* (descend from heaven) into big paying jobs in big business.

There are many interesting terms to describe the bureaucrats, all redolent of the *omote-ura* distinction. Bureaucrats themselves seem to prefer the idea that they are *kuroko*, the kabuki stagehands who "assist" the actors in various ways during a performance and who are dressed in black in order to be inconspicuous.[9] Some former bureaucrats are less flattering. Kakizawa Kōji, formerly of the Ministry of Finance who resigned to run for the Upper House in 1977 as a member of the New Liberal Club, calls them the *megane o kaketa dobunezumizoku* (scurrying rats wearing spectacles).[10] And yet they do have power and talent and are interesting because of that. Japan may be the only country in which popular authors of best-selling novels choose topics such as *Nihon ginkō (The Bank of Japan)* or *Kanryō-tachi no natsu (The Summer of the Bureaucrats).*[11] It seems unlikely that an American novel called *Federal Reserve Bank* or *The Summer of Mickey Kantor* would have much appeal. Thus, the countless weekly and monthly articles in Japan detailing shifts in the *kanryō jinmyaku chiri* (geography of personal networks among bureaucrats) are testimony to the existence of the *ura* and its potency.[12]

This quick survey of the Japanese polity is intended to suggest that what is required of a translator of Japanese political writing is not just a good knowledge of the language. Equally, if not more important is a fluency in comparative politics and an awareness that while Japanese institutions and practices may have "functional equivalents" in other societies—bureaucrats in Japan perform some of the same intermediating functions that lawyers do in the United States—the differences are much more important, and it is these differences that the skillful translator must bring out. The language of the Japanese political economy is no more difficult to translate than the language of other areas of Japanese life, but the Japanese polity remains conceptually difficult. Readers of translated Japanese are too often allowed to forget this fact, and the specific tradeoffs of Japanese political organization remain a subject on the frontiers of political science. It is unfortunately true, as Umesao Tadao has put it, that "There are certain stars in the universe whose properties are so strange as to be almost beyond belief. . . . Since they cannot, in principle, be seen because the gravitational field prevents photons from escaping, they are referred to as 'black holes.' . . . Is not Japan in its own way also a 'black hole' in the world? From the outside one can infer that tremendous amounts of energy are being unleashed but no signal of any sort is being transmitted from the object."[13]

The nuances of *omote* and *ura* are not the only problems that face the political and economic translator. The pages immediately following detail and illustrate eighteen specific areas where I have encountered problems in my own research. This is not a scientific survey or a linguistic analysis. It is rather one reader's report (or confession) of *curvas peligrosas* discovered through the actual experience of having to brake sharply or go off the track. Following this survey, I shall return to some larger issues by looking at the language of the most famous "translation" of them all in the political field—the Constitution of 1947.

1. *False friends.* This term will be instantly familiar to all students of French or users of French-English dictionaries; it refers to words that are especially liable to be mistranslated on account of their apparent resemblance. Thus, *nouvelle* means "news, tidings, fresh information," not "novel," which in French is *roman.* Similarly, a *libraire* is a bookseller, not a librarian *(bibliothécaire).* The problem comes up in Japanese because of the very large number of foreign, usually English, words that have entered the language and because of the existence of *wasei eigo,* or Japanese-created English which does not exist in English (q.v. numbers 5 and 6 below). A few examples include *bukku-mēkā,* which means a hack writer, not a "bookmaker"; *surendā* means "slender," not "surrender"; *konsento* is not "consent" but an electric wall outlet; *kanningu* means "cunning" but the Japanese understand the word to mean "cheating," e.g., *Kare wa kanningu o shite taikō saserareta* (He was expelled from school for cheating);[14] a *komisshon* is a "bribe," not a "commission"; *noruma* comes from the Russian and does not mean "norm" or "standard" but "quota"; and *dorai* and *uetto* mean dry and wet, but they also mean "businesslike" and "sentimental." All of these words are written in *katakana* (the Japanese syllabary used for foreign words), but there are occasional false friends written in *kanji* (Chinese characters), e.g., *yukiotoko,* literally a "snowman," but meaning an "abominable snowman" or a *yeti.*

A problem different but related to that of false friends might be called *"katakana* opacity." Suzuki Takao refers to Japan as a "guessing culture" *(sasshi no bunka),* and I know what he means.[15] In Japan one evening, my wife and I were inattentively watching a symphony orchestra on the NHK second channel when a sign came up on the TV screen announcing in *katakana* the next piece to be played. I said positively, "It's called 'Rolling Green.' Must be some English pastoral music by Vaughan Williams or someone like that." The orchestra then began the overture to *Lohengrin!* There is a warning to the translator in this story. A *fūzu-fū* does not look much like it but is a "who's who," and *rokafura* is not a rendering in Japanese of the name "Rockefeller" but Hawaiian music in a rock arrangement. A nice political coinage that loses much of its bite when written in *katakana* instead of *kanji* is *zaruhō*, literally "bamboo basket law," or a law with many loopholes.

One final false friend that is important in politics is *tarento*. It means "talent," but it also specifically refers to TV anchormen or movie actresses whom the LDP has nominated for the upper house's national constituency in order to trade off their notoriety with the voters. Examples of successful *tarento* candidates in the House of Councillors include the famous TV comic storyteller *(rakugo)* Matsuoka Katsuyoshi and the star of TBS television Santō Akiko. The opposition parties have naturally followed suit and now boast such *tarento* Diet members as Den Hideo, Nozue Chinpei, and Aoshima Yukio.

2. New terms for old. Abel and Marguerite Chevalley write, "Each generation requires new 'current use' dictionaries, not only of its own language but still more definitely of other languages comparable with its own. New words appear on both sides. Old words take on in each tongue a new and unforeseeable color, and the equivalents of yesterday are no longer equivalent today."[16] In Japan the current use dictionaries come out each year, not each generation.[17] Given the pace of change in Japan, the appearance of new words and phrases is not unexpected but it does pose problems for the translator. The great divide is, of course, the war. Some terms for the same thing have changed— for example, a tank used to be a *sensha* but is today a *tokusha*, reflecting the sensitivities of the Defense Agency; and democracy used to be *mimponshugi* but is today *minshushugi*, avoiding the Confucian connotations of the old term. Other words have remained the same but have taken on new meanings—for example, *kakushin* used to mean reform in the direction of fascism and totalitarianism but today refers to the opposite, socialism and communism. Still other words have changed even though their translations remain the same—thus, what before and during the war was called *kigyō seibi* became after the war *sangyō gōrika* (even though the term existed from at least the 1920s), both meaning "industrial reorganization."

Some postwar expressions varied according to the political preferences of the user: thus, leftists preferred *taikyaku* for "retreat" while conservatives favored *tenshin*, "shift army field positions." Similarly, those on the left referred to the defeat of 1945 as *haisen* while those on the right spoke of *shūsen*, "termination of hostilities"; and the American occupiers were either (left) the *senryōgun*, "army of occupation," or (right) *shinchūgun*, "forces stationed (in Japan)."

Some words have been given new meanings by important writers, perhaps the best known social science example being *amae* and *amaeru*. Thanks to Doi Takeo, both words now mean "dependency" in a specifically psychosocial context rather than "to presume upon another's love."[18] Translators working with materials from the second and third decades of the Shōwa era should be alert to changes in basic concepts.

3. Conceptually difficult terms. There are many special conceptual terms in Japanese, and I have chosen only a few to discuss that are particularly relevant to politics and economics. *Yuchaku* is a medical term meaning "adhesion, union, conglutination, healing up," but it is used in political discourse to mean specifically the cooperative relationship between the government and big business. Thus, *kanmin yuchaku* (the growing together of the public and private sectors) is one well-established phrase for what foreigners have labelled "Japan Incorporated."[19] Sakakibara Eisuke, on leave from the Ministry of Finance and serving as a professor at Saitama University, also uses *yuchaku* to refer to collaboration between the bureaucracy and the Liberal Democratic Party.[20] Another medical term, *myaku* (a vein, the pulse), is in constant use today to describe *ura* connections and relationships among the conservative leadership—for example, *jinmyaku* (personnel networks),[21] *kinmyaku* (money channels), *kimyaku* (kindred spirits, meeting of the minds), *sanmyaku* (a range of mountain peaks, specifically former Prime Minister Ikeda's closest associates), and *meimyaku* (life pulse, the "mainstream" line of descent in the LDP from Yoshida to Ikeda to Satō).[22]

Closely related to *myaku* is a much more common word, *suji*, that has been expanded into a large number of political terms and concepts. *Kenkyūsha* (fourth ed.) gives some thirteen meanings for *suji*, ranging from muscle, tendon, string, and line through plot, logic, coherence, and nature. Some of its compounds include *kampen-suji*, "government circles"; *sujigane*, as in *sujigane iri no kyōsantōin*, a "dyed-in-the-wool communist"; *kaisha-suji*, a "high official in a company"; *sono suji*, the "competent authorities" (as in *sono suji no mei ni yori tachi-iri kinshi,* or "no trespassing"); and *kansoku-suji* or *shōsoku-suji,* both meaning "informed sources." Words similar to *suji* in their numerous uses and nuances are *hara* (belly, spirit) and *koshi* (the hip). All three should be signals to the translator to proceed with care.

The most important genuine political concept I want to discuss here is *chōsei,* meaning variously regulation, adjustment, reconciliation, control, and coordination. It is, for example, the term used in phrases such as to "tune" a piano or to "tune up" an engine. The Chōsei Kyoku of the Economic Planning Agency is officially translated by the Japanese government as the "Coordination Bureau." *Chōsei* occurs in countless official and bureaucratic uses, often as a euphemism for "control" in the titles and provisions of post-war economic laws. More important, it is the subject of serious discussion in learned books and articles, either as a function performed by the bureaucracy or as a characteristic that the highly compartmentalized Japanese executive branch lacks. On the one hand, Sakakibara Eisuke, a bureaucrat, writes that "Among all the functions of officials, by far the most important is *chōsei."* Its fundamental basis, he believes, lies in the *honne* of social conflict, and its objective is to produce balance through *nemawashi* ("digging around the roots," maneuvers behind the scenes). Although the famous practice of official "administrative guidance" *(gyōsei shidō)* is not one of the legal powers granted to the bureaucracy, according to Sakakibara, it nonetheless is included in the bureaucracy's *chōsei kengen* (coordinating authority).[23]

On the other hand, Ōkōchi Shigeo, a scholar, argues that the greatest problem of Japanese governmental organization since the Meiji period has been the *chōsei* of "sectionalism" within the government, the need for coordination and regulation created by the *hōken-teki kakkyosei* (feudal rivalry among local barons) inherited from the past. In his view, the numerous prewar, wartime, and postwar attempts to create coordinating organs at the cabinet level were only formal, and were without real substance. He agrees with the well-known political scientist, Rōyama Masamichi, that the concept of coordination does not really exist in Japanese, despite numerous terms approximating it—including, *chōsei, sōgō chōsei, renraku chōsei, tōsei* (3536,

2436),[24] *chōsetsu,* and *tōgō* (to "combine," as in *tōgō sanbō honbu,* "joint chiefs of staff").[25]

The point of this discussion is that a translator of political or economic writing encountering the term *chōsei* should become instantly alert. It is a euphemism for the most important *ura*-world activities of the bureaucracy, and it refers to an executive power that has been sought but never fully achieved by prime ministers throughout this century, notably and tragically former Prime Minister Tōjō. Some characteristic contemporary uses of *chōsei* include *chōsei-ritsu* (literally "adjusted rate," the fixed minimum daily interest rate charged on loans to metropolitan banks by the Bank of Japan), *jishu chōsei* (the "voluntary controls" that a company may enforce over its own production),[26] *tōshi-chōsei-karuteru* (an "investment-control cartel"), and *chōseihi* ("adjustment expenses," the Ministry of Finance's euphemism for political expenditures forced on it by the LDP).[27]

4. *Straight translation can be meaningless.* When a term has no equivalent in English or the equivalent does not make sense, then a translator must supply an explanation rather than a translation. For example, *kuroi kiri* means "black mist" but in fact refers to suspected corruption or to mysterious events related to politics. Similarly, *tōyū* means "party friend" but dates only from the 1978 expansion of associate memberships in the Liberal Democratic Party and the complications this brought to the intraparty elections for president. Prime Minister Ōhira was the first beneficiary of the "party friend" system, a system so totally *ura* that it completely baffled the national newspapers' public opinion polls at the time of Ōhira's election. The Jichishō, which became a ministry in July 1960, is literally the "Ministry of Self Government" or "Ministry of Autonomy" (the term autonomy being an awkward American invention inherited from the occupation) but is best, and officially, translated as "Ministry of Home Affairs," not of course to be confused with the old Ministry of Home Affairs (Naimushō), the former pride of the bureaucracy that the Americans broke up after the war. These cases are not hard, but they do require care in providing accurate explanations.

5. *Wasei eigo (and other gairaigo).* As already noted, Japanese-coined English is a prime source of false friends; but even when not false to English, *wasei eigo* (Japanese-manufactured

English) may call for a translation into different English. Thus, *gōruden-awā* (golden hour) is "prime time" on TV; *beddo-taun* is a "bedroom community"; *ōrudomisu* a "spinster"; *sain* "to autograph"; and *sarariman* a "white-collar worker." Probably the most commonly encountered *gairaigo* ("term from abroad") on the campuses of the 1960s was *geba,* short for *gebaruto,* from the German *Gewalt* (violence). It has been turned into a verb, *gebaru* (to use violent tactics), and combined with other terms to produce *geba-gakusei* (violent students), *uchigeba* (internal violence), and numerous other expressions. Some *wasei eigo* seem to defy anything other than straight translation, e.g., *imēji daun* (the collapse of one's, or a company's, public image), *maihōmu-shugi* (Seidensticker and Matsumoto say "family-first principle," but I prefer something like "consumer-age uxoriousness"), and so forth.

A difficult, contracted *wasei eigo* is *bea,* from *bēsu-appu* (base up), meaning to raise the base on which seniority wages are calculated, what the unions attempt to do in the *shuntō* (spring labor offensive). Seidensticker and Matsumoto give the following example: *Rōdō kumiai wa ni-man-en no bea yōkyū o shita,* "the union demanded a twenty-thosuand yen pay raise." Readers should not confuse *bea* with *purasu arufa* (plus alpha) (s.v. under number 7). One of the most deliciously obscure *gairaigo* was discovered by Don C. Bailey—namely, *arusaro,* from *arubaito saron,* a "coffee shop or cabaret employing part-time student help" (from the German *Arbeit* and the French *salon*).[28]

6. *Hybrid* wasei eigo. According to one analyst, some 15 to 20 percent of the words entering Japanese from foreign languages are combined with native Japanese words to form hybrids—e.g., *chingin-katto* (a pay cut).[29] These words do not usually pose problems of translation, but they can be sources of confusion. Thus, for example, the Japanese will use different terms for a strike by a labor union (the imported *suto,* from *sutoraiki,* or the indigenous *tōsō*) depending on the hybrid—as in *abekku-tōsō* (French *avec* combined with *tōsō*), a labor dispute in which several unions have joined forces; in contrast to *jigen-suto* ("time-limited strike," a work stoppage for a fixed period of time only), or *jūnan-suto* ("flexible strike," one using a variety of tactics such as time delays, work-to-rules, general strike, etc.). Other typical examples include *bamubamu-genshō* ("bam-bam phe-

nomenon," i.e., a sonic boom, not *bangubangu* since *bangu* means "bangs," a hair style, not "bang," a noise), *shinobiyoru-infure*, "creeping inflation" (from *infurēshon*), and *wariate-karuteru*, a "quota cartel."

7. *Business jargon*. Sometimes the terms in this category display the wry Japanese sense of humor, as well as many Japanese business concepts and practices that are unfamiliar in English. Thus, for example, *jitensha sōgyō* is not the "bicycle business," but sales below production costs to avoid the bankruptcy that would occur if production stopped. The metaphor is that of a bicycle's falling over if it stops moving. One rather hard business term is *purasu-arufa* (plus alpha), which means approximately the same thing as the use in English of the letter "n" as a symbol for an indefinite number (as in "to the nth degree") plus another amount. Bailey's explanation, "those aspects of management-labor dealings and relations which, not being specified in the contract, fall within the discretion of management," is much too restricted to a particular context.[30] More typical is *ichiritsu-purasu-arufa*, "uniformity plus alpha," meaning a uniform minimum wage plus special increments for length of service, age, experience, etc. *Purasu-arufa* is also used sometimes merely as a catch phrase for "added advantage," as in the subtitle of Miki Yōnosuke's popular book in the Kappa Business series entitled *Seijiryoku, Jitsuryoku purasu-arufa no himitsu (Political Influence, Secrets of Real Plus Alpha)* and here meaning something like "Machiavellianism for business executives."[31] *Purasu-arufa* always requires care in translation.

Business jargon ranges all the way from such graphic terms as *shukketsu-yushutsu* ("bleeding exports," or sales-below-costs, dumping) to names for each rise and fall of the postwar business cycle (e.g., the *nabezoko fukyō*, "bottom-of-the-pot recession," July 1957 to June 1958; the *Izanagi keiki*, "boom unprecedented since the legendary god Izanagi mated with Izanami to create the Japanese islands," November 1965 to June 1970; and the *sekiyu shokku igo*, "after the oil shock"). It might be noted in passing that the advertising business in Japan also generates as arcane a jargon as it does elsewhere, only it is specific to Japan and to the psychology of Japanese marketing.

8. *Puns and humor*. This category is too large to be analyzed in detail here; suffice it to say that much Japanese humor relies

on puns and amusing acronyms. One well-known example is *ameshon*, "American urination" (from *Amerika* and *shonben*, "to urinate"), a sarcastic term from the 1950s used to refer to Diet members, movie stars, and others who made quick trips to the United States for the publicity, usually with briefcases already packed with postcards to mail to colleagues and constituents (they were there only long enough to pee). It has spawned such related terms as *amebotan*, "American unbuttoning," and *Parishon*, "Paris urination." A somewhat comparable acronym is *satchon*, "Sapporo bachelor," meaning a married man whose company has sent him to the capital of Hokkaido for a period of duty but who has not brought his wife and family with him; Sapporo is also noted for its extensive night life.

The prodigious amounts of money spent on election campaigns often give rise to political puns. During the 1960s, when the internal factions of the LDP tried to outspend each other in order to gain influence with all possible future prime ministers, the slogan was "Nikka, Suntory *(santorī)*, Old Parr *(ōrudopā)*." This is a pun on the names of three popular whiskies; it means roughly even if politicians take money from two *(nikka)* or three *(santorī)* factions, they are fickle and may still dump your faction (you'll find yourself *ōru-pā*, all wiped out).[32]

Some puns are based on collections of similar sounding words—for example, the *go-seru* (five causatives), or five ways to influence a politician: *kuwaseru* (by dining him), *nomaseru* (by wining him) *nigiraseru* (by bribing him), *dakaseru* (by plying him with women), and *ibaraseru* (by flattering him). The "three-*to* teacher" *(santo kyōshi)* belongs to this genre—i.e., the three ways a teacher makes ends meet: *ribēto* (rebates), *purezento* (presents), and *arubaito* (part-time work).[33] New political puns are generated every election. Some are obvious, others untranslatable.

9. Acronyms and abbreviations. Political and economic abbreviations in English usually take the form of initial capitals, as in IBM, SCAP, YMCA, CBS, or UNESCO. Some may be pronounced as a word (you-ness-koe) or as initials (see-bee-ess). Acronyms occur occasionally, particularly in military jargon (CINCPACFLT, Commander-in-chief of the Pacific Fleet), but they are unusual (note, however, "Pan Am," "Socony," "Amtrak," etc.). In Japanese, initials are rare (although they do exist: for example, *Ken-*

kyūsha lists *jetoro* as a pronounced form of JETRO, the Japan External Trade Organization), whereas the most common form of abbreviation is the acronym. When a single word is being shortened, the abbreviated form tends to become the dictionary entry (e.g., *kone*, a "connection" or "contact" from *konekushon*; or *demo*, a "demonstration," as in *demo-kōshin*, a "demonstration march"). Acronyms in Japanese are numberless, and they can confuse even the most skilled reader. *Zaitō*, for example, is the common abbreviation for *zaisei tōyūshi keikaku* (the Fiscal Investment and Loan Plan of the Ministry of Finance), in which even the full term contains an acronym for *tōshi* (investments) and *yūshi* (loans).[34] Acronyms are standard for the names of trade union federations (e.g., Seirōkyō, for Seifu Kankei Tokushu Hōjin Rōdō Kumiai Kyōgikai, Council of Labor Unions of Governmental Public Corporations) and for many banks (Kaigin, for Kaihatsu Ginkō, the Development Bank).

Acronyms are also used in the names of basic policies—e.g., *seikei bunri* (the separation of politics and economics, Japan's basic policy toward China and other countries during the 1960s). Personal names of politicians are sometimes shortened in the newspapers (*kaku-fuku*, for Tanaka *Kaku*ei and *Fuku*da Takeo), and this can be confusing. In standard *kanji* dictionaries, there are 318 characters that can be read *"yoshi,"* 226 *"nori,"* and 189 *"akira."* Before the war there were two ministers in the cabinet named Yoshida Shigeru (one from the Home Ministry and one from the Foreign Ministry, who after the war became prime minister) and their names were distinguished in the *kampō* (government gazette) as Yoshida (1053, 2994) and Yoshida (1050 on top, 868 on the bottom, plus 2994)![35] Faced with the obscure acronym or name, there is no substitute for experience and many dictionaries.

10. *Political jargon.* Common political language is important as a window into the *omote-ura* distinction. The Diet, for example, is constitutionally the most powerful organ of the state, but to some observers it is the scene of *dobuita-seiji* (the politics of putting boards over ditches, i.e., insignificant, local matters) and is merely a *gyōseifu no shitauke kikan* (subcontractor of the administrative branch of government). One of the most common forms of political and economic jargon is the military metaphor. Thus, it is quite normal to read that with former Prime Minister

Satō's election to a fourth term, the LDP had entered its *sengoku jidai* (warring states period), in which the post-Satō *senretsu* (battle line-up) included Miki, Fukuda, Tanaka, Nakasone, and Ōhira. Each of them was engaged in *ikinokori senryaku* (survival tactics) or *honryū warikomi senryaku* (breaking into the mainstream tactics). Political funds are called *heitan* (war supplies), foreign firms do not open branches in Japan but "hit the beaches" *(jōriku-suru),* and contests between oldsters and newcomers after a merger are between the *domingun* (native army) and the *hakengun* (expeditionary army). None of this penchant for military terms is indicative of violence in the society, only of the significance of the relationships involved.

11. *Technical political terms.* Some technical expressions arise from peculiarities of Japanese parliamentary practice—e.g., a *hensoku kokkai* (abnormal Diet), one in which the majority carries on business as usual even though one or more opposition parties is boycotting; or a *rantō kokkai* (free-for-all Diet), one in which members engage in fistfights or throw inkwells at each other, a rather common occurrence after the war but rare today. Other terms come from the peculiarities of Japanese bureaucratic practice—e.g., *dōkisei zen'in yūtai* (all classmates voluntarily resign together), which refers to the custom that when one man from an entering class of officials in a ministry becomes vice-minister, all his classmates or those superior to him resign in order to give him absolute seniority in the ministry.[36] An example from public finance is *hikiage-chōka,* or *age-chō,* meaning an overbalanced national budget, or the conservative fiscal practice of holding treasury revenues in excess of disbursements, which Japan pursued until 1965 (this term is misleadingly translated in *Kenkyūsha* under *age-chō*). In order to translate these types of expressions, the translator must understand both the language and the institutions of Japan.

12. *Japanized Chinese.* When Chinese words, phrases, and proper nouns are printed in Japanese books and journals, they pose no problem—except, of course, for the various simplifications of the Han characters that have occurred in recent years in both Chinese and Japanese. However, when Chinese is spoken in Japan, the situation is radically altered. Chinese is pronounced in Sino-Japanese readings of the characters. Thus, the *Wen Hui Pao* newspaper comes out *Bunkaihō,* Ch'en Tu-hsiu's name is

pronounced Chin Doku-shū, Mao Tse-tung is Mō Taku-tō, and Chiang Ch'ing is heard as Kō Sei. It makes no difference that these pronunciations are unintelligible to Chinese; they are pronounced in the Japanese way in Japan, except of course by Chinese linguists. Again, this is no problem for the Japanese, but it is a problem for anyone who must use the Latin alphabet to put Sino-Japanese into English—and that, of course, is what a translator does. This problem has been further aggravated by the introduction in China of the *pinyin* romanization system and its widespread adoption throughout the English-speaking world. The Ch'ing Dynasty is now officially the Qing Dynasty! This is a problem that seems to get more complicated every year. Soon it will require at least a first-year knowledge of Chinese to look up a book by a Chinese author in the card catalogue of an English-language library. Even so, this problem is also a very old one; I know of at least one American university library that for years had the English works of Chiang Kai-shek (Cantonese)—or Shō Kai-seki (Japanese), Chiang Chieh-shih (Wade-Giles), Jiang Jie-shi (pinyin)—filed under "shek." In short, translators of Japanese materials on China or on Sino-Japanese relations, need to know how Chinese is romanized in English; and the Japanese can offer no help since they pronounce Chinese in a way that is unintelligible in either Chinese or English.

   13. Concepts unstandardized in Japanese. Some abstract political concepts are covered by standardized reference terms in English but not in Japanese, and vice versa. Let me consider only three from the Japanese side—consensus, civilian, and authority. It is astonishing to record that there is no standardized term in Japanese for "consensus," given the fact that it is probably the most commonly used expression in English to describe Japanese "decision-making," and the first trait that a foreign novice is taught about the Japanese political culture. Some writers approximate it with *manjō-itchi-shugi* or *enman* or *dōchō*, while others use variations of *gōi*, *sōi*, and *dōi*. The approved solution to this problem today appears to be the use of *konsensasu*.[37] The lack of a widely accepted term for consensus in Japan may suggest the need for foreigners to use caution in arguing that it is prevalent there.

   The problem with "civilian" comes up because in English it is both an adjective and a noun and because in Japanese compounds with *bun* in them suggest that they have something to do with literary culture. Even so, Japanese does not have a single term for civilian. Instead, it has *bunmin* (as in *bunmin-yūi no gensoku,* the principle of civilian dominance over the government), *bunkan* (as in *bunkan ni yoru kanri seido,* the system of civilian control), *shimin* and *ippan shimin* (as in *shimin no jiyū,* civil liberty), and *minkan* and *minshū* as adjectives. A translator must be careful not to "overtranslate" these terms.

"Authority" and "authoritarian" are words so commonly misused in English today as to make the range of terms available in Japanese probably preferable. Nonetheless, the translator can be confused by the differences between *shihai* (as in *karisuma-teki shihai,* charismatic authority), *kengen* (2360, 4987) (authorized limits of power), *kengen* (2360, 825) (a claim or title), *kennō* (to be authorized or empowered to act), and *ken'i* (as in *ken'i-shugi,* authoritarianism). Again, like consensus, authority is a term to be used with care in the Japanese context, despite the Japanese heritage of authoritarianism.

14. Bureaucratic euphemisms. Bureaucrats invent and use euphemistic language (e.g., they prefer "remains" to "corpse"); this is a natural tendency among them given their need for security and for protection from possible interference in their activities by politicians or the public. But euphemisms are hard to translate. In fact, some English bureaucratic euphemisms come out charmingly concrete when translated into Japanese—e.g., "nepotism" is *keibatsu* (bedroom cliques), and "integration" is *kuroshiro kyōgaku* (joint schooling of blacks and whites). The problem for the translator from Japanese to English is to penetrate the euphemism but not to make it so concrete as to mislead the foreign reader. I have already discussed one typical bureaucratic euphemism, *chōsei* (s.v. under number 3 above). Another is *ikusei* (rearing), an ubiquitous Japanese government term for bureaucratic initiative and control in the development of a new industry. A good example of disguise of intent is the use of *tekiseika* (to make proper) and other words with *ka* added to them, as in article 1 of the ill-fated Special Measures Law for the Promotion of Designated Industries (Tokushinhō) of 1963. In that law the Ministry of International Trade and Industry proposed to *tekiseika* the management and operations of industries it thought needed to have their efficiency raised *(nōritsuka)*. Despite these euphemisms, the law drew forth cries of protest and it was never passed.[38]

15. Coexistence of foreign and Japanese words. Often the existence of foreign and domestic terms meaning the same thing is just a matter of fashion or of an author's style. But the translator often wonders why one word was chosen instead of another. Thus, the Japanese have available *baron-desse (ballon d'essai)* and *dashin-kikyū* (a trial balloon), both sometimes used to mean "leak" (to the press) as much as "probing action." Similarly, *erīto* coexists with *senryō* (elite), and *fōramu* with a plethora of Japanese words meaning a forum or meeting. These terms do not pose problems for a translator except to be sure that he or she understands a writer's meaning.

16. Marxist concepts. While many technical foreign words are used in *katakana,* most Marxist terms have been domesticated and are written in *kanji.* I recall that in 1961 my language tutor in Tokyo, who was then a graduate student at Tokyo University in economics, said to me that if he had to read Marx for an examination, he would read him in Japanese translation; but that if he wanted to understand Marx, he would read him in English translation. Terms such as *kyūbōka riron* (the theory of pauperization) and *mannen kyōkōron* (the doctrine that conditions will increasingly worsen as capitalism develops) are hard to understand in *kanji* and can easily be mistranslated unless it is recognized that they are technical Marxist expressions. Don Bailey, for example, mistranslates *taishū-rosen* as "people's route" when it is, in fact, the standard term for "mass line." Moreover, some Japanese writers use well-known words with special Marxist meanings—e.g., Miki Kiyoshi's use of *antoroporogī* in the sense of Marx and Engels's historical materialistic interpretation of the family. For "anthropology" in the normal sense, the Japanese use *ningengaku* or, most commonly, *jinruigaku.* Some years ago the Japanese Communist Party changed certain key terms in order to "soften" the party's image. Thus, what used to be the "dictatorship" *(dokusai)* of the proletariat has turned into proletarian "control" *(shihai),* and "violent revolution" *(bōryoku kakumei)* has been moderated to "revolution by compelling power" *(kyōseiryoku kakumei).*[39] The point is that a translator of works using Marxist terms should know his or her Marxism.

17. Distinctions in Japanese not made in English. English distinguishes among wages, salary, pay, income, stipend, remuneration, honorarium, etc., and so does Japanese, only in different ways. But in many cases Japanese distinguishes things that English does not. These are among the most important problems of translation. Thus, the distinctions among *kyoka, ninka, tokkyo,* and *menkyo,* all of them meaning generally to "permit" or "license," though with critical differences, are important for bureaucratic practice.[40] *Kisei* (4285, 683), *kisei* (4285, 27), and *kisei* (4285, 2436) all mean "to regulate," but here too there are differences. The first means to regulate in the sense of street demonstrations or exhaust gasses. The second means to regulate in the sense of the Political Funds Regulation Law (to ensure fairness). And the third is somewhat rarer but has been used in postwar laws with the sense of "to bring order" (as in the regulation of black market dealings in food).[41] Some distinctions are too rarified to make much sense in English—as, for example, among *shunin no daijin, shumu daijin,* and *shokan daijin,* all meaning "the minister with jurisdiction" over a particular matter but all occurring in different laws. Finally, it is worth paying attention to those small suffixes *-ra, -tō,* and *-nado* meaning "and so forth" or "and the like." Bureaucrats often add these terms to laws in order to protect themselves and then invoke them when a Diet member accuses them of exceeding their jurisdiction.[42]

18. Culturally circumscribed language. In a sense all the terms discussed thus far are culturally circumscribed. But I am concerned here with one particular aspect of Japanese culture—namely, Suzuki's idea that Japan is an *omoiyari no bunka,* or "consideration culture." This means that "Because it is considered essential to identify with the other and feel as he feels, a free exchange of opposing views between individuals is restrained to the utmost."[43] This is part of the Japanese language. But the *omoiyari no bunka* is further complicated by the split between *omote* and *ura;* the consideration that is shown in one is not the same consideration that is shown in the other. Many of the terms considered to this point belong to the *ura* world. Thus, one further task is to discuss the difficult language of the *omote* world: the arena where form is everything and content little.

Perhaps the best political example of *omote* is a Diet Budget Committee hearing. It is virtually impossible to "translate" the formalities that occur there. First of all, there are two types of hearings: the *sōkatsu shitsumon,* where all inclusive questions are asked, and the *ippan shitsumon,* where questions about specific issues are asked. The prime minister and all other cabinet members, together with high-ranking bureaucrats, attend the first; only the minister, perhaps only the parliamentary vice-minister, together with middle-ranking bureaucrats, attend the second. The prime minister and other ministers often answer questions only from LDP members, bureaucrats from opposition party members. The administrative vice-minister *(jimu-jikan)* of a ministry rarely, if ever, speaks at either of these sessions. At the *sōkatsu shitsumon,* bureau and department chiefs answer for the bureaucracy, while section chiefs may speak at the *ippan shitsumon.* The committee council *(rijikai)* allots time in advance to each member for his questions. All cabinet members and officials have *sōtei mondō shū* (hypothetical question-and-answer booklets) in front of them, prepared by the ministries, and except for an occasional *bakudan shitsumon* (bomb question), everything is prearranged. Bureaucrats refer to Diet members as *sensei.*

Masters of the political *omote* world can speak at these hearings politely and at length without saying anything of substance. Shiina Etsusaburō, himself once the vice-minister of Munitions, twice MITI minister, and vice-president of the LDP, was such a master. It would take too much space to give a full example, but when he was MITI minister he filled Diet records with his correct but only rarely substantive remarks. No less a person than former MITI vice-minister and later president of the Japan Petroleum Development Corporation Tokunaga Hizatsugu, once commented that Shiina managed to look *bōyō* (vague), even though he was extremely intelligent.[44] In his autobiography, Shiina himself supplies a useful comment on the life of a bureaucrat. As a young section chief in the old Ministry of Commerce and Industry, Shiina had to *hanko* (stamp a seal) daily on the numerous documents that flowed across his desk. He ordered his assistant to do this for him until he was reprimanded and forced to do his own stamping. After that, he did the job "looking at knotholes in the ceiling, using as little physical strength and intelligence as possible. I call this approach my 'knothole philosophy' *(fushiana tetsugaku)."*[45] The language that led to Shiina's *fushiana tetsugaku,* or, more exactly, the language of bureaucratic *omote,* even of *menjū-fukuhai* (follow orders to a superior's face, reverse them in the belly), is among the hardest political Japanese to read—or to translate.

The eighteen potentially "dangerous curves" discussed thus far deal mostly with lexical problems, that is, with the challenges and charms of Japanese vocabulary, the changing stock of words and phrases. Still to be discussed is the more difficult, even if better known, category of syntactical problems, under which I include the famous "ambiguity" of Japanese, the problem of equating the topic classifier *wa* with the subject of an English sentence, the problem of understood (or in any case unwritten) subjects and objects, and similar issues well known to students of the language. One way to illustrate some of these difficulties in the field of politics is to look at the language of the Constitution of 1947. I choose the Constitution for various reasons: its supreme importance to the life of the people (ambiguity here, if any, should be intentional and not merely syntactical); the fact that we possess an authoritative English version, which was the actual basis of the Japanese version, and that therefore excludes any argument about the accuracy of a "translation" of the Japanese back into English; and the equally significant fact that the Constitution, regardless of its origins in the Occupation and the speed with which both versions were produced, has secured a firm foundation in the political consciousness of the Japanese as their fundamental charter. The Constitution may yet be amended, but the time is past when it could be repudiated on purely nationalistic grounds.[46]

Japanese is ambiguous. Let us take an example from the second paragraph of the preamble: *Warera wa, heiwa o iji-shi, sensei to reijū, appaku to henkyō o chijō kara eien ni jokyo-shiyō to tsutomete iru kokusai shakai ni oite, meiyo aru chii o shimetai to omou.* In English this reads officially, "We desire to occupy an honored place in an international society striving for the preservation of peace, and the banishment of tyranny and slavery, oppression and intolerance for all time from the earth." The problem is: who does the striving, "we" or "an international society"? It must be admitted that the English version would be better if there were a comma after "society," thereby making it clearer that it is "we" who wish to occupy an honored place and who are also "striving." But the Japanese version certainly leaves the matter open. "We" is the subject of the sentence, but "striving" modifies "international society" *(tsutomete iru kokusai shakai)*, suggesting that the Japanese are, in fact, circumscribing the kind of international society in which they would like to occupy an honored place, perhaps in this one and no other.

A major source of ambiguity, even of incomprehension and unintelligibility, is the separation that occurs in long Japanese sentences between the subject, verb, and object. Thus, for example, the third paragraph of the preamble begins in English, "We believe that [straightforward subject, verb, and object] no nation is responsible to itself alone . . . ," etc. However, the Japanese begins *"Warera wa"* and goes on for four lines before ending *"to shin-zuru."* There is a great deal of complex language about the "laws of political morality" being allegedly universal and "sovereign relations with other nations" before the reader finds out what *warera* is thinking of doing about it all. At least for a constitution, it would seem better to have ended the whole paragraph with *warera wa shin-zuru.*

This problem is not just one of difficulties in comprehension due to length, but also of genuine ambiguity. Thus, for example, article 69: *Naikaku wa, Shūgiin de fushinnin no ketsugian o kaketsu-shi, mata wa shinnin no ketsugian o hiketsu-shita toki wa, tōka inai ni Shūgiin ga kaisan-sarenai kagiri, sōjishoku o shinakereba naranai.* In official English, "If the House of Representatives passes a non-confidence resolution, or rejects a confidence resolution, the Cabinet shall resign en masse, unless the House of Representatives is dissolved within ten (10) days." It seems clear enough that in both Japanese and English, the subject is "the Cabinet" *(Naikaku wa)* and the verb is "shall resign" *(sōjishoku o shinakereba naranai).* But a problem arises in Japanese: who or what is the subject of *kaketsu-shi* and of *hiketsu-shita,* who "passes" and who "rejects"? A careless reader could certainly be forgiven for thinking that it was the Cabinet rather than the House that does these things. The context is the only basis for accurate translation in this case. Again, the meaning of the article would be improved if it were altered to end with *Naikaku wa sōjishoku o shinakereba naranai.* As it is, even the most exactingly precise Japanese requires the exercise of judgment in translation.

The Constitution offers many examples of lexical, as well as syntactical, ambiguities. The second sentence of article 15, for example, says: *Subete kōmuin wa, zentai no hōshisha de atte, ichibu no hōshisha de wa nai.* A Japanese reading his or her Constitution in English might be surprised to learn that "All public officials are servants of the whole community and not of any group thereof." The Japanese version omits the word "community," leaving it simply at "the whole" *(zentai)*. This is surely a result of the English version preceding the Japanese, and the Japanese translator giving up on the sociological concept of "community." The idea of community is well known to the Japanese, but it is one of those cases like "consensus" where it has not been standardized (q.v. category 13 above). *Kyōdōtai* (581, 619, 405) is a recent approximation, as are the older terms *mura-ishiki* and *kyōdo-ishiki* (4766,1050, plus *ishiki*). Today, many social scientists prefer *komyuniti* (as, for example, in *komyuniti chesuto,* Community Chest).

Another term Japanese translators are likely to leave out or make more concrete is 'power.' In English, article 76(2) states, "No extraordinary tribunal shall be established, nor shall any organ or agency of the Executive be given final judicial *power*" (italics added). This is rendered as two sentences in Japanese, the final one of which runs, *Gyōsei-kikan wa shūshin to shite saiban o okonau koto ga dekinai.* If retranslated into English, this sentence would read approximately, "An executive organ cannot administer justice as the court of last resort," thus leaving open the possible ambiguity that an executive organ could perform all other judicial functions except that of serving as a court of last resort. The concept of "judicial power" exists in Japanese as *shihōken* but was not used here for reasons that are unclear.

Another example of the problem of "power" occurs in article 77(2): *Kensatsukan wa saikō saibansho no sadameru kisoku ni shitagawanakereba naranai.* Literally, this sentence says, "public procurators shall be subject to the *rules* [italics added] which the Supreme Court establishes," whereas the official English version reads, "Public procurators shall be subject to the rule-making *power* [italics added] of the Supreme Court." Given the confusion surrounding the concept of "power" in American political science, the Japanese may be the preferred version in this case.

Another concept close to the heart of Anglo-American democracy, one that the Japanese finesse, is "majority." In article 79(3) "the majority" (of the voters) is translated *tasū*, which means simply "a great number," whereas in article 95, "the majority" (of the voters) is translated *kahansū* (more than half). *Tasū* is also used in articles 55, 57, and 58 for "a majority" (of two-thirds or more), while in article 56, *kahansū* is the term for "a majority" (of those present). Of all these cases, the most problematic is article 79(3), where *kahansū* should probably have been used instead of *tasū*. In any case, the foreign concept of majoritarianism is hard to square with the indigenous attempts to forge consensual bases of agreement.

Still another interesting ambiguity arises over the use of the term "regulations." Article 92 asserts: *Chihō kōkyō dantai no soshiki oyobi un'ei ni kan suru jikō wa, chihō jichi no honshi ni motozuite, hōritsu de kore o sadameru.* Any clear-headed translator would render *jikō* in this context as "matters," but the English version reads, "Regulations *[jikō]* concerning organization and operations of local public entities shall be fixed by law in accordance with the principle of local autonomy." Moreover, a reader who continued on for two more articles would encounter a different word, *jōrei*, for "regulations" in English. It would be nice to think that *jikō* was substituted for *jōrei* in article 92 in order to enlarge the powers vested in local governing bodies, but the matter is largely moot today because of the great expansion of the powers of the central government.

One final example from the Constitution leads me back to the problems with which I began this discussion—incidents of international misunderstanding involving Japan because of the lack of equivalence not just of languages but also of political cultures. In the famous article 9, sole article of chapter II "Renunciation of War," there occurs the phrase, "land, sea, and air forces, as well as other war potential, will never be maintained." In the Japanese text of the Constitution, the term equivalent to "war potential" is *senryoku*, not *senbi* or *gunbi*; and *senryoku* means "fighting power" or "fighting strength," not "war potential." Many in Japan maintain, with a good deal of evidence, that the Self-Defense Forces, given their present armaments, do not possess credible *senryoku*, even though Japan's tremendous economic development has certainly provided the nation with a considerable degree of *senbi*—but, fortunately or unfortunately depending on your point of view, that is not prohibited, regard-less of what the English version says.

In this discussion, I have not intended to belittle the Japanese Constitution in any manner; it is without question one of the most liberal and deeply legitimized constitutions in existence today. Rather, I have sought to show that it is dangerous to take the English version as authoritative, and I have also tried to illus-trate the problems that can arise when translating Japanese into English in even so controlled a situation. As a general rule, all political language means more than it says, and a good deal of it is euphemistic. A translator must work first with words and only second with connotations, but in cross-cultural politics it will be the latter that are the potent sources of misapprehension and misunderstanding. With political euphemisms, the usual prob-lem is that translators cannot find an equivalent *euphemism* and therefore translate the term in a concrete form. George R. Pac-kard offers an example: " 'Containment policy' was being ren-dered as '*fūjikome seisaku*,' which connoted an active, enclosing or confining motion, whereas the English original had more of a passive, defensive meaning. There are hundreds of such key words that have similar differences of nuance. The difficulties in translation have been an enormous barrier to effective communi-cations in all fields."[47]

From the opposite point of view, the Japanese have on occa-sion sought advantage in the difficulties of their language, just as they have argued that their institutions were incomparably dif-ferent from those of other countries and therefore should be treated differently. This has led to such surly comments as those of the London *Economist*'s editors following the conclusion in 1979 of the Tokyo Round of GATT negotiations: "Nobody (ex-cept the Japanese, who will surely discover convenient linguistic difficulties) will ever again be able to say that he thought it was all right to kill, steal or bear false customs valuations against his neighbor's trade."[48] All this means, or ought to mean, that there is still a steady need for skilled translators in the fields of Japa-nese politics and economics—both to facilitate understanding across cultures and to correct the misunderstandings that are in-evitable.

9

Tanaka Kakuei, Structural Corruption, and the Advent of Machine Politics in Japan

The saga of Tanaka Kakuei and the Lockheed bribery case brings to mind the masks of tragedy and comedy that are often mounted above the proscenium arch of a Western theater. The tragic aspects concern Tanaka personally, the area of Japan he so brilliantly represented in the central government from 1947 until his death on December 16, 1993, and the fact that he brought a measure of populism into the most bureaucratically dominated government of any of the advanced industrial democracies. The farcical aspects center on the Lockheed case itself—for example, the logistical problems of moving ¥500 million in cash from Deak and Company in Hong Kong to Lockheed's Tokyo office in order to pay off Tanaka, and the various receipts for "peanuts," "pieces," and "units" that Marubeni Trading Company gave to Lockheed. Or there was the young rightist porno movie actor who dove his rented airplane into the Tokyo mansion of Lockheed's chief agent in Japan while dressed up as a *kamikaze* pilot and whose last words shouted over the plane's radio were *tennō heika banzai* (Long Live the Emperor). Or consider the origins of the case in the late Senator Frank Church's subcommittee of the Senate Foreign Relations Committee.

Although the Senate's decision to let it all hang out did not have any lasting impact on the politics of Japan, or Italy, or Holland—the countries that were most immediately affected by the

183

Lockheed revelations of 1976—the United States's Foreign Corrupt Practices Act of 1977, which resulted from the Church Subcommittee's hearings, has had the paradoxical consequences of worsening the American balance of payments while enriching several large American law firms. By one estimate, Lockheed's total payments during 1972 and 1973 to more than half a dozen Japanese politicians amounted to slightly more than 3 percent of the $430 million the company expected to receive from the sale of 21 L-1011 TriStar airbuses to All Nippon Airways. This is not really an unreasonable commission for such a sale (which, incidentally, did go through), but the Foreign Corrupt Practices Act has ensured that much future business will probably go to America's competitors instead. To my way of thinking, the implications of the Lockheed scandal in Japan were never as serious as the implications of an American president's national security adviser being on a Japanese retainer, even though Mr. Tanaka received something in the range of $2 million (depending on the exchange rate) while Mr. Richard Allen received only a thousand dollars and three wristwatches. In any event, thanks to the Lockheed case the world today knows a great deal more about Mr. Tanaka's dealings than it does about Mr. Allen's.[1]

The fundamental issue in the Tanaka case is what the Japanese call *kōzō oshoku,* or "structural corruption." It is argued that Lockheed's bribing of Tanaka while he was the prime minister of Japan in order to cause him to influence the Ministry of Transportation and All Nippon Airways to buy Lockheed Aircraft reveals a pattern of influence peddling that is not unique to Tanaka but inherent in the Japanese governmental system, and that it indicates a serious need for reform.[2] I fully agree that the problem is "structural," but I want to reserve judgment until later on the question of whether it constitutes "corruption."

Another major issue is that following his arrest in the Lockheed case, Tanaka, even though forced to resign as a member of the Liberal Democratic Party, nonetheless transformed his personal organization within the party from a faction into a political machine. Before 1976, the group led by Tanaka within the party was a group of Diet members who worked together to advance their own and their leader's interests but who had to seek allies in other groups. By about 1980, Tanaka's group had become the most important influence-and-patronage-dispensing center within the party, totally controlling who would be named prime minister. It also became a new, powerful actor in making public policy for the Japanese nation. This machine—or *gundan* (army corps), the term chosen by the Tokyo press to distinguish the Tanaka "faction" of the 1980s from its predecessor of the 1970s—dominated Japanese politics until February 27, 1985, when Tanaka was partially paralyzed by a stroke. The Tanaka case thus has major significance for several other questions. Who governs in Japan today? And where is Japanese democracy heading? Before we can address these issues, however, we need to know a great deal more about Tanaka—where he came from, whom he represented, and what he did—in every sense of the word.

I

In the introduction to his translation of Kawabata's *Yukiguni (Snow Country)*, probably Kawabata's greatest work and the one that ensured his winning the Nobel Prize in 1968, Edward Seidensticker writes, "The west coast of the main island of Japan is probably for its latitude (roughly, from Cape Hatteras to New York, or from Spanish Morocco to Barcelona) the snowiest region in the world."[3] The place where Kawabata set his work, although he never actually names it, is Yuzawa, a small mountain spa on the Jōetsu railroad line leading to the old castle town of Nagaoka. Nagaoka is today the main city of the Niigata Third Electoral District, which Tanaka continuously represented in the Diet from the time he was first elected on April 26, 1947, at the age of 28, until July 1993, when he was replaced by his daughter, Makiko. The Niigata Third District is a kind of cross between Mississippi and Vermont, a place that is utterly typical of *ura Nippon* (hidden Japan), the part of the country that supplies workers, electricity, and rice (and that used to supply *geisha* and ricksha pullers) for *omote Nippon,* the Pacific Coast of the country typified by the Tokyo megalopolis, and for which Tokyo supplied little in return—until Tanaka came along.

At the turn of the century Niigata prefecture was the most densely populated prefecture in all of Japan; but by 1972, when Tanaka published his *Nihon rettō kaizō ron* (*Plan for the Remodeling of the Japanese Archipelago*), it had been virtually depopulated.[4] The heavy snows, normally about 15 feet, made the place close to impassable in winter, and most of the men had to set out on *dekasegi,* or seasonal work in the big cities, often on construction projects. Until very recently the children of small-town and rural Niigata lived in school dormitories if they attended school at all, and the only people left at home were mothers and old women. In his book Tanaka noted that many towns in Niigata and other Japan Sea prefectures had all-female fire departments.

Old Echigo, the feudal name of Niigata, lying beyond the Mikuni mountain range that collects all the snow from Siberia, had long been exploited by Tokyo, and during the 1930s and immediately after the war its farmers were among the strongest supporters of the left-wing social and land reform movements. These were the people Tanaka organized into his supporters' organization, the Etsuzankai (that is, the Etsu Mountains Association), which is today the model for all Diet members' local organizations, otherwise known as *kōenkai.* The fact that these people became Tanaka's staunchest supporters also illustrates the principle that nobody in the provinces really cares whether a politician is nominally a socialist or a conservative (or, for that matter, honest): what counts is whether he gets results in pressuring the central government to send some resources to the region.[5]

Tanaka was born in Niigata in 1918, the son of a cattle broker who was also a dissolute gambler. One result of this background is that Tanaka was long famous for singing slightly raunchy *naniwabushi,* what might be thought of today as the Japanese equivalent of country-and-western music. He sang them on the radio when he first became a cabinet minister and even at the IMF meeting in Washington in 1962. Although all Japanese commentators acknowledge Tanaka's high intelligence, he is also famous for having never completed high school, the only modern prime minister who failed to receive a university education, in total contrast to the elite bureaucrats and graduates of Tokyo Imperial University who have dominated most of Japan's postwar politics.[6]

Tanaka began his career by leaving Niigata to work as a hustling young building contractor in Tokyo. His breaks came in 1942 and 1945. In 1942 he married a divorcée, Sakamoto Hana, seven years his elder and the daughter of a medium-size construction company owner. Tanaka inherited his father-in-law's company and renamed it Tanaka Construction. Incidentally, at the time of his marriage his 30-year-old wife extracted three pledges from Tanaka that he says he has faithfully fulfilled: that he was never to threaten to throw her out, never to kick her, and that when the time came for him to cross the Nijūbashi into the Imperial Palace to receive the emperor's attestation as prime minister, they would go hand-in-hand.[7] In 1945 Tanaka got lucky in the course of relocating a major Japanese piston ring factory to Korea in order to escape the Allied bombing. The war ended with him in Korea and an enormous amount of money in his official possession, money for a project that no longer mattered but that he, like many others, did not have to account for in the postwar confusion.

Back in his native province, Tanaka used this money to try to run for national office. He failed in his first attempt but succeeded the second time around. Although he ran on the ticket of one of the conservative parties of the time he avoided trying to win support from the local conservative establishment, with which he had not a chance anyway. Instead he courted the Socialist-tending local farmers, who had just gotten title to the land they had long worked as tenants thanks to the occupation's land reform program. He promised to send them highways, schools, reclamation projects, tunnels, railroads, and snow removal services in return for their votes and that's exactly what he did. The Etsuzankai, which came into being during this period, was for a long time more like a local chamber of commerce and civic group than Tanaka's personal organization. It was formally organized as a political organization only in 1961. By the early 1980s it had about 98,000 members, published a monthly magazine, *Gekkan Etsuzan,* had some 313 district organizations based on all the old town and village units, included most of the local transportation and construction companies as contributors (several of them owned by Tanaka), and had penetrated all 33 municipalities in the Niigata Third District. The Etsuzankai's local secretary was known as the "shadow governor."[8]

As a new member of the Diet during the failing Katayama-Ashida socialist coalition, Tanaka gravitated toward Yoshida Shigeru's mainstream of postwar conservatives. This was an

unusual and astute move on Tanaka's part, since Yoshida typified above all others the postwar dominance of Japanese politics
by retired bureaucrats from the central government, a background that was about as different from Tanaka's as any could
be. Politicians of Tanaka's stripe, local leaders without central
government experience, people like Ōno Bamboku and Kōno
Ichirō, tended to fight against the senior bureaucrats from the
Ministries of Finance, or Transportation, or International Trade
and Industry who transferred laterally into parliament when
they retired as officials. Not so Tanaka. He cultivated them,
worked with them, outsmarted them, and used them. In the
1970s Tanaka was quoted as saying that "Eighty percent of a
prime minister's job consists of getting the civil service to do
what he wants," and in his brilliant interview in the July 1983
Japanese *Playboy,* he repeated that his key advice to the then
current prime minister, Nakasone Yasuhiro, whom he had been
instrumental in putting in office, was "Stay on top of the bureaucrats."[9]

Hardly a year after entering the Diet, Tanaka was arrested for
the first time for taking a bribe. This was in connection with the
socialist government's scheme of 1948 to nationalize the coal
mines; the prosecutors charged that Tanaka had been paid ¥1
million by Fukuoka mine interests to vote against it, which was
almost certainly true. More to the point, however, numerous
leaders of Japan at the time were under indictment for having
accepted bribes in the more serious Shōwa Denkō scandal, including the prime minister, Ashida Hitoshi, and Budget Bureau
director Fukuda Takeo, Tanaka's great competitor of later
years. The indictment of Tanaka thus was at least in part a retaliation by the Ashida faction against people who had broken
ranks over the coal issue and a way to get even for *their* having
been indicted in the Shōwa Denkō case. Tanaka had to run his
first reelection campaign from jail; he obtained his release on bail
only a fortnight before the election of January 23, 1949. Eventually both Tanaka and Fukuda successfully appealed their bribery
cases.[10]

It is perhaps worth pausing here to note that Tanaka and
Fukuda, who became two of the leading prime ministers of the
1970s, were not the only postwar Japanese politicians to have

early brushes with the bribery laws. Virtually every major contemporary Japanese politician has had some such experience, including Satō Eisaku and Ikeda Hayato in the shipbuilding scandal of 1954, Ōno Bamboku in almost every scandal that came along, and most of the conservative mainstream in the *kuroi kiri* ("black mist") incidents of the mid-1960s. Tanaka and Kishi actually served some time in prison, where Tanaka met Osano Kenji and Kishi met both Kodama Yoshio and Sasagawa Ryōichi. Osano, Kodama, and Sasagawa, who are what the Japanese call *kuromaku* (we would say "fixers" or perhaps "godfathers"), all figured prominently in the Lockheed case.

The difference between someone like Tanaka and elite bureaucrats like Fukuda, Satō, and Ikeda is that the latter usually found a way to beat the rap. Fukuda was acquitted after testifying that although he had indeed been paid off by the Shōwa Denkō Company, he did not know it was a bribe. Satō and Ikeda were saved when Prime Minister Yoshida ordered Justice Minister Inukai Takeru (himself also a suspect in the shipbuilding case) to suspend prosecution of them. Certainly in 1976, at the time of his arrest in the Lockheed case, Tanaka expected Prime Minister Miki to order Justice Minister Inaba Osamu, who also happened to come from Niigata (Niigata Second District; Nakasone faction), to do the same for him. Tanaka had every reason to expect such a favor, since it had been done often enough in the past for other leaders of the Liberal Democratic Party. The fact that Miki failed to act in the Lockheed case was one reason why Tanaka wanted to get even with him and felt generally betrayed by the old political elite.

After being cleared of the coal mine bribery charge, Tanaka went on to have a brilliant career as a nonbureaucratic leader (and member of the Satō faction) within the bureaucratic mainstream of the conservative party. In 1957, Prime Minister Kishi appointed him postal minister; at age 39 he was the youngest cabinet minister since Ozaki Yukio, also 39, who had served as Minister of Education in the Meiji era. Within the party Tanaka proved to be exceptionally skillful in managing the relations among Yoshida's great protégé, Ikeda, and the two brothers, Kishi and Satō, the three of whom monopolized political power between 1957 and 1972. In 1962 Ikeda rewarded Tanaka by naming him to the most important cabinet post of them all, Minister of Finance, which he held for three years. Kishi and Satō also supported Tanaka's appointment.

It was as finance minister during the key years of the income doubling plan that Tanaka began to show his real abilities. Right at the outset he refused to attend the Finance Ministry bureaucrats' *go-shinkō*, literally a "lecture in the Imperial presence" but actually a euphemism for the orientation meetings where the bureaucrats try to intimidate and instruct a new minister on what he is supposed to do. Tanaka indicated that instead he would tell *them* what to do, and there is no question that he became an effective minister. The bureaucrats came to respect and like him, and his uncannily accurate grasp of the details of public finance and taxation led to his most famous nickname, the "computerized bulldozer," given to him by his follower and his secretary general of the party during 1983, Nikaidō Susumu.

The highly centralized Japanese public finance system involves large central government subsidies to local governments as well as enormous expenditures for virtually all public works projects throughout the nation. As Minister of Finance, Tanaka was in charge of these subsidies. He had long been associated with road building and automobile taxation schemes, but as finance minister he greatly accelerated the payment of direct government subsidies through the Ministries of Transportation and Construction for vitally needed improvements in Japan's infrastructure. As finance minister he also had the authority to sell government-owned land and to initiate major projects to reclaim marginal or otherwise unusable land, both things that he did with great frequency. And, among his many duties, the Minister of Finance is the person in charge of disaster relief funds. Until Tanaka entered the post, the finance minister had never authorized money for a heavy snowfall disaster on the grounds that since it snowed every year, people could not reasonably regard a snowstorm as a disaster, even when it killed people and collapsed houses. Needless to say, Tanaka changed that. Central government budget allocations for Niigata prefecture went from ¥12.1 billion in 1962 (fifth place nationally) to ¥24.1 billion in 1965 (fourth) to ¥53.3 billion in 1970 (third). By 1983 Niigata was first among Japan's 47 prefectures in terms of per capita governmental expenditures for public works.[11]

During the mid-1960s Tanaka's personal wealth also began to grow. He purchased the land for his residence in the exclusive Mejirodai section of Tokyo, and he also bought the land for his villa in the equally exclusive summer resort town of Karuizawa. Perhaps most ominously, he began to set up a series of *yūrei-gaisha,* or "ghost companies"—firms without employees or offices that traded endlessly and profitably in real estate, particularly real estate that was soon to be the site of a government-built power plant or bullet-train right-of-way or reclamation project. Tanaka also did favors for people: in 1964, for example, he approved Osano Kenji's request to export the funds needed to buy the Princess Kaiulani Hotel in Hawaii. Osano had emerged since his 1948 stint in jail as one of Japan's leading hotel investors, and he was now starting to internationalize his empire, even though the export of capital was still highly restricted. In return Osano bought one of Tanaka's companies in the residential construction business for a very high price, even though the company was close to bankruptcy and not considered a sound proposition.[12]

During the late 1960s Tanaka served as the LDP's secretary general, leading it through two successful general elections (January 1967 and December 1969), and in 1971 Prime Minister Satō named him Minister of International Trade and Industry. At MITI Tanaka performed as brilliantly as he had at Finance, bringing the U.S.-Japan textile dispute to a favorable conclusion (large payments to Japanese textile producers compensated them for restrictions on their exports) and using the ministry's bureaucrats to help write up and promote his grand scheme for industrial relocation. Although the press likes to say that Tanaka's plan was never fully implemented, it is undeniable that Tsukuba science city, the tunnel to Hokkaido, the massive bridges to Shikoku, and the new Tokyo airport would never have been started at this time without it.

As for Niigata, by the early 1980s Tanaka had blessed it with an extension of the Shinkansen, the bullet train that now links Niigata city with Tokyo in under two hours; a new railroad station and subdevelopment at Nagaoka; the atomic power plant at Kashiwazaki, the second most important city in the Niigata Third District; and the Kan'etsu and Hokuriku superhighways. How did he do it? Between 1967 and 1970, three of the six Ministers of Construction came from what would later be known as the Tanaka faction, and from 1970 to 1976, all seven Ministers of Construction were Tanaka's men. Between 1972 and 1976, all four Ministers of Posts and Telecommunications were similarly under Tanaka's control. Where did he get the money to finance his faction? To mention only one source, when in 1970 All Nippon Airways (ANA) applied to the Ministry of Transportation for approval of its purchase of new airliners, the minister was Hashimoto Tomisaburō, one of the stalwarts of the Tanaka faction and later secretary general of the party in the Tanaka administration. We know what happened to ANA's application since it constitutes the core of the Lockheed case, a subject to which we shall return. The Tanaka faction within the party began to come into being as an offshoot of the Satō faction during 1970, although it was only formalized in May 1972, two months before the election for the party presidency when Tanaka became prime minister. It is unnecessary here to try to recount the details of Tanaka's political coup of 1972. Suffice it to say that he exploited the shock all Japanese experienced over Nixon's trip to China. Tanaka aligned his own faction with those of Ōhira and Miki; he bought the support of the Nakasone faction; and he left Fukuda Takeo, Satō's intended successor, out in the cold.

Intellectual critics of Tanaka such as Tachibana Takashi charge him with buying the prime ministership, but they should also acknowledge that he probably saved the LDP from its long-term decline in popular support under Satō.[13] When the Tanaka cabinet took over, it was the most popular government in Japan's postwar history, enjoying a 62 percent support rating in the Asahi poll. It is true that 25 months later Tanaka's popularity had fallen to the lowest level yet recorded, 12 percent. Even so, support for an LDP prime minister was destined to fall even further a few years later under Tanaka's rival, Fukuda Takeo. The pattern of movement from the collapse of support for Tanaka to an even lower degree of backing for his successor, after an interregnum, seemed to parallel the pattern in the United States from Nixon to Carter. Miki and Ford presided over the transitions. The key to Tanaka's high popularity in 1972 was, without question, his decisive recognition of the People's Republic of China two months after he had assumed power.

In a major retrospective article on Tanaka and his politics, Professor Nishibe Susumu of the University of Tokyo concluded, "In the effort to apprehend the essence of an age, people single out a particular figure as a type or pattern. . . . Tanaka is precisely such a type. . . . Tanaka's discerning eye saw through the fictions of democracy. He focused on the clear and simple fact that basic decisions involving the law are made outside the legislature. . . . Tanaka's triumph was based on a deep appreciation of this state of affairs and on resolute action. . . . If we credit accounts of Tanaka's unusual degree of knowledge, for a politician, of laws and of computation, he has used lawful methods of control to manipulate the bureaucratic establishment."[14]

I should like to add that what Tanaka's discerning eye saw above all was that money was indeed the mother's milk of politics and that whoever controlled the largest amounts of it in the political system, controlled the system. Everybody needed money—for reelection campaigns, for his faction, for entertaining and cultivating the bureaucrats who made the vital decisions—and everybody needed more of it than was allowed under the various laws that controlled political funds. Tanaka had a lot of money, and he used it—not for himself, as Professor Nishibe also acknowledges, or even exclusively for the people of Niigata, but in order to get things done.

One of Tanaka's standard ways of disbursing funds was under cover of the Japanese custom of gift-giving: summer gifts *(o-chūgen)*, year-end gifts *(o-seibo)*, bon voyage gifts to travelers going abroad, *mochidai* (money for New Year's rice cakes), and regular political contributions.[15] During the summer of 1974, the press charged that Tanaka had handed out *o-chūgen* gifts of from ¥3 to ¥5 million to *every* Diet member and to a good many bureau chiefs in the ministries. Money became so much a part of the system that a jargon built up around it; the chief way to calculate election expenses was in terms of "bullets"—a bullet being ¥100 million—and the word for bullet, *jitsudan*, came to have a secondary meaning, listed in all dictionaries, of "money."

II

Tanaka did not invent the role of money in Japanese politics; in the postwar era its critical role goes back at least to the Kishi cabinet, when the implications of the multi-member electoral system combined with the domination by a huge coalition party began to sink in. Tanaka merely carried the system to its logical conclusion, and equally important, began to ensure that the less naturally well-connected local politicians such as himself were as well oiled with money as the big business-connected exbureaucrats who got all they needed without asking.[16] In the autumn of 1974, the fact that Tanaka had made the implicit rules of the game explicit caught up with him. A team of young investigative journalists associated with the major Japanese magazine, *Bungei shunjū,* blasted forth with two long exposés of Tanaka's "money-power politics." In the storm that followed, Tanaka was forced to resign the prime ministership, although he claimed ill health. Nonetheless, no one was prosecuted, and only a few tax fines were handed out. Tanaka meanwhile devoted himself to expanding his own faction within the party in preparation for a comeback. Cynics concluded that Tanaka's resignation, coming only four months after Nixon's, was merely another pitiable example of Japan's tendency to copy foreign fads, in this case the Watergate incident.

Then, in February 1976, in Washington, D.C., the Senate Foreign Relations Committee released its bombshell. In Japan, the "Lockheed Incident" took center stage as the biggest foreign-connected political bribery case since the Siemens Company of Germany had bribed the Japanese Navy in 1914. The details were shocking not so much because the Lockheed Company had smoothed the way for its sales of airplanes in Japan—there was plenty of evidence that Boeing, McDonnell-Douglas, and Grumman were engaged in similar operations—but because the case took the Japanese back in time, to periods and people they would have liked to forget, to right-wingers and gangsters; and it suggested that the foreigners knew better how to get things done in Japan than law-abiding citizens. The case was serious since it deeply implicated officials of the Transportation Ministry, plus one of Japan's leading trading companies and the prime minister himself. Worst of all, it brought up the name of Kodama Yoshio.[17]

Kodama, born in 1911 in Fukushima, was one of Japan's most notorious prewar political strongmen and postwar unofficial intermediaries between the world of politics and the worlds of gangsters, bullies for controlling stockholders' meetings (so-called *sōkaiya*), and fanatical right-wingers. During the late 1930s he operated in China. In 1939 the Japanese Army and Foreign Ministry hired him as a bodyguard for Wang Ching-wei, China's leading collaborator, and in 1940 the infamous Colonel Tsuji Masanobu used him to work for the Japanese Expeditionary Army in China. In 1941, by now employed as an agent of the Japanese Navy, he set up the "Kodama Kikan" (Kodama Agency) in Shanghai to buy or expropriate supplies of rare metals for the Navy. At the end of the war he returned to Japan enormously wealthy as a result of his operations. He worked briefly as an adviser to Prime Minister Higashikuni before being arrested as a class A war crimes suspect. He was in jail from 1946 to 1948, together with Sasagawa and Kishi, but was never prosecuted. He used his China spoils to help finance the postwar rebirth of Yoshida's Liberal Party, and he also supplied funds to the Hatoyama and Kishi governments. At the time of President Eisenhower's proposed visit to Japan in June 1960, Kishi asked Kodama to help provide informal protection for the American president. This was the man whom the Lockheed Aircraft Corporation in the late 1950s put on a retainer of ¥50 million per annum as its consultant in Japan, a position he held until 1976.[18]

Kodama's first job for Lockheed was to shift its trading company from Mitsui to the new, lean, and hungry number-three-ranked firm of Marubeni. He then set up the purchase, in 1960, by the Kishi government of some 230 Lockheed F-104 Starfighters as Japan's mainstay fighter-interceptor, beating out the competition from Grumman. In the late 1960s Lockheed decided to enter the civilian airliner competition against McDonnell-Douglas and Boeing, partly in order to keep together the design team it had formed for the supersonic transport that had been killed by environmentalist pressures. A commercial transport had not been in Lockheed's product line since the piston-engined Constellation of the 1950s. It ultimately proved so costly that, in light of other cost overruns on its defense contracts, the company had to turn to the U.S. government for loan guarantees, a "bailout" that lasted from 1971 to 1977. Lockheed's airbus, the L-1011 TriStar, is universally acknowledged to be an outstanding aircraft, but Lockheed faced serious difficulties in getting it out fast enough to compete with the DC-10; and these problems worsened in 1971 when its engine supplier, Rolls-Royce, went bankrupt and was taken over by the British government. Since McDonnell-Douglas had already made great inroads in the European market with its DC-10, sales of TriStars in East Asia came to be viewed as Lockheed's last hope for breaking even on the venture.

Lockheed's president, A. Carl Kotchian, and the president of Lockheed Aircraft Asia, John Clutter, took charge of the sales campaign. The big potential buyer in Japan was the country's number two airline, All Nippon Airways, since Japan Air Lines needed longer distance equipment for its international routes. To get the ANA contract, Kotchian and Clutter had to do several things: they had to rid themselves of the then current ANA president, who had already taken an option on DC-10s, and get a new president who favored Lockheed; they had to persuade the Japanese Ministry of Transportation to delay any airbus imports until 1974, when the TriStar would be ready; they had to sell ANA on buying TriStars; and they had to win Transportation Ministry approval of the sale. Kodama put together the campaign, also incidentally modifying his contract to include a special commission on each L-1011 sold.

To make a long story short, Kodama and Kotchian caused the incumbent ANA president to resign through the disclosure of an embarrassing loan and some *sōkaiya* pressure and installed in his place Wakasa Tokuji, a recently retired vice-minister of transportation. Kodama also advised his friend Osano Kenji to move up as an ANA stockholder from 28th to 10th place, thereby guaranteeing information from the inside on what the airline was thinking. This cost ¥5 million and $200,000 in side-payments to Osano. Marubeni executives worked on the government side of things, arranging all the required delays and approvals. As it turned out, the government proved to be rather more expensive than the direct customer, ANA. When it was all over, according to Kotchian's testimony to the Subcommittee on Multinational Corporations, Lockheed had paid a kickback of $50,000 on each airplane to the president of ANA; bribed the prime minister, the secretary general of the LDP, the MITI minister, the chief cabinet secretary, the Minister of Transportation, the chairman of the LDP's Special Committee on Aviation, and both the current and former parliamentary vice ministers of transportation; paid one Shig Katayama, the president and sole employee of the "I-D Corp." of Hong Kong, some $75,000 to forge receipts for Lockheed's books; and paid large commissions to both Marubeni and Kodama, which Kodama failed to report to the income tax authorities. Kotchian also made some 15 trips to Tokyo between 1970 and 1972, arranging all of this.

The case was broken in the United States through a Securities and Exchange Commission investigation, part of the results of which the Church subcommittee made public. The federal courts prevented full disclosure after Secretary of State Kissinger intervened to protest that complete details would not be in the interest of U.S. foreign policy. Court battles continued for years between Lockheed and one of its insurance companies over the question of whether the sealed files of the complete investigation should be opened. The American press hinted that full disclosure would have set off a similar political earthquake in Saudi Arabia.[19]

Kotchian's Senate testimony led the Japanese Diet to conduct its own investigation, the first in 11 years in which witnesses were under oath and therefore vulnerable to perjury charges. The Japanese government then indicted some 16 individuals— politicians, Marubeni employees, plus Kodama and Osano—on charges of perjury, violation of the Foreign Exchange and Foreign Trade Control Law, and bribery. Although Kotchian clearly implicated at least eight politicians, only three were indicted: the prime minister, the LDP's secretary general, and the parliamentary vice-minister of transportation. In a Japanese bribery trial, the prosecution must prove that the defendant actually received the money, that he knew it was a bribe, and that he was in a position of authority to influence official business in favor of the briber. The prosecutors decided that they could not prove all of these things in the cases of five politicians.

All but one of the politicians implicated by Kotchian were resoundingly reelected in the next general election. Except for Kodama, whose trial was suspended because of illness (and who subsequently died on January 17, 1984), all the people indicted were found guilty, the last of them being former Prime Minister Tanaka, who was convicted on October 12, 1983. All appealed their convictions, a process that has already taken more than a decade to complete. The appeal filed on May 29, 1985, on behalf of Tanaka alone ran to some 1.5 million characters and 3,024 pages.

There were several noteworthy aspects to Tanaka's first Lockheed trial. Tanaka himself concluded from the verdict not that he had been caught and convicted of bribery but that he had been made a scapegoat by his political opponents and the left-tending journalistic establishment of Tokyo for practices that are all too common in Japanese political life. For one thing, the defense was never given an opportunity to cross-examine Kotchian, and it was never explained how Senator Church induced a bribe-giver to go public with his allegations against bribe-takers. The prosecutor's case against Tanaka would probably have been thrown out by an American judge because of tainted and hearsay evidence. Moreover, the issue of privileged communications among heads of state was not fully aired at the trial: that is to say, was Prime Minister Tanaka, in 1972, merely trying to respond to requests from President Nixon for more Japanese imports of American manufactured goods because of the deteriorating American balance of payments?

I do not question that the facts presented in the Tokyo District Court are actually facts. But I want to stress that Tanaka believed that he did not do anything out of the ordinary and that his political opponents changed the rules on him in this particular case.[20] For example, during 1979–80, three years after the arrests in the Lockheed case, an almost identical incident again rocked the Japanese government. It was charged that the McDonnell-Douglas Company had paid ¥500 million (the same amount Lockheed paid Tanaka) through the Nisshō-Iwai Trading Company to the director general of the Defense Agency to influence the sale of F-4 military aircraft to the Japanese Air Self-Defense Forces. The director admitted that he had received the money but claimed it was a political contribution and not a bribe. He was not indicted. In fact, during 1980 both he and Tanaka were named as members of the Diet's Disciplinary Committee, which is charged with oversight of the ethics of Diet members. However, the managing director of Nisshō-Iwai committeed suicide by leaping to his death from corporate headquarters. He left behind a suicide note saying, "Long Live Nisshō-Iwai."

Following the Lockheed verdict of October 1983, several business leaders expressed shock that the court had found Tanaka guilty of bribery. They expected that he would be convicted of perjury and of violating the Foreign Exchange and Foreign Trade Control Law, but not of bribery since the ¥500 million paid by Lockheed through Marubeni would normally have been treated as a political contribution. The court established a new precedent when it held that as prime minister Tanaka had the authority to dictate through administrative guidance what airplanes All Nippon Airways should buy. Tanaka was also shocked by this decision. Rather than resigning his seat in the Diet or otherwise showing contrition for the shame he had brought to high public office, he decided to fight back.

The Japanese press likes to give names to each of the general elections as a short-hand way of expressing the main issues in them. The practice goes back at least to the "Bakayarō election" of April 1953, which was held to overcome the political disarray after Prime Minister Yoshida had called a Socialist member a "damned fool" on the floor of the Diet. Following the first Lockheed verdict of October 12, 1983, all the opposition parties boycotted the Diet proceedings for some 38 days because of Tanaka's conviction and Prime Minister Nakasone's refusal to allow a vote on a resolution calling on Tanaka to resign. Nakasone was trapped. To put a resolution before the Diet censuring Tanaka would guarantee the loss of Tanaka's support; yet by going to the polls six months before the term of the lower house was due to expire, Nakasone forfeited the prime minister's power to call an election at the most opportune time. Heavily pressured by the secretary general of the LDP (who was also a leader in Tanaka's faction), Nakasone agreed to hold an election, which Tanaka knew that he, if not his colleagues, could win.

As soon as it was called, the Tokyo press named the election of December 18, 1983, the "Tanaka Verdict Election." Editors of all the leading dailies proclaimed that it was a golden opportunity for the public to hand down its own judgment on Tanaka's behavior and on what the *Asahi* had labeled the "Tanakasone Cabinet." But considering the results and the fact that the only person in the country who really *wanted* an election during December 1983 was Tanaka Kakuei, it would probably be better called "Tanaka's Revenge Election."

The results for the Liberal Democratic Party were disastrous. It lost 36 seats and only retained a majority in the lower house when it admitted to its ranks several conservative independents (including Tanaka and other Lockheed defendants who had resigned from the party in 1976 at the time of their arrests) and formed a coalition with the New Liberal Club. This coalition was doubly ironic since the eight-member NLC was created by a group of dissident conservatives who left the LDP in 1976 to protest Tanaka's "money power" politics. The party's losses temporarily crippled Nakasone's power and popularity.

For Tanaka, however, the election was an unmitigated triumph. He was returned for the fifteenth time by the voters of the Niigata Third District. They gave him some 220,761 votes, a figure that greatly surpassed his highest previous record of 182,681, set in 1972 when he was prime minister. The voter turnout in Niigata, where it was snowing, was 87 percent, compared with 67.9 percent for the nation as a whole. Tanaka even managed to add his son-in-law, Tanaka Naoki, to his faction. The 43-year-old Naoki, in his first time at the polls, came in second in the three-member Fukushima Third District.[21] The Tanaka faction as a whole lost only two seats, while every other conservative faction suffered major losses. As the price of his reelection as prime minister, Nakasone had to promise publicly that he would "eliminate all so-called political influence coming from Mr. Tanaka." Nonetheless, the Tanaka faction contributed six ministers to the second Nakasone cabinet, more than any other faction, as well as the chairman of the party's Executive Council.

Tanaka's personal triumph in Niigata was made even more spectacular because Nosaka Akiyuki, a prominent Tokyo novelist and the darling of the intelligentsia, entered the race against him. Nosaka is a kind of Japanese Norman Mailer, a serious writer but also notorious for his interest in pornography and politics. He is the author of *Erogotoshitachi* (1963, translated into English as *The Pornographers* in 1968) and former editor of a magazine called *Omoshiro hambun*. In July 1972, Nosaka published in his magazine a story allegedly written by the early twentieth century author Nagai Kafū entitled "Yojōhan fusuma no shitabari" (The paper lining of the sliding door in a four-and-a-half-mat room). As a result he and his publisher were indicted for disseminating obscene material. Despite testimony on Nosaka's behalf from well-known authors, he was convicted and fined, a conviction that was upheld by the Supreme Court. Nosaka was thus very much in the public eye during the 1970s.

In June 1983 Nosaka was elected to the upper house of the Diet. The following November he resigned in order to enter the race for the lower house, choosing to offer himself to the voters of the Niigata Third District. Although he was born in Kanagawa, Nosaka had some prior connection with Niigata because his father was a former deputy governor of the prefecture and a one-time member of the Etsuzankai. Nonetheless, in a nine-entrant race for a seat in a five-member constituency, Nosaka never had a chance of ousting Tanaka, who needed no more than 21 percent of the vote to be relected. His entrance merely helped to publicize Tanaka's triumph, since it ensured that the "shadow shōgun" himself would campaign vigorously on his home turf and that both Tanaka and Nosaka would be followed everywhere by hordes of Tokyo reporters. In the end Tanaka outpolled all the other four victors combined (three LDP and one Socialist) and left Nosaka out of the running with only 28,045 votes and sixth place. On the day after the election the *Yomiuri* cartoon showed Kaku-san singing in front of a mansion labeled "Tanaka faction"; the house is surrounded by the ruins of a bad fire but is itself untouched. The caption reads: "Mad laughter amid the devastation." Until his cerebral hemorrhage of February 27, 1985, Tanaka remained the single most powerful politician in the country.

III

This brings me to the final group of questions I want to discuss: What does this situation mean for the LDP and the future of Japanese politics? Do these events of the late 1970s and early 1980s demonstrate the existence of "structural corruption" in the Japanese political system? One astute foreign observer, Karel van Wolferen, the former head of the Foreign Correspondents' Club in Tokyo, argues: "Corruption in Japan is legitimatized by its systematic perpetration. It is so highly organized and has become so much a part of the extra-legal ways of the Japanese system that most citizens or foreign residents do not recognize it for what it is, but accept it as 'part of the system.' "[22] In other words, for van Wolferen the problem is clearly structural, and I agree with him.

The bribery cases that have occurred virtually every year in Japan since the end of the war have mostly been of one type: payments for access by outsiders to the bureaucratic centers where the main decisions for the society are made. Personal corruption is not unknown in Japan, and it is dealt with harshly. But the kind of bribery we have been discussing is related to the existence of a strong, pervasive, relatively insulated bureaucratic state. It should be noted that virtually all abstract or academic notions and definitions of political corruption presuppose the existence of a bureaucratic state. Such corruption is sometimes referred to as "black market bureaucracy," or, in the former Soviet Union, as the "second economy." The problem in all governments in which state activities are pervasive is for relatively unorganized or low priority interests and groups to gain access to the government. The sale of access is probably unavoidable under these circumstances.[23] The more interesting questions therefore become: What is the overall performance record of any given strong bureaucratic state? How is the purchased access actually used? And does the citizenry tolerate the sale of access?

On the first question, I hardly need to remind anyone of the performance of the Japanese bureaucratic state in the postwar world. It has presided over one of the fastest growing industrial economies ever known. For many years the Japanese public seemed willing to tolerate the sale of access by their politicians so long as there was no evidence of corruption in their meritocratic bureaucracy. People like Tanaka actually performed a vital function for the system, redistributing income from the rich sectors to the poor ones and ensuring that high-speed growth did not benefit one group to the exclusion of others. All the East Asian capitalist developmental states (Japan, South Korea, Taiwan, Hong Kong, and Singapore) have been characterized by an unusually equitable distribution of income—and by a certain amount of corruption. Even the Liberal Democratic Party's lucrative subsidization of agriculture has had important income redistributive effects.

Today the Japanese public appears to believe that the sale of access and related phenomena have gone too far. The extensive reemployment of senior bureaucrats in big business and politics after their retirement—what the Japanese call *amakudari*, or "descent from heaven"—has been singled out as an area of needed reform. As just one indication of the power and influence of ex-bureaucrats in Japan, it should be noted that between 1955 and 1966 some 45 percent of the major cabinet members in Japan were former bureaucrats and that of 18 directors of All Nippon Airways at the time of the Lockheed case, five plus the president of the company were former officials of the Ministry of Transportation.

Amakudari could easily be stopped if Japanese leaders wanted it stopped; they need only prohibit by law the reemployment of former government officials after their retirement from public service. But this would not by itself overcome or even have much effect on structural corruption, and it would deny the country the use of some of its most talented managers. More serious as a cause of structural corruption is the deeply factionalized nature of all the political parties and the inability of a majority of citizens to hold any political party accountable for its policies and actions. It is probably true that, according to numerous public opinion polls, an overwhelming majority of Japanese wanted Tanaka to resign from the Diet after his conviction in the first Lockheed trial. But there is no way that public opinion alone can force a change in politics. The reason is structural, not just personal obstinacy on Tanaka's part. Given that the people calling for Tanaka's resignation never voted either for or against him, it is perfectly understandable that he refused to resign.

In fact, the outcome of the election of December 18, 1983, had almost nothing to do with the Tanaka verdict—except in the special case of the Niigata Third District. The big winner in the election was Kōmeitō, which merely applied well-established, Tanaka-inspired principles of electoral organization and moved its highly disciplined voters around to aid Kōmeitō runners-up from the 1980 elections. For example, in the fourth electoral district of Chiba prefecture, Morita Keiichi, a Kōmeitō candidate who had lost by 13,700 votes in 1980, managed in 1983 to draw an additional 30,000 votes to unseat the incumbent LDP candidate, Someya Makoto. After the election a group of citizens in the Chiba Fourth demanded an investigation into allegedly fictitious residence changes by Kōmeitō supporters. Kōmeitō increased its strength in the Diet by some 25 seats, and it did so by astutely playing the margins of Japan's multimember constituency electoral system. This was the real reason for the LDP's losses, not the Tanaka verdict. Kōmeitō's strategy in the December 1983 election was, of course, identical to that long pursued by the Tanaka faction.[24]

The LDP is a conglomerate of five or six factions which, like the nation-states of nineteenth-century Europe, are subject to constant realignment in accordance with shifts in the balance of power. An LDP politician who succeeds in forming a major group becomes the head of the party and then head of the government. This was the normal situation during the 1960s. But then, during the 1970s, the system broke down, just like the old international balance-of-power system at the time of World War I. The faction led by Tanaka gained more influence than had normally been acceptable or possible in factional politics. Tanaka achieved this not through "corruption" but by mastering the principal determinants of the factional system: the multimember constituency and the judicious use of money to render one candidate more attractive than another.

Tanaka's success ended the *balance* of power and led to open warfare between the new order (Tanaka) and the old order (Fukuda). The situation became even more abnormal when Tanaka was indicted in the Lockheed case but still remained a Diet member and *de facto* leader of his faction in the LDP, even though he was no longer a member of the party. Tanaka himself could not be elected head of the party since he was not a member of it, and his faction could not recommend a leader so long as Tanaka headed it. However, support of the Tanaka faction was indispensable for anyone in the party who wanted to become prime minister. Given the public's condemnation of Tanaka, a leader of the majority party could not govern with Tanaka's backing or without it. The result was a lack of decisive leadership in the party, deep voter frustration, and an almost total loss of accountability in Japanese politics.

One example of this impasse in Japanese politics was the reorganization during the spring of 1985 of the Nippon Telegraph and Telephone Company (NTT) from a purely governmental organ, attached to the Ministry of Posts and Telecommunications, into a semiprivate company. Prime Minister Nakasone had chosen Abe Yuzuru, president of Nisshin Steel Company, to be senior vice president of the new NTT and successor to president Shintō Hisashi after two years' time. Both Shintō and Abe were leaders of the private sector, and perhaps because of their lack of strong ties to the government were thought of as liberals in the area of international economic relations. However, Abe declined to accept his appointment after it became clear that the Tanaka faction did not want him. Tanaka's agent within the company was Kitahara Yasusada, an old NTT bureaucrat with ties to the *yūsei-kanryō* (postal ministry bureaucracy), which Tanaka had tried to dominate ever since he was postal minister in the Kishi government. It would seem that American telecommunications companies, in trying to negotiate greater market access in Japan for their products, should have tried to lobby the Tanaka faction, precisely as their Japanese competitors did. Unfortunately for the Americans, Tanaka was in the hospital during the spring of 1985; and he was none too friendly toward Americans in any case, ever since the made-in-America Lockheed case broke over his head in 1976.[25]

IV

Following Tanaka's stroke, most Japanese observers believed that his power—if not his life—had drawn to a close. Thus the Tanaka era in Japanese politics, meaning the period in which Tanaka Kakuei either totally dominated the Japanese political world or was the primary opponent of the political leader in power, may be said to have lasted some thirteen years, from 1972 to 1985. For the first two years of this period Tanaka was prime minister and offered his country uncommon leadership, for a Japanese politician, including recognition of China and major investments in domestic infrastructure. He also caused and was unable to contain an inflationary spiral that was almost out of control even before the first oil shock made it worse. In terms of political power, in 1972 Tanaka took with him from the old 104-member Satō faction (60 from the House of Representatives and 44 from the House of Councillors) some 66 members (37 Representatives and 29 Councillors) to form the new Tanaka faction. Through transfers within the party and the general election of December 10, 1972, Tanaka slowly increased these numbers to 79 in late 1972, 87 in 1973, and 90 in 1974.

During the interregnum years of 1975–78, when Miki and Fukuda personified the LDP's only alternatives to Tanaka, Tanaka himself at first held his own. His faction reached 93 members before the general election of December 5, 1976, but then its strength began to recede. The political damage done to him by his arrest in the Lockheed case and his resignation from the party is reflected in the slippage of his factional strength to 83 following the election of October 7, 1979. However, with the accession to power on December 7, 1978, of his old cabinet associate and political ally, Ōhira Masayoshi, Tanaka started his comeback. Following the election of June 22, 1980, he enlarged his faction to 86 members. His adroit wooing of new Diet members, encouragement of old members, and close attention to local and House of Councillors' elections meant that his faction continued to grow—to a total of 97 in 1981, 105 in 1982, and an unprecedented 114 following the election of December 18, 1983. At the time of his stroke the Tanaka "faction" numbered 121 Diet members and looked like it was headed toward including a member from every electoral district in the country.

Tanaka's purpose in thus enlarging his faction was, first and foremost, to protect himself from being engulfed by the Lockheed case. He had, of course, other intentions, including rewarding his loyal supporters, continuing to serve Niigata, and demonstrating his utter mastery of the Japanese political system. But he had to keep control over the incumbent prime minister in order to ensure that an ally would pardon him if the courts made that necessary. The Suzuki and Nakasone governments came into being because they served this primary Tanaka interest—and everyone in Japanese political life understood that. Nonetheless, if damage control of the Lockheed case was Tanaka's chief aim, the unintended consequences were to introduce into Japan its first real machine politics and, paradoxically, to advance Japan's democratization.

Until about 1975, there is no question who governed Japan: it was the official state bureaucracy.[26] However, during the late 1970s a subtle combination of events started an apparent decline in the power of the bureaucracy and a concurrent rise in the power of the LDP—or, as the Japanese press put it, a trend away from the *kanryō shudō taisei* (bureaucratic leadership structure) and toward the *tō shudō taisei* (party leadership structure).[27] It seems wise to speak of an *apparent* trend because none of the evidence about it is conclusive. There are still powerful ideological pressures in Japan to pretend that the LDP is more influential than it actually is; and the relationship between the bureaucracy and the politicians has historically been cyclical rather than linear, with the bureaucracy regaining power during times of crisis. Nonetheless, I believe that the trend toward a *tō shudō* is real and has three basic causes: (a) excessive "sectionalism" and jurisdictional infighting within the bureaucracy; (b) more expertise about policy among senior LDP politicians than in the past; and (c) a shift in the recruitment of political leadership away from ex-bureaucrats and toward long-incumbent pure politicians, usually from rural constituencies. Each of these developments has been significantly affected by Tanaka's example and his policies.

Sectionalism has long stood in the way of coordinated action by the bureaucracy, but what powers of coordination it does possess seem to have been overtaxed by the particular issues of the late 1970s. The Ministry of Finance, for example, in the name of fiscal restraint has blocked virtually all policies aimed at expanding domestic demand, even though many LDP politicians believe that reflation of the economy would have brought in more revenue and might have made the taxpayers less hostile to a tax increase. Similarly, the Ministry of Agriculture, Forestry, and Fisheries has become a virtual *kamikaze* squad protecting the free world's most heavily subsidized farmers from any form of foreign competition. And MITI fights with everybody in the government to keep or put high-technology industries under the jurisdiction of its industrial policy and to remain the chief arbiter of Japan's so-called market opening measures. This context has presented politicians with numerous opportunities to support one ministry against another, or to profit from the deadlocks by offering real supra-bureaucratic leadership, or in other ways to expand their powers at the expense of the bickering bureaucrats.

Tanaka was always the master of the bureaucracy. For this reason many senior bureaucrats held him in high esteem compared with other politicians. (For example, Yano Toshihiko, the first former vice-minister of MITI to enter politics since the 1940s, was elected to the upper house in June 1983 and promptly joined the Tanaka faction.) When, during the early 1980s, Tanaka began to turn his faction into a machine, he and his staff had all the necessary expertise to extract policies or favors they wanted from the bureaucracy. Kōsaka Masataka writes:

> Let us consider the complicated mechanisms of public administration in Japan, a matter that always comes up in connection with trade friction. In granting permits and authorizations, under the name of "administrative guidance," the various government agencies exercise subtle powers that they may or may not be authorized to exercise. Foreigners denounce these policies as non-tariff barriers. However, the reality is that even Japanese often suffer considerable inconvenience because of these administrative practices. If one is reticent [in the face of the bureaucracy], there is no telling how long he may be kept waiting. In any case these delays always interfere with good timing. Now, when a problem of this sort is taken to the Tanaka faction, the usual outcome is that the Tanaka machine [n.b.: *mashi-in*] goes into action and promptly disposes of it. The significance of the Tanaka machine lies in its accumulated know-how, in its putting the right people together and activating them to solve concrete problems. This machine is popularly known as the *"yossha"* structure [*yossha,* or "O.K.," was Kaku-san's habitual term for agreeing to the proposal of a petitioner or a constituent]. However, we should not forget that it has a rationality and efficiency that is not really revealed by the slang word *yossha*.[28]

Informal discussions in Tokyo led me to conclude that the usual commission charged by the Tanaka machine to get the bureaucracy to act—for example, to get a building permit out of the Ministry of Construction or to slow down the implementation of some market opening scheme from the Ministry of Posts and Telecommunications—was 3 percent of the value of the project.

The "Tanaka School," an informal institution of political education every bit as influential in the Japan of the 1970s and 1980s as the "Yoshida School" was during the 1950s and 1960s, taught Kaku-san's followers how to manipulate and corrupt the bureaucracy. Smart, young conservatives, newly elected to the Diet, gravitated to the Tanaka faction because that was where the action was, never mind the Lockheed case. Those with a little seniority became much more assertive than formerly on the 17 committees, 49 subcommittees, and 32 research councils of the

LDP's Policy Board. Some of them became so expert in their areas of policy specialization that they became the LDP's so-called *zoku* (tribes), those party officials who developed enough knowledge to force the bureaucracy to serve both national and party interests. They included the *bunkyōzoku* (education specialists), who dominated the textbook controversy of 1982; the *nōrinzoku* (agricultural specialists), who are fighting to stop all competitive farm imports; and the *shōkōzoku* (trade and industry specialists), who spearhead MITI's proposals in the party and the Diet.[29]

Needless to say, not all of these party policy specialists came from the Tanaka faction. But it was Tanaka who first showed them how to bring the bureaucracy to heel. As a result of his influence and that of his machine, a condition that I have called "structural corruption" began to pervade the Japanese government, which ultimately led, in 1993, to the LDP's loss of power and attempts to purge the system of corrupt *zoku*.

When it first began, the internal struggle between politicians and bureaucrats produced a kind of impasse, as the bureaucracy became more wary of enunciating general policy and the party was unable to do so. Only the Tanaka faction was consistently able to produce policy outputs, as distinct from grand declarations such as the six different promises of "market opening," the pledge of "defense of the sea lanes," the offer of an "unsinkable aircraft carrier," and the agreement to "internationalize" the financial system. Given this situation, Japanese political scientists worked overtime to invent neologisms that might capture the essence of the changing Japanese political system. These terms were deliberately contradictory. For example, Murakami Yasusuke came up with "compartmentalized competition" *(shikirareta kyōsō)*, Inoguchi Takashi contributed "bureaucracy-led mass-inclusionary pluralism" *(kanryō-shudō taishū-hōkatsu-kata tagen-shugi)*, and Satō Seizaburō has offered "pluralism guided by the integrated party-bureaucratic apparatus" *(jinmin-kanchō kongōtai ni hōkō-zukerareta tagen-shugi)*.[30]

Whatever one chose to call the Japanese system, it began its long slide toward dissolution during the autumn of 1984. Three things happened. First, Nikaidō Susumu, "commander in chief" of the Tanaka *gundan,* an original member of Kaku-san's breakaway group from the old Satō faction, representative of the

Kagoshima Third District for some 13 terms, and vice president of the LDP, chose to offer himself for the party presidency against Tanaka's own candidate (Nakasone) and in the face of the boss's opposition. Second, in February 1985, Takeshita Noboru, former Minister of Construction, Minister of Finance in the second Ōhira cabinet and in both of the Nakasone cabinets, Shimane prefecture's leading representative in the Diet for 10 terms, and one of the genuine "new leaders" picked to take over the reins of politics when Tanaka's generation left the scene, started doing to Tanaka what Tanaka had done to Satō 15 years earlier. He organized a "study group," the Sōseikai, within the Tanaka faction.

These two developments split the Tanaka faction into three groups: the hardcore loyalists *(shimpan giin)*, the fence-sitters *(fudai giin)*, and the rebels *(tozama giin)*. The difference between the last two groups was that the fence-sitters wanted to attend the meetings of Sōseikai but were afraid to do so, while the rebels, well over a third of the faction, went ahead with their plans to create a Takeshita faction. At the height of this confusion, the third and most important event took place: Tanaka suffered a serious stroke, perhaps caused by the spreading rebellion, and retired to Mejirodai, where he died almost a decade later.

With Tanaka's stroke, the Tanaka machine passed to his *deshi* (pupils), particularly Takeshita Noboru, Kanemaru Shin, and Ozawa Ichirō. Their management of his legacy, which I consider in the next essay, led to a series of bribery scandals that rivaled the Lockheed case in the careers they destroyed. The Recruit case brought down Takeshita, the Sagawa Kyūbin case ruined Kanemaru, and the construction industry bid-rigging cases so weakened the LDP as a whole that it split and in 1993 lost its majority in the lower house. When Tanaka died at the end of 1993, the Japanese political landscape looked like a scene out of Kurosawa's *Ran*—a kind of setting of *Lear* in medieval Japan— and Tanaka's image was indelibly tainted with the epithet *kinken-seiji* (power-of-money politics).

In the introduction to this book, I noted that when I began my study of Tanaka I saw him as a figure of great promise for the democratization of the Japanese political system. I still think there was some truth to this idea. Tanaka was the most effective representative of the people to the bureaucratically managed developmental state in the postwar world. But his method was to control the Diet through *zoku,* Diet members who became experts in the work of the bureaucracy and who were personally loyal to Tanaka. The problem was that these *zoku* tended both to corrupt the bureaucracy and to be corrupted by the companies the bureaucracy was charged with supervising. The result was a system so corrupt that it seemed beyond reform, and that disillusioned many citizens with the promise of parliamentary democracy itself. Whatever else Tanaka may have achieved, he did not make Japanese politics accountable to the people.

10

Puppets and Puppeteers: Japanese Political Reform

Since the Japanese election of the summer of 1993 and the fragmentation of the Liberal Democratic Party (LDP), foreign and Japanese scholars and pundits have been busy trying to analyze what it all means. Is political reform imminent, and if so will it be in the direction of greater democracy, openness, and liberalism; or will it be a return to greater reliance on the bureaucracy, rule from above, and conservatism? On February 2, 1994, the *Wall Street Journal* in an editorial on Prime Minister Hosokawa's compromise agreement with the now-in-opposition LDP on how to reform the electoral system stated that "The parallel to Mr. Hosokawa's rejiggering of Japan's electoral system was the British Parliament's Great Reform of 1832. It doubled at a stroke the number of urbanites entitled to vote, and did away with the notorious 'rotten boroughs,' which had allowed many a rural grandee to nominate and elect his own member of Parliament." At almost the same time, the Japanese equivalent of the *Wall Street Journal*, the *Nihon keizai shimbun*, wrote that "The Hosokawa-Kono [president of the LDP] agreement more or less ratifies a plan put forward years ago by the LDP that was designed to preserve the existing power structure while making a gesture to a public angry about political corruption" (*Nikkei Weekly*, January 31, 1994).

In the pages that follow I will present my own distillation of what serious Japanese analysts are saying about political change in Japan and the possibility of "reform." I will also offer two case studies that I believe reflect where the real pressures for substantive political change are showing up. Even though these cases are all but unknown in English writing on Japan, Japanese political analysts argue that they are among the most important developments in a year that also saw the end of thirty-eight years of LDP majorities in the Diet. The first was the appointment (for the first time in modern Japanese history) of a Public Prosecutor General *(kenji sōchō)* who is not a graduate of either Tokyo or Kyoto universities. And the second was the dismissal (for the first time in thirty years) of a sitting bureau chief in the central state bureaucracy by a politically appointed minister. But first, a sketch of the milieu in which these two events occurred.

I

In writing about the systematic corruption that has afflicted Italian government for the past several decades, W. V. Harris notes that "Tangentopoli ["Bribesville"] is a single story rather than a series of discrete events."[1] That is the same point writers of the Kyodo News Agency stress in their book on the alliances of politicians, financiers, bureaucrats, and criminals *(sei, zai, kan, and bō)* that have dominated Japanese politics at least since Prime Minister Tanaka came to power in 1972.[2] The question is, What is the single story and when did it start?

In Italy, which has many similarities to the situation in Japan, it started with the historic elections of April 18, 1948, and the decision of the Italian people to keep the Communists from coming to power. Nonetheless, by allowing the Christian Democratic Party to monopolize power for so long, even with the Socialists holding the balance of power after 1963, the voters in effect became mere spectators. They had to put up with rule by party bosses. The situation began to change only on May 9, 1991, when President Francesco Cossiga, a Christian Democrat, declared that "the government serves as a conduit of organized crime. . . . Its activities are often indistinguishable from the crime syndicates."[3]

Similarly, in Japan, from the founding of the LDP in 1955 until its dominant Takeshita faction split in late 1992, the LDP was created to prevent the Japanese Communists and Socialists from ever coming to power. This came to be known as the "1955 system."[4] The problem is that both prior to and parallel to the reign of the LDP there was actual rule of the country by the bureaucracy. Some writers refer to this as the "1941 system," meaning that all but the symbolic roles were transferred from the politicians to state officials, and bureaucratic powers were greatly strengthened during and after the war.[5] Suzuki Eiji, chair of the latest Council for the Promotion of Administrative Reform (Rinji Gyōsei Kaikaku Suishin Shingikai) and former president of Mitsubishi Kasei, contends that "During the long years of political inertia when we left foreign affairs to the U.S. and followed the Americans in economic matters, there was virtually nothing for our several hundred Diet members to do."[6] What has occurred in Japan over the past thirty-eight years is not the increasingly corrupt rule of party bosses but the increasingly successful efforts by the party to corrupt the bureaucracy.[7]

The turning point in this process was probably the election of Tanaka Kakuei as prime minister in 1972. He represented a Japanese anomaly: a smart politician without a university degree or a background in the bureaucracy. Tanaka nonetheless allied himself with the bureaucratic mainstream of the LDP, working within it to enhance his own power, without breaking the older system of bureaucratic rule. Tanaka trained a group of followers who would later become known as the *zoku giin*, meaning literally "Diet-member tribes," but referring to Diet members who have a specialized knowledge of or a sustained interest in the affairs of a particular ministry or agency, and strong connections with the industries or groups affected by the policies of that ministry or agency.[8]

So-called *zoku* appeared in construction, transportation, agriculture, telecommunications, and a few other sectors. There were no *zoku* for the environment, foreign affairs, science and technology, economic planning, or justice. They did not displace the bureaucrats or seek to have regulations reduced or eliminated. Instead, they simply enriched themselves by seeking and accepting bribes from businesses that needed to get around the regulations. *Zoku* strongholds in the party were the Tanaka faction (and its successors, the Takeshita faction and the Keiseikai) and the Policy Affairs Research Council (Seimu Chōsa Kai), where the LDP attempted to mold bureaucratic initiatives to enrich itself and ensure its own continuity. The Tanaka faction always named the Minister of Construction—Kanemaru Shin was Tanaka's second Minister of Construction—together with Posts and Telecommunications and, after Tanaka's conviction for bribery in the Lockheed case, the Minister of Justice (in order to pardon Tanaka should his conviction ever be upheld). It was Prime Minister Miyazawa's appointment of Gotoda Masaharu as Minister of Justice in the cabinet reshuffle of December 1992 which more than any other single event signaled that the old order was starting to change, a topic to which we shall return.[9]

According to a survey made by the National Diet Library on the amounts of money spent on politics in four leading industrial nations, Japan spends four times more per capita than any other nation. The figures are Japan ¥1,698, Germany ¥506, the United States ¥403, and the United Kingdom ¥94. It calculated these numbers by adding together all income received by political parties and political groups, national government subsidies, annual allowances for politicians, and any other sources of income it could find and then dividing by the total population.[10]

Japan needs all this money because its citizens seek to buy access to the strong Japanese state, because its political culture stresses people and personal relations over parties and abstract principles, because of the costs of personal support groups *(kōenkai)* that politicians must maintain in their districts, and because of factional competition within the LDP. In raising money, politicians have found the construction industry to be the biggest cash cow of them all. For this reason, the premier *zoku* positions are Minister of Construction and Director General of the National Land Agency. The construction ministry's bureaucracy is also not as elite as the power centers of the developmental state—the Ministry of Finance (MOF) and the Ministry of International Trade and Industry (MITI). It is descended from the old Civil Engineering Bureau of the Ministry of Home Affairs (Naimu-shō), the pinacle of the prewar civil service, which was broken up during the Allied Occupation. Some Japanese politicians have proposed "reforming" the current system by restoring the Naimu-shō, which might help stop corruption in the Ministry of Construction but would probably not advance democratic government very much.

Japanese national and local governments spend roughly ¥40 trillion (c. $400 billion) on public works projects each year. This sum is equivalent to almost 10 percent of GNP and is larger than America's annual defense budgets during the height of the Cold War. The Japanese general construction industry (*zenekon* as it is known in the press) also has a labor force of some 6 million workers, some of whom are undoubtedly illegal foreigners but which can still deliver more votes than former Prime Minister Hosokawa's Japan New Party could. According to the authoritative journal *Kankai (Bureaucratic World),* the government expects to invest ¥430 trillion (c. $4 trillion) during 1991–2000 as part of its social infrastructure spending plan, compared with ¥263 trillion during 1981–90.[11] These public projects include some of the largest construction jobs on earth—the Kansai airport being built on an artificial island in Osaka harbor (estimated cost ¥1.4 trillion), the trans-Tokyo Bay tunnel, the Tōzai and Karasuma subway lines in Kyoto—and Tanaka Kakuei and his successors arranged for exactly 3 percent of all such contracts to be paid directly to themselves.

Thanks to a major series of investigative articles by the Kyodo News Service, which were also translated into English and published in the *Japan Times,* we now know in detail how Tanaka pioneered this practice. Former Minister of Construction Amano Kōsei (Nakasone cabinet, 1986–87) told of meeting Tanaka in June 1972 just after he had become prime minister, and going over a list with him of 48 dam projects with a total contract value of about ¥800 billion that were planned by the Water Resources Development Public Corporation (Mizushigen Kaihatsu Kōdan, established in 1962).[12] Attached to the list was a bid-rigging scheme with the names of the firms to be awarded contracts. Amano said to Kyodo News, "I retouched the list when I was construction minister." He added, "I'm for bid-rigging. . . . What's wrong with bid-rigging that helps the construction industry operate smoothly and secures jobs?"[13]

Uera Sukimasa, former chairman of Tobishima Construction Company, was the industry's representative who personally handed over the cash to Tanaka at his Mejiro, Tokyo, estate. Another company executive is quoted as saying that he paid Uera "exactly 3 percent" of the value of the contracts, and that "When an executive of our company delivered money that was missing a fractional amount, Uera complained that he had to make up the difference."[14] Three percent of the water control projects collected by Tanaka over the years comes to about ¥24 billion ($235 million).

Tanaka's power rested on his control of the largest faction within the LDP. He recruited and trained his followers in what he liked to call "the philosophy of numbers" *(sū no ronri)*, by which he meant that to control the largest faction in the party was to control the party as a whole. The key to that was illegal contributions, and the key to that in turn was control of the Ministry of Construction. With control of the party, one could control the Diet and from there try to control the bureaucracy and the nation. His key lieutenants after Nikaidō Susumu, his first chief cabinet secretary, were Takeshita Noboru, who succeeded Nikaidō and ultimately Tanaka himself, and Kanemaru Shin, who succeeded Takeshita as leader of the Tanaka faction after Takeshita was disgraced in the Recruit bribery scandal.

In addition to these stalwarts, there was a remarkable crop of younger men who joined Tanaka in the general election of December 27, 1969. At that time the prime minister was Satō Eisaku and the secretary general of the party Tanaka Kakuei, who had assumed the post in August 1965 at age 47, the youngest person in history to do so. Among the new members of the Satō (later Tanaka, later Takeshita, and later Keiseikai) faction were Ozawa Ichirō, son of former Minister of Transportation Ozawa Saeki in the Yoshida cabinet of 1948; Hata Tsutomu, front man for Ozawa in creating the 1993 coalition government and briefly prime minister in 1994; Kajiyama Seiroku, secretary general of the party under Miyazawa when it lost its majority and one of Ozawa's enemies today; Watanabe Kōzō, a later ally of Ozawa's; and Okuda Keiwa, a later Minister of Posts and Telecommunications and a strong ally of Ozawa's during 1993. In 1969 Tanaka was about to use these men to carry out a *coup d'état* against his leader, Satō, just as Takeshita would later do to Tanaka, and Ozawa to Takeshita. They all learned well from the master.

It is important to understand that within the Tanaka faction, there was a dual structure of power, just as there has been throughout Japanese politics and society since approximately the twelfth century. The Japanese like to distinguish between those who actually wield power and those who take responsibility for the way it has been wielded. The Japanese terms for this distinction are both seemingly endless and very old. They include *tatemae* (pretense) and *honne* (reality), *soto* (external) and *uchi* (in the family), *omote* (formal) and *ura* (hidden), *kagemusha* (dummy general) and *kuromaku* (behind the screen), and *ningyō* (puppet) and *kuroko* (puppeteer).[15]

In recent politics the public positions of Prime Ministers Uno, Kaifu, and Miyazawa can be contrasted with the power-wielders who put and maintained them in office, Takeshita, Kanemaru, and Ozawa. Tanaka himself tried to play both roles, but he groomed some of his lieutenants as front men and others as puppeteers. The line of descent of *kuromaku* went from Tanaka, to Takeshita, to Kanemaru, to Ozawa—what has come to be known in an off-color Japanese pun as the *Kon-Chiku-Shō*, meaning "son of a bitch" but made up of characters from the names of Kanemaru, Takeshita, and Ozawa.[16] One not unimportant reason for the double track in Japanese politics is to make bribery charges hard to prove.

This combination of *uragane* (hidden money), remote-control politics, and the pretense of governmental accountability became unstuck during 1992. The key figure in the story was Kanemaru Shin, born September 17, 1914; successor to Tanaka and Takeshita as the "don" of the construction *zoku;* and deputy prime minister in the Miyazawa cabinet. For whatever reasons—arrogance, stupidity, old age, or indifference—Kanemaru began to make mistakes. He infringed on other people's roles and allowed the public to get a glimpse of the involvement of gangsters in the corrupt triangle of bureaucrats, politicians, and businessmen. The last time gangsters had made the political news was in the Lockheed case, and that had cost the master himself, Tanaka, any chance of ever appearing again in a public political role.

In September 1990, Kanemaru made a trip to North Korea and irritated both the Foreign Ministry and the ultra-rightists. However, he really made a mistake in early 1992 when he infringed on the territory of the Ministry of Finance's Budget Bureau by suggesting that Japan should "expand public finance even by issuing deficit-covering bonds."[17] Kanemaru's final downfall was caused by the Sagawa Kyūbin scandal. It turned out that Kanemaru was not just the "don" of the construction *zoku;* he was also dabbling in the wildly overregulated transportation industry. Sagawa was an up-and-coming trucking company that had profited greatly from Japan's "just-in-time" parts delivery system.[18] On August 22, 1992, the prosecutors revealed that the president of Sagawa had confessed to paying off Kanemaru to the tune of ¥500 million in February 1990, just before the general election. On August 27, Kanemaru resigned as deputy prime minister and as chairman of the Keiseikai, his name for the old Tanaka-Takeshita faction of the LDP. But on September 29, the prosecutors fined Kanemaru a mere $1,820 without even having him come to their office for an interview. This was to have serious consequences for the prosecutors, since they had already indicted the governor of Niigata for taking the same amount of money from Sagawa that Kanemaru had.

On October 14, 1992, Kanemaru submitted his resignation from the Diet and a month later he entered a hospital in Odawara, a standard ploy for Japanese politicians hoping to avoid arrest. On December 18, in a struggle over who was to succeed Kanemaru as chairman of the Keiseikai, Ozawa and Hata split from the faction to create a new organization committed to political "reform." In January 1993, the prosecutors failed to indict Kanemaru for violating the Political Funds Control Law, but two months later they finally indicted and took him into custody for income tax evasion. On March 27, they reindicted him in light of new evidence found in his offices and home. On July 27, 1993, after the LDP's loss of its majority in the lower house, he went on trial.

These events have left very exposed Kanemaru's chief disciple and intended replacement as head of the Keiseikai, Ozawa Ichirō. Ozawa is as vulnerable to arrest as his mentor, since Kajima Construction Company has told prosecutors that for the past several years it delivered ¥5 million to him every six months during traditional Japanese gift-giving seasons.[19] Some Japanese analysts have argued that Ozawa was merely protecting himself and distracting the public and the prosecutors by backing the Hosokawa government and calling for reform of the political system. Others contended he is a real reformer intent on saving the country from its own self-indulgence and that he is determined to turn Japan into an "ordinary country" *(futsū no kuni),* free of its military and psychological dependency on the United

States.[20] In order to evaluate these claims, we must now turn to the details of our case studies.

II

In November 1993, a Mainichi journalist had the following exchange with Gotoda Masaharu, former chief of the National Police Agency, former chief cabinet secretary (Nakasone cabinet), former Minister of Justice, and former deputy prime minister (Miyazawa cabinet). *Journalist:* "One of the things you've been saying for quite a while is, 'If the Liberal Democratic Party doesn't carry out political reform, it is going to be damned.'" *Gotoda:* "I was saying that if the present political situation continues, there will be no end to the corruption surrounding politics, and there would no longer be any clear line between money and politics. There would be a growing distrust of politicians and government among the people, and the end result, I was saying, would be the collapse of parliamentary democracy in this country."[21] Lest someone should mistake Gotoda for a Japanese version of *Mr. Smith Goes to Washington,* it is important to stress that he comes from a background that is almost unimaginable in countries such as the United States, except perhaps for high officials in the defense or intelligence agencies. Gotoda is one of the few remaining representatives in public life of the old Ministry of Home Affairs (Naimu-shō).

Born in 1914, Gotoda passed the Higher Public Officials Entrance Examination in 1938 while he was still a junior in the law school of Tokyo Imperial University. The following year he graduated and entered the Ministry of Home Affairs. Before being dismembered by the Occupation, the Home Ministry was in charge of everything from local government, police, civil engineering, and workers, to thought control, religion, and the colonies. It held a position in the developmental state comparable to the economic ministries after the war. Gotoda served from 1939 to 1973 in the Home Ministry or in one of its postwar spinoffs, the National Police Agency. He worked on labor and commercial policy in different prefectural governments, took on economic police duties during the Occupation (control of the black market, hoarding, and so forth), was chief of the national police from 1969 to 1972, and was appointed deputy chief cabinet secretary in Tanaka's government. This is the most powerful bureaucratic post in the cabinet.

In November 1973, he retired from public service; and in December 1976, he was elected to the House of Representatives from the Tokushima Sixth District, which he has represented ever since. He does not belong to any faction within the LDP (although he was a Tanaka faction loyalist so long as Tanaka was in the Diet) and has been blocked from becoming prime minister by his police background, which the Japanese public still regards with distaste dating from the wartime period. Gotoda has long worried about the corruption of the bureaucracy, the air of scandal that always hovers around the ministries of Construction and Transportation, and the influence of men like Ozawa Ichirō.

One of the main battlegrounds between Gotoda and Ozawa has been over control of another spinoff from the old Home Ministry, the Jichi-shō (literally, Ministry of Self-Government, but officially translated as Ministry of Home Affairs). Like its predecessor, it is in charge of subsidies for and supervision of prefectural and local governments in Japan. Both Gotoda and Ozawa are former ministers of the Jichi-shō—today not nearly as important a position as it was before the war—and both have sought to place their subordinates in important positions in local administrations. Gotoda's people tend to reflect the ethos of the prewar developmental state—conservative, incorruptible, and paternalistic—while those associated with Ozawa reflect the Tanaka-Takeshita-Kanemaru approach to government.

Prefectural and local governments are important intermediaries between the Ministry of Construction and the general construction companies. Well over half of the 47 prefectural governors are former central government officials, and virtually all deputy governors, heads of general affairs bureaus, and financial section chiefs in provincial administrations come from the Jichi-shō. In late 1993, the *Asahi* noted editorially that all of the mayors and governors recently arrested for bribe-taking were former civil servants. It therefore wondered whether transferring more authority to local government offices would contribute to reform at all.[22]

Gotoda and Ozawa had their most famous clash over the control of local government in April 1991 in the course of the Tokyo gubernatorial election. Gotoda's candidate in the election was the three-term incumbent, Suzuki Shun'ichi, then eighty years old. Ozawa backed Isomura Hisanori, a former TV anchorman, in a campaign that tried to portray Suzuki as a doddering old fool. Nonetheless, Suzuki beat Isomura by a huge margin of more than 800,000 votes. Humiliated, Ozawa resigned as secretary general of the LDP.

In December 1992, following Kanemaru's resignation from the Diet, another old ex-bureaucrat, Prime Minister Miyazawa, saw his chance to begin to weaken the Tanaka wing of the party, even though his own tenure had depended on its support. He appointed Gotoda as Minister of Justice. Following Kanemaru's arrest the following spring, he promoted Gotoda still further to the post of deputy prime minister. These moves began a process of genuine, unprecedented change in the organizations that actually govern Japan, something that could plausibly be called "reform," as distinct from the mere mouthing of a commitment to reform. What made these moves possible was something also rather rare in Japan: the influence of public opinion.

The public had been insulted and outraged when the prosecutors failed to indict Kanemaru for having taken a large bribe from the Sagawa company. The press published photographs of citizens throwing inkwells at the Public Prosecutors' Office, and regional prosecutors wrote editorials denouncing their colleagues in the capital for pusillanimity.[23] It was not just that Kanemaru openly admitted taking a shopping basket full of cash from Sagawa, or that the prosecutors had thrown the book at other officials who had taken the same amount. The public knew that such favoritism meant that the fix was in at the Ministry of Justice. Miyazawa and Gotoda knew it too.

As Minister of Justice, Gotoda had the legal authority to appoint and dismiss officials in the Ministry of Justice and in its separate but affiliated agency, the Public Prosecutors' Office (Kensatsu-chō). But he faced two restrictions in doing so. The Public Prosecutor General and the chief of each High Public Prosecutors' Office are *ninmenkan* (Imperial-approved appointments). This gives them cabinet rank and is designed to protect them from flagrant political pressure once in office. The second restriction is the custom within the bureaucracy that dictates the appointments themselves will not be flagrantly political.[24]

In most of Japan's central government ministries, the top official is actually the career vice-minister, but this is not true of the apparatus in justice. The hierarchy there goes from Public Prosecutor General, the top post, to chief of the Tokyo High Prosecutor's Office, to chief of the Osaka High Prosecutor's Office, to senior official in the Supreme Procuracy (which represents the government before the Supreme Court), and then to vice-minister of Justice, who is boss within the Ministry of Justice. The elite among the prosecutors are the investigators of actual cases, and the best of them are concentrated in the Special Investigations Department (Tokusōbu) of the Tokyo District Public Prosecutor's Office. They are responsible for investigating and prosecuting political crimes and violations of trust among civil servants and corporate executives.

Investigators are often admired by the press, the public, and their peers, but they do not normally make it to the top post. That usually goes to an official of the *aka-renga-gumi* ("red-brick gang," those who work inside the old, prewar brick building of the Ministry of Justice in Kasumigaseki, Tokyo). The typical place for a top investigator as distinct from a Justice Ministry insider to end his career is as chief of the Osaka High Public Prosecutor's Office, a dead end. It was this almost unalterable pattern that Gotoda changed.

He put Yoshinaga Yūsuke, a former investigator and chief of the Osaka office, in charge of the Tokyo High Prosecutors, also making him next-in-line as Prosecutor General (a post he achieved in December 1993). It was a bold, imaginative stroke that struck terror in the hearts of construction executives, governors, and mayors throughout the country, the construction *zoku*, and Ozawa Ichirō himself. Yoshinaga had never served in the *aka-renga-gumi*; he is best known as the *Tokusō no ēsu* (Ace of the SID), the man who arrested Tanaka Kakuei in the Lockheed case, chief investigator in the Douglas-Grumman case, and prosecutor of the Recruit bribees. He had paid dearly for these achievements with banishment to places such as Utsunomiya and Hiroshima. He was never expected to be seen in Tokyo again. Even more unusual, he is a graduate of Okayama University, which separates him from all other Prosecutors General, who went to either Tokyo University or Kyoto University.[25]

In the course of Yoshinaga's unprecedented campaign against

the nation's *zenekon* crooks, prosecutors have taken into custody and indicted the mayor of Sendai; the governors of Ibaraki and Miyagi prefectures; officials from Kajima, Tobishima, Hazama, Taisei, and Shimizu construction companies; plus innumerable bag men, money launderers, and flunkies. In March 1994, they arrested Nakamura Kishirō, a former Minister of Construction in the Miyazawa cabinet and the first politician to be arrested while the Diet was in session in 27 years. He was charged with taking a bribe from Kajima Construction Company to help prevent the Fair Trade Commission from filing a criminal complaint against a bid-rigging association (what in *zenekon* jargon is called a "teahouse") in Saitama prefecture headed by a Kajima official. Nakamura, a favorite of Kanemaru Shin, was at the time also deputy chairman of the LDP's Special Committee on the Anti-Monopoly Law. In light of the nature of the evidence used against Nakamura—documents found in Kanemaru's offices and home and the confessions of various construction company officials—many other political leaders, including Ozawa, are liable to arrest.[26]

Yoshinaga is ending his career in a blaze of glory. He formally took up his post as head of the Tokyo High Prosecutor's Office in July 1993; and a mere five months later he was promoted to Prosecutor General, his predecessor having resigned early. Yoshinaga will surely go down as one of the legendary figures of the modern Japanese state, but Gotoda may well have the greater lasting influence. He has reminded his fellow officials and politicians of the beneficent legacy of the old Naimu-shō, as opposed to its wartime, control aspects. It may be that a Japan freed of the psychological influence of the American occupation will recreate the Naimu-shō and that this will be one result of the ending of the LDP's lock on political power.

III

As secretary general of the Shinseitō (Renewal Party), Ozawa is in charge of the organization's strategy and its fund-raising. Shinseitō is the group of former Takeshita faction members who broke away from the ruling party at the end of 1992 and then, during the summer of 1993, decided to back the eminently presentable Hosokawa Morihiro as prime minister. Ozawa would have been the first to notice that Yoshinaga's arrests had probably eliminated the construction industry as the prime source of Japanese political funds. Moreover, the success in January 1994 of the compromise political reform bill meant that Japan would soon be shifting to small, single-member constituencies in order to elect its Diet. It was unlikely that this shift would make Japanese elections less expensive.

As of the end of 1993, Ozawa's chief public source of funds was also a source of embarrassment to him. He is allied with Kōmeitō (the Clean Government Party), which is controlled by the militant, rich, and sometimes unscrupulous religious leader Ikeda Daisaku, head of the fundamentalist Buddhist sect Sōka Gakkai. The press refers to this alliance as the "ichi-ichi line," after the given names of Ozawa and Ichikawa Yūichi, the leader of Kōmeitō. Many liberals find this alliance deeply disturbing, and even faction leaders and power brokers within the LDP, some of whom might themselves want to ally with Ozawa, hold back from doing so because of this connection.[27] Because of this overdependence on Kōmeitō, as well as the construction industry, Ozawa needs a new source of funds.

One possibility to replace construction funds might be clients of the Ministry of International Trade and Industry. MITI controls the three biggest political contributors in the country—the steel, automobile, and electric power industries—and if they could be delivered to Shinseitō, Ozawa's star as the *kuromaku* of the post–Cold War era would really start to rise. The problem is that MITI is not the same kind of agency as the Ministry of Construction. It competes every year with the Ministry of Finance for the position as the most elite ministry in the country. It consistently attracts top graduates in law and economics from the most selective universities, particularly from the Department of Law of the University of Tokyo, which was set up in the 1880s as a training academy for what were then officials of the Emperor.

Equally important, MITI does not control vast amounts of subsidies which it distributes to clients. It is a strategy-making agency—an "economic general staff," as it was dubbed before and during the war—and it is closer in spirit to the American Joint Chiefs of Staff than to the Department of Commerce. MITI men are proud and smart. They are the putative authors of the postwar Japanese economic "miracle." In order to cause these people to serve his interests, Ozawa would have to use different tactics from just assigning a few *zoku* to intermediate between them and the industries they supervise. He would have to take over the ministry itself and put his own men in charge of its day-to-day operations.

One of the things that has made his efforts to do so somewhat plausible is that even elite organizations like MITI are on the defensive in the wake of the LDP's loss of power. There is a strong reaction in Japan to excessive regulation—or so one would gather from the press—just as there is a public suspicion that the great powers of the state may themselves be a cause of the continuous corruption scandals. Because the state is so powerful, people try to buy their way into its good graces. There is also a growing fear that the state made too many mistakes in letting the "bubble economy" get out of control; the reputation of Kasumigaseki is somewhat tarnished. Another element in the growing public criticism of the bureaucracy is anxiety that the disintegration of the LDP may have unbalanced the Japanese governmental system and opened the way to a "bureaucratic dictatorship."[28]

Some of Japan's most astute political analysts continuously stress that "the fundamental political problem of Japan is the need to democratize the bureaucracy in order to democratize policymaking." They contend that "since 1941 Japan has had a bureaucracy-led industrial cooperation system."[29] Prime Minister Hosokawa made "reform" of this system his primary pledge in asking voters to support his new party. During 1993, even the Americans began to bash the bureaucracy as a tactic in their endless struggles to control their trade deficit with Japan. This was unusual for them since they are usually smugly devoted to their "theories" that bureaucrats could not possibly "pick winners" or otherwise help an economy to prosper. They have stuck to such theories through 25 years of trade deficits and in the face of overwhelming evidence to the contrary throughout East Asia until the Japanese themselves made an issue of bureaucratic power.

MITI itself was not blameless in leaving itself open to political manipulation. Like most other ministries, MITI had learned to live with the LDP. Its bureau chiefs dutifully answered the questions put to its LDP minister in the Diet. A few of its officials still resigned from public service and entered politics, always as candidates of the LDP. And when Hosokawa's coalition government was created, MITI leaders, like most other senior bureaucrats, instinctively sided with the those LDP members who defected to join it as members of Sakigake (the Harbinger Party) of Takemura Masayoshi. When Takemura and Ozawa could not get along in the coalition, Ozawa naturally began to think of the bureaucracy as one of his rivals.

Ozawa's true motives in attacking MITI are unknown. Sometime between Kanemaru's resignation from the Diet in November 1992 and the opening of the regular Diet session in late January 1993, Ozawa underwent, in the words of Robert Angel, a "transmogrification that rivaled Saul of Tarsus' experience on the road to Damascus. Shedding his image as a political backroom brawler and fixer *par excellence,* he emerged as Nagatacho's foremost champion of political reform."[30] Perhaps he needed the "screen of political reform" to hide his own involvement in Kanemaru's schemes.[31] He may also have wanted to distract the public from its concern with corruption by jumping on the bandwagon to change Japan's electoral system from one of multi-member constituencies to single-member constituencies. That, after all, has been the position of most liberals in the LDP, including Kaifu and Miyazawa, ever since the Recruit case of 1988–89.

On the other hand, Ozawa may genuinely want single-member constituencies for his own agenda. The biggest event during his tenure as secretary general of the LDP (1989–91) was the Gulf War. Foreign and domestic criticism of Japan's free ride on defense seemed to have convinced him that the constitution must be revised in order to provide the basis for Japan's military participation in future U.N. peacekeeping operations. The single-member constituency system enacted in January 1994 will make it easier to revise the constitution; that is one of the reasons why liberals within the Socialist Party voted against it in the upper house of the Diet. Whatever Ozawa's combination of motives, all of his political plans require money, and he seems determined to try to get it in the same old way, by controlling the relationship between the state and industry. In seeking to do so, he was greatly aided by the mood of criticism of the bureaucracy—a mood, incidentally, that he helped foster by his own actions and writings.[32]

On October 12, 1993, Ozawa launched his effort to make the bureaucracy more politically responsive. What came to be called the Ozawa Plan *(Ozawa kōsō),* which he presented to his coalition partners, called for cuts in the numbers of higher bureaucrats (bureau chiefs and above) who would be allowed to answer questions in the Diet, the upgrading of parliamentary vice-ministers (i.e., Diet members assigned to supervise particular ministries) to the level of "deputy ministers" *(fuku-daijin),* and the addition of some 100 to 160 politicians to key ministries with the rank of bureau chief and the title of "political counselor" *(seimu-shingikan).*[33] He clearly wanted a Japanese version of the American system of presidential appointees. As Oishi Nobuyuki explained, "Unlike the U.S., where as many as 4,000 bureaucrats are politically appointed, the Japanese bureaucrats remain in place from one administration to the next."[34]

Needless to say, the bureaucrats did not like this plan one bit. They charged that it was a blatant effort to politicize Japan's civil service and pointed to numerous statutes governing the bureaucracy that the plan appeared to violate. Former MITI Vice-Minister Morozumi argued that "Politicians are supposed to decide what the nation wants. The administration is supposed to supply information that will assist in making choices, and to implement whatever choices are made." He added his own (and much of the public's) opinion of politicians: "Have you ever heard a Japanese politician express an educated opinion on the current Cambodian problem, or on our relationship with Russia, for instance? No, all they talk about is their success in influencing the outcome of some public project or other."[35]

Like all big Japanese organizations, MITI is internally divided into factions. The longest lasting of these splits, dating from the 1960s, is between the "nationalists" and the "internationalists."[36] This distinction used to have policy implications, but in recent years it has boiled down to an argument over promotions based on "merit" (the internationalists) versus promotions based on "seniority" (the nationalists). Both groups also have liaisons with different groups of politicians.

During 1993 the nationalists at MITI included in their ranks a former vice-minister, the sitting vice-minister, and several bureau chiefs. The internationalists included in their ranks the chief of the secretariat and two people whose names were often in the Japanese press at the end of the year: former Vice-Minister Tanahashi Yūji (MITI class of 1958), and former Industrial Policy Bureau chief Naitō Masahisa (MITI class of 1961). Hosokawa's MITI minister, Kumagai Hiroshi, was himself a former MITI official (MITI class of 1964), a member of Shinseitō, and an ally of Ozawa's. On December 16, 1993, Minister Kumagai asked Bureau chief Naitō to resign, and a week later he did so. Kumagai's firing of Naitō, which is what it was, produced an explosion in bureaucratic and political circles of a sort not seen in Japan since the 1950s, when a powerful politician interfered with bureaucratic appointments in the agriculture ministry.

Kumagai, of course, knew all about the internal factional struggle within MITI; Ozawa had appointed him to the post precisely so that he could exploit it for Ozawa's benefit. Both Ozawa and Kumagai were close to the leaders of the nationalist faction, some younger members of which ghost-wrote major parts of Ozawa's best-seller *Nihon kaizō keikaku (A Plan for the Reform of Japan)*.[37] In 1976, when Kumagai resigned from MITI to enter politics, Tanahashi was the chief secretary. He helped Kumagai by promoting him just before his resignation and by introducing him to the Fukuda faction within the party (Tanahashi had been a secretary to former Prime Minister Fukuda Takeo). In 1977, Kumagai was elected to the upper house with the help of the Fukuda faction, but once in office he broke with Fukuda's forces and joined the Tanaka faction. Ever since, Kumagai and Tanahashi had been distant.

Tanahashi was thought of as an exceptionally strong vice-minister, and he and Naitō were both regarded as "golden boys" within the ministry. They played key roles in the semiconductor negotiations with the United States, and they fought to protect MITI's interests in jurisdictional battles with the postal ministry (over value-added telecommunications networks) and with the education ministry (over computer programming). But Tanahashi was politically vulnerable. He is the son-in-law of Matsuno Yukiyasu, former governor of Gifu prefecture, eight-time LDP representative from the Gifu First District, and former director general of the National Land Agency. Both Tanahashi and his son, Yasufumi, also a MITI official, had their eyes on Matsuno's old and secure electoral district.

In December 1992, young Tanahashi Yasufumi resigned from MITI in order to run for the Diet from his grandfather's district. The chief secretary at the time, Naitō, promoted him to a new post called "planning adviser" within the Secretariat to help flesh out his résumé for the coming election campaign. This was common practice in the ministry; Tanahashi senior had done the same for Kumagai when he decided to enter politics. Unfortunately, Yasufumi ran as an LDP candidate in the July 1993 election and lost.

At about the same time as the election, a series of poison-pen letters began to circulate within the ministry charging that the chief secretary, who was also a close associate of Yasufumi's father, had shown favoritism to the son with his last-minute promotion. They also went on to make some criminal charges, including that some of the funds generated by MITI's control of bicycle racing—which are normally used to promote the machinery industry—had actually gone to LDP politicians. Whatever the truth of these allegations, they helped soften up the ministry for Kumagai's firing of Naitō.[38]

Kumagai said to the press that he had fired Naitō because of his mishandling the case of Tanahashi Yasufumi and because the allegations surrounding him brought confusion to the ministry. The press nonetheles interpreted the firing as a *coup d'état* carried out by Ozawa in his plan to gain control of MITI. As chief of the industrial policy bureau, Naitō was the next in line to become vice-minister and, they argue, would have been able to thwart Ozawa's plans. Despite these maneuvers, many doubt that Ozawa will succeed in bringing MITI under his control. Even Ozawa's deputy secretary general of Shinseitō, Watanabe Kōzō, a former MITI minister, argues that Japan needs MITI more than ever because of the rapidly changing global economy and that "he felt like crying" when he read in the newspapers about how the ministry has been weakened by political interference.[39] Also the powerful group of MITI old boys disapproves of Kumagai and the way he has brought the ministry's internal struggles into the open.

At the same time, the current vice-minister, an Ozawa supporter, has assumed concurrent control of the industrial policy bureau, and the line of succession is open. Ozawa is the man of the hour, and few are shedding tears for Naitō, who became what he called a "political refugee" as a visiting professor at Georgetown University in Washington, D.C. During the autumn of 1993, two of the most experienced insiders of Japanese politics wrote articles about Ozawa, his reputation for strongarm tactics, and his future. One, Hayasaka Shigezō, Tanaka's former chief assistant, compared Ozawa to Ōkubo Toshimichi, the Meiji leader dubbed the "Bismarck of Japan" by his English-language biographer.[40] The other analysis of Ozawa by Yamaguchi Toshio, Diet member from the Saitama Second District, compared him to Sakamoto Ryōma, the reformer at the end of the Tokugawa period who played a key role in forging the alliances that led to the Meiji Restoration.[41] These are evocative and favorable comparisons, but it should also be remembered that both Ōkubo and Sakamoto were assassinated. However long Ozawa remains on the scene, it is undeniable that he has shaken the foundations of one of the pillars of the Japanese bureaucratic establishment. The last person to do that was General MacArthur, and he did so only incompletely.

Professor Yamaguchi Jirō believes that what is so facilely called "reform" would actually require a combination of the French Revolution and the Allied Occupation in order to make much difference in the ways Japanese conduct their public affairs.[42] Perhaps he has overstated the case, but his point is useful in helping to counter the mindless projection onto Japan of American comparisons. When *Time* magazine writes: "He is a charismatic former southern governor-turned-national-leader with a pledge to reform government. . . . Bill Clinton, right? Yes, but also Morihiro Hosokawa" (February 21, 1994), one can only shudder at the possible consequences of such ignorance. In this essay I have sought to show that Japan is undergoing profound changes in its political structures and procedures. Whether these changes add up to "reform" probably depends on the values of the observer. What I hope I have also shown is that to understand what is going on in Japan, it is best to address this very complex country empirically and inductively—as it is, rather than as theorists or propagandists wish it to be.

INTERNATIONAL RELATIONS

11

The Patterns of Japanese Relations with China, 1952–1982

In advanced democracies with high rates of literacy and strong independent mass media of communication, the formulation and conduct of foreign policy is not a neat, relatively technical activity performed by the government. In addition to involving all the usual components of any nation's external relations (the attempt to advance or maintain political and economic security and to ameliorate relations of conflict with allies and opponents), foreign policy in advanced democracies also involves the sometimes uncontrollable elements of public emotion, invidious national comparisons, and the ultimate values of a people. Each of these extra elements offers opportunities for domestic and foreign actors to manipulate or distort policy.

Such emotional elements are not caused by the openness of the democracies; rather, openness makes their existence significant as an opportunity for, or a constraint on, governments. The roots of affect as a potential element in foreign policy are collective memory and value differences among nations. Japan, for example, has extensive economic contacts with the Middle East— during the early 1980s it was the number one or number two trading partner of Saudi Arabia, Kuwait, Oman, Qatar, the United Arab Emirates, and both Iran and Iraq. Japan is able to trade with nations which are bitter enemies of each other because of the almost total lack of emotional involvement on the part of the Japanese people with the disputes of the region.

On the other hand, this is not true of Japanese relations with China. Here all political, economic, and diplomatic ties are subtly skewed by the popular attitudes and aspirations of the Japanese people as these are mobilized by the Japanese press. The dilemma of Japanese flattery *(omoneri)* of China versus Japanese national contempt *(anadori)* for China is as great an influence on Sino-Japanese relations as the changing national calculations of political and economic interest.

Any attempt to study Sino-Japanese relations in the postwar era must, therefore, address not only the "objective" complementarities between the two nations and their respective governmental policies, but also the pressures of public opinion, an influence that is infinitely greater on the Japanese side (a media-dominated mass society) than on the Chinese side (a relatively closed and controlled Leninist country). I believe that since the creation of the People's Republic of China (PRC) in 1949 and Japan's regaining of independence in 1952, relations between the two neighbors can be analytically divided into three distinct phases: (1) the period of Japanese dependency and contrition, 1949–71; (2) the period of China euphoria (or panda-mania), from the Nixon Shocks to the Baoshan Shock, 1971–81; and (3) the return of "Banquo's ghost," high-school history textbooks in hand, to haunt the celebration, 1982 and after.

Three themes (at least) also emerge from this history: (1) between the mid-1950s and the late 1970s, Japan's peculiar attitude toward China permitted the PRC to take political advantage of Japan in their bilateral relations; (2) China's manipulation of Japan emotionally and Japan's accumulated experience in dealing with post-1949 China led during the 1980s to a more realistic understanding between the two nations; and (3) despite China's manipulation of Japanese guilt and greed vis-à-vis its continental neighbor, Japan's postwar China policy has been subtle, sophisticated, and largely successful. The following elaboration of these themes is written primarily from a Japanese point of view; the division into periods and the emphases would undoubtedly differ in a Chinese perspective.

RELATIONS BEFORE 1971

Several decades ago, Ogata Sadako made the important point that "not many Japanese regard Communist China as a 'cold war' enemy, nor do they accept the 'China-communism-enemy' equation that is so widely held in the United States."[1] As governmental archives have begun to be opened concerning the critical Korean War years when the basic structure of postwar international politics in East Asia was fixed, new evidence of this discrepancy between Japanese and American views is coming to light. It is now clear that Japanese Prime Minister Yoshida Shigeru fought a vigorous, rear-guard action against the chief American peace-treaty negotiator, John Foster Dulles, in order to avoid recognizing the Taipei government instead of the Beijing government—the price Dulles extracted from Japan for a peace treaty with the non-Communist allies of World War II. In discussions between the two leaders during 1951, Yoshida firmly held to the views that the American policy of containment of China was wrong, that Chinese communism had its roots in Chinese nationalism, that the Sino-Soviet alliance would not last, and that Japan could play an important role in weaning China away from communism. It now seems that the "Yoshida letter" of December 24, 1951, promising that Japan would recognize the Nationalist government on Taiwan, was written not by Yoshida but rather by Dulles and forced on the Japanese prime minister. One of Yoshida's biographers, Kōsaka Masataka, believes that Yoshida accurately foresaw the Sino-Soviet split, and that the 1952 peace treaty between Japan and Nationalist China is harder to justify than other arrangements of the early years of the Japanese-American alliance.[2]

Prior to the signing of the San Francisco Peace Treaty, British diplomacy supported Yoshida's position against that of Dulles, primarily because Britain feared that if Japan did not regain its access to the China market, Japan would compete with and ultimately drive British products from Southeast Asia—which is, of course, precisely what happened. (During the 1930s China was Japan's third-largest source of imports, after the United States and Korea, and its biggest export market.) Britain also argued that a closer tie between Tokyo and Beijing would help to create a counterweight to the Soviet Union in Asia and possibly facilitate the early development of Chinese "Titoism." Before his final meeting with Dulles, Yoshida (a former ambassador to Great Britain) tried to play the British off against the Americans; and during the 1960s he quietly encouraged Macmillan and De Gaulle to increase economic exchanges with China in order to bring China more into non-Communist international society. As early as 1951, Yoshida had said in the Diet that "if Communist China is agreeable, Japan would like to establish a trade office in Shanghai," and that he regarded "the Republic of China as merely a local government."[3]

This "ancient" history is still important today for various reasons. First, Yoshida's views were not his alone. They were widely, if privately, held throughout the mainstream of Japanese conservative politicians for the next two decades, and they were imparted to later prime ministers of the so-called Yoshida School—particularly Ikeda, Satō, and Tanaka. Second, regardless of the contents of the Yoshida letter, the Japanese Foreign Ministry internally interpreted it to mean that Japan had recognized Nationalist China only because it held the seat reserved for China in the United Nations. During the 1960s and early 1970s, Japan's diplomacy was much more attuned to the PRC's rising fortunes in the United Nations than it was to the strategic and anti-Soviet motives of Zhou, Mao, Nixon, and Kissinger in their moves toward each other. As a result, after the PRC replaced Taiwan in the United Nations during October 1971, Japan acted more quickly and decisively to recognize Beijing than did the United States.[4] And third, Japan's basic policy during the 1950s and 1960s of trading simultaneously with mainland China, Taiwan, and the United States, under the camouflage of *seikei bunri* (the separation of politics and economics), and in spite of the confrontations of the Cold War, represented a de facto implementation of Yoshida's political strategy toward China and not, as is so commonly supposed by Americans, evidence of Japan's lack of a principled foreign policy. Let us elaborate on these points, since they all conditioned and even determined the "normalization" of 1972.

The key to Japan's strategy toward China down to the Nixon Shocks was the use of pro-Beijing members of the ruling Liberal Democratic Party (LDP) to open separate channels to the mainland, while simultaneously having the leaders of the party take pro-Taiwan positions in order to placate the Americans. This strategy was not easy: the pro-China Diet members were a heterogeneous group with diverse motives for engaging in "private" diplomacy; the factionalization of the LDP meant that non-ruling factions often exploited foreign policy issues to embarrass the factions in power, even when there was no basic disagreement among them over foreign policy goals; and the Chinese were afforded innumerable opportunities to manipulate the process by threatening to shut down the private channels.

Nonetheless, in my opinion, this strategy was one of the most skillfully executed foreign policies pursued by Japan in the postwar era—a clever, covert adaptation by Japan to the Cold War and a good example of Japan's essentially neo-mercantilist foreign policy. The strategy eventually broke down after the Chinese and the Americans raised the stakes and when the interests of Japanese politicians, journalists, and businessmen could no longer be contained within the strategy's very personal and very Asian boundaries. The left-wing opposition parties in Japan also tried repeatedly to manipulate the China issue in domestic politics, but "it is the 'pro-China' conservatives, led by former Prime Minister Ishibashi Tanzan, the late Takasaki Tatsunosuke, and veteran M.P. Matsumura Kenzō, who must be given more credit than all of the left wing for advancing trade with China."[5] As one measure of their success, during 1965 Japan replaced the Soviet Union as China's leading trading partner; and from 1965 to 1973 Japan's total trade with China was worth $7.67 billion ($1 billion in Japan's favor) and with Taiwan $8.3 billion ($3.2 billion in Japan's favor).[6] Needless to add, this success was not due solely to Japanese efforts; it also reflected the development of the Sino-Soviet dispute and China's then prevailing hostility both to the Soviet-led and American-led blocs. The first sign of China's later openness to the capitalist democracies was its acceptance (or toleration) of Japan as its major source of imports.

The leading pro-China Diet members within the ruling party were Matsumura Kenzō (1883–1971), a politican whose career spanned the prewar, wartime, and postwar governments, and who was a personal friend of Zhou Enlai and Liao Chengzhi; Takasaki Tatsunosuke (1885–1964), vice-president of Manchurian Heavy Industries during the Pacific War and the Japanese partner in setting up the Liao-Takasaki (L-T) informal trading relationship of 1962 to 1967; Utsunomiya Tokuma, a sort of leftist Japanese version of former U.S. Senator Wayne Morse within the conservative party, whose father, General Utsunomiya Tarō (a collaborator of Sun Yat-sen's in the 1911 revolution), had given him a classical Chinese education; Ikeda Masanosuke, a nationalist of the old school—he continued to use the derogatory term "Shina" (for China) after the war—and one who shifted from a pro-mainland to a pro-Taiwan position during the 1960s; Fujiyama Aiichirō, the foreign minister in the Kishi cabinets who underwent a *tenkō* (conversion) to a pro-China position in 1966 and who succeeded Matsumura as the chief negotiator with the Chinese; Furui Yoshimi, Matsumura's number one aide and the man who bore the brunt of all Chinese humiliations during the Cultural Revolution and the later years of the Satō cabinets in order to keep the trade alive (in 1972, the year of Sino-Japanese normalization, he lost his seat in the Diet because he had so stoically endured these national humiliations); Tagawa Seiichi, Matsumura's secretary and the principal scapegoat along with Furui whenever the Chinese demanded a Japanese kowtow (Tagawa left the LDP for the New Liberal Club in 1976 as a protest over the Miki cabinet's stalling on a treaty of peace and friendship with China); and Okazaki Kaheita, a former Shanghai-based banker and the successor to Takasaki as guarantor of the "memorandum trade office" that followed the L-T arrangement.[7]

On the Chinese side the chief negotiator was Premier Zhou Enlai. Zhou was particularly close to Matsumura and Takasaki because they did not spend all their time apologizing to him for earlier Japanese behavior in China, and sometimes offered candid criticisms of such things as the Great Leap Forward and the inefficient management of Chinese enterprises.[8] Zhou's chief lieutenants, many of whom were purged during the Cultural Revolution but came back during the 1970s, were Liao Chengzhi (1908–1983), the son of Sun Yat-sen's closest colleague, Liao Zhongkai, and who, like his father, was educated in Japan (at Waseda, Matsumura's university—according to Furui, Liao was more fluent in Japanese than in Mandarin); Sun Pinghua, director of the China-Japan Friendship Association; and various Japan specialists in the Foreign Ministry such as Xiao Xiangqian, in 1972 head of the Memorandum Trade Office in Tokyo and a decade later the first Chinese official to launch the attack against Japan for its alleged revisions of high-school history textbooks.

Many American observers like to say that Zhou Enlai's diplomacy was "pragmatic," but it seems to me that some Japanese analysts have come closer to its reality. According to the distinguished China specialist Ishikawa Tadao, the Chinese insist on basing their foreign policy on some abstract governing principle *(gensoku-shugi)*; when this principle no longer coheres with reality, or fails to advance then-current Chinese interests, the Chinese try to maintain the principle anyway, while looking for face-saving formulas within which actually to do business. Thus, according to Ishikawa, a foreign power approaching China will be most successful if it adroitly finds ways to let the Chinese pretend to maintain their principles while compromising them in practice.[9]

Another equally distinguished China specialist, Etō Shinkichi, generalizes on a different dimension. In his view, Beijing, in conducting its foreign policy, gives exceptional weight to the personal character of a foreign head of state, particularly whether he is or is not a "friend" of China. Thus, according to Etō, changes in Chinese foreign policy can sometimes be engineered by changing the head of state of a nation that is dealing with the Chinese, even if there is no difference between the actual policies of the two leaders. "Beijing," Etō writes, "had indulged in too much abuse of Satō to be able to adopt a moderate line with the Satō Cabinet without losing face." By shifting from Satō to Tanaka in 1972, the Japanese presented the Chinese with an opportunity to reverse their extremely anti-Japanese views of the previous few years—and this they promptly did.[10]

Whether or not these generalizations about Chinese diplomacy truly preceded Japanese actions during the 1950s and 1960s, they seemed to be the ones actually governing Sino-Japanese interaction in that period. Trade got started during the 1950s when Japan took up the opportunities afforded by Chinese invitations through leftist channels to Japanese businessmen and by Zhou's Bandung diplomacy. The Chinese then cut off trade in May 1958, using the Nagasaki flag incident (the desecration of the PRC flag by Japanese youths in a Nagasaki department store, May 2, 1958) as a pretext, but actually because of

Kishi's 1957 visit to Taiwan, the first by a Japanese prime minister to the Republic of China. As soon as Ikeda had replaced Kishi, Zhou reestablished trade using the "friendly (Japanese) companies," which led to the L-T arrangements and the financing of Chinese purchases by the Japanese Export-Import Bank. Ikeda himself maintained a public hard-line, anti-PRC position to placate the United States, but he privately supported the Matsumura group in fostering trade and added his faction's chief adviser, Ogawa Heiji, to Matsumura's 1962 delegation to China. (Ironically, in 1982 Ogawa was serving as minister of education when the textbook controversy arose, and the Chinese retaliated by cancelling a new invitation for him to visit Beijing.)

These channels began to narrow following Yoshida's reassurances to Taiwan in May 1964, the onset of the Cultural Revolution in China in 1966, and Satō's visit to Taiwan in 1967. During the rest of the decade, with China now furiously attacking "revived Japanese militarism," Furui and Tagawa played their parts. They kept the trade going by placidly agreeing to any and all of Zhou's demands for gestures of Japanese obsequiousness—a Japanese stance that I call *"fumie* diplomacy." (A *fumie* was a tablet with a crucifix on it that the Tokugawa military government at the time of the census forced people to stamp their foot on to prove that they were not Christians; by extension, the term refers to any loyalty test not freely taken.)[11] Although Furui and Tagawa were ritualistically attacked within the LDP and truly ridiculed by the United States for the things they signed in China, many Japanese understood that they were merely treading on a *fumie* in order to maintain the Sino-Japanese connection. Trade continued throughout the Satō era, and then expanded dramatically after Tanaka came to power. During 1972 the Chinese quickly discovered that Japanese militarism was nonexistent, although a decade later they reignited the charge for a different but analogous purpose.

As mentioned earlier, I believe that Japan's diplomacy toward China in this period was a creative adaptation to the Cold War and the ongoing Communist revolution in China. It maintained Japan's short-term interest in trade, kept open Japan's options for normalization in the long term, and avoided alienating the United States, the PRC, or Taiwan. However, precisely at the height of its implementation, internal intellectual and journalistic trends were facilitating conditions that during the following decade made China diplomacy much harder for the Japanese to control and much easier for the Chinese to manipulate. The 1960s witnessed the high tide of Japanese intellectual flattery of China, an attitude that turned into positive intoxication during the Cultural Revolution. Japanese scholars and critics filled the monthly magazines with paeans to and justifications of everything the Chinese did. As Nakajima Mineo notes, little of this writing was analytical or scientific; it projected onto China the feelings of war guilt that bothered many Japanese, or offered a vehicle for their anti-American attitudes during the Vietnam War, or provided a utopian contrast to their own increasingly bureaucratized society.[12] Such commentary on Chinese affairs was almost invariably sentimental and tendentious. "Progressive intellectuals," in Ogata's words, "consider Japan's rise to the status of a great power as having been attained through the sacrifice of China, and argue further that since Japan's military aggression launched China on the course of its 'national liberation' movement, Japan is morally obliged to approve China's present government."[13]

In 1964, further complicating these trends and ensuring that the Japanese public would hear only one side of the China story, the major Japanese newspapers obtained an agreement, through the good offices of the Matsumura group, to exchange journalists with Beijing. This was a major coup for the Japanese press, and during the early stages of the Cultural Revolution Japanese journalists made a significant contribution to the outside world's understanding of what was happening there. However, the Chinese soon began applying political tests to Japanese journalists, expelling those that China regarded as unfriendly. By 1970 China had reduced the number of Japanese papers represented in China from nine to one (the *Asahi*). From then on Japanese journalists were admitted to China only if they adhered to Zhou Enlai's three principles: they must not (1) pursue a hostile policy toward China, (2) participate in any plot to create "two Chinas," or (3) obstruct the normalization of Sino-Japanese relations. With much less reason than Furui had for his *fumie* diplomacy, the Japanese press accepted these conditions and reported Chinese news in a manner indistinguishable from official Chinese media.[14] This was also an issue that would come back to haunt Japan during the textbook controversy.

Such journalistic and intellectual developments laid the foundation for mass pressure on Japan's China policies during the 1970s. When, during 1971, the United States revealed that it was engaged in secret diplomacy with Beijing and the PRC replaced Taiwan in the United Nations, the Japanese public was ready not just for "normalization" of relations with China but for a love affair that would last almost a decade. The "China boom" unleashed by Nixon and Tanaka eclipsed information on China's pervasive political instability and on the strategic concerns that had brought the Chinese and Americans together. In contrast to the careful balancing of Japanese interests and Chinese principles during the 1960s, Japanese leaders now found themselves propelled forward by Chinese campaigns aimed at a domestic Japanese audience; and they agreed to several Chinese proposals (such as the "anti-hegemony clause" and the Long-term Trade Agreement) that, with the benefit of hindsight, indicated the need for greater caution.

RELATIONS 1971–81

The sensational announcement of July 1971 that the American president's national security adviser had met secretly with the Chinese leadership in Beijing, and that the president himself had accepted an invitation to visit China the following year, set off what the Japanese call "China fever" *(Chūgoku fībā)*. A little more than a year later, in September 1972, the new Japanese prime minister, Tanaka Kakuei, flew to Beijing and signed with Zhou Enlai a nine-point communiqué that ended "the abnormal state of affairs which has hitherto existed between the People's Republic of China and Japan" (article 1). This "normalization" of relations was without question a momentous development in the history of modern East Asia, but it was neither as directly caused by the initiatives of Richard Nixon and Henry Kissinger as has been commonly supposed, nor was it as utterly an unmixed blessing for Japan as many Japanese journalists and businessmen profess to believe. In addition to making open and explicit the economic policies that the LDP had long carried out toward China through private channels, the specific terms of normalization also began Japan's involvement in the Sino-Soviet dispute, further intruded China into Japan's domestic political processes, and set the stage for the competitive scramble among capitalist nations at the end of the decade to help China in its belated modernization efforts.

The standard interpretation of these developments is that "until the summer of 1971 the policy of the Japanese government toward the PRC remained generally consistent in its studied passivity and inaction. . . . During his seven and a half years as prime minister, Satō Eisaku was preoccupied in the field of foreign policy mainly with the reversion of Okinawa . . . the normalization of relations with South Korea . . . and the textile dispute with the United States. . . . Under the circumstances Satō had neither the will nor the time to take the initiative in reorienting Japan's posture of political noninvolvement toward the PRC, until he was jolted by the 'Nixon shocks' of the summer of 1971 into a reluctant reappraisal of the situation."[15]

From what has come to light since 1971–72, it seems that much more was going on within the Satō cabinet regarding China policy than this standard interpretation allows. Partisans of, and participants in, Satō's China policy-making group argue that the Satō cabinet actually laid the basis for Sino-Japanese normalization and that Tanaka's hasty diplomacy of August and September 1972, together with his extensive use of opposition party intermediaries with the Chinese, produced terms of normalization that were much less advantageous to Japan than were possible, given China's urgent need to open itself to the West.[16]

On January 22, 1971, before either Ping-Pong diplomacy or the Kissinger trip, Satō said in the Diet that Sino-Japanese normalization was on the political agenda for the near future, and for the first time used China's official name, the People's Republic of China. Satō continued to speak out in this vein throughout 1971, thus allowing the Chinese in January 1972 to halt their campaign against "revived Japanese militarism." Equally important, working through his personal secretary Kusuda Minoru, Satō welcomed the creation of an "international relations study group" *(kokusai kankei kondankai)* to formulate a new China policy. This group included such mainstream academics in the fields of China and international relations as Ishikawa Tadao (Keiō University), Imahori Seiji (Hiroshima University), Ichiko Chūzō (Ochanomizu University), Umesao Tadao (Kyoto University), Etō Shinkichi (Tokyo University), Etō Jun (Tokyo Institute of Technology), Kamiya Fuji (Keiō University), Kanamori Hisao (Economic Planning Agency), Kōsaka Masataka (Kyoto University), Nakajima Mineo (Tokyo University of Foreign Studies), Miyashita Tadao (Kobe University), Nagai Yōnosuke (Tokyo Institute of Technology), and Yamazaki Masakazu (Kansai Gakuin University). The group first met formally on August 26, 1971.

Among the study group's most important activities, presided over by Nakajima Mineo, was writing a letter for the signature of Hori Shigeru (1901–1979), the LDP secretary general and the alleged "brains" of the Satō cabinet, to be sent to Zhou Enlai offering Japanese recognition of the PRC as the sole legitimate government of China. This was the highest official approach yet made by Japan to China. Minobe Ryōkichi, the "progressive" mayor of Tokyo, delivered the letter personally, for which he earned from the press the nickname of "Minobenjyā"—a pun on his and Henry Kissinger's names, and a reflection of the Japanese public's desire for a home-grown version of Kissinger. Hori himself had inaugurated the letter-writing effort as a result of secret talks he had had with Tagawa Seiichi, one of Matsumura Kenzō's chief lieutenants. Tagawa also introduced Hori to some Chinese officials in the Memorandum Trade Office in Tokyo.[17]

As it turned out, Zhou made a tactical decision to reject Hori's initiative, and went further to declare: "Even if Satō accepted the three basic principles as the basis of opening talks with us, we shall not accept Satō as a negotiating partner. However, any successor of Satō's will be welcome in Beijing as long as he accepts the three basic principles."[18] With this action Zhou intruded himself and the China issue directly into Japanese politics. He seems to have understood that because of the public infatuation with China, he could force Satō out of office and bring to power a Japanese leader who, even if he did not differ from Satō on fundamentals, would be to some extent beholden to Zhou for his political popularity. Tanaka was a politician of the Yoshida school, and neither he nor his associate, Ōhira Masayoshi, belonged to any of the China-policy organizations, whether pro-Beijing or pro-Taipei, within the LDP. Moreover, Tanaka did not initiate normalization; when he came to power during July 1972, recognition of the PRC was already a foregone conclusion, because of Satō's acceptance of a "one China" policy and because of Nixon's stance at Shanghai in February 1972.

However, Tanaka was a man in a hurry, having based his successful campaign for the presidency of the LDP on the slogan, "Don't miss the boat to China." Thanks to Zhou Enlai's willingness to receive him in Beijing, Tanaka had become as popular in Japan during 1972 as Nixon was in the United States, before the latter's landslide reelection in November 1972. Tanaka had no strong views of his own on Japanese policy toward China. As a master of factional politics within the conservative party, he was responding more to party disarray over the Nixon Shocks, and to attempts by other faction leaders (e.g., Miki) to exploit the China issue, than to the substantive changes in East Asian international relations. Tanaka ignored the study group and turned China policy over to the Ministry of Foreign Affairs, which was itself split between pro-Chinese and pro-American bureaucrats because of "China fever." The results were inevitable: normalization occurred on Zhou Enlai's terms; the LDP remained divided between the Tanaka and Fukuda factions (Satō had intended Fukuda to be his successor) for the rest of the decade; and many nations in Asia and North America became concerned about Japan's seemingly precipitate embrace of the Chinese. It is here that the true significance of the Nixon Shocks is to be found.

The final three articles (numbers 7, 8, and 9) of the communiqué that Zhou Enlai and Tanaka Kakuei signed at Beijing, September 19, 1972, established the agenda for Sino-Japanese relations down to the Baoshan Shock of 1981.[19] Article 7 committed both Japan and China not to seek "hegemony" in the Asia-Pacific region and to oppose efforts by any other nation to do so. Tanaka and his staff made no demurral to the inclusion of this article since Kissinger had welcomed a similarly worded article in the Sino-American Shanghai communiqué, and the Ministry of Foreign Affairs chose to regard it as merely a general platitude of international relations.[20] The fact that "anti-hegemony" was the Chinese code word for signing up allies in the Sino-Soviet dispute became clear only six years later when its implications for Japan threatened to scuttle the negotiations for a Sino-Japanese treaty of peace and friendship, which had been called for by article eight.

Article 9 was of less significance, but it soon gave the Japanese a foretaste of the troubles implicit in articles 7 and 8. Article 9 stated that "the Government of the People's Republic of China and the Government of Japan agree to hold negotiations aimed at the conclusion of agreements on trade, navigation, aviation, fishery, etc., in accordance with the needs [sic] and taking into consideration the existing nongovernmental agreements." Negotiations over the aviation agreement produced two years of acrimonious wrangling after the Chinese declared it intolerable that their aircraft should use the same Japanese airport as, and be parked alongside, airliners from Taiwan. The internal Japanese debate greatly strengthened pro-Taiwan forces in the LDP, abetted by the formation of an ultranationalist group in the Diet (the Seirankai), and caused Japan Air Lines to lose its second most lucrative route, the one between Tokyo and Taipei. Foreign Minister Ōhira eventually resolved the dispute through his agreement of April 20, 1974, which permitted PRC airplanes to use Tokyo's new Narita airport and Taiwan's planes to land at the more convenient Haneda airport, and which led to the creation of a dummy airline, wholly owned by JAL, to fly between Taipei and Tokyo. The Taiwan government retaliated by stopping all flights for a period (it even threatened to shoot down Japanese airliners that intruded into Taiwanese air space), but eventually flights resumed between Tokyo and Taipei and between Tokyo and Beijing on the basis of Ōhira's formula. Ōhira's air treaty is one of the best examples of Japan's helping the Chinese to preserve their sacred principles while concretely violating them.

In September 1974, Tokyo and Beijing agreed to begin talks leading to a basic treaty of peace and friendship between the two countries. To Japan's pleasant surprise the initial discussions revealed that China would not raise the Taiwan issue in the negotiations, but in January 1975 Zhou Enlai in a meeting with Hori Shigeru (now turned openly pro-China) revealed China's true agenda. Zhou said to Hori that opposing superpower hegemony was a fundamental principle of Chinese foreign policy, and that since the principle had been agreed to by the Americans and by Tanaka it should certainly form the bedrock of future Sino-Japanese relations.[21] This immediately set off a new crisis in the Japanese government, one that lasted until 1978.

The issue, only slowly appreciated by Japanese politicians and the public, was that the USSR did not regard Sino-Japanese normalization as merely a warm reunion among people who shared *dōbun dōshu* (a common script and a common race), the standard Japanese cliché for the basis of Sino-Japanese friendship. Gromyko made flying trips to Tokyo in January 1972 and January 1976 to see if he could prevent the Chinese from using normalization against the Soviet Union. Japan in this period actually possessed considerable leverage over the Soviet Union for a possible resolution of its Northern Territories dispute (in 1976 Gromyko talked about renewing the old Soviet offer to return two of the four northern islands if Japan would refuse to go along with the Chinese anti-hegemony clause).[22] The Japanese missed these opportunities, and the Soviets eventually retaliated by strengthening their Pacific fleet and stationing military forces on the islands claimed by Japan. By raising anti-hegemony Zhou Enlai neatly ensnared Japan in the Sino-Soviet dispute; and although the Japanese knew it was a trap, they never discovered how to avoid it.

China always held the whip hand in the negotiations. In December 1974, Miki Takeo replaced Tanaka as prime minister; and even though Miki was a long-time enthusiast for improved Sino-Japanese relations, his political backers, Fukuda Takeo, Shiina Etsusaburō, and Nadao Hirokichi, used the anti-hegemony issue to thwart him. (Ironically, it was Fukuda of all people who eventually accepted the anti-hegemony clause.) Miki was further discredited in Chinese eyes when he expressed condolences over the death of Chiang Kai-shek in the spring of 1975 and allowed former Prime Minister Satō to attend the funeral on Taiwan. The peace treaty talks deadlocked in March 1975. Beijing then responded with a full-blown people-to-people campaign to influence Japanese public opinion against the Japanese government. In a preview of the textbook controversy, the Chinese

> intensified their people's diplomacy vis-à-vis every element of Japanese politics and especially the press. They repeated familiar arguments supporting anti-hegemony, stating that Japan's equi-distance policy was unrealistic and that China would patiently wait till Japan came around to accepting her position. Peking invited foreign correspondents, including Japanese, to visit the so-called "death pits" in Tatung where thousands of Chinese miners died during the Japanese

occupation in the 1930s and 1940s. They were also invited to interview some of the survivors about Japanese atrocities and examine human skeletons. Chinese guides told the reporters that China had not sought war reparations from Japan because she "recognized that the broad masses of Japan were not to blame for what happened in cities like Tatung." The reporters were given clear hints that China had been generous toward Japan and it was now Japan's turn to return the favor by agreeing to China's terms on anti-hegemony.[23]

China's final ploy was a carrot-and-stick maneuver offering remarkable economic gains if Japan agreed to the anti-hegemony clause, or endless territorial hassles over places like the Senkaku islands if Japan refused.[24] The economic carrot, in terms of a substantial enlargement of trade, had become available as a result of the death of Mao Zedong in September 1976 and the subsequent overthrow of the so-called Gang of Four. Hua Guofeng tried to consolidate his tenuous legitimacy as Mao's successor by proposing a massive industrialization effort based on imported capital equipment. He published his scheme as the "Outline of the Ten-Year Plan for the Development of the National Economy, 1976–1985."[25] Hua's plan greatly excited the various Japanese *zaikai* (big business) groups, who had been active on the Chinese scene since 1971, even to the extent of conducting their own "private" diplomacy with the Chinese. Increasing trade friction with the Western democracies, and the prospect that Chinese oil sales would give the Chinese the cash to buy Japanese products, made the lure of the China market irresistible. As early as 1975 Miki's chief foreign policy adviser, Hirasawa Kazushige, opined that China could soon supply about 15 percent of Japan's annual oil imports (the actual Chinese shares for 1979, 1980, and 1981 were 3.1 percent, 3.8 percent, and 4.8 percent, respectively).[26]

The breakthrough in the deadlocked talks came in February 1978, when Inayama Yoshihiro, the vice president of Keidanren, and Li Xiwen, the Chinese vice minister for trade, privately negotiated and signed a Long-term Trade Agreement that committed both sides to some $20 billion worth of commercial deals over the next eight years. The following September, Minister of International Trade and Industry Kōmoto Toshio and Vice-Premier Li Xiannian extended the agreement to 1990 and raised the total amount to $60 billion. Fukuda Takeo, who had replaced

Miki as prime minister in December 1976, remained hostile to the Chinese terms for a treaty, both because many in his faction were pro-Taiwan and because he still resented Tanaka's use of the China issue against him in 1972. But China's sweetening of the pot through the trade agreement made the treaty inevitable, and Fukuda now looked only for some face-saving way to accept the anti-hegemony clause.

In the five-article Treaty of Peace and Friendship, signed August 12, 1978, Japan agreed to the anti-hegemony clause (article 2), but in return demanded from the Chinese article 4: "The present treaty shall not affect the position of either contracting party regarding its relations with third countries." The Japanese had made a valiant effort to square both the Chinese and the Soviets, but it did not work. The Russians threatened "retaliatory action" against Japan and noted that "the future will show whether Japan will be able to pursue an independent foreign policy."[27]

For the next two years, two mutually exclusive tendencies dominated the international relations of East Asia, not to mention LDP politics in Japan and presidential politics in the United States. First, the Japanese and the Americans (who recognized Beijing four months after the Japanese peace treaty) proclaimed that their policies had inaugurated a new era of peace and stability in the region and that, as the Japan External Trade Organization (JETRO) put it, "The world is witnessing [in China] the transition of a closed society governed by whimsical political principles into an open system based on sound economics."[28] Second, following China's playing of its "America card," rivalries among Asian Communist nations exploded: the Soviets strengthened their ties with Vietnam, the Vietnamese in turn invaded Cambodia, the Chinese invaded Vietnam, the Soviets invaded Afghanistan, and the Communist militarization of the area advanced to the strategic level (Backfire bombers, SS-20 missiles, long-range Soviet naval patrols, and so forth).

The attempted Japanese and American reconciliations with the Chinese in the late 1970s were not, of course, narrowly motivated or lacking in historical perspective and political imagination. But after their execution, with every passing day it became clearer that they were based on flimsy and often self-deluding premises. The process of change in China—the turmoil surrounding the deaths of Zhou and Mao, the politics of succession, the Chinese estimate of the Soviet threat, and the attempt to find an economic development strategy compatible with continued Communist party dominance—was more complex, and its course less predictable, than the simplifications of panda-mania, political junkets to the Great Wall, and foreign press enthusiasm for "Xidan democracy" (the high tide of liberalism in 1979 following the death of Mao) could encompass.

For the Japanese, the moment of truth came on the economic front, whereas for the Americans it was the Taiwan issue and the Chinese failure to cooperate strategically against the USSR. Only three months after the extension of the Sino-Japanese Long-term Trade Agreement to the year 1990 and to the $60-billion level, the Third Plenary Session of the Eleventh Chinese Communist Party Central Committee (December 1978) scrapped its economic guidelines. Chen Yun and Deng Xiaoping shifted Chinese economic priorities from heavy industrialization to agriculture and consumer-oriented light industries. On September 7, 1980, the party officially abolished Hua Guofeng's Ten-Year Plan for the Development of the National Economy and forced Hua to resign as Chinese premier. What replaced Hua's plan was an ever-lengthening period of "economic readjustment," dominated by fractious debates over the realities of China's economic and political geography. China had expected to pay for Hua's capital imports through oil revenues, but Chinese oil production failed to meet expectations, at least in the short term, and the low quality and refining difficulties of Chinese oil made it uncompetitive with Middle Eastern crude. On top of that, China's educational deficiencies, inherited from the Cultural Revolution, stood in the way of China's absorbing much of the technology that Japan and the West had to offer. Bureaucratic conflicts among different Chinese power centers—national and local governments, rural and urban interests, civilian and military needs, educated and political cadres, new and old bureaucracies—dominated every attempt to come up with a new plan. Perhaps most important of all, the fact that no one had a theory or a foreign example of how to develop a society made up of a billion people meant that great caution had to be exercised not to unleash uncontrollable expectations or unprecedented socio-economic forces.

The Baoshan Iron and Steel Complex near Shanghai symbolized these internal contradictions. As the showcase Sino-Japanese development project, it formed the heart of Hua Guofeng's Ten-Year Plan. Nippon Steel was the prime contractor, and Baoshan was to be a Chinese replica of the Pohang works in Korea and Nippon Steel's plants at Kimitsu and Oita—that is, among the most modern steel-producing facilities on earth. China signed all the contracts to build Baoshan, but then found that it simply could not pay for it. Within the Chinese government, Vice-Premiers Chen Yun, Bo Yibo, and Yao Yilin launched attacks on Hua's economic allies, Li Xiannian, Yu Qiuli, Gu Mu, and Kang Shen. Deng's men charged that the plant was located on soft and sandy soil, that it was too far from coal supplies, that it was situated on Yangtze estuaries too shallow for large ships, and that in general it had been badly bungled. Nippon Steel, then Japan's biggest single enterprise, and Inayama Yoshihiro, its former president, were humiliated. They both replied that the plant was well designed and would produce as specified if the Chinese would only go ahead and build it. During the Sino-Vietnamese war of February 1979 China froze all contracts with Japan and asked for new Japanese financial concessions. The Japanese were thus forewarned. But given the expectations that "China fever" had aroused, nothing could really have prepared the Japanese for the Baoshan Shock.

On January 19, 1981, China unilaterally cancelled signed contracts with Japan worth about ¥300 billion, including the entire second phase of the Baoshan complex (thus making it economically inefficient) and some fifteen petrochemical complexes throughout the country. Work on most of the contracts was already under way, and in several cases Japanese firms had already manufactured and delivered the ordered equipment. The companies affected included Nippon Steel, Mitsui Engineering, Mitsubishi Heavy Industries, the trading companies of Mitsubishi, Mitsui, and C. Itoh, and hundreds of smaller subcontractors, some of whom were threatened with bankruptcy if they were not paid.

"The prospect that China is abandoning all major projects that need big industrial plants," wrote the *Japan Economic Journal,* "poses grave concern for the future of the bilateral long-term trade agreement which essentially consists of barter deals of

Chinese crude oil for Japan's industrial plants. . . . 'Their sheer ignorance of international business practices and rules is amazing,' both businessmen and government officials say."[29] With the cancellation of the contracts Inayama's "private" trade agreement became a governmental headache, and during the summer of 1981, Japanese ministerial representatives shuttled back and forth to Beijing trying to get the Chinese at least to pay penalties for default. The Chinese listened politely, threatened to take their business to the European Community, and asked the Japanese to advance them another ¥300 billion to pay for Baoshan alone. The Japanese government agreed, and in September 1981 work resumed. But Japanese confidence in the China connection had been gravely shaken, and in many industrial quarters the old attitudes of contempt for China reappeared.

THE TEXTBOOK CONTROVERSY

During the summer of 1981, in the middle of the Baoshan Shock, the director of JETRO's China Section mused out loud: "Perhaps they [the Chinese] are counting on support from the sentimentalists in Japan. Remembering China's waiver of wartime reparations, the sentimentalists believe the issue should be solved on a higher, political dimension. In other words, they believe Japan should extend a helping hand as a neighboring country to help China overcome its current hardships."[30] Little could the director have imagined that only a year later the Japanese press would hand China an issue with which to mobilize the "sentimentalists" and humiliate the Japanese government to a greater extent than it had ever been able to do in the past. The "sleeping issues" of Sino-Japanese interaction—such questions as why Japan was a rich nation and China a poor one, what actually had been the state of relations before "normalization," and whether or not Japanese should still feel guilty about China—were about to be reawakened. Although farcical in its concrete details, the textbook controversy hit the Japanese in an area of great emotional vulnerability, and brought home to some of them the risks of continuing to base their foreign policy solely on short-term economic advantages rather than on political principles to which they were committed and that they wanted to see prevail. The textbook controversy conditioned and accompanied a sharp turn in Japanese political leadership of the postwar era, the change from the ceremonial government of Suzuki Zenkō to the verbally activist government of Nakasone Yasuhiro. It also signaled that recriminations about the past will continue to be manipulated by all the nations of the area.

On June 26, 1982, the *Asahi shimbun, Mainichi shimbun,* and *Yomiuri shimbun,* and on June 27 the *Sankei shimbun,* all carried headlines proclaiming that the Ministry of Education had forced the revision of high school history textbooks, changing in particular the word "aggression" against China to "incursion" into China in discussions of the Sino-Japanese War of 1937–45. In other words, the ministry was accused of changing *shinryaku* (literally, "invade and plunder") to *shinkō* (literally, "enter and assault")—or even to the utterly neutral *shinshutsu* (literally, "advance"), a combination of characters that does not exist in this sense in Chinese.[31] Much more was to come before the summer was over, including charges that the Education Ministry had deleted from the texts the number of Chinese casualties in the Japanese "Rape of Nanking" of 1937, that it had ordered the Korean independence struggle of 1919 to be characterized as a "riot," and that it had in general sought to "prettify atrocities," as Beijing's *Renmin ribao* of August 15 (the thirty-seventh anniversary of Japan's surrender) put it. Japanese Foreign Ministry officials declared the whole incident to have been the worst since normalization and to have set back friendly Sino-Japanese relations by at least ten years.[32]

There are many complex aspects to the textbook controversy, but the first point to make is that the initial reports were all untrue: no textbooks had been revised during 1982. On September 7, the *Sankei* carried headlines saying, "We Apologize Deeply to Our Readers," and went on to explain how it and other papers had made a serious mistake in their initial reports. On September 19 the city editor of the *Asahi* also printed an unusually opaque apology for his paper's error; but meanwhile at the Education Ministry, members of the press club covering it tried unsuccessfully to expel the *Sankei* reporters for admitting publicly that they had all been mistaken.[33]

The end, and apparently intended, result of these stories was the humiliation of Japan and of Prime Minister Suzuki Zenkō, who was scheduled to visit Beijing from September 26 to Octo-

ber 2 to celebrate the tenth anniversary of Sino-Japanese normalization. Throughout August and much of September the Chinese
press lambasted a "handful of rightists" in Japan, who were allegedly trying to revive militarism, and the Chinese government
twice rejected official Japanese explanations of the incident and
demanded immediate correction of the school books. When he
finally got to China, Suzuki spent a third of his meeting with
Premier Zhao Ziyang talking about textbooks, and was forced
to reassure party leaders Deng Xiaoping and Hu Yaobang that
Japan was not reverting to its old ways. In his speech to the
Twelfth Party Congress (September 1–11), Chairman Hu dwelt
on the dangers of revived Japanese militarism, but when Suzuki
expressed Japanese misgivings to him and Deng about a possible
Sino-Soviet rapprochement, Hu summarily rejected them.

During February 1983, Suzuki's successor, Nakasone
Yasuhiro, felt he had to say to the Diet that the Sino-Japanese
War of 1937–45 was a "war of aggression" started by Japan;
and Nakasone sent LDP Secretary General Nikaidō Susumu to
Beijing to reassure the Chinese that Japan had its "remnant
militarist forces" under control. On February 19, as Nikaidō
was preparing to leave China, Premier Zhao advised Japan "to
limit its military capability to its defensive needs."[34] Needless to
say, the facts that China maintains the world's largest standing
army, has developed and deployed thermonuclear weapons, and
chose the time of Suzuki's visit to test-fire its first submarine-
launched missiles were not mentioned in either the Chinese or
the Japanese press. A good many Japanese could be forgiven for
thinking that they had been grossly maligned by either their own
press, or a foreign government, or both.

The screening of textbooks by the Japanese government has a
long and checkered political history. It began in 1949, and was
strengthened in 1953 with the revision of the School Education
Law, empowering the minister of education to examine and au-
thorize all school textbooks. He does so by appointing academics and school officials to the Textbooks Screening Research
Council (Kyōkayō Tosho Kentei Chōsa Shingikai), set up in May
1950. These textbook examiners make two kinds of comments
on the new texts submitted for possible adoption to the ministry
by authors and publishers: *kaizen iken,* which are merely suggested improvements and are not mandatory; and *shūsei iken,*

which are required corrections of erroneous facts or figures. Part of the controversy of 1982 focussed on the ministry's allegedly making its recommended changes to the history books *shūsei iken,* although no one knows for sure, because of the confusion in press reports and the ministry's reticence in discussing the matter.

On June 16, 1982, the Education Ministry delivered one sample copy each of some 593 different, newly-authorized elementary and high school textbooks to the ministry's press club. In accordance with established practice, the journalists divided the labor of reading them among the sixteen newspaper and television companies represented in the club. Each paper checked its batch and then shared its reports with all the others. One journalist's report, later identified as coming from Nihon TV, claimed that a world history textbook published by the Jikkyō Shuppan Company had changed "aggression" to "attack"; all the other press services then reported this news without checking it out. When they did look into it, the author of the text denied that his statements had been edited, and claimed that he had been misunderstood and misquoted when interviewed by Nihon TV, although he acknowledged that he did not have his original manuscript with him at the time of the interview.[35]

The Ministry of Education was silent on this subject until July 30, when Minister Ogawa denied that any changes had been made in 1982, adding that over the previous thirty years the ministry had often recommended and had accepted changes of wording similar to those the press was now making such a fuss about, but had not done so this year. On August 10, a leaked education ministry internal policy document revealed that the ministry did think that textbooks should be standardized in using one word for "invasion"; that the Korean independence movement of 1919 did involve "riots" *(bōdō);* and that the number of deaths at Nanking in December 1937 was in dispute.[36]

The real background to this controversy was the decades-long dispute between the Communist-dominated Japan Teachers' Union (Nikkyōso) and the Liberal Democratic Party's conservative education-policy specialists *(bunkyōzoku)* over the political content of educational materials.[37] In postwar Japan, textbooks normally have been written with a leftist bias in an attempt to get the teachers to adopt them, and then the LDP has pressured the

Ministry of Education to remove the leftist bias via its screening and recommending procedures. This struggle became a national cause célèbre in 1965 when the leftist historian Ienaga Saburō sued the minister of education over changes ordered in a new edition of a history textbook that he had written. He also claimed that the screening procedures violated article 26 of the constitution (freedom of education). In 1970 Ienaga won his suit in the Tokyo District Court, but the ministry informed local school boards that the court's decision was not binding on them and nothing actually changed; and in March 1986 the Tokyo High Court ovreturned the district court's decision and ruled that state screening of textbooks did not and does not run counter to the constitution.[38] During 1981 the LDP's Textbook Problems Subcommittee announced a draft bill to strengthen the screening system, and began deliberating it with various party and Diet groups. Some Japanese writers believe that the 1982 controversy was Nikkyōso's counterattack against the LDP's plans—a way of warning the Education Ministry's press club about the screenings.[39]

Although the Japanese press published its first revelations on June 26, no newspaper or government official in China took up the issue politically until July 20. That was the day on which the LDP's Special Council for International Economic Policy (Jimintō Kokusai Keizai Taisaku Tokubetsu Chōsa Kai), headed by former MITI Minister Ezaki Masumi, arrived in Taipei after a tour of Southeast Asia. The Sino-American negotiations over American arms sales to the Republic of China were then at their most delicate stage (the U.S.-PRC joint communiqué attempting to compromise the issue was released on August 17, 1982); and this evidence that Japan was improving its economic ties with Taiwan clearly ran counter to Beijing's strategy. Furthermore, Deng Xiaoping was fighting off internal attacks from party and military rivals who were trying to embarrass him over his U.S. policy and the Taiwan issue before the opening of the Twelfth Party Congress. He could not appear soft on anything having to do with Taiwan, and also needed a diversionary issue.[40] It thus seems doubtful that the Chinese government was truly interested in Japanese school textbooks, but there can be no doubt that it found in the textbook controversy a convenient lever to try to bring the Japanese government to heel, in which it was largely successful.

Beyond China's concerns, however, the textbook controversy opened old wounds in other parts of Asia that genuinely shocked and mortified the attentive Japanese public. Protests against Japan's cavalier attitude toward its earlier imperialism (regardless of the actual details of textbook revisions in Japan) erupted in Singapore, Hong Kong, Okinawa, and particularly the Republic of Korea. If the Chinese reaction was staged by the government for its own purposes, the Korean reaction—including mass demonstrations, boycotts, and threats to break off diplomatic relations—clearly had a popular basis.[41] Since many of the LDP's educational specialists belong to the Fukuda, Kōmoto, and (former) Nakagawa factions and are strong supporters of Japanese-South Korean cooperation, they were appalled by the evidence of Korean outrage over Japanese insensitivity to the past. These Asian reactions were further stimulated by new developments in Japan: former Prime Minister Kishi's poorly timed proposal to build a monument on Mt. Fuji honoring Japanese who had worked in Manchuria; the publication and serialization in *Akahata* (organ of the Japanese Communist Party) of Morimura Seiichi's *Akuma no hōshoku (The Devil's Gluttony)*, which details medical-experiment atrocities committed by Japanese against Chinese and Korean prisoners during World War II; and the première on August 7, 1982 of Tōei's popular motion picture *Dai Nippon teikoku (The Empire of Great Japan)*, which glosses over questions of Japan's responsibility for the war.

By September 1982 the Chinese and the Koreans had accepted Japan's apologies and promises to re-revise its (actually unrevised) textbooks, and the textbook controversy was officially over. But within Japan it continued, and took on a deeper and more serious dimension. Various writers revealed that even thirty years ago, at the height of postwar contrition, textbooks made no mention at all of the history of Korea between 1910 and 1950 or of the Rape of Nanking, and that because the Japanese educational system is so oriented toward preparing students for entrance examinations, few students ever actually read their texts on post-Meiji history since the examination questions normally concentrate on earlier periods.[42] The most important follow-up investigations centered on the failings of the Japanese press: its obsequiousness toward China, its persistent leftist bias, its failure to report serious news events that do not square with its ideological tendencies, and its unchecked power to influence and occasionally even determine Japanese foreign policy.[43] Nonetheless, if the openness of Japanese democracy had caused the nation some embarrassment during 1982, the result was a victory for still more openness: previously delicate subjects such as Japan's ambivalence toward the rest of Asia, the ease with which other nations make it a scapegoat, and the responsibilities of the press in a modern mass democracy were finally being aired.

CONCLUSIONS AND PROSPECTS

In 1885 Fukuzawa Yukichi wrote a famous essay entitled *Datsuaron,* or "Getting Out of Asia," in which he advocated that Japan renounce its Asian heritage in favor of all-out modernization on the Western model.[44] A century later it appears that Japan has followed Fukuzawa's advice to the letter: it remains geographically an Asian country, but has become, in fact, a global economic power in terms of the markets it depends on both for its resources and sales. The interesting thing about Japan's process of *datsua,* however, is that it became most pronounced in the postwar period. Before and during the war, Fukuzawa may have wanted Japan out of Asia, but Japanese idealists, colonialists, and militarists ensured that it stay in.[45] However, from 1952 down to sometime after the normalization of relations with China, Japan was preoccupied with developing new markets to replace those it lost as a result of war and revolution, and it paid little or no attention to East Asia, intellectually or politically, except insofar as it had to, as a result of American leadership or pressure. Except for a few specialists, the Japanese people also seemed to forget about the concrete details of their earlier Asian period. To the extent that they thought about Asia at all, it was in terms of abstractions about their own feelings of guilt, or as a tool for criticizing American policies that nonetheless they profited from and followed, or as a place to go for cheap vacations.

This collective Japanese amnesia about Asia, uncontaminated

by much in the way of serious political analysis or reflection, began subtly to change during the 1970s. The opening to China was the major cause of change, but other factors also figured, including Japan's achievement of economic great-power status, the Nixon Shocks, the oil shocks of 1973 and 1979, the anti-Japanese riots of 1974 in Southeast Asia, the emergence of newly industrialized countries in non-Communist East Asia as potential economic rivals to Japan, and the United States' growing irritation with Japan's inability to declare itself sincerely as part of the democratic alliance.

The Vietnamese war was also important. Its similarities to Japan's disastrous intervention on the continent a quarter-century earlier were obvious to many older Japanese, and the fact that it ended with the United States' humbling defeat helped lighten Japan's guilty conscience about its own earlier behavior in a guerrilla war in China. The Western allies of World War II, and particularly the United States, had long castigated Japan for its conduct of the war in China; but now in light of Americans' own self-reflection, it seemed that perhaps Japan's policies in China had been merely mistaken instead of being morally reprehensible, as the postwar Japanese generation had come to think. The parallel was not exact, of course. Public opinion in the United States had been an important influence on the American decision to disengage from Vietnam, whereas domestic views had played no part at all in Japan's forcible eviction from China, Korea, and the rest of its former empire.[46]

During the early 1980s Japan's domestic foreign policy debate became much livelier and more candid than it had been fifteen years earlier. Rearmament, the Soviet threat, the real terms of the Japanese-American "alliance," and the ambiguities of China's Communist development schemes were put on the record for Japanese public and political debate, eventually perhaps even for Japanese decision and commitment.

The Sino-Japanese relationship is central to each of these important issues. There are grounds for optimism in that Sino-Japanese economic and technological collaboration continues and also because Japan and China seem to be understanding each other more realistically. Equally important, however, the events of the late 1970s and the early 1980s—particularly the textbook controversy—stimulated new forms of nationalism both in

China and Japan. In China, nationalism has been the most potent emotional force in domestic politics since at least the 1930s. Leaders such as Mao Zedong and Zhou Enlai, whose nationalistic credentials were unassailable, could on occasion ignore or deflect the nationalist issue when it suited their purposes to do so—as, for example, in Zhou's handling of the Taiwan issue with Kissinger or in the PRC's position on the status of Macao at the time of the 1974 Portuguese revolution. But after the deaths of Mao and Zhou in 1976, and particularly after Deng Xiaoping launched the regime on a liberalizing course, the nationalist issue again became salient in domestic political struggles. No Chinese leader, including Deng, could allow himself to be made vulnerable on questions of slights or challenges to Chinese sovereignty. The textbook controversy, like the revived dispute with the United States over the status of Taiwan and the dispute with Great Britain over the status of Hong Kong, showed that the Chinese leaders had to put China's nationalistic self-esteem ahead of other goals, even when this potentially threatened the country's substantive modernization efforts.

About the same time as the revival of the nationalist issue in China, a new form of Japanese national pride, and a growing irritation with foreign politicians' making Japan a scapegoat whenever it served their immediate interests, appeared across the East China Sea. Japan was no longer responding with contrition or silence to charges of reviving militarism, unfair trade practices, a uniquely barbarous imperialist past, or inadequate defense expenditures. This new Japanese attitude was reflected internally in the virulent polemics about press behavior in the wake of the textbook controversy, in the unending tide of books about Japan's unusual social institutions, and in the novel thought for many postwar Japanese that foreign critics might be interfering in Japan's domestic affairs.

As of the early 1980s, neither a revived Chinese nationalism nor a new Japanese nationalism was so advanced as to pose serious obstacles to international cooperation and compromise on many different planes. China's opening to the democratic capitalist nations and its efforts to modernize both its economy and its ideology were among the most significant developments of the second half of the century; and Japan clearly recognized that its role in helping the Chinese was logical, complementary, and in the interests of all the peoples of the region. Both China and Japan need a relatively long period of peaceful commercial and cultural interaction. This will help to underwrite China's new course with real achievements and to put the past issues of imperalism and revolution into a more analytical and less emotional perspective. To achieve such a period of steady development, both sides must avoid exploiting nationalistic issues for short-term political satisfactions. That they will do so is, however, in no way guaranteed by the logic of their mutual interests.

12

Reflections on the Dilemma of Japanese Defense

Nakasone Yasuhiro, prime minister of Japan from 1982 to 1987, is the only postwar prime minister who also served earlier in his political career as director general of the Bōei-chō (Japanese Defense Agency). Nakasone is very interested in defense issues and proud of his service at the Bōei-chō. In his commencement speech to the 1985 graduating class from the Defense Academy at Yokosuka, Nakasone reminded his audience that it is his calligraphy, from the time he headed the Defense Agency, that hangs in the great hall of the Defense Academy. His writing is composed of six kanji (characters), *fūu shinzan garyō*, that mean, approximately, "Amid wind and rain, hidden deep in the mountains, there lies a reclining dragon."

In his speech Nakasone indicated that he meant by these words that the Japanese Self Defense Forces (SDF) are always ready for emergencies, something like "semper fidelis," the slogan of the U.S. Marine Corps. But the beauty of Chinese characters is that they are open to a variety of interpretations. *Garyō*, for example, means "reclining dragon," but it also has the connotation of a great man who has had no opportunity to display his real talents, a possible reference to Nakasone himself in 1970–71 when he was director-general of the Defense Agency, or to the postwar Japanese army itself. In fact, the whole phrase conjures up an image of a group of samurai patiently waiting for the time when their talents would again be needed. The thought that the woods of Japan might harbor some old-style Japanese warriors in SDF uniforms was a constant theme of the Japanese defense debate of the 1980s, and it seems to pose a major dilemma for Japan and its allies.[1]

A dilemma is a situation that requires a choice among unpleasant alternatives. The first horn of the contemporary Japanese defense dilemma, then, refers to the fears—real, pretended, and imagined—of the citizens of Japan, the nations Japan invaded during World War II, and the United States and the former USSR that Japanese rearmament is imminent and that it will lead to "revived Japanese militarism." From the moment Nakasone took office as prime minister, his critics raised suspicions that he intended to end Japan's alleged pacifism and eliminate the postwar political barriers that some Japanese think prevent a return to militarism. These barriers include the war-renouncing clause (Art. 9) in the Constitution of 1947; the three non-nuclear principles (*hikaku sangensoku*—"Japan will not produce, possess, or let others bring in" nuclear weapons) that Prime Minister Satō first enunciated in 1968; and the ceiling on defense expenditures of 1 percent of gross national product (GNP) that Prime Minister Miki established in 1976. Nakasone himself certainly contributed to the suspicions about his intentions by his repeated statement that he would like to bring about a "general settling of accounts concerning postwar politics" *(sengo seiji no sōkessan)*, which in context was a clear euphemism for reform of Japan's postwar pacifist and dependent foreign policy.[2]

As an example of the kind of criticism Nakasone received, during September 1985 the well-known Japanese commentator and literary critic Katō Shūichi charged that three events of that past summer actually signaled the "rebirth of a militaristic Japan." The three events were an alleged breeching of the 1 percent barrier, Nakasone's formal visit to Yasukuni Shrine (a religious war memorial in Tokyo), and the Liberal Democratic Party's introduction in the Diet of a draft Official Secrets Law.[3] As it turned out, the 1 percent ceiling was not broken; Nakasone was damned if he did and damned if he did not go to Yasukuni, much like the situation President Reagan faced on his visit to the Bitburg military cemetery in Germany in May of that same year; and the Official Secrets Law was intended, at least in part, to control flagrant industrial espionage in Japan by the Soviet Union and other powers.[4] The idea that these three events added up to a "militaristic Japan" was anything but self-evident.

Katō Shūichi's was not the only voice raised against the apparent trend of events. In the United States one of the biographers of the famous novelist Mishima Yukio—whom Nakasone had aided when he was head of the Defense Agency and who committed *seppuku* on November 25, 1970, after seizing control of the main army base in Tokyo—commented on a recently released film of Mishima's life. Henry Scott Stokes wrote that the Mishima case personified for him the dangers of Japanese rearmament. In Scott Stokes's view, "Today Japan has no strategic forces at all: no nuclear submarines, no aircraft carriers, no nuclear-tipped ICBMs. I do not know what is to come in Japan. But I am sure of this: the world is in enough trouble as it is without adding to its infinite complications the terrifying prospect of a suicidal, nuclear-armed Japan." Henry Scott Stokes clearly believes that Mishima was not so much an aberrant Japanese as an extreme but exemplary metaphor for Japan's frustrations with its dependent foreign policy and that this was the reason Nakasone befriended him.[5] Some people in China spent the fortieth anniversary of the end of the Pacific War saying over and over again essentially the same thing as Scott Stokes.[6]

Fear of revived militarism, then, constitutes the first horn of the Japanese defense dilemma. The other horn of the dilemma is, of course, the persistent charge that Japan is taking a "free ride" on the backs of the Americans, Koreans, Taiwanese, and all the other people of the Pacific Basin who take seriously their responsibilities to try to maintain a stable and secure environment. This free ride is doubly galling since no nation profits more from international political and military security than Japan. Certainly, if one views the issue of national defense expenditures without taking into account military threats, the geographical aspects of strategy, or possible non-defense-budget contributions to security, Japan does not seem to be carrying its share of the regional or global security burden (see Table 12-1). By comparison with South Korea, for example, Japan's contribution is minimal. With a population of about 40 million and a per capita 1982 GNP of $1,734 (compared with Japan's 119 million people and a per capital income of $8,975), Korea was still able to devote some 6 percent of its GNP to defense and to maintain some 540,000 men under arms. In 1983, Japan's total armed forces personnel amounted to 241,000, leading one commentator to observe: "The Japanese Self-Defense Force has never attained its maximum strength of 270,000, turnover is unacceptably high, and the proportion of officers to NCO's and of NCO's to enlisted men is ridiculously high—indeed, no forces of the size of the JSDF sport a comparable contingent of generals and admirals."[7] American congressmen who enjoy "Korea-bashing" because of Korea's favorable balance of trade with the United States and who erroneously characterize it as "another Japan" should be reminded of this major difference between Korea and Japan.

It was comparisons such as the one between the Korean and Japanese defense burdens that, on September 9, 1985, caused U.S. Undersecretary of State for Political Affairs Michael Armacost openly to criticize Japan for remaining within the 1 percent ceiling in setting the fiscal year 1986 budget for defense

TABLE 12-1   Defense Expenditures, Selected Nations, 1982

NATION	TOTAL (BILLIONS US$)	PER CAPITA	PERCENTAGE OF GOVERNMENT EXPENDITURES	PERCENTAGE OF GNP
U.S.	215.9	$938	29.2	7.2
USSR (1981)	191.0	713	11–13.0	8.4–15.0
West Germany	28.5	461	27.9	4.3
Britain	24.2	432	11.9	5.1
France	22.0	408	17.5	4.1
Japan	10.8	91	5.2	0.93
Israel	8.2	2,060	40.7	37.9
Canada	6.0	247	9.2	2.0
South Korea	5.2	132	35.0	7.6
Taiwan	3.3	183	39.4	7.3
Sweden	3.0	365	6.9	3.1
Switzerland	2.0	320	21.4	2.1

Sources: PHP Kenkyūjo, *Za dēta fairu 1984* (Tokyo: PHP Kenkyūjo, 1984), pp. 60–61, 286; Japan Institute for Social and Economic Affairs, *Japan 1983, An International Comparison* (Tokyo: Keizai Kōhō Center, 1983), p. 75.

spending. And on September 12, Secretary of Defense Weinberger declared himself "disappointed" with Japan. Looking at these same figures, however, Soviet Communist Party Secretary Gorbachev blasted "the militant forces of imperialism" that were "pressing for the remilitarization of Japan and for the establishment of an aggressive Washington–Tokyo–Seoul grouping."[8]

Like the charge of "revived Japanese militarism," the charge that Japan is enjoying a "free ride on defense" requires closer scrutiny. When, for example, Edward Olsen argues that it is the American taxpayer who pays for Japan's military protection, he is simply wrong.[9] Whoever is paying for the American armed forces, it is assuredly not the American taxpayer. United States budget outlays for national defense in 1983, 1984, and 1985 were $209.9 billion, $237.6 billion, and $272 billion, respectively. Corresponding to these expenditures, the United States government's budget deficits for these three years were $195.4 billion, $177.8 billion, and $179.0 billion.[10] It is no secret that for the first half of the 1980s Americans consumed a great deal more than they produced and paid the difference by borrowing from foreigners. One major source of American consumption was its defense establishment, and the leading foreigners helping out their American friends were the Japanese. During 1984 alone, Japan exported some $49.7 billion in long-term capital, most of it destined for the United States, where high interest rates promised good returns. Japan could plausibly argue that it was itself paying for about a quarter of the American defense burden and that this was no free ride inasmuch as the Japanese loans to the United States were denominated in dollars, with each percentage point of decline of the dollar against the yen being also a percentage point of pure loss for Japanese investors. Critics of Japan's free ride never seem to remember that no one was actually *paying* for the Reagan defense buildup. Payment was being put off for future generations to deal with.

A different objection to the free-ride argument is that the Americans do not seriously want Japanese rearmament and are, in fact, as alarmist as the Chinese or the Filipinos about a real Japanese military awakening. What the Americans want is for Japan to buy more airplanes and other weapons from the United States in order to relieve the Americans' bilateral trade deficit. In the American mind there has always been an unacknowledged linkage between trade and defense, and the so-called free ride on defense only occurred to the Americans as they thought about the trade issues. This is a point on which the Japanese have been much more candid than the Americans. Kataoka Tetsuya, for example, argues that what the United States wants from Japan is not rearmament or even a real military alliance but "defense cooperation," meaning Japanese purchases of American weapons but no Japanese input into strategy or policy. In Kataoka's view the "conservative pacifism" of Japan "is not a matter of real commitment, but a studied and cerebral posturing that reciprocates the prejudice of the senior partner toward Japan. It is a species of nationalism inverted. . . ." Kataoka believes that American "hegemonism" and Japanese "pacifism" are two sides of the same coin, and that demands for change in one without a change in the other are fruitless. Similarly, he dismisses the concept of comprehensive security advanced by the mainstream conservatives in Japan as "a code word embellishing the status quo with slightly increased foreign aid and a little more active diplomacy such as an Olympic boycott."[11]

What Kataoka and others of his persuasion are concerned about is that the Japanese-American Security Treaty is anything but an alliance between equals. It commits the United States to come to the aid of Japan if it is attacked, but it does not require that the Japanese do anything at all if the United States is attacked. No doubt there are Japanese who do not want a real alliance with the United States, but what is much less widely appreciated is that there are also Americans who do not want a real alliance either. They like the current arrangements in which the Japanese are clearly guided in their foreign policies by the State Department and the Pentagon. Many Americans seem more attracted to the idea of an expansion of Japanese economic aid to the Third World than to the idea of a genuine Japanese-American alliance.[12] A Japanese reflection of such views is Masuzoe Yoichi's contention that the mainstream of the LDP maintains the "one-percent-of-GNP" ceiling on defense expenditures primarily as a form of nationalistic resistance to heavy-handed American pressure tactics.[13]

Like its classical archetype, Scylla and Charybdis, the Japanese defense problem is a genuine dilemma. On the one hand, there is the possibility that an open commitment to rearmament might escalate out of control; on the other hand, there is international resentment about Japan's niggardly contributions to the common defense. Like all real dilemmas, this one cannot be solved by favoring one view over the other. In classical mythology the rock of Scylla and the whirlpool of Charybdis were things that one had to navigate between. Nakasone, the first prime minister since Hatoyama and Kishi of the 1950s who had anything at all interesting to say on the subject of Japanese defense, tried to be such a navigator. Therefore, in order to assess Japan's real contributions to northeast Asian security, we must look at what the Nakasone government tried to do and what it actually accomplished.

BACKGROUND TO THE NAKASONE ADMINISTRATION

On June 12, 1984, in testimony before the U.S. Congress, the assistant secretary of state for East Asian and Pacific affairs, Paul Wolfowitz, said concerning Japan, "The days of 'economic giant, political pygmy' are over."[14] It is not at all clear that Wolfowitz believed that this was true—Americans are accustomed to a certain degree of hyperbole in the assertions of their bureaucrats—but if Japan is at least beginning to play an expanded political role in international affairs, the process of change began during the Carter administration. During the last years of President Carter's administration, analysts of Japan noted "a new assertiveness that arises not simply from an awareness of the country's economic power but from a new sense of confidence in the strength of the nation's economic, social, and political institutions and in the Japanese way of doing things." Not unconnected with this new assertiveness, the last Carter years were also a time when "Japanese leadership groups share[d] a general lack of confidence in American leadership."[15]

The Carter administration was the first elected post-Vietnam government in the United States, and the particular lessons it chose to learn from Vietnam were those associated with the neo-isolationism of the domestic antiwar movement.[16] Most particularly, the Carter administration drew an analogy between Vietnam and Korea and then publicly declared its intention to withdraw all U.S. ground forces from Korea. Probably nothing else ever said or done by the United States in the postwar world so seriously alarmed mainstream Japanese opinion as this American decision unilaterally to give up maintaining the balance of power on the Korean peninsula. Japan protested directly and privately to the president, who reversed himself, but the episode was instructive to both sides. It confirmed in the minds of Americans that the Japanese would take initiatives (e.g., prepare to defend themselves) only when they were forced to do so by U.S. decisions.

Ronald Reagan's 1980 election as president only accelerated Japan's reappraisal of its situation. Like other American allies, the Japanese were poorly informed about Reagan and the mood of the Americans who voted for him. The Japanese tended to think of Reagan as a former movie actor rather than as a former two-term governor of California. When President Reagan then ostentatiously received as his first Asian visitor to the White House the president of the Republic of Korea, the Japanese knew that the Japanese-American relationship was under some strain.

Interestingly enough, however, the alleged "new assertiveness" of the Japanese never amounted to anything substantive until 1982, which was the turning point. The replacement of Alexander Haig with George Shultz as secretary of state signified, among other things, the ending of any serious attempt by the Americans to build a strategic relationship with the Chinese. There would continue to be military exchanges between Chinese and American leaders, as well as growing economic and cultural ties, but it became apparent that the Chinese did not want closer ties and that the Americans could not find in China a substitute for their own efforts in Asia. It was in this context that in November 1982 Nakasone Yasuhiro became prime minister of Japan, and he more than any other recent Japanese leader began to give some substance to Japan's "new assertiveness."

Nakasone had long been identified with the domestic school of political opinion that advocated revision of the postwar Constitution in order to allow Japan openly to build its own defense forces. Until the 1980s, however, the issue was more a matter of national self-respect than of national security, since Japan had no credible enemies. China and the Soviet Union did not threaten Japan directly, even though the situation in Korea did. But at the time the Korean War erupted, Japan was still an occupied country. The U.S. presence in Korea was a great boon to Japan, but Japan had not caused the American intervention there, and nothing Japan could have done would have altered the situation. For at least 25 years the United States extended its defense umbrella over Japan, but Japan did not really need it since the weather was fair.

By the time Nakasone became prime minister, the weather had changed. Beginning in the late 1970s, Japan's relations with the USSR seriously deteriorated, and, for the first time since the Russo-Japanese War, a Russian military threat in the Pacific became a new element in the politics of the region. The causes of this deterioration included the Sino-Japanese treaty of 1978, which the USSR regarded as hostile; the Soviet invasion of Afghanistan and the subsequent U.S.-initiated anti-Soviet sanctions which the Japanese joined; the Soviets' support of Vietnamese imperialism throughout Indochina; the USSR's military buildup in East Asia, including the construction of military bases in the southern Kurile Islands claimed by Japan and the deployment of at least 135 SS-20 IRBMs at some 13 Siberian bases; and the shooting down on September 1, 1983, of Korean Air Lines flight 007 over the Sea of Japan.[17] Only a minority in Japan doubted any longer that Japan had a security problem, but Japanese opinion was by no means united on the proper response to this development.

There were several schools of thought. One held that since the Soviet Union had no leverage or influence in East Asia other than military intimidation, it would be better to try to shift the contest to economic grounds rather than to compete on Russia's terms. Most Japanese were openly derisory of the performance of the Soviet economy, and thought it would be unwise to overreact to Russia's military provocations. Moreover, since it was impossible for Japan to compete militarily with the USSR, a low-risk low-profile foreign policy seemed the optimum choice.

Nakasone did not necessarily differ from this position in terms of fundamentals, but he was very different in atmospherics. He recognized that the Reagan administration was rebuilding American military capability, and he moved decisively to identify Japan with Reagan's policies and to re-cement the Japanese-U.S. alliance. In some seven summit meetings with Reagan,

Nakasone developed a special "Ron and Yasu" relationship (i.e., a personal friendship). He also supported Reagan's deployment of Euromissiles, took measures to defuse trade friction between Japan and the United States, and in many ways demonstrated a statesmanship that few Americans had thought possible from a Japanese leader. By the time Nakasone and Reagan were both reelected for second terms (the first time in the United States since Nixon and in Japan since Satō), every American official had come to regard Nakasone as virtually the best Japanese prime minister that Americans had encountered in the postwar world.[18] Concomitant with the flowering of the Ron-Yasu relationship, it became de rigueur for U.S. diplomats to declare on every appropriate occasion that Japan was the "cornerstone" of U.S. policy in East Asia.

The problem remained that Nakasone was not nearly as popular in Japan as he was in the United States. In Japan he suffered from his "hawkish" reputation, from the fact that his tenure in office depended on continued support from "Tanaka, Inc." (the faction of the ruling party that until Tanaka's stroke on February 27, 1985, actually ran the country), and from his allegedly un-Japanese personality, meaning his ability to speak articulately with foreigners without lapsing into panic-stricken silences as his predecessor was wont to do. Nonetheless, through his bold initiatives with Korea (Nakasone was the first Japanese prime minister ever to visit Seoul) and his sensitive diplomacy with China and Southeast Asia, Nakasone slowly gained in public opinion. The fact that the Americans were impressed with him also raised his value in Japan, if only on instrumental grounds. Nakasone could not easily deliver on all the things the foreigners expected of Japan, nor could he prevent external interest groups from using Japan as a scapegoat or diversion (as, for example, in the "textbook controversy" of 1982). But to the extent that Japan was no longer perceived as a political pygmy, this achievement was due almost entirely to Nakasone's leadership.

According to the Jiji Press's October 1985 poll of public opinion, 48.1 percent of the population gave their support to the Nakasone cabinet, up slightly from the 47.9 percent recorded during September. The support rate for the ruling Liberal Democratic Party was also high, at 37.2 percent, but well under that given to the party's leader. Support for the largest opposition party, the Socialists, dropped from 7.8 percent to 6.4 percent during the same period, the lowest rating in three years.[19] There are virtually no other cases of Japanese cabinets whose popularity went up after three years in office, particularly since Nakasone's faction within the party was only the fourth largest and was not a major distributor of patronage or influence. The astonishing thing about Nakasone's popularity was that he was without question the most nationalistic and the most militarily realistic leader of Japan for at least 25 years, even though Japan claims loudly and publicly to be a pacifist nation.

NAKASONE ON DEFENSE

Nakasone's defense policy can be broken down into four large components: steady increases in defense expenditures, close cooperation with the United States, an attempt to reengage the Soviet Union diplomatically, and a major effort at public education. Let me briefly survey each of these.

During each of Nakasone's first three years in office the military budget went up by at least 4.6 percent in real terms. This achievement was extraordinary in that Nakasone imposed flat budgets on virtually all other government expenditures as a matter of fiscal restraint. His defense increases were also made in the face of public opinion polls from his own Prime Minister's Office showing that 54.1 percent of the public did not see any reason to change defense spending, while only 14.2 percent wanted to increase it and 17.7 percent wanted to cut it.[20] He also had to learn to live with the one-percent-of-GNP ceiling. He said that he would like to get rid of it, but every time he did so, the other faction leaders in the ruling party championed it and formed tactical alliances against him. Table 12-2 details the general trend of Japanese defense expenditures since the creation of the LDP in 1955. It reveals that although Nakasone greatly increased the amount spent on defense, he did not increase Japan's defense burden, given Japan's continuing economic growth. None of the percentages in the table show significant change since about 1980.

The year 1985 saw two major fights over defense expenditures that offer insights into Nakasone's methods. The first was over enactment of a five-year defense procurement plan for 1986 to

TABLE 12-2   Trends in Level and Share of Japan's Defense Expenditures, 1955–84 (fiscal years)

	DEFENSE EXPENDITURES (BILLION ¥)	CHANGE IN AMOUNT OVER PREVIOUS YEAR	RATIO TO GNP	RATIO TO GENERAL ACCOUNT BUDGET
1955	134.9	−3.3%	1.78%	13.61%
1960	156.9	0.6	1.23	9.99
1965	301.4	9.6	1.07	8.24
1970	569.5	17.7	0.79	7.16
1975	1,327.3	21.4	0.84	6.23
1977	1,690.6	11.8	0.88	5.93
1978	1,901.0	12.4	0.90	5.54
1979	2,094.5	10.2	0.90	5.43
1980	2,230.2	6.5	0.90	5.24
1981	2,400.0	7.6	0.91	5.13
1982	2,586.1	7.8	0.93	5.21
1983	2,754.2	6.5	0.98	5.47
1984	2,934.6	6.5	0.99	5.80

Source: Japan Institute for Social and Economic Affairs, *Japan 1984: An International Comparison* (Tokyo: Keizai Kōhō Center, 1984), p. 86.

1990. It was to replace the Defense Agency's Midterm Program Estimate for 1983–87, which was merely an internal plan of the Agency. In Nakasone's original scheme, the new five-year-plan was to be formally adopted by the National Defense Council and the cabinet, both of which would also simultaneously scrap the 1 percent ceiling. The main goal was to make the defense procurement plan an officially endorsed policy of the cabinet, something it had never been in the past. As it turned out, the proposal to abolish the 1 percent rule produced a storm of criticism, and Nakasone had to change his tactics. Under intense pressure from the Suzuki faction and Nakasone's coalition partner, the New Liberal Club, Nakasone divided the 1 percent ceiling from the five-year procurement plan and dealt with them separately, even though the five-year plan would ultimately breech the barrier if enacted unchanged. On September 18, 1985, Nakasone had his victory. A joint session of the cabinet and the LDP's Executive Board approved Nakasone's plan to spend 18.4 trillion yen on defense for the period 1986–90, even though this amount was 1.04 percent of the government's estimated 1,772 trillion yen GNP for the five-year period. Nonetheless, Nakasone had to promise to keep at least the first year's expenditures under 1 percent of GNP.

His solution was some statistical but face-saving sleight of hand. During early October the Economic Planning Agency released a new official estimate of the growth of Japan's GNP using fiscal year 1980 rather than fiscal year 1975 as the base year for its calculations. On this basis the EPA was able to boost estimated GNP for 1986 by about 7 trillion yen, enough to cover the first year's increase in defensive outlays and still keep them at an official 0.9371 percent of estimated GNP.[21] Needless to say, 1 percent of the GNP of the world's second largest economy is both a large amount of money and a moving target, particularly when it is realized that Japan does not include pensions for retired servicemen in the defense budget as is the normal practice in the West. The five-year plan included 187 F-15 Eagles by the end of the period and 100 P3C antisubmarine aircraft. Not least of Japan's defense expenditures was about $1.2 billion per annum for the upkeep of U.S. forces in Japan, including plans for two squadrons of F-16s at Misawa, the first of which arrived there during September 1985.

The second fight of the summer came over the actual defense budget for fiscal 1986. The primary contestants here were on the one hand Takeshita Noboru, then minister of finance, one of the leaders of the dominant Tanaka faction, and an active candidate to succeed Nakasone, and on the other, Katō Kōichi, the director general of the Defense Agency. Takeshita and his ministry habitually opposed increases in the defense budget, giving first priority instead to reducing the large government deficits, and they knew that their views were popular with the public.

Nakasone's answer to both the Ministry of Finance and his factional rivals in the party was to appoint younger politicians known for their great promise but from dovish factions to head the Defense Agency. Such directors seem to work harder than older politicians at forcefully representing their agency; and because they are thought to be future leaders, they receive the enthusiastic backing of their fellow faction members regardless of ideology. This was precisely the case with Director General Katō. Appointed by Nakasone in November 1984, Katō was then only 46 years old. In 1960, he was an active demonstrator at Tokyo University during the Security Treaty riots, which is an unusual background for a Defense Agency chief, to say the least. He was a former foreign ministry official, having served as a vice consul in Hong Kong before turning to politics. He had been elected five times from the Yamagata second district and was a member of the Suzuki faction.

Katō turned out to be a vigorous, hard-working defense chief. After bitter bargaining and a face-to-face confrontation on July 26 between Katō and Takeshita that lasted until 3 A.M., the Ministry of Finance agreed to a defense budget request for fiscal 1986 of 3.36 trillion yen, which was a 7.3 percent increase over fiscal year 1985 and only slightly under the 8 percent increase Katō had originally requested. At the same time the ministry cut all other government expenditures except in the favored areas of foreign aid, energy projects, high-tech research and development, and personnel costs. In the final fiscal 1986 budget adopted by the cabinet, defense survived at 3.34 trillion yen, a jump of 6.58 percent over 1985. The year 1986 was the sixth year in a row that major defense spending increases occurred.

In addition to spending increases, another major element of the Nakasone defense policy was his strong commitment to the Japanese-American alliance. The broad political aspects of this matter have already been discussed. In concrete terms, the United States asked Japan in 1983 to assume primary responsibility for three sectors of defense in its adjacent waters: control of the seas south to the Philippines and Guam; the ability to mine and blockade the straits connecting the Sea of Japan with the Pacific Ocean; and the building of an air defense screen across the Japanese islands to interdict Soviet long-range bombers, fighter bombers, and tactical aircraft. In order to fulfill these tasks, the United States estimated that Japan would need 14 squadrons (350 airplanes) of F-15 interceptors, 70 destroyers, 25 submarines, and 125 P3C antisubmarine aircraft.[22] Nakasone on different occasions agreed to these three operational tasks; his five-year defense procurement plan, although not identical with U.S. estimates of needs, was intended to provide the means. Under Nakasone, joint exercises between Japanese and American forces were also expanded; F-16s were deployed on the Japanese home islands; the Japanese agreed to install over-the-horizon radar on Iwo Jima, providing surveillance over much of eastern Siberia; and an effective (if not implemented) agreement was concluded between Japan and the United States on the transfer of militarily relevant technology.

The third element of Nakasone's defense policy was the diplomatic attempt to reengage the USSR in a dialogue about mutual problems. The goal here was to bring some of Japan's economic leverage to bear on Soviet behavior. This attempt required close cooperation and coordination with the Reagan administration—one reason why Nakasone, in his 1985 New Year's visit with Reagan, strongly endorsed U.S. policies aimed at restarting negotiations with the USSR over strategic arms reductions.

Nakasone started his Soviet campaign in November 1984 at the funeral of Indira Gandhi. He had a meeting with then Soviet Premier Nikolai Tikhonov, which seemed to lead to an improved climate at the December 12–14, 1984, meeting of the Japan-Soviet Business Cooperation Committee. Nakasone also wanted to end the Soviets' freezing out of Japan such as occurred at the Brezhnev funeral, when Andropov met some five foreign leaders but refused to give the Japanese prime minister even ten minutes. Change on this front began in March 1985, when Mikhail Gorbachev met Nakasone in the Kremlin. In January 1986 the new Soviet foreign minister, Eduard Shevardnadze, visited Japan for bilateral talks. However, for Nakasone's opening to the USSR to have any lasting effect, the Russians must show some flexibility on the Habomai and Shikotan islands in return for a Japanese renunciation of its claim to the two southernmost Kurile Islands.

The final element of Nakasone's defense policy was his attempt to change the long-standing Japanese consensus on defense. He has tried to do this sometimes through bold gestures (such as his trip to Korea in 1983 and his agreement to supply $4 billion in economic aid to Korea over a five-year period), sometimes through unusual diplomatic ploys (such as his speech to the U.N. General Assembly on October 23, 1985, in which he apologized for Japan's actions during World War II), and sometimes by actions that were certain to arouse controversy (such as his leading the entire cabinet in an official visit to Yasukuni Shrine on August 15, 1985). Virtually every political commentator in Japan attacked Nakasone for his "political mistake" in visiting Yasukuni. But the visit did not seem to have hurt him with the public, and it did help open up Japan's rather constipated discussion of responsibility for the war.

Popular attitudes, including the widespread belief in Japan that it was the "victim" in World War II, remain the greatest single obstacle to a realistic defense policy in Japan. For example, a major Japanese-American public opinion poll of July 1985 found that 79 percent of the Americans questioned believed that the United States would come to the defense of Japan if it were attacked. However, only 42 percent of the Japanese had such a belief, and 54 percent explicitly said that the United States would not defend Japan.[23] Similarly, the eleventh edition of the Defense Agency's annual report, released on August 7, 1985, pointed out that according to a poll taken in November 1984, fewer than 10 percent of Japanese "believe the Self-Defense Forces are effective in maintaining the security of the nation." Most citizens considered the military's principal role to be disaster relief.[24] Nakasone was the first leader since the 1950s even to begin to make a dent in such attitudes.

In short, I believe that Nakasone offered some skillful navigation between the rocks of "revived Japanese militarism" and a "free ride on defense." Few of his predecessors and virtually none of his declared (and actual) successors even challenged the "conservative pacifism" that Yoshida Shigeru laid down as fundamental Japanese policy 35 years ago. It is possible to think of Nakasone as reckless—a nationalist who committed his nation to more unpayable IOU's than any other postwar leader. It is also possible to regard him as the first Japanese statesman of international stature since Yoshida.

Today the world actually knows how the dilemma of Japanese defense will end. The trend of events is unmistakable. By the turn of the century Japan will be a fully independent nation-state, the size of at least two Germanies, defending itself. If Japan is still allied with the United States, the alliance will have a different and as yet unknown basis from the Cold War–oriented Security Treaty. What the world does not know is how to get there. It will take a great deal more Nakasone-style leadership to make the transition from the Self-Defense Forces of today to a national security force for tomorrow. Whether the Japanese political system can produce such leadership will greatly affect the prosperity and stability of the Asia-Pacific region.

13

Rethinking Asia

People around the world, particularly those in the United States and the rich capitalist countries of East Asia, seem to be having great difficulty in understanding how radically different the world has become after the Cold War and the end of superpower bipolarity. Americans continue to fantasize about being the "lone superpower" without realizing that unipolarity renders the global dimension of strategic competition irrelevant. All conflicts are now regional. The Japanese continue to believe that what Donald Hellmann has called their "grotesquely unbalanced 'partnership'" with the United States is still viable and that free trade can be maintained, even though Japan itself refuses to budge on its Gargantuan trade surpluses and does nothing about its "fortress" *(yosai)* economy, to use the name applied to it by Sony chairman Morita Akio.

Meanwhile, major changes challenge almost all received wisdom. The Republic of Korea, for example, has gotten its military back into the barracks after thirty years of what Frank Gibney has described as "hard-as-nails authoritarian government." Just as Japan is recognized as the economic model for the rest of East Asia, South Korea may become the political model for the democratization of these so-called miracle economies.

Korea's achievement in managing the transition to democracy is comparable to Spain's transition from fascism to democracy, both of them involving changes of a revolutionary magnitude. Similarly, China after the 14th Party Congress of 1992 has a political economy that is structurally similar to that of Park Chung Hee's Korea—authoritarian politics combined with market economics—and produces similar rates of growth, except that a Chinese economy growing at 10 percent a year will very quickly alter both the regional and the global balance of power. These developments are conceptually difficult, their implications almost unfathomable without a new framework of understanding. The "vision thing," as George Bush so notoriously put it, is a bigger problem than ever.

In this essay I propose, first, to sketch in some of the things that the end of bipolarity logically entails in America's relations with Japan, Korea, and China; second, to offer a few theoretical generalizations about the related phenomena of transnational economic integration and subnational ethnic fragmentation; and third, to review some of the scenarios for the maintenance of peace and stability in Asia and the Pacific in an era of fundamental structural change.

It is today a cliché to say that the global political economy presents troubling options for the United States. Americans do not know any longer how to order their priorities, but without some new basis for doing so they are in danger of following the former USSR into domestic chaos. The demands of the Cold War led what is now Russia into imperial overstretch and disintegration of its empire, and those same demands weakened the United States, turning it into the world's biggest debtor nation. Neither former superpower could have maintained the old priorities even if the Cold War had continued. The pretensions of superpowerdom are absurd in a period in which Russia, even if it still has nuclear weapons, has become an underdeveloped hinterland, and in which the nature of power has shifted radically from coping with short-term military threats to long-term technological threats. During 1989–91 the United States did not so much "win" the Cold War as jump from the frying pan into the fire. Soviet communism set for the United States a low standard of economic comparison; Germany and Japan have raised the economic stakes considerably.

The Southern Center for International Studies in Atlanta set five questions for the Clinton administration as it began to address the United States' new external environment.[1] Should the United States concentrate on solving its own domestic problems or should it concentrate on the United States' global role and position? What role should the United States play in the global economy, the choices ranging from what Alan Tonelson calls an "intelligent economic nationalism," to a revivified international free trade regime, to North American economic regionalism as a response to the European Community and to massive Japanese investment in Asia?[2] Under what conditions and circumstances should the United States intervene militarily overseas? To what extent should the United States act unilaterally, or in concert with the United Nations and other multilateral international institutions? And, finally, what kind of a new international order is desirable and what kind is possible, ranging from a unipolar conception of renewed American hegemony, to a G-3 of regional trading blocs, to a polycentric world in which peace is maintained, if at all, only by the *balance* of power? These questions are interesting today because the answers that made sense in the Cold War are now irrelevant.

BILATERAL CHANGES

Let me begin with some salient aspects of United States' relations with Japan, South Korea, and China. State Department officials freely concede that our bilateral economic relations with Japan are "out of control."[3] With the trade deficit running at around $60 billion per annum and every arrow in the economists' quiver already fired—Action Plans, MOSS Talks, Plaza Accords, Maekawa Reports, and Structural Impediments Initiatives—nobody knows what to do next. It is increasingly apparent that what the Japanese call "excess competition" *(kato kyoso)*—caused by cartels, male job security, administrative guidance, and other features of the Japanese economy—results in Japan's exporting the unintended consequences of its rigged economic structure. It does not produce the "mutually beneficial exchange" of the economists' textbooks. For Japan actually to change would mean changing Japan's political structure, ending the vested interests and bureaucratic careers devoted to perpetuating the postwar developmental system. However, the end of the Cold War opens up the possibility of a new solution.

Throughout the Cold War the United States exerted consistent *gaiatsu* (foreign pressure) on Japan to keep the Liberal Democratic Party (LDP) in power and to keep the Japan Socialist Party (JSP) out. The reasons for this were obvious. The JSP had never evolved into a reliable supporter of democracy against communist totalitarianism, as did the Social Democratic Party of Germany. The JSP has remained committed to neutralism and the end of the Japanese-American Security Treaty. However, with the end of the Cold War, none of this matters any more. A non-LDP government in Japan would do a lot to break up the cozy relationship that now exists among politicians, bureaucrats, and insider industrialists, and to correct the inequities of the "rich Japan, poor Japanese" syndrome.

There is another reason why the United States should cool the support it has given the LDP throughout the Cold War. As a report of the Australian Senate on Japan's defense policy put it,

> The only conceivable quarter from which political support for a resurgence of an independent military role for Japan might come is the large number of ultranationalist associations. These groups, estimated to have an active membership of around 23,000 and often having their origins in the patriotic societies of pre-war Japan, share many if not all of the following objectives: the revision or abolition of the Constitution; restoration of the pre-1945 imperial system; the development of a more powerful military force, including nuclear weapons; a strong belief in the racial superiority of Japanese; fierce anti-communism; and a resentment of foreigners and foreign involvement in Japanese affairs. The criminal underworld provides these associations with much of their funding, facilitating their persistent and vocal campaigns on issues which offend their beliefs.[4]

Unfortunately, the report then proceeded to dismiss the influence of such groups on the grounds that "These ultranationalist groups have no systematic links or support within the government, the bureaucracy, business, or other power elites in Japan." This is not true. The Nomura scandal of 1991 revealed the major influence that *yakuza* (mobsters) had on Japan's largest financial securities firm, and the Sagawa Kyubin scandal of 1992 detailed the close ties between virtually all members of the LDP and both the criminal underworld and right-wing groups.[5] An end to the LDP's monopolization of Japanese political power might help break up these affiliations as well as provide for the possibility of a non-threatening independent military role for Japan.

American relations with South Korea also face an equally changed landscape. Beginning in 1950 and continuing to the present time, American military involvement on the Korean peninsula was always based on the United States' global concerns, never on Korea itself. We became involved in the Korean conflict because of that war's potential impact on the worldwide balance of power. With the end of the Cold War and China's opening of diplomatic relations with the Republic of Korea, the United States' interest in Korea as a global issue no longer exists. For this reason alone the American ground forces, stationed in Korea for the past forty-three years, should be withdrawn. However, there are also other reasons.

First, those ground forces have no further military purpose. The threat from the north, to the extent that it still exists, is today nuclear and not conventional. It can be countered by American nuclear forces available to the Seventh Fleet, and ultimately removed only through inspection, negotiation, and political reunification. In my opinion, North Korea is probably developing a nuclear option only as a bargaining chip, as leverage to obtain aid for the development of an atomic power capability. Russia's cut-off of petroleum supplies and China's requirement that it be paid in hard currency have created an acute energy crisis for the north. The nuclear threat also keeps open channels of communication to the International Atomic Energy Agency, Seoul, Tokyo, Washington, and the private Americans who travel to Pyongyang under the pretense of negotiation. A North Korean use of atomic weapons is unlikely, particularly in the face of Chinese opposition, but the idea that it might possess such weapons keeps Cold War bureaucracies working a little longer.

Second, to leave American ground forces in Korea makes them hostage to a possible future conflict and threatens the stability of United States' relations with Japan. As one of Japan's most seasoned diplomats, Okazaki Hisahiko, observed, "If a war were to occur on the Korean peninsula, Americans would shed their blood, but Japanese would not be willing to do the same."[6] Actually there is no need for either American or Japanese soldiers to get involved. South Korea has a population of 43 million, as against North Korea's 22 million, and is fully capable of defending itself.

Beyond these military considerations, the U.S. troops should be removed because they are an obstacle to Korean democratization. The United States has applauded the progress toward democracy and civilian rule that began with Roh Tae Woo's declaration of June 29, 1987, leading to the election of Kim Young Sam as president on December 19, 1992. But the United States tends to forget that its own toleration of both Chun Doo Hwan's coup d'état and his massacre of civilians at Kwangju in May 1980 is one of the reasons why democracy took so long in coming in Korea. As Frank Gibney puts it,

> The Kwangju bloodletting was the Korean equivalent of China's Tiananmen massacre—no less ruthless for having been perpetrated by an ally. . . . More than any other factor or event, it set in motion an undercurrent of anti-American feeling, which persists among Korean students to this day, for America's passive acquiescence in the massacre was held by many Koreans to mean active support.[7]

The errors of both the Carter and Reagan administrations cannot be corrected at this late date, but the American troops should be withdrawn as a small, belated gesture toward the consolidation of civilian rule in Seoul. The end of the Cold War makes it possible and the future importance of Korea in an emerging Asian balance of power makes it desirable.

China offers further variations on these post–Cold War themes. In 1989, China had a per capita income of $547, or 2.6 percent of that of the United States; and a total GNP of $603.5 billion, or 11.6 percent of ours. China's population of 1.1 billion people is more than four times that of the United States. These numbers mean that China could fairly easily produce an economy the same size as the United States' while still having a relatively low per capita income. If China achieved a per capita GNP even one-fourth that of the United States—approximately the level of Korea's today—it would have an absolute GNP greater than that of the United States. With the high growth and savings rates achieved in recent years, matching the per capita income of South Korea today is not an unrealistic goal for China.[8]

Americans like to believe that economic growth is desirable in and of itself, regardless of the natural resources that may be destroyed in the process. They also believe that economic growth inevitably leads to democratization—important because it allegedly makes people happier and because democracies are said to go to war with each other rarely, if at all. The conservative Heritage Foundation states this as if it were a Newtonian law: "The law of supply and demand is as immutable as the law of gravity: as a country moves up the economic ladder, political freedoms almost always follow."[9] Let us not dwell on the fact that the law of gravity does not operate in the "almost always" realm. What is interesting about this remark is that it is explicitly directed to the East Asian newly industrialized countries, even though most of them are anything but democratic. When they do advance toward democracy, as in the case of South Korea, their economic growth tends to slow down.

What these American ideologues fail to understand is that democracy is a peculiarly effective way of making decisions under conditions of significant heterogeneity. Since economic development will normally produce greater social differentiation, democracy is a logical response to these conditions. But if the heterogeneity can be mitigated—through fairly equitable income distribution, restrictions on immigration or emigration, or an overarching ideology of uniqueness and exceptionalism—democracy may not be necessary for effective government, and the tradeoff between economic growth and democratic development can then be postponed.

In the past the Chinese Communists have been wary of using market mechanisms for economic growth precisely because they feared that the Americans were right, and that it would lead to the collapse of communist authoritarianism. One reason why in recent years they have accepted those mechanisms is that evidence from the high-growth economies of South Korea, Taiwan, and Singapore suggests that authoritarianism (sometimes disguised by a facade of democracy) is compatible with high levels of per capita income.

During the Cold War it made sense for the United States to promote China's economic development because it reinforced the strategic triangle with the USSR. Today, by giving China most-favored-nation access to the American market, the United States is actively helping China to become as big as the United States itself—but with no guarantee that its people will be satisfied with a per capita income only a quarter of America's, or that democratic government will become unavoidable in the Chinese context. It may well be that the United States should promote Chinese development anyway, but it is time to start thinking about the need to balance China's future power, and to recognize that the presumed relationship between economic development and democracy is not as certain as the law of gravity.

THE GLOBAL CONTEXT

American relations with Japan, Korea, and China appear in a very different light when seen only on their own terms, omitting any thought of a global, bipolar conflict. The United States no longer needs to support a corrupt and isolationist party in Japan just because it is anticommunist. The United States no longer needs to intervene in a Korean civil war. The United States no longer needs a unified, economically viable China as a counterfoil to a hostile USSR. But the United States still has a vital interest in a peaceful, stable East Asia—where its three biggest wars of this century began—and in mutually beneficial economic relations with the world's main manufacturing center. How, then, should it alter or maintain its current relations in the area?

Before addressing that question, one needs a clear understanding of the direction of global change and the forces driving it. It seems to me that there are two general tendencies in international relations in the wake of the Cold War. The first trend is the spectacular growth of transnational economic integration, caused by technology, the validation of capitalism by the outcome of the Cold War, the shift from the primacy of military to economic power, and the desire of lagging parts of the world to compete with East Asia. This integration takes the form of both new regional markets—the European Community, NAFTA, the ASEAN free trade agreement—and so-called borderless economies, multinational corporations, the global communications village, and the wired world of capital flows from one market to another. Many believe that this integration contributes to the unification of the world and is therefore an unqualified good.

The second trend is toward social fragmentation—the phenomenon of a single political unit dividing into several, as in the former USSR, former Czechoslovakia, and former Yugoslavia.

Fragmentation also involves a sharp rise in the politicization of ethnicity in many parts of the world, leading to what some have called a "retribalization." Examples include the Serbian campaigns of "ethnic cleansing" against their former Muslim and Croat fellow citizens, attacks by Hindus against Sikhs and Muslims, and persistent rural-urban warfare in Cambodia. Georgie Anne Geyer has called this trend the "death of citizenship," a malady not unknown in the United States.

These two trends are interrelated, through their combined effects on the state. The end of the Cold War has produced a crisis for the old state system and its particular distribution of sovereignties. Old borders are coming down—producing integration—while new ones are being built—leading to fragmentation. The Institute for the Study of International Politics in Milan summed it up well in its 1992 annual report:

> It is true that economic and financial integration weakens (or, better, makes relative) the divisions between states, but rather than unifying the world this causes new divisions to arise. . . . The extension of economic relations simultaneously guts both sides [of an existing state]. On the one hand it knocks down the division between states because it unites that which in their universe would be divided: citizens and foreigners. On the other hand, the fall of the outer division cancels exactly that element which permitted the internal divisions among groups (national, ethnic, or racial), living next to each other under the same rules, to remain unseen. . . . The multiplication of economic relations not only increases the interconnection of peoples, but at the same time diminishes the political solidarity of each people.[10]

Several implications follow from these trends. One is that the powerful movements toward economic regionalism are also generating two equally powerful counterreactions: fears of the strongest partner and fears of being left out. Europeans fear German dominance, Latin Americans fear United States' dominance, Southeast Asians fear Japanese dominance. Even within some integrated markets, such as that being forged by ASEAN, there is a fear of "Indonesianization"—dominance by the largest partner. But the fear of being left out is equally strong. It lies at the heart of Australia's promotion of APEC (Asian-Pacific Economic Cooperation) as against Malaysian Prime Minister Mahathir's EAEC (East Asian Economic Caucus). The latter would exclude the English-speaking nations, Australia and New Zealand as well as the United States and Canada, because NAFTA excludes Southeast Asian nations.

There is no way to know how this process of integration and fragmentation will resolve itself. The former superpowers have been reduced to armed impotence. The United States alone certainly does not have the resources to establish its own hegemonic order. The new political configuration of the world will probably not be known for decades. Meanwhile we are likely to see high levels of conflict because of weakened foundations for both domestic and international order. The world will also witness many attempts at reaggregation, in the form of movements toward political union (e.g., the Maastricht Treaty), or cultural unity (e.g., the Kurds in Iraq, Turkey, and Iran), or semi-imperial hegemony (e.g., "Greater China," or some sort of new Greater East Asia Co-Prosperity Sphere). Finally, global commerce will acquire the logic of war. This has always been true for the developmental states; it will now become true for all states. The most logical way to promote peace, stability, and continued prosperity under these conditions will be through some form of the balance of power.

CHOICES

In an interview published in the house organ of the Japanese Ministry of Foreign Affairs, former ambassador Okazaki Hisahiko commented, "I think that China will never be truly close to Japan even in the future." Even though Japan has been courting China in recent years with a soft stance on human rights, an imperial visit, and the full range of economic inducements, Okazaki is probably right. This means that a new version of Japan's Greater East Asia Co-Prosperity Sphere, even one not forged at the point of a bayonet but based on real prosperity, is not in the cards. China appears unwilling to become another goose in Japan's notion of the Asian economies flying in formation behind Japan, the lead goose. Equally important, barring extensive institutional reform and rejuvenation of its political system, Japan is not truly capable of offering leadership in Asia, even if China acquiesced.

Donald Hellmann argues that "Japan's affluence is accompanied by a Midas-like incapacity for international leadership that is rooted in a reluctance and/or inability to define in a credible way a national purpose beyond narrow economic self-interest."[11] Kenneth Pyle suggests why this is so:

> Harmonizing Japanese institutions with international practice recalled U.S. Commerce Secretary Baldrige's assertion to the Japanese: "You will have to change your culture." The century-long pursuit of equality with the West had left its mark on all of Japan's institutions. They were designed to promote a uniform and disciplined national effort to achieve this goal. They were also designed to insulate Japan from direct foreign influence by foreign companies and individuals. To reform these institutions and practices would constitute a challenge to central features of Japanese culture, social relations, and political structure.[12]

None of this means that China and Japan will not continue to enjoy a flourishing commerce, but there will also always be political tension between them. Could this be overcome through some form of collective security arrangement in which neither nation took the lead? This, too, seems highly unlikely for various reasons. First of all, the very concept of collective security rests on dubious logic. In cases where it has been said to work, such as NATO in Europe, hegemonic and balance of power considerations operated beneath the rhetoric of collective security.

Equally important, East Asia has had almost no experience with what Richard Betts calls "integrative organizational forms," certainly nothing like the experience of Europe from the time of the Marshall Plan. Whereas virtually all American policies in postwar Europe were multilateral, in Asia they were normally bilateral and did not contribute to a web of relationships that might persist once the Americans are gone. Despite the history of failures of multilateral treaties and organizations intended to preserve peace and security in the Pacific—from the nine-power Treaty of Washington (1922) to the Southeast Asia Treaty Organization (1954)—many Western leaders profess to see a need for a "Pan-Asian Security Organization." This would apparently be modeled on the Council for Security and Cooperation in Europe (CSCE) and would be an answer to Japan's calls for an Asian security "dialogue."

However, there is no consensus in Asia on norms, or on what

a supranational order in the region should look like. In ASEAN, for example, nations close to Vietnam, such as Thailand, favor cultivating China as a counterweight, whereas those further away, such as Indonesia, favor cultivating Vietnam as an obstacle to Chinese influence. Where nations cannot agree on who constitutes a threat, collective security is unlikely to work.

The remaining security alternatives all hinge on the role of the United States. Richard Ellings and Edward Olsen consider three scenarios.[13] The first they call a "new multilateral constabulary," which turns out to be not multilateral at all but a continuation of the current Japanese-American Security Treaty. One of its main purposes, in fact, would be not so much security *cooperation* with Japan as continued American engagement with Japan in order to see that Japan does not rearm, continues to transfer military technology to the United States, and contributes to security in an acceptable way. The intent is to perpetuate the American role in the Pacific much as it was during the Cold War but with some slight savings in American costs. Whether it would be acceptable to Japanese public opinion, to the other nations of the region, and to the American public are all open questions. Its greatest weakness is that it perpetuates the American military's artificial separation between the military and economic aspects of security and leaves the United States in the untenable position of defending nations to whom it is simultaneously going into debt.

The second Ellings and Olsen Asian security alternative is a complete American withdrawal from the region. This could be justified on grounds that the area is sufficiently stable to do without an American presence; and the logic of the Cold War, never well formulated for the Pacific in any case, no longer applies. The main issue that destabilized the region and gave communists an opening was the dismantling of colonial empires. That issue is now history, and new problems that might develop—caused by the integration and fragmentation that the end of the Cold War unleashed—are not solvable by the United States.

The objection to U.S. withdrawal is precisely that America's security threats have become economic and technological; if the United States is not totally to lose control over its own national security, it must regain its economic competitiveness, and in order to do so, it must remain active in the world's economic center of gravity. Thus, it is argued that the United States should use its unique ability to project military power to influence events in Asia, and that to withdraw from the area would, through evolutionary economic changes, pose the greatest possible threat to its own security.

The third Ellings and Olsen alternative is a balance of power, with the United States cast in the part of "engaged balancer," somewhat like the role Britain played in the nineteenth century. Under such a policy the United States would be committed not to any particular Asian nation or subregion, but to ensuring that no single power could achieve hegemony. It would exert influence primarily though its good offices, but would have the capacity to use force in cooperation with other nations when necessary. Normally this force would not be based in the region but would be of the sort supplied by a carrier task force.

Commentators differ on the elements in such a balance of power. Ellings and Olsen see the major players as China, India, Japan, Russia, and the United States, but it seems to me that India and Russia will not have political influence until they have some economic clout. They are also among the states most affected by the twin post–Cold War trends of integration and fragmentation, and are likely to be internally preoccupied for a long time. Richard Betts has a similar conception, but sees the need for a balance only among China, Japan, Russia, and the United States.

My own conception is somewhat more complicated. I would seek a balance among China, Japan, and ASEAN, with the United States shifting its strength in order to achieve and maintain it, while supporting Korea and Vietnam as the two most important buffer states in East Asia. Such a policy would obviously require American recognition of the Socialist Republic of Vietnam as soon as possible, greatly enhanced American attention to ASEAN, and a new commitment to the intrinsic, not just the derivative, importance of Korea in the Asian balance of power.

In all of these places the United States desperately needs new policies. In Vietnam the United States should participate along with Japan in the country's debut into high-growth capitalist Asia. The United States also needs to provide whatever external reassurances are appropriate to ease Vietnam's relations with, and possible membership in, ASEAN. With regard to ASEAN itself, the United States should offer it access to the American market at least equal to that enjoyed by Japan and China. NAFTA need not be an obstacle to American-ASEAN relations, and it could evolve into an instrument for helping to ensure ASEAN's prosperity. The United States also needs to support the economic development of the Philippines, not for nostalgic reasons but to ensure that the Philippines is not dumped by foreign investors, and that it becomes a healthy member of ASEAN.

Korea requires particular attention. While it no longer needs American ground forces, it may require American assistance in managing unification with the north, including reassuring China, the power with the greatest stake in the Korean peninsula, that a unified Korea will not adversely affect it. The United States can help ensure that China's stake is recognized. China has always had trouble living with one Korea. Korea will also need financing to integrate the two economies, and the United States knows how to create the international syndicates that can supply this.

We can also help both Korea and ourselves in other ways. Korea needs to regain its economic dynamism. To do so it needs above all to achieve greater equality in its distribution of wealth. As the World Bank puts it,

> The perception that the economic gains of Korea's rapid growth have not been fairly enough distributed is . . . causing difficulties in the labor market, where workers are not merely trying to capture productivity gains in their wage settlements, but are also trying to appropriate a portion of the gains they feel have eluded them in the past.[14]

This is perfectly just. A more equitable distribution of wealth correlates directly with high rates of growth and savings, and is the main reform that Korea must undertake. Americans could help by joining in strategic alliances to produce new products and to fight against Japan's structural trade surpluses.

Korea's former Minister for Science and Technology, Kim Jin Hyun, observed in a speech delivered in Washington:

> The United States and Korea . . . have much to offer each other through mutually beneficial cooperation. If the basic sciences and advanced high technologies of the United States are grafted onto the production and manufacturing technologies of Korea, it will make both of our countries competitive technologically as well as industri-

ally. [This will lead] to balanced trade relations in the Asia-Pacific region, especially with Japan, which is the common challenge facing our two countries.

An American move to take up Minister Kim's proposals for technological cooperation would be an important signal to Japan, perhaps causing it to become more internationally responsible.

In 1955, not long after the U.S. occupation of Japan had ended, the Communists had defeated the Kuomintang in China, the Korean conflict had come to a halt, and the French had been driven from Indochina, Edwin O. Reischauer—then a professor at Harvard and later to become ambassador to Japan—published a book called *Wanted: An Asian Policy*. He did so, he wrote, because "We take a frantic interest in individual crises when they develop, but appear strangely indifferent to the basic ills that have caused them. Worse still, we are easily diverted from our problems in Asia to more trivial matters."[15] Much the same could be said today. The costs of an American failure to change, either due to myopia or the influence of vested interests in the system as it presently exists, could be catastrophic. At the same time the possible benefits of a stable, developing Asia are as great today as they were in the decades after Reischauer wrote.

14

History Restarted: Japanese-American Relations at the End of the Century

The peculiar Cold War relationship between Japan and the United States lasted from approximately 1950 to 1990. Today it continues only through inertia, without any foundation in grand strategy or in response to a common threat, despite a high degree of economic interdependence. Japan and the United States are today, as Nakanishi Terumasa puts it, merely "paper allies."[1] Both the Japanese and the Americans have profited greatly from their forty-year alliance, but they have also deluded themselves about its foundations and are emerging from it crippled in certain major respects. One of the most striking asymmetries between Japan and America in the aftermath of the Cold War, and largely caused by it, is Japan's weakness in taking a larger role in world affairs and the United States's weakness in reestablishing the industrial and economic foundations on which its claims to global leadership rest. To talk about Japanese-American relations at the end of the century, then, means first of all to understand the delusions and dependencies with which they are emerging from the fog of the Cold War.

Amid the welter of political and academic verbiage concerning the collapse of communism and the end of bipolarity, two theses stand out for their insight and originality. One is Francis Fukuyama's "The End of History?" and the other Alan Tonelson's "What Is the National Interest?"[2] Both reflect diametrically opposite views of the nature of the Cold War, and they therefore differ on the significance of its end.

After one strips away the Hegelian camouflage, Fukuyama's argument can be reduced to an unabashed American victory cry: We won. According to Fukuyama, the Cold War was not simply a political and military contest between the Soviet and American empires; it was, above all, a contest between advocates of the primacy of the state and advocates of the primacy of society. In terms of economic ideology, the battle was between V. I. Lenin and Adam Smith, between a state-led command economy and a state-as-referee laissez-faire economy. "The triumph of the West, of the Western *idea*," Fukuyama writes, "is evident first of all in the total exhaustion of viable systematic alternatives to Western liberalism."

Looking out of the corner of his eye, Fukuyama can see that Japan does not fit this schema. But he defines the problem away (just as many Japanese critics of the United States think that Americans are also doing): "Many Americans are now aware that Japanese industrial organization is very different from that prevailing in the United States or Europe, and it is questionable what relationship the factional maneuvering that takes place within the governing Liberal Democratic Party bears to democracy. Nonetheless, the very fact that the essential elements of economic and political liberalism have been so successfully grafted onto uniquely Japanese traditions and institutions guarantees their survival in the long run." This is of course a restatement of the official American position that Japan was reborn in the image of the United States during the Allied Occupation and that, in the long run, the two will converge as liberal democratic countries. If one accepts Fukuyama's proposition that the bedrock of modern history was a struggle between Leninism and liberalism, then liberalism (including Japan) won, and history—at least until some new dialectical paradigm emerges—is over.

By contrast, Alan Tonelson is more in the neorealist mode. He would agree with Robert Gilpin that the Western strategy in the Cold War encompassed (1) a series of alliances (NATO, the Japan–U.S. Security Treaty) based on "a common assessment of the Soviet threat"; (2) an extended deterrence that "united the industrial democracies militarily"; and (3) the Bretton Woods system of economic cooperation, its last vestige today being

GATT-style "free trade," that was intended to overcome "economic nationalism."[3] However, Tonelson goes further and argues that the essence of American policy was a "strategy of smothering the foreign policy (and economic) independence of Western Europe and Japan." During the Cold War, the United States sought to meet "all the major needs—principally those for security and prosperity—that historically led the Western European countries and Japan to conduct their own foreign policies in the first place." The intent of this policy, most clearly evident in the Bretton Woods arrangements, was two-fold: to rehabilitate Western Europe and Japan as markets for American goods and allies against the USSR, and to prevent the reappearance of a pre-1914 multipolar balance of power, "which had proved highly unstable and in fact had collapsed into two terrible conflicts." In contrast to Fukuyama, Tonelson stresses that the Western strategy in the Cold War was aimed above all at preserving a bipolar world.

Today, Tonelson believes the "smothering strategy" of the United States has become completely unsustainable because (1) it requires the continued "hemorrhaging of U.S. economic strength," and (2) Western Europe and Japan are no longer interested in going along. Contrary to James Fallows's important argument that with the end of the Cold War, the United States must "contain Japan," Tonelson thinks that this is precisely what the United States has been doing for the past forty years.[4] Kissinger made a similar case to Chou En-lai in 1971; and many Americans see the Security Treaty today as a safeguard for the rest of Asia and the Pacific "against the possibility of a more assertive Japanese profile in the region backed by military force."[5] In Tonelson's conception, the Cold War amounted to a smothering of history (its suspension if not its literal end), and the revolutionary events of 1989–91 portend its restarting. He concludes that "increased Western European and Japanese independence will undoubtedly make the world less stable," and that the United States should "focus on coping with the consequences of a less stable world."[6] Tonelson's article is a work of policy advocacy; he does not dwell on whether the United States *can* wean itself away from its Roman pretensions (even though it can no longer afford them) or on what grand strategy Japan might pursue, if it is capable of formulating one.

I believe that the mode of thought exemplified by Fukuyama's article characterizes what passes for strategy in Washington these days and that the mode of thought exemplified by Tonelson's piece characterizes what passes for strategy in Tokyo. If my contention is even close to the truth—and, as we shall see, there are many serious people in Tokyo other than the stridently neo-nationalist Ishihara Shintarō who subscribe to it—then it is reasonable to conclude that during the 1990s Japan and the United States are on a collision course.[7] Needless to say, just as when the navigator of a ship warns of a collision course he is not predicting a collision, I am not *predicting* a collision. But I want to lay out the perceptions, capabilities and lack of capabilities, and asymmetries that the Cold War relationship between Japan and the United States fostered. And I want to point out that, other things being equal, without reform in both countries they portend conflict. Let me divide this complex whole into three subdiscussions: (1) the New World Order; (2) the movement from GATT to economic regionalism and perhaps toward a new version of the Greater East Asia Co-Prosperity Sphere; and (3) the problem of what the Japanese call "emotional friction" *(kanjō no atsureki)* or the possibility that the Japanese and Americans do not *want* any longer to be allies.[8]

I

One of the ironies of the Persian Gulf War, 1990–91, is that—although it did not look like it—Japan actually supported the United States in an international military venture more fully than it had ever done in the past. Never before—during the Korean War, the defense of Taiwan, the defense of South Korea, the fight against the communist insurgency in the Philippines, the defense of South Vietnam, the Arab-Israeli War of 1973, and the Iran-Iraq War of the 1980s—had Japan concretely supported the United States' use of force in areas where its own national interests could also be said plausibly to be involved. Nonetheless, it was during the Gulf War that Americans concluded from Japan's reluctant contributions that the Japanese were not serious allies and that the Americans and the Japanese harbored different values concerning the "New World Order." The Gulf War thus served as a catalyst in Japanese-American relations, turning numerous impressions and irritations that each country had about the other into more hardened stereotypes. As William Watts put it, "The picture many Japanese have of America is one of a society beset with internal problems and at times virtually out of control, while the counterpart American image of Japan is one of a nation of humorless workaholics, bowing before higher authority."[9] These views color what each side thinks is a plausible version of a post–Cold War international system and of Japanese-American relations now that the threat of communism no longer unites them.

The basic Japanese position has been well and candidly stated by Ogura Kazuo of the Ministry of Foreign Affairs:

> The United States has lost a considerable amount of economic influence in the world. The United States no longer has the money or the manpower to see its global ideals realized. In order to realize its own global dreams, the United States must now turn to other countries. . . . [But] the United States is too proud to admit that it relies on other nations. For better or worse, the nations of the world are becoming more dependent on each other economically and politically. This is only now beginning to sink in. However, the people of the United States refuse to accept their new predicament. . . . The American people do not want to be dependent on the Japanese.[10]

The question remains why the United States has lost economic influence and must rely on others to help it out. Is it merely because Western Europe and Japan have caught up with the United States, or is the United States in actual decline?

Today, virtually all Japanese seem convinced that the United States is in decline, even though they differ on what Japan should do about it. Until the Gulf War there were roughly three schools of thought in Japan: those who felt it was in Japan's own interest to help prop up the United States; those who had read Paul Kennedy's *Rise and Fall of the Great Powers* closely and concluded that it was a waste of resources to try to prop up the United States; and those who took the position that even though the United States was in decline, since it refused itself to admit it or do anything about it, Japan should continue to profit from the old relationship as long as possible.[11] The Japanese are aware that any real program of domestic reform in the United States would involve costs to them: a genuine American "peace dividend" would mean a reduction of U.S. military commitments in the Western Pacific; the development of a U.S. economic strategy would mean serious American demands for reciprocity in market access, investment, and environmental protection on the part of its trading partners; and a true free-trade agreement with Mexico might mean some strategic closing of the American market to Asian exporters. But so long as the United States continues to waver on these issues, the Japanese believe they must work on the proposition that America's days as a superpower are numbered.

For years Japanese leaders and analysts have been hammering away at conditions in America that they think disqualify it from continuing to exercise leadership. These include Washington's fiscal deficits, the country's low economic competitiveness, drug-ridden cities, violent crime, and a miserable public education system. Former Prime Minister Nakasone, for example, merely reflected the common wisdom when he remarked that "drug abuse [in America] has reached alarming proportions."[12] A 1991 symposium of distinguished Japanese officials, professors, and industrialists—some of them educated in America and all of them familiar with it—contended that credit-card abuse in America was causing "middle class families to give up," that the "homeless live in tents put up even near the White House in Washington," and that the Harvard Business School was only good at training financiers for Wall Street, i.e., for "hollow work" *(kyogyō)*.[13] Professor Saitō Seiichirō of Rikkyō University summarized the opinions of the group: "I believe that the United States is a 'vegetating nation' [*shokubutsu kokka*]. The troubles are seen by everyone, but they are not healed by anyone. The situation is worsening. It is not worsening all at once but it is worsening gradually. The Americans have grown used to it. But then they coerce us into lending them money. The United States is heading in the direction of a vegetating nation."[14]

Even though some of the popularity of these views can be ascribed to the nationalistic pleasure of comparing conditions in the United States with those in Japan, today they are widely held by Japanese opinion leaders, not just by neonationalist fringe groups. Some authorities on the United States, such as Homma Nagayo, emeritus professor of the University of Tokyo and former head of that university's American Studies Center, even warns of a possible "U.S. collapse from internal problems," a development he fears the Americans might blame on Japan. In Homma's view, Japan should try to find a "graceful exit" *(hanamichi o tsukuru)* for the United States from its role as hegemon.[15] Until that occurs, many Japanese regard the United States with growing contempt—as the world's "credit-card policeman," or as what Christopher Layne has called a "Potemkin-village superpower."[16]

With these attitudes as a background, the spectacular success of the American-led Blitzkrieg against Iraq came as a shock to Japan. Nonetheless, the combination of "smart bombs but dumb VCRs" simply caused many influential Japanese to conclude that the United States and the former USSR had more in common than they had previously thought: both countries overtaxed their domestic economies to support their privileged military-industrial complexes. For example, Funabashi Yōichi of the *Asahi shimbun,* sees parallels between the disintegration of the European Communist economies and the 1987 collapse of the American stock exchange.[17] The Japanese are well aware that their intervention prevented the stock market collapse from turning into a panic. On the Gulf War itself, Funabashi vacillates between seeing it as America's Suez or as an example of "macho unilateralism" aimed at disguising weakness and at intimidating the Japanese.[18] Other Japanese writers have taken a similar line. In one discussion, Nakanishi Terumasa of Shizuoka University argued that President Bush's decision to use force in the Persian Gulf was "a kind of historical coup d'état against the new order, an attempt to reverse the trend toward multilateralism in the post–Cold War world." Etō Jun added that "The United States is now becoming dependent on Japan at an accelerating rate for the advanced technology that it needs to sustain its military interventions."[19]

Before considering the Japanese prescriptions for a New World Order in light of these conditions, let me turn briefly to the corresponding American impressions of the Japanese. These are, in essence, that Japan is a "unidimensional economic superpower," which fails "the test of good global citizenship, much less leadership."[20] In William Barnds's view (and it should be noted that he is a recent past president of the Japan Economic Institute, one of the Japanese government's prime information

agencies in Washington), "Japanese policy [in the Gulf War]—
and the government went beyond what most of the public supported—demonstrated that Japan remains insular, still sees its
role in the world largely in terms of its narrow economic self-
interest, and remains politically unwilling and unable to assess
and act on its interests in a broader international context, especially during a crisis. When one of the world's key nations fails to
set policies that help maintain the international system, the system is in trouble."[21]

Why do the Japanese behave this way? For many Americans
the answer is that the Japanese and the Americans see the world
and the maintenance of order in it differently. The Americans
hold to "principles" whereas the Japanese respond only to pressure, such as the notorious American *gaiatsu* or what many Japanese masochistically delight in calling "Japan-bashing." A good
example of these views comes from former Assistant Secretary of
Defense Richard Perle: "Even before the question of sending
Self-Defense Forces to the Gulf became an issue, what surprised
the American people is that even when the Japanese government
had decided to send some medical teams, there were hardly any
volunteers. Doesn't 'contributing' mean realizing one's own international responsibilities and then trying to meet those responsibilities, not just doing something because the United States
wants you to? I find it hard to understand why Japan doesn't
realize this."[22] From a Japanese point of view, the Gulf War virtually began with an outburst of *gaiatsu* (foreign pressure). According to the *Yomiuri shimbun*, a letter from U.S. Secretary of
Defense Dick Cheney dated August 10, 1990, eight days after
Saddam Hussein's invasion of Kuwait, to Director General of
the Japanese Defense Agency Ishikawa Yōzō, stated: "At this
time evidence is needed to show that the U.S.-Japan relationship
continues to be firm. . . . [Without such evidence, the U.S. government cannot refute the argument that] the two nations no
longer have a relationship."[23] In the *Yomiuri*'s assessment, the
Kaifu cabinet read this letter as a threat, one that moved its members much more profoundly than the menace of Saddam Hussein.

Japanese political scientists explain this reliance on *gaiatsu* as
a consequence of America's smothering strategy during the Cold
War, a strategy that was implemented most forcefully against

Japan in the wake of the Security Treaty riots of 1960. In the analysis of Professor Sasaki Takeshi, postwar Japanese politics should be divided into three phases: (1) 1945–60; (2) 1960–85; and (3) 1985–present. In the first phase, "politics retained its ideological dimension"; but in the second phase, when Japan put further constitutional development on hold and devoted itself to high-speed economic growth, "Japanese politicians began to lose interest in the high politics of diplomacy and national security, and competition among political parties became a mere formality, adding momentum to the political apathy of the people." During the third phase, changes in Japan's external environment and its own growing wealth forced it to think about reforming its political system. But its politicians, literally having forgotten their function, persisted in their factional battles, or in arranging for their sons and grandsons to succeed them, or in "pork-barrel politics." Japan's "foreign policy continued to be oriented exclusively to economic issues and it took virtually no initiatives in other fields."[24]

A major unintended consequence of the United States' hegemonic smothering strategy, then, was the atrophy of the Japanese political system. To quote Sasaki again, in responding to the demands of the Gulf War, Japan's political leadership

> found itself in serious conflict with the deeply entrenched domestic interests catered to over the decades. Stable though it might outwardly seem, Japanese politics began to suffer from chronic, structural instability. . . . Japanese political leaders today are a product of the second phase. . . . In the second phase . . . the role of politics actually contracted, and systems emerged through which the burdens of politics were taken over to a considerable degree by other organizations and actors [the bureaucracy, big business, and the United States]. . . . The bureaucracy has cultivated involvement in the people's daily lives incomparably deeper than that attempted by politicians, and the structures of that involvement are firmly established.

Reliance on *gaiatsu* is thus one Japanese adaptation to American hegemony, and Japanese officials themselves often invite and orchestrate it by prompting their normally uninformed American counterparts. "It is often said that the Bush Administration has acted at times like an opposition party and even at times like the ruling party itself."[25] During the Gulf War, a common pun in

Tokyo was that Kaifu was busy using his "Bush-button phone" to call the White House. As we shall see, the Americans do not normally acknowledge that this situation exists because it contradicts their view that Japan is a democratic ally who has freely joined in a "global partnership" based on Japanese-American "burden-sharing." But the leading external, non-American analyst of *gaiatsu*, Aurelia George, concludes:

> U.S. pressure has become a powerful catalyst for change in the Japanese economy, polity, and society. . . . U.S. pressure is now penetrating the inner reaches of the Japanese policymaking process. Almost all the government's major decisions are held up for scrutiny in terms of their possible impact on Japan's relations with the United States. . . . In many respects the United States is itself an actor in the Japanese policy process: as a surrogate opposition party presenting the only true set of alternative policies to the government's, as an interest group representing the voice of Japanese consumers, and as an alternative power base for Japanese prime ministers seeking to overcome both shortfalls in their factional strength and domestic resistance to change.[26]

During the Cold War, Japan and America learned roles that they played with each other quite successfully; but these roles have become anachronistic. Nonetheless, most Japanese and Americans are not ready to give them up and learn new ones. The Japanese still like leaving their external security needs to the Americans, and the Americans still enjoy the Roman appurtenances of power. The situation is comparable to the last decades of the Edo *bakufu* (military government), when the samurai were still deferred to by the merchants who were simultaneously their financiers. "In Washington," writes Thomas Ginsburg, "those who continue to see the United States as the global hegemon are reluctant to share international decision-making."[27] Joseph Nye subtly reinforces their position by his arguments that even though the Americans are making no efforts to check their decline, they still control a vast reservoir of "soft power" with which to keep their erstwhile allies in line.[28]

In Tokyo, too, even such neonationalists as Nakanishi change their tune when writing in English: "No matter how much may be said and written about the end of the Cold War, there will be no fundamental change in the Japan-U.S. relationship unless there are basic changes in the strategic, political, and economic context governing the relationship."[29] But, of course, it is precisely those "basic changes in the strategic, political, and economic context" that have started to occur: the Russians are no longer a military threat; both Koreas are now members of the United Nations and perhaps on their way toward some form of unification; and a combination of Mt. Pinatubo and the Filipino Senate have closed down America's last outposts in its former colony. The time for a New World Order is now.

Japanese thinking about what kinds of institutional arrangements should replace those of the Cold War is actually more advanced than that of the Americans. They call these new arrangements "pax consortis," a concept invented by Professor Inoguchi Kuniko and now widely used, although with varying definitions, throughout Japanese policy-making circles.[30] Former Prime Minister Nakasone defines it as "peace achieved through the cooperation of many nations led by the United States."[31] In a different context, Nakasone added that the specific members of the consortium should be the G-7 advanced industrial democracies. "Despite the spectacular allied victory in the Persian Gulf," he wrote, "a new world order is nowhere in sight. . . . Superpower America is in economic decline. . . . We are entering the age of Pax Consortia . . . [a] transition from economic to comprehensive summitry. . . . The Group of Seven will have to serve as the world's banker, gendarme, and environmentalist."[32] Satō Hideo agrees with this formulation, but he warns that it will not be easy to achieve: "The United States would have to reject hegemony."[33]

Inoguchi herself does not include a leadership role for the United States. "The shape of the world order," she writes, "will not be a unipolar Pax Americana; it will be a system of joint management by a consortium of industrial nations."[34] Unfortunately, there are several obvious objections to this sort of reasoning. It fails to specify *why* the various nations should cooperate with each other and is, therefore, as flawed as the original idealism that prompted the so-called neorealist school to develop the theory of hegemonic stability.[35] For example, why should not the U.N. Security Council, with of course the addition of Japan and Germany as members, play the role given by these theorists to the G-7 democracies? Is not any global "pax consortis" already upstaged by the emergence of the expanded European Community, the North American Free Trade Area, and the probable recreation of the Greater East Asia Co-Prosperity Sphere?

The American response to these proposals has been ambiguous. Americans thus far seem to prefer the term "burden-sharing" in talking with their former Cold War clients about future relations, but this phrase tends to alarm the Japanese, who see it as a ploy to get them to pay for American foreign policy without participating in its formulation. In any case, proposals for burden-sharing (*futan no wakachiai* in Japanese) sound to Japanese like invitations to join a sinking ship, and they violate Japan's oldest instinct about foreign affairs: *nagai mono ni wa makareyō* (move with the powerful).[36] It should be recalled that Japanese foreign policy in the twentieth century has been based on bilateral alliances with the nation that Japan deemed to be the most powerful in every sense, including cultural. This led to the Anglo-Japanese Alliance, 1902–22; the Axis Alliance with Germany, 1940–45; and the Japanese-American Security Treaty, 1952–present. Japan has never been drawn to alliances with nations in decline. The Americans would therefore be wise to abandon the term "burden-sharing," because it both reeks of American self-righteousness and amounts to a self-advertisement of America's declining ability to carry out an independent foreign policy.

Another dubious concept favored by some Americans in dealing with Japan is "global partnership." The term is prominently featured in a so-called policy consensus report of August 1991 on "the future of U.S.-Japan relations," which was endorsed by a large number of former American officials who reside in Washington, D.C., including Alexander Haig, Melvin Laird, Charles Percy, William Proxmire, Paula Stern, Robert Strauss, and Paul Volcker. References to an "equal partnership" (allegedly established by Reischauer when he was ambassador), or a "potential partner" (as co-builder of the FSX and supplier of advanced technology to the Department of Defense), or a "global partnership" (undefined) are all mixed up.[37] No one knows exactly what "global partnership" means except that the two nations should continue to get along so long as neither has to make any sacrifices.

As of the end of the Gulf War the New World Order was quite

recognizably the old world order, continuing through inertia but visibly slowing down. Ambassador William Gleysteen summarized the situation as follows: "Certain inherent American strengths and Japanese liabilities are working against a radical switch in global influence from the United States to Japan in the forseeable future. . . . [Japan will temporarily remain an] almost equal ally [even though it has] largely replaced the United States as the [Asia-Pacific] region's creditor and provider of assistance, as the source of the most useful technology, and as an appropriate model for economic development."[38]

II

In talking about economic issues in the Asia-Pacific region, one must begin by largely discounting or ignoring the opinions of economics professors in English-speaking countries. This is because they failed to anticipate the growth of great wealth in the area, still cannot adequately explain it, and are today concerned more with defending their arcane theories than with studying the nature and potentialities of Asian capitalism. It is more than likely that history will come to judge English-language academic economics as having the same relationship to Asian capitalism that academic Marxism-Leninism taught in the USSR until August 1991 had to the Soviet economy.

I raise this issue at the outset because one of the major controversies at the heart of the various economic disputes between Japan and the United States is what theory applies and whether the East Asian and North American capitalist economies even belong to the same species. And the answer has direct implications for policy. If the two economies belong to the same species of capitalism, then there is every reason to suppose that problems might be solved or ameliorated through such measures as macroeconomic coordination, exchange and interest rate adjustments, deregulation, market-opening agreements, and foreign direct investment. If they are not members of the same species, then such measures are likely to make the situation worse— which arguably has been the case since the so-called Plaza Accord of 1985.

GATT and the Uruguay Round are a case in point. If the economists' doctrine of free trade actually has some validity, then the attempt to extend and force a conclusion to the Uruguay Round after the negotiations collapsed in Brussels in December 1990 makes sense. But if GATT during the most recent past two decades was really based on a political doctrine—the willingness of a hegemonic power, the United States, to exchange economic benefits for political and security backing as part of a grand strategy against the Soviet Union—then the Uruguay Round collapsed because the Cold War is over. As Lawrence Krause has observed, "The rest of the world has seen the U.S. make too many mistakes—both in the economic and political arenas—to comply with U.S. desires now that they no longer require a protective U.S. military umbrella."[39] It is as plausible to conclude that this was the calculation made by Japan and the European Community (EC) at Brussels in 1990 as to contend that they have benightedly missed the point of the lessons taught by Adam Smith, David Ricardo, and their followers two centuries ago.

The Japanese are extremely well informed about "the nearly fanatical loyalty to 'free trade' that has characterized America's bipartisan foreign policy establishment."[40] In the past they have verbally respected it and tried to turn it against the Americans whenever the latter sought reciprocity in bilateral economic relations. But times have changed. The Japanese no longer care what the Americans think. When, in March 1991, Japanese government officials threatened to "arrest and prosecute" American rice exporters for merely displaying three different kinds of rice that are grown in the United States at a privately sponsored International Food and Beverage Fair held in Chiba city, Japan, the Cold War relationship between the two countries was clearly over.[41] As John Ruggie has pointed out, "A very different and much more politicized international trading game is emerging, one that is not well illuminated by the conventional free-trade/protectionism discourse."[42]

Trade between Japan and the United States will of course continue, but it will be managed trade—something that has long been true for the Japanese side but that the Americans must now learn. Interestingly enough, the 1991 Japanese-American agreement concerning trade in semiconductors is an excellent example of successfully managed trade. Article 10 of the agreement states: "The Government of Japan recognizes that the U.S. semiconductor industry expects that the foreign market share will grow to more than 20 percent of the Japanese market by the end of 1992 and considers that this can be realized." The very definition of managed trade is negotiated market shares. Nonetheless, in order to protect their ideological *amour propre,* the Americans inserted into the preface: "The purpose of this Agreement is to enhance free trade in semiconductors on the basis of market principles and the competitive positions of the U.S. and Japanese industries and in accordance with established principles of the General Agreement on Tariffs and Trade."[43]

More intellectually serious than the trade issue is the problem of structural differences between the Japanese and American economies. "To what extent," asks I. M. Destler, "is major systemic variation politically tolerable, consistent with the notion of a 'fair' overall relationship?"[44] It is unnecessary here to rehearse the extensive attacks on and defenses of *keiretsu,* administrative guidance, structural corruption, infringements of intellectual property rights, industrial policy itself, and many other features of the Japanese economic system that have commanded the attention of Japanese and Americans for the past two decades.[45] Actually, it has long been recognized that structural differences need not in themselves be an obstacle to economic exchange, as the years of expanding trade and investment among the command economies, the reformed command economies, the capitalist developmental states, and the laissez-faire economies demonstrate. The question of structural differences between Japan and the United States has become salient because it embarrasses the U.S. government's economic advisers. Their advice has been based on the idea that structural differences did not exist, or that evolutionary change was reducing them, or that such tactics as the Structural Impediments Initiative (aimed at Japan's retail trade industry, its lax antitrust laws, spending on public works, and other more or less innocent bystanders) would take care of the problem.

The fighting issue at the heart of the structural differences question is "revisionism" and the possibility that those whom the Japanese government, and American hangers-on, label "revisionists" may turn out to be correct. Peter Ennis has defined "revisionism" as the "view that Japan's economy and society are not organized around classical notions of free markets, in which the direction of the economy is determined by the independent actions of consumers and corporations all operating to maximize their profits and incomes. This challenges the conventional wisdom (hence 'revisionism') among American policymakers that Japan is fundamentally similar to the United States and other Western capitalist democracies."[46]

Until the early 1990s the Japanese establishment stigmatized the views of anyone who suggested that Japan had a different history of industrialization, a different role for the state in the economy, a different evaluation of economic affairs in the overall scheme of things, and different ways of financing industry or dealing with labor-management problems than was taught in English-language textbooks. Even today some Japanese writers warn of revisionism's dangers. Iida Tsuneo, for example, himself a staff member of the primary semiofficial agency for contending that Japan is incomparable, still wants the economy declared off limits for discussion. He also insists that Japan's economy is just like other capitalist economies: its trade surpluses are temporary, *keiretsu* are not important, and the revisionists who "say the Japanese economy is capitalist in form only and actually operates on non-market principles" are making arguments that are "polemical and overdrawn."[47]

But what is new and important is that many Japanese writers and economists are beginning to acknowledge that there are major differences between Japan and the United States. This is important for international relations because it puts the Japanese-American relationship on a new ideological footing, one that in my opinion is more realistic than the old one and that will have to abandon the condescending efforts of American *gaiatsu* to force the Japanese to reform their economy using the American economy as a model. As Harry Gelber puts it, "Marx was clearly wrong—at least so far—in arguing that 'the mode of production of material life determines the general character of the social, political, and spiritual processes of life,' for neither industrialism nor post-industrialism have made Japanese society akin to Germany or France like Britain."[48] Some Japanese are starting to agree.

The late Foreign Minister Ōkita Saburō, one of Japan's most distinguished economists, in what may also be a mild parody of President Bush's rhetoric, writes: "There are many rooms in the house of capitalism. . . . [Japan may occupy] some kinder gentler middle ground between a centrally controlled economy and a laissez faire market-driven economy. The Japanese experience is thus studied as one point of light."[49] Sakakibara Eisuke in a recent book characterizes Japan as a "non-capitalist market economy."[50] Noda Masaaki lists seven principles that he believes distinguish Japan's "samurai capitalism" from its Anglo-American relatives, number seven being that "national prosperity is in the hands of state bureaucrats."[51] Terasawa Yoshio confesses that "Japan is not really the pure survival-of-the-fittest American-type of capitalism. It is half socialism . . . and the government is in control. . . . On the surface Japan is a capitalist system like that of the United States, in other words a free competition, survival-of-the-fittest system; but on the inside it is different."[52]

Not all of this new candor will please Americans. Every once in a while a Japanese writer contends that Japan's superior economic performance vis-à-vis the Americans was not just a matter of market forces and getting the prices right but a form of retaliation against the United States for its hegemony. Or neonationalist writers argue that Japan's economic performance demonstrates the superiority of the Japanese "race," while deriding "mongrel" nations such as the United States and Brazil. For example, Professor Aida Yūji of Kyoto University has suggested that "Iberian and African cultural traits seem to impede industrialization," and that the United States "with its vast human and technological resources . . . could become a premier agrarian power—a giant version of Denmark, for example—and the breadbasket of the world."[53]

These views are important for international relations, I believe, because they signal that Japan is consciously drawing away from the American example and beginning to see itself as a model for other Asian economies (and perhaps Eastern Europe and Russia as well). It seems significant that when, in September 1991, the Russians suggested that they might be willing to return the Northern Territories to Japan, MITI minister Nakao Eiichi replied that his ministry was ready to offer Moscow the benefit of its own postwar reconstruction experience in rebuilding the economy.[54] Such advice might be more valuable than any currently being proffered by the IMF or the World Bank.

Japan is not of course a *potential* model for East Asia. It is already the prototype of the capitalist developmental states—

Taiwan, South Korea, and Singapore in the first tier, the ASEAN states in the second—that have transformed Pacific politics. The most important fact about the post–Cold War Asia-Pacific region is Japan's growing economic dominance and the degree to which it is integrating all the nations of the region (including mainland China) through trade, direct investment, aid, financial services, technology transfer, and Japan's continuing role as a developmental model. The high yen *(endaka)* caused Japan to enter for the first time into a genuine horizontal division of labor with the other nations of East Asia. Today there is no doubt that Japan has the capacity to create a yen-based regional economic grouping in the Asia-Pacific region, and that it has been moving in that direction as a way of responding to the expanded market that the EC has created and to the North American free-trade area. Japan understands, without openly acknowledging it, that the European and North American agreements came into being when they did in part as responses to the challenge of Japan's own neomercantilism; but it does not want to exacerbate the situation by a precipitate move toward a yen bloc. Moreover, many Japanese leaders warn against any action that could disrupt relations between Japan and North America and Europe. Former Prime Minister Nakasone has declared, "It is impossible to imagine a secure Asia without a U.S. presence."[55]

There are many speculative aspects to the growing trend toward economic regionalism. Europeans, Latin Americans, and Southeast Asians all ask themselves whether they can really trust putting their respective destinies in the hands of Germans, Americans, or Japanese. Equally important, existing institutions have the capacity to transcend or redirect regionalism in potentially less exclusive directions. NATO, OECD, the G-7 democracies, APEC, and PECC already exist and are functioning. Nonetheless, I believe that these considerations are not strong enough to stand in the way of regionalism, and that by the end of the century the world is likely to be reduced to a G-3: a Japan-dominated Asia-Pacific region in which the United States has only observer status; a German-dominated Europe that includes Austria, Scandinavia, and probably Poland, Czechoslovakia, and Hungary; and a U.S.-dominated North American region that may well be preoccupied with economic and demographic disasters in Mexico and elsewhere.[56] But I acknowledge that there are many contingencies that could alter this prediction and that the world of the future might be only G-2: Europe and an Asia-Pacific region that includes both Japan and the United States. There are powerful influences promoting this configuration, including the fact that two-fifths of Japan's overseas direct investment is in North America. There is also the negative factor that whereas the United States is feared and envied in Latin America, Japan is feared and envied in Southeast Asia, making each an ideal counterweight for the other.

One further question has not received enough attention but constitutes perhaps the most important intellectual issue in assessing Japan's future role in the world. What are Japan's intentions, or is Japan even capable of having strategic intentions? All intelligence estimates are based on a combination of three sets of data—past behavior, current capabilities, and future intentions—with a conscious attempt to avoid all forms of theorizing since these may skew or warp the data. In the case of Japan, past behavior and current capabilities are so extraordinary and so formidable as to cause any other nation or people to be concerned about its future intentions. As we have already noted, many of Japan's allies and trading partners believe that during the Gulf War and with regard to the Uruguay Round of GATT negotiations Japan displayed an inexplicable inability to discern its own national interest. This aspect of Japan of course contrasts markedly with its well-known ability at the level of industry and finance to develop and pursue long-term strategies with intense competitiveness.

Perhaps the most articulate proponent of the view that Japan is incapable of formulating strategic intentions is Karel van Wolferen. He comes to the same conclusions as Professor Sasaki Takeshi quoted earlier, but he sees the paralysis of the Japanese government as more serious and less easily corrected than do Sasaki and other Japanese political scientists. For van Wolferen, Japan is without a compass and without brakes. He writes:

> I distinguish administrative decisions, which involve adjustments to an existing policy, from political decisions, which introduce new commitments or major changes in the way a country orders its domestic affairs or relates to the rest of the world. Japan's administrators (government bureaucrats as well as the bureaucrats in the indus-

trial federations, the financial institutions and the corporate groupings) are among the world's most capable administrators. But like
bureaucrats anywhere in the world, they can of necessity only be
concerned with very limited areas of policy-making. What makes
Japan special is the inability of its politicians to come up with the
necessary political input, even when that would seem to serve the
national interest.[57]

In my opinion, this political paralysis is an unintended consequence of the way in which the United States exercised its hegemonic role in the Cold War, what Tonelson earlier called the
"smothering strategy." But when it comes to Japan's movement
toward a new Greater East Asia Co-Prosperity Sphere, I believe
that Japan may know exactly what it is doing, that its bureaucrats are quite capable of guiding the nation in this direction, and
that its seeming indecision merely reflects a delicate sense of timing and excellent camouflage for its long-range intentions. Since
1987, according to *The Economist,* "Officials at MITI, the Ministry of International Trade and Industry, have been studying the
economic prospects of the Pacific basin. They have concluded
that greater political and economic integration of the region is
inevitable. They are groping for a way to harness that development for Japanese interests."[58] As mentioned earlier, former
Prime Minister Nakasone opposes such a grouping if it would
exclude the United States, but others such as Kakizawa Kōji, the
former ruling party's leading foreign affairs specialist, favor it.[59]
Japan has already supported the floating of two different trial
baloons. In Seoul, in January 1989, it backed former Australian
Prime Minister Bob Hawke's original proposal for an APEC without the United States. And at the end of 1990, Malaysian Prime
Minister Mahathir Mohamad proposed an East Asian Economic
Group that, in Hadi Soesastro's terms, "is perhaps the first time
after World War II in which a leadership role in East Asia is
handed to Japan on a silver platter by another Asian country."[60]
    Japan has not (yet) formally endorsed any proposal that
would start to separate it from the markets of North America
and Europe. But it is clearly thinking much harder about this
issue than it is about, for example, the Uruguay Round of the
GATT talks. In a speech in Los Angeles during the summer of
1991, Japanese Ambassador to the United States Murata Ryōhei
issued this warning:

I'd like to tell you that there is an apprehension in Asia that the EC and a North American free-trade area might form introverted, less open economic entities. This is why some Asian leaders have proposed the formation of economic entities in Asia, which would exclude non-Asian developed nations such as the United States. However, I sincerely hope that the North American free-trade area will be an open, extroverted system, rather than closed and introverted. If the latter is pursued, it may lead to inattention on the part of the United States regarding the Asia-Pacific region. This inattention could conceivably result in the advocacy of economic regionalism in Asia.[61]

In my opinion, much more important than the European single market or the North American Free Trade Agreement as an influence on Japanese thinking was the Plaza Accord of 1985. It raised the value of the yen from 235 yen to 1 U.S. dollar to approximately 135 yen to 1 U.S. dollar. Although this devaluation of the dollar was expected to give North American and European firms a window of opportunity to compete with Japan, they failed to capitalize on it and the opportunity has now passed. At the same time Japan undertook a major restructuring of its industries, including massive investments domestically and overseas. Out of this experience came Japan's conception of a new regional order, a new and much more prosperous version of the Greater East Asia Co-Prosperity Sphere; and it has not been distracted from that goal by Americans' harping on the GATT negotiations or the Persian Gulf War. If I am right it may be that just as the people of Moscow and East Berlin now joke that socialism was the shortest route from capitalism to capitalism, the people of the Pacific will soon be saying that Asian capitalism was the shortest route from the Greater East Asia Co-Prosperity Sphere to the Greater East Asia Co-Prosperity Sphere.

III

One further reason why I think the future may see three distinct economic regions rather than a renewal of the Japanese-American alliance is that Japanese writers have begun to prepare the public emotionally for a rupture of that alliance. This is not a bilateral but primarily a Japanese initiative. It started in Japan in the wake of the Gulf War. Despite a growing interest in and fear of Japan as an economic competitor, most Americans have until recently paid little attention to Japan. They supposed that Japanese-American relations were at least as good as those with Europe and considerably better than with some long-standing American friends such as Israel. But from Japan come cries of alarm and an outpouring of emotionalism that William Watts sees as a "communications disconnect."[62] Murakami Kaoru warns that "The watchword of the Congress is bash Japan, but meanwhile in Japan a new nationalism is gathering strength."[63] Some of this writing deserves serious consideration, even if evaluating its influence is still quite difficult.

Ogura Kazuo, then head of the Cultural Exchange Department (Bunka Kōryū Bu) of the Foreign Ministry, is interested primarily in the differences in values held by Japanese and Americans and the place of value judgments in relations among foreigners. He writes:

> Both countries are democratic and have market economies. . . . However, that is not the point. These two countries have taken an entirely different *approach* to these values at home and abroad. . . . Many Japanese find the concepts behind personal liberty, democracy, and free market economics to be outlandish [*batakusai,* exotic, foreign]. . . . The Japanese people do not have a common set of ideals and values. They do not share any "universal" religious beliefs or political ideals with other peoples in the world. The Japanese have not exported their "gods" to other countries. . . . Japan has been interested only in earning respect and status in the world community. Will Japan ever change its mind and sacrifice human life for other causes? The answer is no.[64]

Without doubt this argument is overdrawn; the ethical principles involved in *on, giri,* and *ninjō* (roughly translated, obligation, duty, and human emotions) are as ubiquitous in Japan as any set of ethics ever can be in a given society. But the essence of Ogura's argument is that Americans expect the Japanese to adopt *their* values. The Japanese, however, are not interested in American values, are not trying to proselytize their own ones, and resent America's trying to make Japan a "psychological colony."[65] The idea that Japanese do not have "fundamental" values, only situational ones, is an old theme of Western writers about Japan from Ruth Benedict to Karel van Wolferen. One

Japanese writer, who refers to Japan as a "secular superpower," goes so far as to say,

> In international settings, Japanese never seem to know what's going on. Even at home, our mass media often miss the significance of world events. Lacking a system of principled beliefs—call it religion or ideology—we misjudge the values and motivations of other people. We have a superficial, sometimes distorted view of global politics. The simple truth is that we are uncomfortable with philosophical concepts. Japanese love making money, but if you ask us why we toil, we shug our shoulders; hard work and affluence seem to be ends in themselves. Questions about the meaning of life elude us.[66]

These views are relevant to the alliance because, as Iriye and Cohen observe, in the postwar world Japanese have defined themselves in relation to the United States whereas Americans perceive Japan only insofar as it reflects American values. Americans are actually little interested in Japanese realities.[67] These conditions have existed throughout the postwar period, but the disparities in power between the two countries and their common interests in the Cold War kept any tensions thus generated under control. The Gulf War shattered the old complacency. "One must realize," writes Okamoto Yukio (formerly of the Ministry of Foreign Affairs), "that American expectations toward Japan had risen considerably under the concept of 'global partnership.' . . . [Japan failed to live up to these expectations.] But there's more to the situation. Unfortunately, Japan's basic posture was questioned. Americans interpreted Japan's actions as being completely void of any human convictions about the need to defend peace and order. . . . In addition, Japan decisively left the impression that it reacts only when pressured by the United States and never takes the initiative in coping with problems as if they were its own."[68]

A particular virulent form of the rising concern with value differences among Japanese and Americans is racism. Ishihara Shintarō has long harped on American racial prejudice as "the root cause of Japan-bashing," and in the Persian Gulf War many Japanese felt that the differences between American criticism of the Japanese and of the Germans reflected racism.[69] There may be some truth to this, but it also ignores and deflects attention from the differences between Germany and Japan. Germany has real political parties compared with Japan's façade of political accountability; Germany is embedded in the European Community whereas Japan has hardly begun to respond to its neighbors' concerns; Germany is actively engaged in helping a distressed area of the world, East Europe, whereas much of Japan's foreign aid is as valuable to its general trading companies as it is to the designated recipients; and Germany clearly expressed its differences with the Bush administration's strategy toward Iraq while the Japanese debate centered only on what would satisfy the Americans. In light of these considerations Americans are tired of being called racists or Japan-bashers for trying to understand accurately what is going on in Japanese policy-making circles.

At the same time Americans suspect that Japanese charges of American racism reveal a Japanese preoccupation with race. The long series of racial slurs uttered by former Prime Minister Nakasone Yasuhiro, by LDP faction leader (and during 1992 Foreign Minister) Watanabe Michio, and by former Justice Minister Kajiyama Seiroku are only the most obvious examples. But this preoccupation with racial categories is revealed in many other, more subtle ways. For example, the *Asahi shimbun* recently noted that a Japanese citizen, Professor Iriye Akira, was in 1988 elected president of the 18,000-member American Historical Association, and then added, "It is inconceivable that a similar thing could happen in Japan any time soon."[70] Another example was the statement by Sassa Atsuyuki, the former head of the Cabinet Security Office and a strong critic of Japan's lack of military cooperation in the Gulf crisis, that Japan "underestimated the ferocity of the Anglo-Saxons" *(angurosakuson no sugosa no kashō-hyōka).*[71] An American is tempted to respond that it is not accurate to refer to American citizens as Anglo-Saxons, since the United States is a polyethnic society. But the Japanese might also have noticed that neither the chairman of the American Joint Chiefs of Staff (General Colin Powell), nor a field commander with the surname of Schwarzkopf, nor many of the troops can plausibly be thought of as Anglo-Saxons. Japan may have underestimated the ferocity of the Americans, but it is alarming that they conceive of them in racial terms.

I do not believe that the Japanese-American alliance is unraveling because of value differences alone. The comments quoted here are, however, symptomatic of the changing emotional and psychodynamic foundations of the relationship. My own position is much like that of Ogura Kazuo: I expect foreigners to have "foreign" values.[72] As for Japan's lack of involvement in the Gulf War, I agree with Henry Kissinger when he wrote: "I told a highly educated and sophisticated friend that I could not imagine any American rationale that would encourage Japan to place its forces at a great distance from its home islands when there was no Japanese urgency to do so. He didn't understand. He said that any nation as powerful economically as Japan had a duty to participate, otherwise it is taking a free ride. Now that is an approach to foreign policy that might work if everybody had the same interests, but it is also historically unsound."[73]

Nonetheless, it seems to me that the emotional tinder discussed here has a potential for fueling the larger, more substantive disputes between Japan and the United States discussed earlier. As Barnds puts it, "What appears likely is not a rupture or a complete breakdown of the relationship, but a gradual drifting apart in terms of psychology, trust, and political cooperation. There is as little evidence of American willingness to accomodate Japan's growing (potential) power as there is of Japanese willingness to exercise a measure of leadership."[74]

One sample of the possible future course of the U.S.-Japan relationship was President Bush's disastrous visit to Tokyo in January 1992. Bush had earlier canceled a November 1991 trip to Japan because of American criticism that he was neglecting domestic policy, a cancellation that had the incidental effect of weakening the new prime ministership of Miyazawa Kiichi. When the trip was rescheduled for January 1992, the president decided, as an act of political expediency, to link Japan and the issue of American unemployment; and he took with him twenty-one leaders of American industry, including the outspoken chairman of Chrysler, Lee Iacocca.

On January 19, 1992, Sakurauchi Yoshio, the speaker of the Japanese House of Representatives, replied to Bush and his companions, "It is really pathetic that America is becoming a subcontractor to Japan. The reason for the trade imbalance is that U.S. workers won't work hard and are unproductive and often illiterate."[75] This was followed by Prime Minister Miyazawa's remark that the United States had lost its "work ethic," sparking a retort from Senator Ernest Hollings of South Carolina that

American workers should "draw a mushroom cloud and put underneath it: made in America by lazy and illiterate Americans and tested in Japan."[76]

Perhaps more significant is the growing evidence in both Japan and the United States that such political epithets and stereotypes are gaining greater currency among normally uninterested sectors of the two populations. In Japan, the Gakken Company, a publisher of popular and sensational books, brought out a heavily illustrated mass-market paperback called *Nihon basshingu ron (On Japan Bashing)*, subtitled in English "Latest Trends in Japan Bashing," which plays to the Japanese public's sense of grievance that it is merely being used as a scapegoat for the failings of others. As if in retaliation, Japanese sports enthusiasts launched an openly racist attack on a Hawaiian contender for the rank of *yokozuna* (grand champion) in sumo wrestling merely because he was a foreigner.

Meanwhile in the United States, Americans were objecting strenuously to efforts by the Nintendo Company of Japan to buy a Seattle baseball team. And in Los Angeles, a popular revolt from below stopped city authorities from completing a contract to buy Japanese-made trolley cars. In many regions of the United States a campaign to buy American automobiles showed unexpected strength. And across the nation a novel by Michael Crichton entitled *Rising Sun*, which deals with the challenge of Japan, became an instant best-seller. Crichton's novel carries as a final epigram a statement by Morita Akio of Sony: "If you don't want Japan to buy it, don't sell it."

These sorts of developments can be read as symptoms of the intrinsic situation that has developed between the two countries because of the end of the Cold War and the ability of vested interests—intellectual, military, and economic—to block needed reforms. As I stated at the outset, the Japanese-American relationship continues today only through inertia, without any foundation in grand strategy or in response to a common threat. Obviously, the spread of *kembei* (contempt for America) in Japan and so-called Japan-bashing in America beyond the circles of policy specialists, and largely because of their myopia and neglect, complicates any attempt to find solutions.

According to one important scenario, the situation is already beyond repair. In their wrongly neglected book *The Coming*

War with Japan (neglected in the United States but not in Japan, where by early 1992 it had sold around 400,000 copies), George Friedman and Meredith LeBard write:

> It is easier [for the U.S.] to force Japan to limit its exports of cars to the U.S. and to increase its purchase of U.S. cars than to increase the efficiency of Detroit. This is the trap of empire. Empire is first won by the most efficient and industrious. It is then maintained by political and military efforts, not economic efficiency. Thus, economies atrophy while armies and navies grow. This military power is used to transfer wealth from colonies and allies, rather than going to the political effort of rebuilding the domestic economy. At each point, the imperialist power has a choice of solving an economic crisis through internal effort or increased exploitation. The latter, being the path of least resistance, is the usual choice. The result is frequently a vast military force with a hollow socio-economic center, an empire in collapse.[77]

This view of course owes a great deal to Paul Kennedy's *Rise and Fall of the Great Powers,* although it stresses the consequences of the decline of the American economy for the Pacific. Whether the failure to correct this decline leads to an American policy of extortion to maintain its superpower status and eventually to war is an open question, but Friedman and LeBard are neither wrong nor sensationalist to draw attention to the possibility.

In my opinion it is not hard to imagine a renewed alliance between Japan and the United States, one based on their current interests and strengths and not on those that existed when the Security Treaty was first negotiated. Such a renewed alliance would first and foremost attempt to institutionalize the economic interdependence of the two countries while recognizing their political and ideological differences. On the American side, two things at least are needed: first, a legal framework for managing our trade with Japan (section 301 of the Trade Act of 1988 would do: if the law had been implemented against Japan over its closed rice market, we would probably today have much more friendly relations with Japan). Second, we need an industrial policy to ensure that American manufactured goods are attractive to American (and overseas) buyers, thereby avoiding protectionism, which would merely cheat everybody.

But although a newly formulated Japanese-American alliance

is not conceptually difficult to imagine and is clearly in the economic interests of the peoples involved, it would be politically difficult to forge. It would require fundamental changes in the systems of corporate governance, antitrust law, education, and political representation of both countries and an intense analytical effort on the part of the United States. It may well turn out that the two different states—the one military and regulatory and the other economic and developmental—cannot overcome their differences. In any case a renewed alliance would require leadership of at least the 1949 variety, and that unfortunately is in short supply on both sides of the Pacific.

Notes

INTRODUCTION

1. For the concept of a dictatorship of development, see Richard Lowenthal, "Development vs. Utopia in Communist Policy," in Chalmers Johnson, ed., *Change in Communist Systems* (Stanford: Stanford University Press, 1970), pp. 35, 39.

2. Robert Kuttner, "The Pacific Rim: Why Clinton Is at Sea," *Business Week,* December 13, 1993.

3. Philip G. Cerny, *The Changing Architecture of Politics: Structure, Agency, and the Future of the State* (London: Sage Publications, 1990), p. 12.

1 *La Serenissima* OF THE EAST

1 Chalmers Johnson, *MITI and the Japanese Miracle* (Stanford: Stanford University Press, 1982), p. 311. Some of the more important comparative studies of Japan are: Reinhard Bendix, "Preconditions of Development: A Comparison of Japan and Germany," in R.P. Dore, ed., *Aspects of Social Change in Modern Japan* (Princeton: Princeton University Press, 1967), pp. 27–68; Cyril E. Black, et al., *The Modernization of Japan and Russia* (New York: Free Press, 1975); Marius B. Jansen, "On Foreign Borrowing," in Albert M. Craig, ed., *Japan: A Comparative View* (Princeton: Princeton University Press, 1979), pp. 18–48; Robert E. Ward and Dankwart A. Rustow, eds., *Political Modernization in Japan and Turkey* (Princeton: Princeton University Press, 1964).

2. James Morris, *The World of Venice,* rev. ed. (New York: Harcourt Brace Jovanovich, 1974), pp. 14, 31, 32, 33, 34, 44, 208, 256. See also John Julius Norwich, *A History of Venice* (New York: Knopf, 1982). Note Donald C. Hellmann's generalization that the Japanese have concentrated more "on aims appropriate to an expanding international trading company" than on those of a nation; see his *Japan and East Asia* (New York: Praeger, 1972), pp. 61–62.

3. "Japan Official Criticized for Trade Views," *Los Angeles Times,* April 9, 1982.

4. Benjamin Ward, *The Conservative Economic World View* (New York: Basic Books, 1979), p. 19.

5. Morris, *op. cit.,* p. 96.

6. Winston Davis, "The Secularization of Japanese Religion," in Frank E. Reynolds and Theodore M. Ludwig, eds., *Transitions and Transformations in the History of Religions: Essays in Honor of Joseph M. Kitagawa* (Leiden: E.J. Brill, 1980), p. 265.

7. Ward, *op. cit.,* p. 18.

8. Murakami Yasusuke, "The Age of New Middle Mass Politics: The Case of Japan," *Journal of Japanese Studies* 8 (Winter 1982): 29–72.

9. On "oligarchy" in contemporary Japan, cf. Lawrence W. Beer, "Constitutional Revolution in Japanese Law, Society, and Politics," *Modern Asian Studies* 16 (1982): 40, 52.

10. Morris, *op. cit.,* p. 73.

11. "Japan's Strategy for the 80's," *Business Week,* December 14, 1981, p. 119.

12. Namiki Nobuyoshi, *Nihon-kata keizai o toku (Explaining Japanese-type Economies)* (Tokyo: President, 1981), pp. 104 ff., 292–301.

13. Komiya Ryūtarō and Yamamoto Kōzō, "The Officer in Charge of Economic Affairs in the Japanese Government." Unpublished paper, January 1979, p. 28.

14. Ward, *op. cit.,* p. 5. Cf. "The Crisis in Economic Theory," *The Public Interest,* special 15th anniversary issue, 1980.

15. Between 1969 and 1992, 31 economists have been awarded Nobel prizes in Economics: 1 each from The Netherlands, France, and the former USSR; 2 each from Norway and Sweden; 4 from the U.K.; and 20 from the United States.

16. Namiki, *op. cit.,* pp. 15, 46–49.

17. (Tokyo: Chūō Kōron Sha, 1979).

18. W. G. Beasley, "Modern Japan: An Historian's View," in Beasley, ed., *Modern Japan* (Berkeley: University of California, Press, 1975), pp. 20–21.

19. Nakamura Takafusa, *The Postwar Japanese Economy,* trans. Jacqueline Kaminski (Tokyo: University of Tokyo Press, 1981), p. 17.

20. *Ibid.,* p. 18.

21. *Ibid.*

22. *Ibid.*

23. Minabe Shigeo (Hiroshima University), "The Strength and Weakness of the Japanese Economy: Free Labor Services as Lifetime Employment Insurance," *United Malayan Banking Corporation Economic Review* 17/2 (1981): 5–6.

24. *Ibid.,* p. 7. Professor Minabe has no illusions about a trade-off in Japanese enterprise familism: "Japan is a heaven for mediocre people, but hell for those who are especially blessed" (p. 9).

25. Nakamura, *op. cit.,* p. 19.

26. Johnson, *op. cit.,* pp. 204–07.

27. Nakamura, *op. cit.,* p. 48.

28. See Suzuki Yoshio, *Money and Banking in Contemporary Japan* (New Haven: Yale University Press, 1980).

29. For views critical of Japan's alleged capital liberalization, see Leon Holl-

erman, "Japan's New Banking Laws," *The Banker,* January 1982, pp. 1–3. During 1981 the Diet enacted a law to identify and record the amount of money each Japanese citizen had in tax-free savings accounts (the so-called Green Card System). The intent was to end the flagrant tax evasion that the old system had been generating. However, the mere threat of bringing the system under control has raised the specter of savers withdrawing some 9 trillion from bank deposits, 4 trillion from money market trusts and 14 trillion from postal savings, and investing it in gold, land, or sending it abroad. See "Moves to Dump 'Green Card' Rise to a High Pitch." *Japan Economic Journal,* April 13, 1982.

30. Kataoka Tetsuya, *Waiting for a Pearl Harbor: Japan Debates Defense* (Stanford: Hoover Institution, 1980).

31. S.J. Kaufmann, "What Really Bothers Foreign Businessmen in Japan," *Japan Times Weekly,* April 3, 1982.

32. See Yamamura Kozo, "General Trading Companies in Japan: Their Origins and Growth," in Hugh Patrick, ed., *Japanese Industrialization and Its Social Consequences* (Berkeley: University of California Press, 1976), pp. 167–68, 184.

2 Social Values and the Theory of Late Economic Development in East Asia

1. Umehara Takeshi, "The Civilization of the Forest," *New Perspectives Quarterly* 7:3 (Summer 1990): 29–30.

2. Kim Yoon Hyung, "An Introduction to the Korean Model of Political Economy," in Lee-Jay Cho and Yoon Hyung Kim, eds., *Korea's Political Economy: An Institutional Perspective* (Boulder, Col.: Westview, 1994), p. 45.

3. I distinguish the state-guided capitalist economies, which I call "capitalist developmental states," from the Anglo-American examples, which I call "capitalist regulatory states," in *MITI and the Japanese Miracle* (Stanford: Stanford University Press, 1982).

4. Max Weber, *The Religion of China,* trans. Hans H. Gerth (Glencoe, Ill.: Free Press, 1951), chap. 8, "Confucianism and Protestantism."

5. Cf. Robert Bellah, *Tokugawa Religion* (Boston: Beacon Press, 1957).

6. See, e.g., John Brewer, *The Sinews of Power: War, Money, and the English State, 1688–1783* (New York: Knopf, 1989); Grace Goodell, "The Importance of Political Participation for Sustained Capitalist Development," *Archives of European Sociology* 26 (1985): 93–127; and J. H. Plumb, *The Growth of Political Stability in England, 1675–1725* (Harmondsworth, Middlesex: Penguin, 1973).

7. Kim Yoon Hyung, *op. cit.,* p. 47.

8. Winston Davis, "Religion and Development: Weber and the East Asian Experience," in Myron Weiner and Samuel P. Huntington, eds., *Understanding Political Development* (Boston: Little, Brown, 1987), pp. 221–80, esp. p. 269. This article contains a bibliography of Davis's other works.

9. Albert O. Hirschman, *Rival Views of Market Society and Other Recent Essays* (New York: Viking, 1986), p. 123.

10. Robert N. Bellah, in Institute of East Asian Studies, ed., *The Japanese*

Challenge and the American Response: A Symposium (Berkeley: Institute of East Asian Studies, University of California, 1982), p. 112.

11. Albert O. Hirschman, *Essays in Trespassing: From Economics to Politics and Beyond* (Cambridge: Cambridge University Press, 1981), p. 3.

12. Thorstein Veblen, *Imperial Germany and the Industrial Revolution* (1915; reprinted University of Michigan Press, 1966); Joseph Schumpeter, *Imperialism and Social Classes* (1951; reprinted Philadelphia: Porcupine Press, 1991); Alexander Gerschenkron, *Economic Backwardness in Historical Perspective* (Cambridge, Mass.: Harvard University Press, 1962) and *Bread and Democracy in Germany* (1943; reprinted Cornell University Press, 1989); Alice H. Amsden, *Asia's Next Giant: South Korea and Late Industrialization* (New York: Oxford University Press, 1989); Jung-en Woo, *Race to the Swift: State and Finance in Korean Industrialization* (New York: Columbia University Press, 1991); and Robert Wade, *Governing the Market: Economic Theory and the Role of Government in East Asian Industrialization* (Princeton: Princeton University Press, 1990).

13. See Chalmers Johnson, "Political Institutions and Economic Performance: The Government-Business Relationship in Japan, South Korea, and Taiwan," in Frederic C. Deyo, ed., *The Political Economy of the New Asian Industrialism* (Ithaca: Cornell University Press, 1987), p. 143.

14. Gordon A. Craig, Introduction, in Eckart Kehr, *Economic Interest, Militarism, and Foreign Policy: Essays on German History,* trans. Grete Heinz (Berkeley: University of California Press, 1977), p. xi.

15. *Ibid.,* pp. 118–19. Kehr also writes, "The characteristic and distinctive feature of the Bismarckian Reich lies in the peculiar way in which the relationship between the state and nation was arranged, the method of regulating relations between the federal states, and the attribution of legal sovereignty to the *Bundesrat,* while real hegemony was reserved to the Emperor and Prussia," chap. 1. The exact nature of the conservative alliances in prewar Japan was the focus of one of the most important Marxist debates in this century. See Germaine A. Hoston, *Marxism and the Crisis of Development in Prewar Japan* (Princeton: Princeton University Press, 1986).

16. Cf. Chalmers Johnson, "South Korean Democratization: The Role of Economic Development," *The Pacific Review* 2:1 (1989): 1–10.

3   COMPARATIVE CAPITALISM

1. See Peter Passell, "Economic Scene," *New York Times,* December 17, 1992 (where Tyson is said not to be among the "wisest economic heads" of this generation); James Fallows, "Commentary," National Public Radio, January 5, 1993; James Risen, "Economists Watch in Quiet Fury," *Los Angeles Times,* January 8, 1993; and Alice H. Amsden, "From P.C. to E.C.: Now, Economic Correctness," *New York Times,* op-ed., January 12, 1993. For excerpts from Tyson's columns as a member of the *Los Angeles Times'* Board of Economists, see *Los Angeles Times,* December 20, 1992.

The economists also attacked Robert Reich, Clinton's appointee as secretary of labor, because he does not have a Ph.D. in economics but was trained as a lawyer. See Louis Uchitelle, "Clinton's Economics Point Man," *New York*

Times, November 21, 1992. It seems never to have occurred to either the economists or the journalists taking down their complaints that one place on earth where national economic policy is made by lawyers and where economists are asked to keep their distance is 1-3-1 Kasumigaseki, Tokyo, the headquarters of Japan's Ministry of International Trade and Industry.

2. Chalmers Johnson, Laura D'Andrea Tyson, and John Zysman, eds., *Politics and Productivity: How Japan's Development Strategy Works* (New York: Harper Business, 1989).

3. Paul R. Krugman, "What Do Undergrads Need to Know About Trade?" (Cambridge, Mass.: M.I.T., n.d.), typescript, 10 pp.

4. These are titles of influential books. See Richard Pascale and Anthony Athos, *The Art of Japanese Management* (New York: Warner Books, 1981); Rodney Clark, *The Japanese Company* (New Haven: Yale University Press, 1979); and Frank Gibney, *The Pacific Century* (New York: Scribner's, 1992).

5. Kenneth B. Pyle, *The Japanese Question: Power and Purpose in a New Era* (Washington, D.C.: AEI Press, 1992), p. 43.

6. C. Fred Bergsten, "The World Economy After the Cold War," *California Management Review,* 34:2 (Winter 1992): 53.

7. "The Purging of Japan," *The Australian,* April 11–12, 1992, p. 19.

8. John J. Curran, "Why Japan Will Emerge Stronger," *Fortune,* May 18, 1992.

9. Hoshino Shinyasu, "The Japanese Model: Maturing 'Miracle,' " *NIRA Library: International Crossroads,* May 1992.

10. Shimada Haruo, " 'Jyapan moderu' wa shinazu" [The "Japan Model" Will Not Die], *Bungei shunju* (February 1992), pp. 138–49. Also see former Foreign Minister Okita Saburo, "Japan's Catch-up Capitalism," *World Link* (September/October 1992), pp. 27–29.

11. See Shimada Haruo, "Japan's Industrial Culture and Labor-Management Relations," in Kumon Shumpei and Henry Rosovsky, eds., *The Political Economy of Japan: Cultural and Social Dynamics* (Stanford: Stanford University Press, 1992), pp. 267–91.

12. *Bungei shunju* (February 1992), p. 148.

13. World Bank, Press Release No. 16, October 15, 1991, p. 6.

14. "Japan Wants Strings on Aid: At Odds with U.S., Tokyo Urges Managed Economics," *International Herald Tribune,* March 9, 1992. In its 1991 World Development Report, the World Bank for the first time allowed the possibility of "market-friendly state intervention." It also authorized several major studies, funded by the Japanese, on why this idea was no longer heresy.

15. Morita Akio, " 'Nihon-kata keiei' ga abunai" ["Japanese-style Management in Danger"], *Bungei shunju* (February 1992), pp. 94–103.

16. "Corporate Values Reassessed," *Japan Update* (June 1992), p. 9.

17. Katayama Osamu, et al., "Nihon-kata keiei wa machigatta ka" ["Is Japanese-Style Management Mistaken?"], *Voice* (May 1992), pp. 82–112.

18. *Bungei shunju* (February 1992), p. 97.

19. *Bungei shunju* (April 1992) pp. 176–93.

20. *Voice* (May 1992), pp. 106–09.

21. *Bungei shunju* (April 1992), pp. 176–93.

22. Transcript of interview given by Senior Minister Lee Kuan Yew to James Impoco, Tokyo Bureau chief of *U.S. News & World Report*, August 27, 1992.

23. (Tokyo: Nihon Seisansei Honbu, 1983); translated as *The Rise of the Japanese Corporate System: The Inside View of a MITI Official*, trans. Thomas I. Elliott (London: Kegan Paul International, 1991). Quotations are taken from the English translation.

24. *Bungei shunju* (February 1992), pp. 138–39.

25. In Japanese, Shimada's terms are, *"sangyo no ikusei, shido, kantoku."* *Ibid.*, p. 145.

26. Thomas K. McCraw, "The Trouble with Adam Smith," *The American Scholar* (Summer 1992), p. 371.

27. Amaya as quoted by Clyde V. Prestowitz, Jr., "Beyond Laissez-Faire," *Foreign Policy*, 87 (Summer 1992): 80. On the distinction between producer and consumer economics, see Lester Thurow, *Head to Head: The Coming Economic Battle Among Japan, Europe, and America* (New York: Morrow, 1992), pp. 113–51.

28. Robert Zielinski and Nigel Holloway, *Unequal Equities: Power and Risk in Japan's Stock Market* (New York: Kodansha International, 1991), p. 12. On the financial dimensions of comparative capitalism, also see Michael E. Porter, "Capital Disadvantage: America's Failing Capital Investment System," *Harvard Business Review* (September/October 1992): 65–82.

29. W. Carl Kester and Timothy A. Luehrman, "The Myth of Japan's Low-Cost Capital," *Harvard Business Review* (May/June 1992): 135.

30. Eamonn Fingleton, "The Gaijin and Gyosei Shido," *Institutional Investor* (October 1990): 71–76.

31. Sakakibara Eisuke and Noguchi Yukio, officials of the Ministry of Finance, quoted by Pyle, *op. cit.*, p. 43.

32. Peter Gourevitch, *Politics in Hard Times: Comparative Responses to International Economic Crises* (Ithaca: Cornell University Press, 1986), p. 238. Cf. Mark Kesselman, "How Should One Study Economic Policy-making?" *World Politics*, 44/4 (July 1992): 645–72.

33. Manuel Castells, "Four Asian Tigers with a Dragon Head: A Comparative Analysis of the State, Economy, and Society in the Asian Pacific Rim," in Richard P. Appelbaum and Jeffrey Henderson, eds., *States and Development in the Asian Pacific Rim* (Newbury Park, Calif.: Sage Publications, 1992), p. 56.

34. *Ibid.*, p. 57.

35. *The American Scholar* (Summer 1992), p. 371.

36. Michael Lind, "The Catalytic State," *The National Interest* (Spring 1992), pp. 3–12.

37. James Kurth, "Things to Come: The Shape of the New World Order," *The National Interest* (Summer 1991), p. 11.

4 TRADE, REVISIONISM, AND THE FUTURE OF JAPANESE-AMERICAN RELATIONS

1. The quoted remark is from Miles Kahler, "The International Political Economy," in Nicholas X. Rizopoulos, ed., *Sea-Changes: American Foreign*

Policy in a World Transformed (New York: Council on Foreign Relations Press, 1990), p. 106.

2. The term "revisionism" applied to Japan was invented by Robert C. Neff in *Business Week*, August 7, 1989. On Japanese reactions to revisionism, see, *inter alia*, Homma Nagayo, "Nihon 'tasharon' no kiken," *Gaikō Forum*, October 1989, pp. 12–20; *Newsweek* (Japanese language ed.), October 26, 1989, pp. 8–15; "Gaikō no ketsuraku tsuku 'minaoshi ron,' " *Aera*, January 30, 1990, pp. 10–11; and Omori Minoru and George R. Packard, *Nichi-Bei shōtotsu e no michi* (The Road to a Japan-U.S. Collision) (Tokyo: Kōdansha, 1990). For a response, see " 'The Gang of Four' Defends the Revisionist Line," *U.S. News & World Report*, May 7, 1990, pp. 54–55.

3. *Nihon keizai shimbun*, September 28, 1989, p. 1.

4. *Ibid.*, October 21, 1988; cited in Frank K. Upham, "Legal Regulation of the Japanese Retail Industry: The Large-Scale Retail Stores Law and Prospects for Reform," Program on U.S.-Japan Relations, Harvard University, Occasional Paper 89–02, 1989, pp. 2, 42.

5. "Japanese Pay More When the Label Reads 'Made in Japan,' " *Los Angeles Times*, November 8, 1989.

6. Editorial, *Los Angeles Times*, November 12, 1989.

7. "Government Offices Slam Task Force on Price-gap Issue," *Daily Yomiuri*, December 12, 1989.

8. U.S. Congress, Joint Economic Committee, *Restoring International Balance: Japan's Trade and Investment Patterns* (Washington, D.C., 1988), pp. 34–35.

9. Speech of Clayton Yeutter, November 30, 1988. *U.S./Japan Economic Agenda*, No. 9 (February 1989), p. 3.

10. Sekiguchi Waichi, "Intellectual Property Trade in U.S.-Japan Relations," Program on U.S.-Japan Relations, Harvard University, Occasional Paper 89–10, 1989, p. 1; and Marie Anchordoguy, *Computers, Inc.: Japan's Challenge to IBM* (Cambridge, Mass.: Harvard East Asian Monographs, 1989), pp. 149–50.

11. See "American Business and the Japanese Patent System," *Congressional Record* (Senate), April 13, 1989.

12. "U.S. Chip Gets Patent in Japan," *New York Times*, November 22, 1989; "Patent News Keeps Bolstering Texas Instruments Stock," *Los Angeles Times*, November 23, 1989; and "Japan Grip Still Seen on Patents; Chip Award Offers Lesson in Frustration," *New York Times*, November 24, 1989.

13. Richard T. McCormack, Under Secretary of State for Economic Affairs, "Challenges to the International Economy in the 1990s," U.S. Department of State, *Current Policy*, No. 1223 (October 30, 1989), p. 4.

14. Speech in Tokyo, September 20, 1989. British Information Service, Policy Statement 49/89.

15. See Chalmers Johnson, "Rethinking Japanese Politics: A Godfather Reports," *Freedom at Issue*, November-December 1989, pp. 5–11.

16. Alexander Gerschenkron, *Bread and Democracy in Germany* (Ithaca: Cornell University Press, 1989), foreword by Charles S. Maier, pp. vii, xvii, xx.

17. Sam Jameson, "Three Rivals for Japanese Premiership Assess U.S. Frictions," *Los Angeles Times*, August 6, 1989.

18. *Japan Economic Journal*, November 25, 1989.

19. "Japan's Land Prices: A Blessing Becoming a Curse," *Japan Economic Journal,* January 20, 1990. Also see Robert L. Cutts, "Japan's New Land Standard," *The American Chamber of Commerce in Japan Journal,* March 1990, pp. 25–33, and "Power from the Ground Up: Japan's Land Bubble," *Harvard Business Review,* May-June 1990, pp. 164–72.

20. *Japan Economic Journal,* December 2, 1989.

21. *Japan Economic Journal,* December 9, 1989; "Japan Building Firms, U.S., Settle Bid Rigging Case," *Los Angeles Times,* November 24, 1989; "Settlement By Japanese Builders: They Agree to Pay $32.6 Million to U.S. in Navy Bid Rigging," *New York Times,* November 24, 1989.

22. Editorial, *Japan Economic Journal,* December 9, 1989.

23. John McMillan, "Dangō: Japan's Price-fixing Conspiracies," *Economics and Politics* 3:1 (November 1991): 201–18.

24. *Ekonomisuto,* July 18, 1988, p. 52; and Mitsubishi Sōgō Kenkyūjo, *Zenyosoku: 90 nendai no Nihon (A Total Forecast: Japan in the 1990s)* (Tokyo: Daiyamondo Sha, 1989), pp. 17–19.

25. "Tokushū: kensetsu 'dangō' no jitsuryokusha" (A Special Issue: Powers in Construction Dangō), *Zaikai tembō,* September 1989, p. 68. Also see letter to the editor by an official of the tax collecting division of a city in Saitama Prefecture, *Japan Times,* November 29, 1989; "A Rigged System," *Asahi shimbun,* ed., *Asahi Evening News,* October 6, 1989; *Sentaku,* May 1989; "Construction Door Still Seen as Shut," *Japan Times,* May 17, 1989; Uchiyama Kōzō, *Dangō mondai e no shiten (A View of the Dangō Problem)* (Tokyo: Tōshi Bunka Press, 1988); " 'Dangō' Underpins Construction Bid System," *Japan Economic Journal,* October 10, 1987; "The Tightest of Closed Shops Still Prospers," *Far Eastern Economic Review,* June 11, 1987; "Construction in Japan Runs on Dangō: Collusive Inner Circle Hurdle for U.S. Firms Despite Recent Pact," *Los Angeles Times,* April 3, 1988; and Robert L. Cutts, "The Construction Market: Japan Slams the Door," *California Management Review,* vol. 30, no. 4 (Summer 1988), pp. 46–63.

26. "U.S. Won't Impose Sanctions on Japan for Trade Barriers in Construction," *Los Angeles Times,* November 23, 1989; and "Japan Lashes Back at U.S. Criticism of Bidding Barriers," *Los Angeles Times,* November 25, 1989. Hills may have caved in on the Japanese construction industry in order to help reelect the LDP. The LDP's then secretary general, Ozawa Ichirō, said to the press that on October 12 he asked Hills not to create problems for the LDP and that she agreed. *Jiji Press,* Tokyo, November 28, 1989. Why even a conservative U.S. government would think that reelecting the LDP is in its interests is unclear.

27. McMillan, "Dangō: Japan's Price-fixing Conspiracies."

28. *Japan Economic Journal,* December 2, 1989.

29. R. Taggart Murphy, "The Crisis of Japan's Global Financial Dominance," Speech to the American Management Association and the Japan Management Association, Chicago, November 9, 1989; and Upham, "Legal Regulation of the Japanese Retail Industry," p. 27.

30. "A Lesson in Industrial Policy from Japanese Ministry," *Washington Post,* December 12, 1989; and Namiki Nobuyoshi, *Tsūsanshō no shūen (The Last Moments of MITI)* (Tokyo: Daiyamondo-sha, 1989). (Namiki is a former MITI official.) Also see "Fujitsu Offers Apology for Cutthroat Contract Bids,"

Los Angeles Times, November 21, 1989; and "Tokyo Warns 2 Big Japanese Computer Firms on Bidding," *Los Angeles Times,* November 25, 1989.

31. "Credibility of Computer Industry Is Shaky in Wake of ¥1 Bids to Land Major Contracts," *Japan Times,* January 6, 1990.

32. "Nihon tataki no shinsō," *Ashi shimbun,* January 6, 1990; "Pickens Still Pushing for Corporate Change," *Japan Times,* January 5, 1990; "Pickens Suing Japan Concern," *New York Times,* January 15, 1990.

33. *Japan Economic Journal,* November 11, 1989.

34. During the period 1987–89, various Japanese organizations bought—i.e., became the owners of—the following American properties (data from *Japan Economic Journal,* November 11, 1989):

BUYER	ACQUISITION	PRICE (BILLION ¥)	DATE
Sony Corp.	Columbia Pictures	644	9/89
Bridgestone Tire	Firestone Tire	333.7	3/88
Sony Corp.	CBS Records	269.7	11/87
Dai-Ichi Kangyō Bank	CIT Group Holdings	200	9/89
Sumitomo Corp.	Cook Cable TV	190	2/89
Aoki Construction	Westin Hotels	190	10/87
Nippon Mining	Gould	148.5	8/88
Mitsubishi Real Estate	Rockefeller Center	120	10/89
Fujisawa Pharmaceutical	LyphoMed	105	8/89
Nippon Mining	Conoco	100	4/88
Bank of Tokyo	Union Bank, Calif.	97.5	2/88

35. S.I.A., *The Semiconductor Industry Association: Key Facts and Issues* (Cupertino: S.I.A., 1987), p. 8.

36. Lawrence B. Krause, "Our System of Managed Trade," written for *Nihon keizai shimbun,* July 1, 1988. Also note the comment of Under Secretary of State for Economic Affairs McCormack: We have "de facto managed trade within the GATT rules themselves, violating the spirit, though not the letter, of the GATT." McCormack, "Challenges to the International Economy."

37. In a speech, T.N. Srinivasan and Hamada Koichi of Yale University analyzed econometrically why Japan imports so few manufactured goods. Dissatisfied with their results, they had to tidy up some loose ends: "The existence of *keiretsu* may be working against flexibility of the price mechanism. As a group, Japanese firms engage often in implicit contracts with a time horizon longer than in the United States. This will result in greater inertia to the response of most Japanese firms to changes in marginal cost advantages by switching customers or suppliers. Criticism of this type of inertia can go too far. After all, the Japanese live on a small island [*sic*]. Business practices in an open land with lots of frontier opportunities—as pictured in Western movies—are not easily

transferred to the village economy where people stay for life in a small community and therefore cannot afford to betray long term friends or clients. Only the exposure to international competition will slowly change this Japanese Corporate behavior." "The U.S.-Japan Trade Problem," Unpublished paper, December 1989, p. 30.

38. U.S. Congress, Joint Economic Committee. *Restoring International Balance,* p. 32.

39. Quoted by Upham, "Legal Regulation of the Japanese Retail Industry," p. 32.

40. James Fallows, "Containing Japan," *The Atlantic,* May 1989, pp. 43, 48.

41. Ishihara Shintarō and Morita Akio, *"No" to ieru Nihon (Japan That Can Say "No")* (Tokyo: Kōbunsha, 1989), pp. 59–73; *Los Angeles Times,* August 6 and November 25, 1989; ABC News, "Nightline: Japanese Investment in the United States," Transcript of Show #2233, December 13, 1989 (Watanabe).

42. Quoted in Henri-Claude de Bettignies, "The Globalization of the Japanese Economy: Implications for Europe and the United States," Unpublished paper, University of Southern California, April 1989, p. 7.

43. Ivan P. Hall, "Stop Making Excuses for Japan's Insularity," *Wall Street Journal,* July 6, 1987. The "mutual understanding industry" is also engaged in lobbying and public relations. See John B. Judis, "The Japanese Megaphone," *The New Republic,* January 22, 1990, pp. 20–25; Judis, "A Yen for Approval," *Columbia Journalism Review,* January-February 1990, pp. 42–45; and Judis, "Conflicting Japan Policy and a Conflict of Interest," *In These Times,* January 17–23, 1990, p. 6.

44. *Commentary,* September 1989, p. 71.

45. *U.S./Japan Economic Agenda,* No. 9 (February 1989), p. 5.

46. Kuroda Makoto, "Super 301 and Japan," Unpublished paper, c. December 1989, p. 10; Ishihara and Morita, *"No" to ieru Nihon,* pp. 128–29.

47. "Trade Ministry Gets an Earful of Complaints," *Los Angeles Times,* September 14, 1989. Also see "Japan: Can It Cope?" cover story, *Business Week,* April 23, 1990.

48. "Business Luncheon Notes," Japan Society, New York, September 7, 1989.

49. James Fallows, "Getting Along with Japan." *The Atlantic,* December 1989, pp. 60–62.

50. See, e.g., Hanai Hitoshi "Kō shite umareru tai-Nichi kyōi ron" (How the Japan-Is-a-Menace View Emerged), *Chūō kōron,* August 1989, pp. 269–77. Hanai has studied at the University of Southern California.

51. "Japan Invades Hollywood," *Newsweek,* October 9, 1989, p. 66.

52. S.I.A., *The Semiconductor Industry Association,* p. 9.

53. Nukazawa, "Containing Japan Is Not the Answer," *Japan Times,* August 30, 1989; Glen S. Fukushima, "The Liberalization of Legal Services in Japan: A U.S. Government Negotiator's Perspective," *Law in Japan,* vol. 21 (1988), p. 8.

54. (New York: Random House, 1988). Cf. Kunii Toshiyasu, *Pax Japonica* (Tokyo: President, 1988). On the theory of "hegemonic stability" and its relationship to the Japanese-American trade conflict, see, *inter alia,* Inoguchi

Kuniko, *Posuto-haken to Nihon no sentaku (Japan's Choices in the Post-hegemonic Era)* (Tokyo: Chikuma Shobō, 1987); Chalmers Johnson, "The End of American Hegemony and the Future of US-Japan Relations," *Harvard International Review,* 10th Anniversary Issue (1989), pp. 126–31; Steven Schlosstein, *The End of the American Century* (New York: Congdon & Weed, 1989); and Richard Rosecrance, *America's Economic Resurgence* (New York: Harper & Row, 1990).

55. Ishihara and Morita, *"No" to ieru Nihon,* pp. 12–21; and Karatsu Hajime, "Nichi-Bei no 'tokushu' o iu no wa tome yo" (Let's Not Talk of "Peculiarities" of the U.S. and Japan), *Chūō kōron,* January 1990, pp. 81–90. On Karatsu in English, see Doi Ayako, " 'America-Bashing,' Japanese Style," *Washington Post,* July 16, 1989. For a serious study of the role of technology in the Japanese-American competition, see Yakushiji Taizō, *Tekunohegemoni (Technological Hegemony)* (Tokyo: Chūō Kōron-sha, 1989).

56. See Murphy, "The Crisis of Japan's Global Financial Dominance"; and Karel van Wolferen, *The Enigma of Japanese Power* (New York: Knopf, 1989), pp. 422–25 *et passim.*

57. *The Atlantic,* May 1989, p. 41.

58. McCormack, "Challenges to the International Economy."

59. U.S. Congress, Joint Economic Committee, *Restoring International Balance,* p. 20.

60. Omae Ken'ichi "Amerika yo, Nihon ni wa keizai yokushiryoku ga aru" (Hey America, Japan Has the Power to Control the Economy), *Chūō kōron,* August 1989, pp. 256–67.

61. Sen. John Heinz, "The United States and Japan in the 21st Century." Speech to the Japan-U.S. Business Council, New York, July 10, 1989.

62. *The Atlantic,* December 1989, p. 64.

63. Geza Feketekuty, "U.S. Policy and Super 301," Unpublished paper, c. December 1989, p. 5.

64. Sen. Heinz, "The United States and Japan"; Sen. Jay Rockefeller, "Trade Policy Still Comes Last," *Journal of Commerce,* December 5, 1989.

65. Takahashi Jōsen, *Nihon keizai ga ugoku (Japan's Economy on the March)* (Tokyo: Keizaikai, 1989), pp. 193–97.

66. Edward Lincoln, "U.S.-Japan Trade Talks: Hope for Progress," *The Heritage Lectures,* No. 234 (Washington, D.C.: Heritage Foundation, December 12, 1989).

67. The phrase "deft political orchestration" is from Bruce Stokes, "Trade Report," *National Journal,* June 17, 1989, p. 1563.

68. The indispensable work on the Reagan trade policy is Clyde V. Prestowitz, Jr., *Trading Places: How We Allowed Japan to Take the Lead* (New York: Basic Books, 1988).

69. Quoted in Samuel C. Patterson, Jessica R. Adolino, and Kevin T. McGuire, "Continuities in Political Research: Evidence from the *APSR* Since the 1960s; Report of the Managing Editor of the *American Political Science Review* for 1988–89" (Columbus, Ohio: American Political Science Association, August 21, 1989), p. 10.

70. Jagdish N. Bhagwati, "United States Trade Policy at the Crossroads," *The World Economy,* vol. 12, no. 4 (December 1989), p. 476, note 62, and pp. 463 and 467–68. For an analysis of Japan's trade by an economist who is sensitive to the data, see Edward J. Lincoln, *Japan's Unequal Trade* (Washington, D.C.: Brookings Institution, 1990).

71. Robert Wade. "Industrial Policy in East Asia: Does It Lead or Follow the Market?" Lecture, Swarthmore College, November 30, 1989; and Chalmers Johnson, "The Japanese Political Economy: A Crisis in Theory," *Ethics & International Affairs,* vol. 2 (1988), pp. 79–97.

72. Cf. Chalmers Johnson, "Japan: Their Behavior, Our Policy," *The National Interest,* no. 17 (Fall 1989), pp. 17–27.

73. Francis Fukuyama, "The End of History?" *The National Interest,* no. 16 (Summer 1989); "The Triumph of Capitalism," *New Perspectives Quarterly,* vol. 6, no. 3 (Fall 1989); and Edwin Feulner (president, Heritage Foundation), "Conservatism: The Agony of Victory," *New York Times,* October 27, 1989.

74. James Fallows, *The Atlantic,* December 1989, p. 56.

5 The Foundations of Japan's Wealth and Power

1. Karel van Wolferen, "Wrong on Japan," *The National Interest* (Fall 1993), pp. 85–92.

2. See Thomas M. Huber, *Japan's Strategic Economy* (Boulder, Col.: Westview, 1994). From a different point of view, also see Kasaya Kazuhiko, *Samurai no shisō: Nihon-kata soshiki tsuyosa no kōzō (Warrior Thought: The Structural Strength of Japanese-type Organizations)* (Tokyo: Nihon Keizai Shimbunsha, 1993).

3. The quotation is from General Carl E. Mundy, Jr., Commandant of the Marine Corps. See "The Marines Want Singles Only, But They Are Quickly Overruled," *New York Times,* August 12, 1993. On the division of labor within Japanese households, see Iwao Sumiko, *The Japanese Woman: Traditional Image and Changing Reality* (New York: Free Press, 1993).

4. See, e.g., John E. Fitzgibbon, Jr., *Deceitful Practices: Nomura Securities and the Japanese Invasion of Wall Street* (New York: Birch Lane Press, 1991).

5. An example of this kind of writing by an established economist is Robert Z. Lawrence, "Japan's Different Trade Regime," *Journal of Economic Perspectives* 7:3 (Summer 1993): 3–19.

6. Andrew Vincent, *Theories of the State* (Oxford: Basil Blackwell, 1987), pp. 11 and 38 (on Habermas).

7. See, e.g., J. Mark Ramseyer and Frances McCall Rosenbluth, *Japan's Political Marketplace* (Cambridge, Mass.: Harvard University Press, 1993); Kent E. Calder, *Strategic Capitalism: Private Business and Public Purpose in Japan* (Princeton: Princeton University Press, 1993); and Samuel Kernell, ed., *Parallel Politics: Economic Policymaking in Japan and the United States* (Washington, D.C.: Brookings Institution, 1991).

8. See, e.g., Karel van Wolferen, "Ribijyonizumu wa katta ka" (Has Revisionism Won?), *Global Business,* August 15–September 1, 1993, pp. 16–19;

James Sterngold, "For Japan, the Old Slurs Are the New Party Line," *New York Times,* August 15, 1993; "Nihon shijō wa heisa-teki" (Japan's Markets Are Closed), *Asahi shimbun,* August 11, 1993; and Yasuba Yasukichi, "Fiscal Policy and the Burden of the National Debt in Japan Since 1982: Indicting MOF's Crime Against Humanity," Discussion Paper, Faculty of Economics, Osaka University, July 1993.

9. Karel van Wolferen, *The Enigma of Japanese Power* (New York: Vintage Books, 1990); Glen Fukushima, *Nichi-Bei keizai masatsu no seijigaku (The Political Science of Japanese-American Economic Friction)* (Tokyo: Asahi Shimbun Sha, 1992); James Fallows, *Looking at the Sun* (New York: Pantheon, 1994); Pat Choate, *Agents of Influence* (New York: Knopf, 1990); Marie Anchordoguy, *Computers, Inc.: Japan's Challenge to IBM* (Cambridge, Mass.: Harvard University Press, 1989); Michael Crichton, *Rising Sun* (New York: Knopf, 1992); Clyde Prestowitz, *Trading Places* (New York: Basic Books, 1989).

10. Kenneth B. Pyle, *The Japanese Question: Power and Purpose in a New Era* (Washington, D.C.: AEI Press, 1992), pp. 122–23.

11. *Ibid.,* p. 26.

12. Ozawa Ichirō, *Nihon kaizō keikaku (Plan for the Reform of Japan)* (Tokyo: Kodansha, 1993), p. 102.

13. Ozawa Ichirō, "Ima, nani o subeki na no ka" (What Should We Do Now?), *Bungei shunju,* August 1993, pp. 134–43.

14. John A. Hall, "Nationalisms: Classified and Explained," *Daedalus* (Summer 1993), pp. 1–28.

15. Liah Greenfeld, "Transcending the Nation's Worth," *Daedalus* (Summer 1993), pp. 47–62.

16. Fukuzawa Yukichi, *Autobiography* (1899; New York: Columbia University Press, 1980).

17. Ozawa, *Nihon kaizō keikaku,* p. 17.

18. Greenfeld, *op. cit.,* p. 59.

19. Ellis S. Krauss, "Normative Approaches to Economic and Trade Issues," in Joel H. Rosenthal, ed., *Moral Education III* (New York: Carnegie Council on Ethics and International Affairs, 1993), p. 69.

20. Ishihara Shintarō, *The Japan That Can Say No* (New York: Simon and Schuster, 1991), pp. 21, 42. On whether Japan really has a "technology card" in the context of the FSX controversy, see Jeff Shear, *The Keys to the Kingdom* (New York: Doubleday, 1994).

21. Krauss, *op. cit.,* pp. 67, 70.

22. See Patricia Boling, "Private Interest and the Public Good in Japan," *The Pacific Review* 3:2 (1990): 138–39.

23. Oishi Nobuyuki, "Descent from Heaven Unchanging for Bureaucrats," *Nikkei Weekly,* October 4, 1993.

24. Murata Takashi, "Sendai, Ibaraki wa hyōzan no ikkaku" (Sendai and Ibaraki Are Only the Tip of the Iceberg), *Shūkan tōyō keizai,* August 14–21, 1993, pp. 16–18.

25. See Sōmu-chō Gyōsei Kanri Kyoku, ed., *Tokushu hōjin sōran, Heisei gennen-han (Directory of Special Legal Entities, 1989 edition)* (Tokyo: Gyōsei Kanri Kenkyū Senta, 1989), pp. 171–73.

26. Byron K. Marshall, *Capitalism and Nationalism in Prewar Japan: The Ideology of the Business Elite, 1868–1941* (Stanford: Stanford University Press, 1967), p. 3.

27. Boling, *op. cit.*, pp. 141, 142.

28. For other examples, see Essay 8 below.

29. For an important analysis using some of the concepts listed here, see Kubo Kōshi, "Hosokawa shintaisei no kenryoku kōzō" (The Power Structure of Hosokawa's New Order), *Shokun*, October 1993, pp. 68–79.

30. See Chalmers Johnson, "The Tremor: Japan's Post–Cold War Destiny," *The New Republic*, August 9, 1993, pp. 21–27.

31. Eugene B. Skolnikoff, "Knowledge Without Borders? Internationalization of the Research Universities," *Daedalus* (Fall 1993), p. 232.

6   Japan: Who Governs?

1. Maruyama Masao, *Thought and Behaviour in Modern Japanese Politics*, ed. I. Morris (London: Oxford University Press, 1969), pp. 128–29.

2. Nagai Yōnosuke, "Social and External Factors Influencing Japanese Foreign Policies during the 1970's," Unpublished paper for the Japan Institute of International Affairs and the International Institute for Strategic Studies.

3. Taguchi Fukuji, "Pressure Groups in Japanese Politics," *The Developing Economies* 6 (1968): 471.

4. J. A. A. Stockwin, *Japan: Divided Politics in a Growth Economy* (New York: Norton, 1975), p. 281.

5. For a first report of this project, see "MITI and Japan's International Economic Policy," in R. A. Scalapino, ed., *The Foreign Policy of Modern Japan* (Berkeley: University of California Press, 1977), pp. 227–79.

6. Vogel, ed. *Modern Japanese Organization and Decision-Making* (Berkeley: University of California Press, 1975); Ari, et al., *Gendai gyōsei to kanryōsei (Modern Administration and the Bureaucratic System)* (Tokyo: Tokyo Daigaku Shuppankai, 1974), Vol. 2 (Vol. 1 concerns administration in foreign countries).

7. Albert M. Craig, "Functional and Dysfunctional Aspects of Government Bureaucracy," in Vogel, ed., *Modern Japanese Organization*, p. 3.

8. Kawanaka, "Nihon ni okeru seisaku kettei no seiji katei" (The Political Processes of Policy-making in Japan), in *Gendai gyōsei*, Vol. 2, 3–6, 34–37; and Kojima, "Gendai yosan seiji shiron" (A Sketch of Modern Budgetary Politics), in *ibid.*, pp. 121–25.

9. P. B. Stone, *Japan Surges Ahead, The Story of an Economic Miracle* (New York: Praeger, 1969), p. 186.

10. *Japan Times*, August 12, 1974.

11. See Matsumoto Seichō, *Gendai kanryō ron (On Modern Bureaucrats)*, 3 vols. (Tokyo: Bungei Shunjū Sha, 1963–66); and Fukumoto Kunio, *Kanryō* (Tokyo: Kōbundō, 1959). As an example of the popular Marxist writing on Japan in the West, see E. J. Hobsbawm, "Vulnerable Japan," *New York Review of Books*, July 17, 1975, pp. 27–32.

12. Rinji Gyōsei Chōsa Kai, *Gyōsei no kaikaku* (Tokyo: Jiji Tsūshin, 1967), p. 10.

13. *Japan Times,* December 13, 1971.

14. Ota Kaoru, *Yakunin o kiru (Cutting Down the Bureaucrats)* (Tokyo: Tōyō Keizai Shinpōsha, 1973), pp. 10, 16–17.

15. On *amakudari,* see Essay 7 below.

16. Ōta, *Yakunin o kiru,* pp. 106–07. Sahashi Shigeru, a former administrative vice-minister of MITI, 1964–66, believes that "sectionalism" (his term) is one of the most serious shortcomings of the bureaucracy. He states flatly that "Bureaucrats are officials of the various ministries before they are servants of the nation." Sahashi, "Kanryō shokun ni chokugen suru" (Straight Talk to the Gentlemen of the Bureaucracy), *Bungei shunjū,* July 1971, p. 108. In an interview with the author in Tokyo, September 5, 1974, Sahashi said further that no measures of reform of jurisdictional competition have yet been effective. He believes that the combining of ministries into new organizations is useless; it only produces territorial competition among bureaus. He feels that only a wholesale change of attitude among officials will help.

On the other hand, sectionalism may be the most effective restraint on the powers of the bureaucracy. Hollerman argues: "If 'the government' of Japan were actually a highly coordinated set of agencies, its powers could be applied with overwhelming force. Instead, partly as a result of sheer ambition for status and partly as a result of divergent interests within the society itself, there is intense rivalry and jealousy among the ruling agencies and their personnel. In competing for power, they tend to neutralize one another's authority to some extent. It is this offsetting effect, rather than the absence of specific powers of internal control, and also 'rule by personalities' as opposed to 'rule by law,' which provides the degree of freedom in Japan's peculiar species of enterprise economy." Leon Hollerman, *Japan's Dependency on the World Economy* (Princeton: Princeton University Press, 1967), pp. 160–61.

17. See, for example, Craig, in Vogel, ed., *Modern Japanese Organization,* p. 20.

18. See, in particular, Yamamoto Masao, ed., *Keizai kanryō no jittai, seisaku kettei no mekanizumu (Facts About Economic Bureaucrats, the Mechanisms of Policy-making)* (Tokyo: Mainichi Shinbun Sha, 1972), pp. 24–27, 98–100.

19. Fukumoto, *Kanryō,* p. 143; Matsumoto, *Gendai kanryō ron,* Vol. 1, p. 50; Yamamoto, *Keizai kanryō,* p. 115.

20. Ōta, *Yakunin o kiru,* p. 142.

21. On Fukuda's fame as a budget bureaucrat, see Fukumoto, *Kanryō,* pp. 142–143; and Honda Yasuharu, *Nihon neo-kanryō ron* (Tokyo: Kōdansha, 1974), p. 100.

22. Interview, Tokyo, September 5, 1974. Yamamoto Masao uses the same term, *kakuremino,* to describe the deliberation councils. *Keizai kanryō,* p. 21. Also see pp. 46–49, 74–76.

23. See Ehud Harari, "Japanese Politics of Advice in Comparative Perspective," *Public Policy* 22 (1974):537–77; and Yung Ho Park, "The Governmental Advisory Commission System in Japan," *Journal of Comparative Administration* 3 (1972): 435–67.

24. Kawanaka, in *Gendai gyōsei to kanryōsei,* Vol. 2, p. 7.

25. The two best collections of memoirs of vice-ministers and bureau chiefs in the field of trade and industrial policy are Sangyō Seisaku Kenkyūjo, ed., *Tsū-sanshō 20-nen gaishi (An Unofficial Twenty-year History of MITI)* (Tokyo: Sangyō Seisaku Kenkyūjo, 1970); and Seisaku Jihō Sha, ed., *Kaikoroku sengo tsūsan seisaku shi (Reminiscences of the History of Postwar Trade and Industry Policy)* (Tokyo: Seisaku Jihō Sha, 1973).

26. John Locke, *Two Treatises of Government,* ed. Cook (New York: Hafner, 1947), p. 122.

27. Ralf Dahrendorf, *Society and Democracy in Germany* (Garden City, N.Y.: Doubleday, 1967), p. 218.

28. See, *inter alia,* T. J. Pempel, "The Bureaucratization of Policy-making in Postwar Japan," *American Journal of Political Science,* November 1974, pp. 647–64.

29. Isomura Eiichi and Kuronuma Minoru, *Gendai Nihon no gyōsei* (Tokyo: Teikoku Chihō Gyōsei Gakkai, 1974), p. 11.

30. *Ibid.,* p. 18.

31. Sahashi, *Bungei shunjū,* July 1971, p. 112.

32. Sahashi Shigeru, *Ishoku kanryō (An Exceptional Bureaucrat)* (Tokyo: Daiyamondo Sha, 1967), pp. 219–21.

33. Ōta, *Yakunin o kiru,* pp. 164–67.

34. Sahashi, *Bungei shunjū,* July 1971, p. 109.

35. Misonō, "Keizai kanryō no kinō to kongo no hōkō" (The Functions of the Economic Bureaucracy and Its Future Course), *Keizai hyōron* 17 (February 1968):13.

36. Robert M. Spaulding, Jr., *Imperial Japan's Higher Civil Service Examinations* (Princeton: Princeton University Press, 1967), p. 293.

37. Ide Yoshinori and Ishida Takeshi, "The Education and Recruitment of Governing Elites in Modern Japan," in Rupert Wilkinson, ed., *Governing Elites* (New York: Oxford University Press, 1969), p. 109.

38. Isomura and Kuronuma, *Gendai Nihon no gyōsei,* p. 3.

39. Yoshino, *Shōkō gyōsei no omoide (Reminiscences of Commercial and Industrial Administration)* (Tokyo: Shōkō Seisaku Shi Kankō Kai, 1962), pp. 114, 249–50.

40. John M. Maki, "The Role of the Bureaucracy in Japan," *Pacific Affairs* 20 (1947):391.

41. Shinobu Seizaburō, "From Party Politics to Military Dictatorship," *The Developing Economies* 5 (1967):681.

42. Itō Daiichi, "The Bureaucracy: Its Attitudes and Behavior," *The Developing Economies* 6 (1968):450. While figures broken down for each ministry are not readily available, the total number of departments *(bu)* and bureaus *(kyoku)* throughout the bureaucracy jumped from 160 in 1955 to 173 in 1956, the biggest one-year change between 1952 and 1972 except for 1961–62, when they rose from 187 to 201. (The income-doubling plan and trade liberalization began to be implemented during 1961–62.) These figures do not necessarily support Itō's point, however, because 1955–56 also saw an across-the-board 20 percent cut in personnel and sections for all agencies, ordered by the Administrative Management Agency. The total numbers of sections *(ka)* and offices *(shitsu)* dropped from 916 in 1955 to 734 in 1956. No section chiefs were let go; they

were retained in newly created positions called "management officers" *(kanri-kan)*, of which a total of 459 were established in the government in 1956. For the aggregate figures, see Isomura and Kuronuma, *Gendai Nihon no gyōsei*, p. 338. For the reduction-in-force and establishment of *kanrikan*, see Tsūsanshō Daijin Kanbō Chōsaka, *Tsūshō sangyō shō shijū nen shi* (Tokyo: Tsūsan Shiryō Chōsa Kai, 1965), pp. 681–82, 685–87.

43. Ōta, *Yakunin o kiru*, pp. 9, 140–47.

44. Misawa Shigeo, "Seiji kettei katei no gaikan" (An Outline of the Political Policy and Decision Making Process), in Nihon Seiji Gakkai (Japan Political Science Association), ed., *Gendai Nihon no seitō to kanryō (Political Parties and Bureaucracy in Contemporary Japan)* (Tokyo: Iwanami Shoten, 1967), p. 15.

45. Byron K. Marshall, *Capitalism and Nationalism in Prewar Japan* (Stanford: Stanford University Press, 1967), p. 111.

46. Supreme Commander for the Allied Powers, *Historical Monographs,* Vol. 10, Part C, "Reform of Business Enterprise: Elimination of Private Control Associations" (Washington, D.C.: National Archives, 1951), pp. 57, 89, 93. N.B.: This monograph was omitted from the original fifty-five volumes microfilmed and made available to the public by the National Archives. It was retrieved and specially microfilmed for the author by the National Archives on June 4, 1974. The National Archives explained that they had not microfilmed and given it a volume number in the original project because of a handwritten notation on the cover, "This draft was *rejected* and not included among the finished monographs sent to Washington for publication and it is considered wildly unreliable and misleading. WEH." WEH is presumably William E. Hutchinson, editor of the historical monographs project. From internal evidence the monograph was written by George Tays. In my view this monograph is no more or less reliable than any of the others; it does differ, however, in being by far the most candid of any of the SCAP monographs. It is for this reason, I suspect, that it was rejected. There is also included in the typescript of the monograph a four-page single-spaced letter praising the work. It is signed by MEH, presumably Marvin E. Habel of the historical monographs staff.

47. *Ibid.,* p. 16.

48. *Ibid.,* p. 103.

49. Quoted in Shiba Kimpei and Nozue Kenzo, *What Makes Japan Tick* (Tokyo: Asahi Evening News Co., 1971), p. 32. Also note the comment of Takahashi Makoto, "The wartime economic controls are of special importance in that through them were established both a state-operated fiscal mechanism in the monetary phase of finance and banking, and a direct system of control. These were continued essentially in the postwar period as 'legacies of the wartime economic controls,' and a structure of state economic control supported mainly by the fiscal mechanism has been reorganized. Direct control, meanwhile, has been modified or gradually abolished along with the reconstruction of capitalism." "The Development of Wartime Economic Controls," *The Developing Economies* 5 (1967):650–51.

50. Gary D. Allinson, *Japanese Urbanism* (Berkeley: University of California Press, 1975), p. 88.

51. Tsuji, "Kanryō kikō no onzon to kyōka" (The Preservation and Strength-

ening of the Bureaucratic Structure), in Oka Yoshitake, ed., *Gendai Nihon no seiji katei* (Tokyo: Iwanami Shoten, 1958), pp. 109–25. Excerpted in *Journal of Social and Political Ideas in Japan* 2:3.88–92 (1964).

52. Maki, "The Role of the Bureaucracy," p. 397.

53. Supreme Commander for the Allied Powers, *Historical Monographs,* No. 13 "Reorganization of Civil Service" (Washington, D.C.: National Archives, 1951), p. 24.

54. Foster B. Roser, "Establishing a Modern Merit System in Japan," *Public Personnel Review* 11:4.201 (1950).

55. Jinji Gyōsei Chōsa Kai, *Kōmuin jinji gyōsei no hensen (Official Personnel Administration in Transition)* (Tokyo: Jinji Gyōsei Chōsa Kai, 1972), pp. 47–57. Also see Watanabe Takeshi, *Senryōka no Nihon zaisei oboegaki (Notes on Japanese Finance Under the Occupation)* (Tokyo: Nihon Keizai Shimbun Sha, 1966), pp. 156–60, 220–23.

56. See Chalmers Johnson, *Conspiracy at Matsukawa* (Berkeley: University of California Press, 1972), chaps. 1 and 2.

57. Maki, "The Role of the Bureaucracy," p. 405.

58. *Gendai Nihon no gyōsei,* p. 12; and Yamamoto, *Keizai kanryō,* pp. 185–204.

59. For brief descriptions of the most important public corporations, see Gyōsei Chōsa Kai, ed., *Gyōsei yōran (Administrative Handbook)* (Tokyo: Gyōsei Chōsa Kai, 1974), pp. 107–82.

60. *Bungei shunjū,* July 1971, p. 115.

61. See Isomura and Kuronuma, *Gendai Nihon no gyōsei,* pp. 220–21; and K. Bieda, *The Structure and Operation of the Japanese Economy* (Sydney: Wiley, 1970), pp. 104–05.

62. For a list of all *tokushu hōjin* during 1968 and 1969, the ministries and sections of the central government that supervise each of them, dates of establishment, and other data, see Gyōsei Kanri Chō (Administrative Management Agency), *Gyōsei kanri nenpō,* Vol. 13 (April 1969), pp. 225–53. Also see Yoshitake Kiyohiko, *An Introduction to Public Enterprise in Japan* (Beverly Hills, Calif.: Sage Publications, 1973).

63. *Japan Times,* March 21, 1974. Iwatake Teruhiko, MITI 1934–59, describes in his memoirs how much he disliked seeing old colleagues who had gone to a *kōdan* or to a private business coming back to the ministry for favors and how much he dreaded his own *amakudari.* However, he became a director of Kobe Steel Company. Iwatake, *Zuihitsu Toranomon (Toranomon Jottings)* (Tokyo: Tsūsan Sangyō Chōsa Kai, 1960), pp. 306–07. Sahashi is the only MITI vice-minister who refused to *amakudari.* See Kusayanagi Daizō, "Sahashi Shigeru, amakudaranu kōkyū kanryō," *Bungei shunjū,* May 1969, pp. 162–74.

64. Seisaku Jihō Sha, *Tsūsanshō, sono hito to soshiki (MITI: Its People and Organization)* (Tokyo: Seisaku Jihō Sha, 1968) contains a short biography and comments on the reputation of every official in MITI at the rank of section chief and above. For Hiramatsu Morihiko, see p. 149.

65. See the list in Yamamoto, *Keizai kanryō,* pp. 205–16.

66. Naikaku Sōri-daijin Kanbō Kōhō-shitsu, *Kōmuin ni kan suru seron chōsa*

(Public Opinion Poll Concerning Public Officials) (September 1973), pp. 30–31, 32–39.

67. Randall Bartlett, *Economic Foundations of Political Power* (New York: Free Press, 1973), pp. 26, 63.

7 THE REEMPLOYMENT OF RETIRED GOVERNMENT BUREAUCRATS IN JAPANESE BIG BUSINESS

1. *Asahi shimbun,* March 16, 1974. With regard to the situation in public corporations, some unions of the 35,000-member Council of Governmental Special Corporation Employees went on strike March 20, 1974, demanding higher wages and protesting the practice of employing *yokosuberi* officials. The union charged that in 61 public corporations, 303 of a total of 384 governing board members were retired government officials. *Japan Times,* March 21, 1974. On *chii riyō,* see *Asahi shimbun,* June 5, 1974.

2. *Asahi shimbun,* March 27, 1974. The official title of the National Personnel Authority's report is "Eiri kigyō e no shūshoku no shōnin ni kan suru nenji hōkokusho" *(Annual Report Concerning Approvals of Employment in Profit-making Enterprises).*

3. Ino Kenji and Hokuto Man, *Amakudari kanryō, Nihon o ugokasu tokken shūdan (Descended-from-heaven Bureaucrats, The Privileged Groups That Move Japan)* (Tokyo: Nisshin Hōdō, 1972), p. 167; and *Asahi shimbun,* March 27, 1974.

4. For a discussion of the Yano case and a list of all descents from the Ministry of Finance and MITI during 1973, see *Sandē mainichi,* April 14, 1974.

5. See "Taiyō Kobe Bank Supplement," *Japan Times,* October 1, 1973; and Okurashō Hyakunenshi Henshūshitsu (Editorial Office for the Hundred Year History of the Ministry of Finance), ed., *Okurashō jinmeiroku (Who's Who of the Ministry of Finance)* (Tokyo: Okura Zaimu Kyōkai, 1973).

6. Romanization of names is in accordance with the *Jinji kōshinroku,* 26th edition, 1971. For Mr. Morozumi's activities on behalf of Prime Minister Tanaka, see *Japan Times,* October 11, 1973.

7. On the Sumitomo Metals Incident, see, *inter alia,* "Gyōsei shidō no jittai o arau" (Probing the Realities of Administrative Guidance), *Tōyō keizai,* no. 3796, April 6, 1974, pp. 28–33; and Eugene J. Kaplan, U.S. Department of Commerce, *Japan: The Government-Business Relationship* (Washington, D.C.: Government Printing Office, 1972), pp. 146–48 (note Kaplan's remark that "unlike other steel companies, Sumitomo has not employed former government officials" on p. 146).

8. Cf. Kusayanagi Daizō, "Sahashi Shigeru, amakudaranu kōkyū kanryō" (Sahashi Shigeru, A Top-level Bureaucrat Who Did Not Descend from Heaven), *Bungei shunjū,* May 1969, pp. 162–74.

9. For a list of prewar army and navy officers holding top positions in big business, see T. A. Bisson, *Japan's War Economy* (New York: Institute of Pacific Relations, 1945), p. 257 *et seq.* For the active duty and post-retirement attitudes

and activities of prewar civil officials, see the memoirs of Yoshino Shinji, vice-minister of commerce and industry from 1931 to 1936 and minister in the first Konoe Cabinet, *Shōkō gyōsei no omoide (Recollections of Commercial and Industrial Administration)* (Tokyo: Shōkō Seisaku Shi Kankō Kai, 1962).

10. Supreme Commander for the Allied Powers, *History of the Nonmilitary Activities of the Occupation of Japan* (Washington, D.C.: U.S. National Archives, n.d.), Vol. 13, "Reorganization of the Civil Service," unpaginated, microfilm.

11. Shibuzawa Kijirō, *Kōkyū kōmuin no yukue, minkan amakudari to rikkōhō seigen mondai (The Activities of High-level Public Officials, The Problems of Descent-from-heaven to Civilian Life and the Qualifications of Election Candidates)* (Tokyo: Asahi Shimbun Chōsa Kenkyū Shitsu, Internal Report No. 120, May 10, 1966), p. 12.

12. For a summary of proposals for reform, see *Japan Times,* editorial, December 13, 1971. For criticisms of *amakudari,* see *Japan Times,* March 16, 1974; March 27, 1974; and March 29, 1974 (editorial). For an excellent article in English on the uses and ironical implications of the term *amakudari,* see V. Dixon Morris, "The Idioms of Contemporary Japan: Amakudari," *The Japan Interpreter,* VII:3–4 (Summer–Autumn 1972), pp. 383–86.

13. Shiba Kimpei and Nozue Kenzō, *What Makes Japan Tick* (Tokyo: Asahi Evening News Co., 1971), p. 174.

14. Cf. Urata Tomoo, "Sangyōkai ni haishutsu suru kanryō shusshinsha" (The Proliferation of Alumni from the Bureaucracy in the Industrial World), *Keizai ōrai,* October 1973, pp. 146–53.

15. See "Tsūsanshō to sekiyu gyōkai" (MITI and the Petroleum Industry), together with a chart listing 48 former senior officials of MITI and their present positions in various petroleum firms, *Asahi shimbun,* April 16, 1974.

16. *Nihon keizai shimbun,* May 30, 1974.

17. See Marie Anchordoguy, *Computers, Inc.: Japan's Challenge to IBM* (Cambridge, Mass.: Harvard University Press, 1989), pp. 50, 59.

8 *Omote* (Explicit) and *Ura* (Implicit)

1. Mainichi Daily News, *Fifty Years of Light and Dark: The Hirohito Years* (Tokyo: Mainichi Newspapers, 1975), p. 182. For a version of this famous incident from an Allied perspective, see John K. Emmerson, *The Japanese Thread* (New York: Holt, Rinehart and Winston, 1978), p. 237. Since the characters for *mokusatsu* mean silent kill, most informed commentators believe that the Allies did not mistranslate Suzuki. If he really meant "no comment," that is not what he said—and *mokusatsu* does not imply it, even obliquely. However, the fact that the Japanese and Emmerson maintain that Suzuki's nuance was misunderstood illustrates the tendency of the Japanese to take refuge in alleged mistranslations.

2. Nagai Yōnosuke, "Social and External Factors Influencing Japanese Foreign Policies During the 1970s," Unpublished paper, the Japan Institute of International Affairs, p. 10.

3. I. M. Destler, Fukui Haruhiro, and Sato Hideo, *The Textile Wrangle, Conflict in Japanese-American Relations, 1969–1971* (Ithaca: Cornell University Press, 1979), pp. 134, 136n.

4. Nawa Tarō (Asahi Shimbun), *Tsūsanshō* (MITI) (Tokyo: Kyōiku Sha, 1974), p. 45. Although Nawa does not use the term, he implies that Satō's language was an example of *kanchō yōgo* (literally, "official jargon"), which usually means an official's saying yes to an inquiry but taking no responsibility for its outcome.

5. Suzuki Takao, *Japanese and the Japanese* (Tokyo: Kōdansha, 1978), p. 60.

6. Kunihiro Masao, "U.S.-Japan Communications," in Henry Rosovsky, ed., *Discord in the Pacific, Challenges to the Japanese-American Alliance* (Washington, D.C.: Columbia Books, 1972), p. 167.

7. For references to Ikeda's *hōgen*, see Honda Yasuharu, *Nihon neo-kanryō ron (On Japan's New Bureaucrats)* (Tokyo: Kōdansha, 1974), Vol. I, p. 21; and Tsūsanshō Kisha Kurabu, *Tsūsanshō* (Tokyo: Hōbunsha, 1956), p. 20.

8. Even today the prime minister is occasionally referred to as a "portable shrine." See the discussion of *shushō mikoshi* in Yomiuri Shimbun Seijibu, ed., *Sōri-daijin (The Prime Minister)* (Tokyo: Yomiuri Shimbun Sha, rev. ed., 1972), p. 50.

9. See, for example, Hashiguchi Osamu (during 1973, director of the Budget Bureau of the Ministry of Finance and later the first vice-minister of the National Land Agency), *Shin zaisei jijō (New Financial Conditions)* (Tokyo: Saimaru Shuppankai, 1977), p. 122. In Hashiguchi's view, *kuroko* (a term he translates as "prompters") must be distinguished from *shironuri* (white-painted ones). It is all right for *kuroko* to comment from the shadows on the *shironuri,* but it is unseemly for them to make public statements through the mass media as if they were *shironuri.*

10. Quoted by Kanayama Bunji, "Seiiki no okite, kanryōdō no kenkyū" (Rules of the Sacred Precincts, Research on the Way of the Bureaucrat), *Chūō kōron,* July 1978, p. 230. *Kanryōdō* is, of course, a play on the term *bushidō.* On Kakizawa Kōji and his troubles with the Ministry of Finance, see Satō Seiichirō, "Ōkurashō no chinbotsu" (The Sinking of the Ministry of Finance), *Shūkan bunshun,* May 26, 1977, p. 58.

11. *Shōsetsu Nihon ginkō* (Tokyo: Kadokawa Bunko, 1971) and *Kanryōtachi no natsu* (Tokyo: Shinchōsha, 1975), both by Shiroyama Saburō. For an appreciation of Shiroyama, see Ezra Vogel's review of his *The War Criminal* in *The Japan Interpreter,* vol. 12, no. 1 (Winter 1978), pp. 145–47. For translations of some of Shiroyama's stories, see Tamae K. Prindle, *Made in Japan, and Other Japanese Business Novels* (Armonk, N.Y.: M. E. Sharpe, 1989).

12. For examples, see any issue of the magazine *Gekkan kankai (Monthly Bureaucratic World).*

13. Umesao Tadao, "Escape from Cultural Isolation," *The Japan Interpreter,* vol. 9, no. 2 (Summer-Autumn, 1974), pp. 141–42.

14. This example is from Edward G. Seidensticker and Matsumoto Michihiro, *Nichibei kōgo jiten (Japanese-American Colloquial Dictionary)* (Tokyo: Asahi Shuppan Sha, 1977), pp. 236–37.

15. Suzuki, *Japanese and the Japanese*, p. 146.

16. *The Concise Oxford French Dictionary* (Oxford: At the Clarendon Press, 1934), p. iii.

17. For example, Asahi Shimbun Sha, *Shimbungo jiten (Dictionary of Newspaper Language)*, annual.

18. For a succinct discussion of *amae* and many other terms, see Doi Takeo, "*Amae*: A Key Concept for Understanding Japanese Personality Structure," in Takie Lebra and William Lebra, eds., *Japanese Culture and Behavior* (Honolulu: University Press of Hawaii, 1974), pp. 145–54.

19. For a typical use, see Kusayanagi Daizō, "Tsūsanshō: tamesareru sutā kanchō" (MITI: A Star Bureaucracy on Trial), *Bungei shunjū*, August 1974, p. 120.

20. " 'Gyōsei kaikaku' no hinkon" (The Poverty of "Administrative Reform"), *Shokun*, November 1977, p. 74.

21. Former MITI vice-minister Sahashi Shigeru uses the term *jinmyaku* synonymously with *habatsu* (faction) in *Tsūsan jyānaru (rinji zōkan)*, May 24, 1975, p. 39. Also see Saisho Fumi, *Eigo ni naranai Nihongo (Japanese That Does Not Translate into English)* (Tokyo: Kenkyūsha, 1971), p. 56.

22. For *kimyaku, sanmyaku,* and *meimyaku,* see Yomiuri Shimbun, *Sōri-daijin,* pp. 96, 144, and 207.

23. *Nihon o enshutsu-suru shinkanryō-zō (A Portrait of the New Bureaucrats Who Direct Japan)* (Tokyo: Yamate Shobō, 1977), pp. 76, 85–89.

24. For those who want to check the *kanji,* these numbers refer to characters in Nelson's *The Modern Reader's Japanese-English Character Dictionary,* rev. ed. (1962).

25. Ōkōchi, "Nihon no gyōsei soshiki" (Administrative Organization in Japan), in Tsuji Kiyoaki, ed., *Gyōseigaku kōza (Lectures on the Science of Public Administration)* (Tokyo: Tokyo Daigaku Shuppankai, 1976), II, pp. 77–110.

26. The phrase "voluntary controls" is, of course, a euphemism in both English and Japanese; the controls are ordered by the government and are involuntary.

27. See John Creighton Campbell, *Contemporary Japanese Budget Politics* (Berkeley: University of California press, 1977), p. 177 and n. 8.

28. *A Glossary of Japanese Neologisms* (Tucson: University of Arizona Press, 1962), p. 8.

29. *Ibid.,* p. vii.

30. *Ibid.,* p. 120.

31. (Kōbunsha, 1970).

32. Yomiuri Shimbun, *Sōri-daijin,* p. 93. The slang word *pā* may be derived from the French negative particle *pas.*

33. John H. Boyle, "The Idioms of Contemporary Japan," *The Japan Interpreter,* vol. 7, no. 2 (Spring 1972), pp. 193–94.

34. Inoue Kanae, *Taikei kanchō kaikei jiten (Dictionary of Official Accounting)* (Tokyo: Gihōdō, 1973), pp. 44–45.

35. Ishiguro Osamu, "Jinmei no kanji" (The Characters of Personal Names), *Seikai ōrai,* May 1976, pp. 92–93.

36. Sometimes bureaucrats balk and refuse to resign "voluntarily." A case in MITI, that of Hayashi Shintarō, rocked the ministry. For the case and the expression, see Kusayanagi, *Bungei shunjū,* August 1974, p. 126.

37. See, in particular, Kojima Akira, "Gendai yosan seiji shiron" (A Sketch of Contemporary Budgetary Politics), in Ari Bakuji, Ide Yoshinori, *et al., Gendai gyōsei to kanryōsei (Modern Administration and the Bureaucratic System)* (Tokyo: Tokyo Daigaku Shuppankai, 1974), II, pp. 122, 124. For an example of the use of *konsensasu,* see Honda Yasuharu, *Nihon neo-kanryō ron,* Vol. II, p. 126.

38. On the Tokushinhō, see Nakamura Takafusa, "Sengo no sangyō seisaku" (Postwar Industrial Policy), in Niida Hiroshi and Ono Akira, eds., *Nihon no sangyō soshiki (Japan's Industrial Organization)* (Tokyo: Iwanami Shoten, 1969), p. 312. For the draft law, see *Shūgiin shōkō iinkai kiroku* (House of Representatives, Records of the Commerce and Industry Committee), Forty-third Diet, May 21, 1963.

39. See John K. Emmerson, "The Japanese Communist Party After Fifty Years," *Asian Survey,* vol. XII, no. 7 (July 1972), p. 571.

40. The popular writer Matsumoto Seichō notes that in the division of labor between the Fair Trade Commission and MITI over approving cartels, MITI must first "approve" *(ninka)* them and then the FTC "permits" *(nintei)* them. He then asks rhetorically, *"Ninka to nintei to dō chigau no ka"* (What is the difference between *ninka* and *nintei?*). *Gendai kanryō ron (On Modern Bureaucrats)* (Tokyo: Bungei Shunjū Sha, 1964), II, p. 114. Only the bureaucrats know the answer.

41. For this and many other distinctions, see Kojima Kazuo, *Hōrei ruiji yōgo jiten (Dictionary of Synonymous Terms in Laws and Ordinances)* (Tokyo: Gyōsei K.K., 1975), pp. 73–75.

42. For a case of a bureaucrat relying on *nado* in the face of an apparent violation of law, see *Sangiin yosan iinkai dai-ni bunkakai* (House of Councillors, Budget Committee, Second Subcommittee Meeting), Fifty-eighth Diet, April 10, 1968, p. 7.

43. Suzuki, *Japanese and the Japanese,* p. 146.

44. Seisaku Jihō Sha, ed., *Kaikoroku sengo tsūsan seisaku shi (Recollections of the History of Postwar Trade and Industrial Policy)* (Tokyo: Seisaku Jihō Sha, 1973), pp. 92–93.

45. Nihon Keizai Shimbun Sha, ed., *Watakushi no rirekisho (My Personal History)* (Tokyo: Nihon Keizai Shimbun Sha, 1970), vol. 41, p. 179.

46. As a text, I have used the facing Japanese and English versions in *Kenkyū-sha's Current English Dictionary* (Tokyo: Kenkyūsha, 1948), pp. 490–519. Gotoda Teruo, a graduate student in political science at the University of California, Berkeley, assisted me during 1978 in studying the language of the Constitution.

47. "A Crisis in Understanding," in Rosovsky, ed., *Discord in the Pacific,* p. 126.

48. *The Economist,* April 21, 1979, p. 96.

9 TANAKA KAKUEI, STRUCTURAL CORRUPTION, AND THE ADVENT OF MACHINE POLITICS IN JAPAN

1. Cf. Donald Kirk, "The Allen and Tanaka Scandals: Japanese Money Politics," *The New Leader*, vol. 64, no. 24 (December 28, 1981), pp. 3–5. The Foreign Corrupt Practices Act of 1977 prohibits American companies from making payments to foreign officials in order to promote their products. It provides for corporate fines of up to $1 million and individual punishments of fines up to $10,000 and five years in prison.

2. For the concept "structural corruption" as applied to Japanese politics, see in particular Tachibana Takashi, *Tanaka Kakuei kenkyū: zenkiroku (Research on Tanaka Kakuei: The Complete Report)* (Tokyo: Kōdansha, 1982), Vol. II, pp. 413–14. (Tachibana is the author of the original exposé of Tanaka's "money-power politics," published in *Bungei shunjū*, November 1974.) An equally important writer on "structural corruption" is Murobushi Tetsurō. See his *Oshoku no kōzō (The Structure of Corruption)* (Tokyo: Iwanami Shoten, 1981).

3. Kawabata Yasunari, *Snow Country*, trans., with an introduction, by Edward G. Seidensticker (New York: Knopf, 1956), p. v.

4. On the populations of the various prefectures as of December 31, 1903, see E. Papinot, *Historical and Geographical Dictionary of Japan* (1910; Tokyo: Tuttle, 1972), p. 803.

5. The classic work in English on *kōenkai,* although he does not mention the Etsuzankai, is Gerald L. Curtis, *Election Campaigning Japanese Style* (first published 1971; Tokyo: Kōdansha International, 1983). The most important materials on the Etsuzankai are the series of articles that appeared in the Niigata edition of the *Asahi shimbun* from June 16 to October 25, 1981, under the title *Kusa no toride (A Grass Fortress)*. These have been collected and edited as Asahi Shimbun Niigata Shikyoku, ed., *Tanaka Kakuei to Etsuzankai: shinsō no kōzu (Tanaka Kakuei and the Etsuzankai: The Layout of the Depths)* (Tokyo: Yamate Shobō, 1982). Also see Niigata Nippō, ed., *Kakuei no fūdo (Kakuei's Home Turf)* (Niigata City: Niigata Nippō Jitsugyōsha Shuppan-bu, 1983); Niigata Nippō, ed., *Za Etsuzankai* (Niigata City: Niigata Nippō Jitsugyōsha Shuppan-bu, 1983); and Kobayashi Kichiya, *Jitsuroku Etsuzankai (True History of the Etsuzankai)* (Tokyo: Tokuma Shoten, 1982).

6. Tanaka was much closer to and more influenced by his mother than his father. On the early years of his life, see Tanaka's autobiography in *Watakushi no rirekisho* (Tokyo: Nihon Keizai Shimbunsha, 1967), Vol. 28, pp. 7–107; Saki Ryūzō, *Etsuzan Tanaka Kakuei (Tanaka Kakuei of the Etsu Mountains)* (Tokyo: Asahi Shimbun Sha, 1977), pp. 74, 79, 102ff.; Kodama Takaya, in *Mainichi Daily News*, November 9, 1974; and Mayumi Yoshihiko, *Ningen Tanaka Kakuei (Tanaka Kakuei the Person)* (Tokyo: Daiyamondo Sha, 1972).

7. Tanaka, *Watakushi no rirekisho*, p. 98. In my one face-to-face meeting with Tanaka at Mejirodai, June 8, 1984, I wanted to ask him how in 1942 his wife knew that he would one day be prime minister, but after Tanaka started talking I was never able to put in another word.

8. Fukuoka Masayuki, "Tanaka Kakuei's Grass Roots," *Japan Echo,* vol. X, no. 1 (Spring 1983), pp. 33–39; and Jichi-shō Senkyo-bu (Ministry of Home Affairs, Elections Department), ed., *Seiji dantai meibo (Register of Political Organizations)* (Tokyo: Ōkura-shō Insatsu-kyoku, 1983 ed.).

9. *Time,* Aug. 1, 1983, p. 29; and "Tanaka Kakuei moto-shushō ningen dokyumento" (A Human Document from Former Prime Minister Tanaka Kakuei), *Pureiboi,* July 1983, pp. 40–67, 207–09.

10. The Shōwa Denkō scandal came to light in April 1948, when opposition party members charged several government officials with accepting bribes from the Shōwa Denkō Company, at the time Japan's largest fertilizer producer, in return for arranging a low-interest loan from the Reconstruction Finance Bank. For a study of this and ten other major political corruption scandals, see Aritake Shūji, *Seiji to kane to jiken to (Politics, Money, and Scandals)* (Tokyo: Keizai Ōrai Sha, 1970). Also see *Kōdansha Encyclopedia of Japan,* Vol. 7, p. 173.

11. In 1982 each resident of Niigata paid an average of $541 in taxes, while per capita spending on public works was $1,644. By contrast, the per capita tax payment in Tokyo was $3,060, whereas the per capita public works spending was just $815. Steve Lohr, in *New York Times,* February 27, 1984. Also see Kent E. Calder, "Kanryō vs. Shomin: Contrasting Dynamics of Conservative Leadership in Postwar Japan," in Terry E. MacDougall, ed., *Political Leadership in Contemporary Japan* (Ann Arbor: Michigan Papers in Japanese Studies, 1982), pp. 1–28; and Shimizu Minoru, in *Japan Times Weekly,* October 8, 1983.

12. Takahashi Ichio, *Osano Kenji wa shinazu (Osano Kenji Lives)* (Tokyo: Yamate Shobō, 1981), pp. 106–12, 191–95, 210–12.

13. Tachibana, *Tanaka Kakuei kenkyū,* Vol. I, pp. 44–49.

14. Nishibe Susumu, "Tanaka Kakuei no shakai-teki hiyō (The Social Cost of Tanaka Kakuei), *Chūō kōron,* March 1983, pp. 72–83; trans. as "Tanaka Kakuei, Product of Japanese Democracy," *Japan Echo,* vol. X, no. 2 (Summer 1983), p. 67.

15. One of the most difficult problems in the study of Japanese political corruption is the almost universal payments of illegal "gifts" to public officials (e.g., schoolteachers and doctors in national university hospitals). On this subject, see in particular, Befu Harumi, "Bribery in Japan: When Law Tangles with Culture," in Elinor Lenz and Rita Riley, eds., *The Self and the System* (Los Angeles: UCLA Extension, 1975), pp. 87–93.

16. In my opinion, the best works on the postwar Japanese political process and how money came to play the predominant role in it are Gotō Motoo, Uchida Kenzō, and Ishikawa Masumi, *Sengo hoshu seiji no kiseki (Loci of Postwar Conservative Politics)* (Tokyo: Iwanami Shoten, 1982); Itō Masaya, *Jimintō sengoku shi (The History of the Liberal Democratic Party's Wars)* (Tokyo: Asahi Sonorama, 1982, 1983), 2 vols.; Masumi Junnosuke, *Sengo seiji (Postwar Politics)* (Tokyo: Tokyo Daigaku Shuppankai, 1983), 2 vols.; and Masumi, *Gendai seiji (Contemporary Politics)* (Tokyo: Tokyo Daigaku Shuppankai, 1985), 2 vols.

17. One of the best studies of the origins of the Lockheed case is Larry Warren Fisher, "The Lockheed Affair: A Phenomenon of Japanese Politics," Ph. D.

dissertation, University of Colorado, Boulder, 1980. Also see John T. Noonan, Jr., *Bribes* (New York: Macmillan, 1984), pp. 655–80.

18. See Onda Mitsugu, *Kuromaku no jinsai kanrijutsu: Kodama Yoshio kara nani o yomitoru ka (A Kuromaku's Ways of Human Control: Reading Between the Lines on Kodama Yoshio)* (Tokyo: Kanki Shuppan, 1982), pp. 85–86, 189–212.

19. See "Lockheed Resists Insurer's Request for 1970s Data on Overseas Payoffs," *Wall Street Journal,* October 3, 1983.

20. Many in Japan have questioned the fairness of the first Tanaka trial. See, in particular, Watanabe Shōichi, " 'Kakuei saiban' wa Tōkyō saiban ijō no ankoku saiban da" ("Kakuei's Trial" Was More of a Black Court Than the Tokyo Trials), *Shokun,* January 1984, pp. 48–67; Ishijima Yutaka, " 'Kakuei saiban' wa shihō no jisatsu da" ("Kakuei's Trial" Means the Suicide of the Administration of Justice), *Shokun,* May 1984, pp. 24–72 (Ishijima is perhaps Japan's most prominent criminal lawyer); Inoue Masaharu, " 'Kakuei saiban' wa shuken no hōki da" ("Kakuei's Trial" Is an Abandonment of Sovereignty), *Shokun,* June 1984, pp. 42–67; and "Tachibana Takashi no daihanron" (Tachibana Takashi's Big Counterargument), *Shokun,* July 1984, pp. 24–60. The most politically potent criticism of the trial came from former Minister of Justice Hatano Akira in his book *Nani ga kenryoku ka: masukomi wa rinchi mo aru (What Is power? Lynchings by the Mass Media)* (Tokyo: Kōdansha, 1984). See also Kitakado Masashi, *Isshin yūzai nishin muzai (First Trial, Guilty; Second Trial, Acquittal)* (Tokyo: Yamate Shobō, 1982).

21. Kaku-san adopted Tanaka Naoki (born Suzuki, a former official of Nippon Kōkan Steel Co.) in 1969 upon the latter's marriage to Tanaka's partly American-educated daughter, Makiko. Makiko and Naoki together played a prominent role in the battle following Tanaka's stroke over who would manage his affairs. It was Makiko who removed Tanaka from Tokyo Teishin Hospital on April 28, 1985, and returned him to Mejirodai to be cared for by her and his wife. On June 6, she and Naoki also closed Tanaka's central Tokyo office, keeping open only his offices in the Diet building and at his residence. These actions brought into the open the growing feud between Makiko and Naoki on the one hand and Tanaka's faithful secretary and spokesman, Hayasaka Shigezō, and the financial secretary of the Etsuzankai, Satō Akiko, on the other. The press also revealed that Satō was Tanaka's mistress and that it was this relationship above all that Makiko wanted to interrupt. The closing of the office run by Hayasaka and Satō signified to the political world the *de facto* end of the Tanaka faction as a political machine. In addition to numerous press accounts, see in particular Kaminogō Toshiaki, "Joketsu: Tanaka Makiko to ketsuzoku no tatakai" (Heroine: Tanaka Makiko and the Battle Among Relatives), *Gendai,* July 1985, pp. 82–94.

22. Karel van Wolferen, "Reflections on the Japanese System," *Survey* (London), vol. 26, no. 1 (Winter 1982), p. 137.

23. Cf. Noonan, *Bribes,* p. 623.

24. For further details, see Hans H. Baerwald, "Japan's December 1983 House of Representatives Election," *Asian Survey,* vol. 24, no. 3 (March 1984), pp. 265–78.

25. On the part played by the Tanaka faction in the "liberalization" of the

telecommunications industry, see "Seme no yūsei, shiren no denden" (Postal Ministry on the Attack, NTT on Trial), *Nihon keizai shimbun,* October 22, 1984; interview with Satō Megumu (former Postal Ministry bureaucrat, chairman of the House of Representatives' Telecommunications Committee, postal minister during 1984–85, and member of the Tanaka faction), *Gekkan kankai,* May 1983, 102–08; Ōuchi Takao, "Yūsei vs. tsūsan: kono hateshi-naki arasoi" (Postal Ministry vs. MITI: A Battle Without End), *Gekkan kankai,* June 1984, pp. 136–45; *Zaikai tembō,* August 1984, pp. 39–61; and Sam Jameson, "Executive Refuses Key Job at NTT," *Los Angeles Times,* March 21, 1985.

26. Cf. Essay 6 and Chalmers Johnson, *MITI and the Japanese Miracle* (Stanford: Stanford University Press, 1982), chap. 2.

27. See the 16-part series entitled "Tanaka's Decline and LDP Maneuvers," published in the *Daily Yomiuri,* June 12–27, 1985.

28. Kōsaka Masataka, "Tanaka jidai no owari ga hajimatta" (The Ending of the Tanaka Era Has Begun), *Shokun,* May 1985, pp. 56–57.

29. The best study of *zoku* to date is Inoguchi Takashi and Iwai Tomoaki, "Jimintō rieki yūdō no seiji-keizai-gaku" (The Political Economy of the LDP's Interest-based Guidance), *Chūō kōron,* March 1985, pp. 128–62.

30. For these terms, see Satō Seizaburō and Matsuzaki Tetsuhisa, "Jimintō etchōki seiken no kaibō" (Autopsy on the Super-long-term Reign of the LDP), *Chūō kōron,* November 1984, pp. 66–100, particularly 70, 73–74.

10 PUPPETS AND PUPPETEERS

1. W. V. Harris, "Italy: Purgatorio," *New York Review of Books,* March 3, 1994, p. 38.

2. Kyōdō Tsūshin Sha, Shakai-bu, ed., *Riken yuchaku: seizaibō kenryoku no kōzu (The Union of Interests: A Map of Political, Financial, and Underworld Power)* (Tokyo: Kyodo News Service, 1993).

3. Giuseppe Saco and Angelo Codevilla, "The End of the Italian Republic?" *Wilson Quarterly* (Autumn 1992), pp. 134–35.

4. See, e.g., Hans H. Baerwald, *Party Politics in Japan* (Boston: Allen & Unwin, 1986). On the end of the 1955 system, see Chalmers Johnson, "The Tremor," *The New Republic,* August 9, 1993, pp. 21–27.

5. See, e.g., Yamaguchi Jirō, "Kanryōsei no minshuka o dō susumeru ka" (How Do We Promote the Democratization of the Bureaucratic System?), *Ekonomisuto,* August 24, 1993, p. 19.

6. Suzuki Eiji and Morozumi Yoshihiko, " 'Seiji' ga kanryōsei o haizumete kita" (Politics Has Warped the Bureaucratic System), *Ekonomisuto,* August 24, 1993, p. 26.

7. See, e.g., Ikuta Tadao, "Jimintō seiken hōkai de tōrai shita 'kanryō dokusai' " ("Bureaucratic Dictatorship" in the Wake of the Collapse of the LDP), *Foresight,* August 1993, pp. 6–9.

8. Mitsumori Takeshi, "Sei-zai-kan yuchaku kaitai e no mitsu no kadai" (Three Topics Concerning the Break-up of the Political-Financial-Bureaucratic Collusive Triangle), *Ekonomisuto,* August 24, 1993, pp. 30–33; "Kanryō seido kaikaku" (Reform of the Bureaucratic System), *Asahi shimbun,* December 1,

1993, morning edn.; and Steven C. Clemons, "The Committee System of Japan's National Diet: Sound and Fury Signifying Something?" *Journal of Northeast Asian Studies* VI:1 (Spring 1987): 46–61.

9. Yoshida Shigeto, "Zoku giin no yusuri to takari" (Extortion and Blackmail by *Zoku* Diet Members), *Bungei shunjū*, May 1993, pp. 106–10; and Yamaguchi, *op. cit., Ekonomisuto*, p. 21.

10. Kakeya Takeo, Nagatsuma Akira, and Koyanagi Tatsuhiko, *Nikkei Business*, August 30, 1993, pp. 16–19.

11. Hakozaki Michio, " 'Dangō' ni amai shakai ni wakare o tsuge yo" (A Society That Is Sweet on Bid Rigging Should Give It Up), *Kankai*, June 1993, p. 110.

12. On the Water Resources Development Public Corporation, see Chalmers Johnson, *Japan's Public Policy Companies* (Washington, D.C.: American Enterprise Institute, 1978).

13. "Bidding for Influence," *Japan Times,* January 29, 1994.

14. "Bidding for Influence," *Japan Times,* February 1, 1994.

15. For an excellent discussion of the dual structure of power, see Kubo Kōshi, "Hosokawa shintaisei no kenryoku kōzō" (The Power Structure of the Hosokawa New Order), *Shokun,* October 1993, pp. 68–79.

16. See Kunihiro Masao, "Omoi shittaka Ozawa Ichirō" (The Ozawa Ichirō I've Come to Know), *Shūkan bunshun,* February 3, 1994, pp. 44–46. Kunihiro, an aide to former Prime Minister Miki and a Socialist member of the upper house, voted no on January 21, 1994, against the Hosokawa electoral reform bill.

17. Uchida Michio, *Shūkan tōyō keizai,* July 17, 1993, pp. 54–58.

18. See Nihon Ryūtsū Shimbun, ed., *Chōsen suru Sagawa Kyūben (The Challenger: Sagawa Kyūben)* (Tokyo: Nihon Ryūtsū Shimbun Sha, 1983); Sataka Makoto and Itō Hideko, *Sagawa kyūben jiken no shinsō (The Truth of the Sagawa Kyūben Case)* (Tokyo: Iwanami Shoten, 1993); and Japan Socialist Party, *Tettei kyūmei: Sagawa jiken (Thorough Research: The Sagawa Case)* (Tokyo: Socialist Party, 1992).

19. *Nihon keizai shimbun,* November 5, 1993, p. 1; *Nikkei Weekly,* November 8, 1993. Hazama Construction Company also acknowledges that it bribed Ozawa to get the contract for the Hyūga Dam in his native Iwate prefecture. Evidence of the bribe is on a floppy disk that the company gave to the prosecutors. *Japan Digest,* December 23, 1993.

20. See Ozawa's best-selling book *Nihon kaizō keikaku (A Plan for the Reform of Japan)* (Tokyo: Kōdansha, 1993). Many writers, officials, and scholars claim to have been the source for the ideas in Ozawa's book. See, e.g., Yamaguchi, *op. cit., Ekonomisuto,* p. 24. The idea and the terms for Ozawa's plan to put politicians in the ministries seems to be straight from Yamaguchi's *Seiji kaikaku* (Tokyo: Iwanami Shinsho 281, 1993). On the possible meanings of *futsū no kuni,* see Uji Toshihiko, "Riberaru-ha no kenen" (Fears of the Liberals), *Tokyo shimbun,* February 2, 1994.

21. "Kono hito to ichi jikan: Gotoda Masaharu" (An Hour with This Person: Gotoda Masaharu), *Ekonomisuto,* November 9, 1993, p. 40.

22. "Kanryō ga chihō o seiha suru" (Bureaucrats Conquer the Regions), *Asahi shimbun,* editorial, September 27, 1993.

23. See Socialist Party, *Tettei kyūmei: Sagawa jiken,* pp. 25, 44.

24. See Suda Shinichirō, "Kenshō kensatsu-kan" (Investigating and Prosecuting Officials), *Foresight,* December 1993, pp. 24–27; Mukaidani Susumu, *Chiken tokusōbu (Regional Special Investigation Departments)* (Tokyo: Kōdansha, 1993); and Charles Smith, "Gunning for Graft," *Far Eastern Economic Review,* December 30, 1993, p. 20.

25. "Yoshinaga Yūsuke o kenji sōchō no̱ reru ni hiki-ageta Gotoda hōshō no nerai" (Justice Minister Gotoda's Aim in Putting Yoshinaga Yūsuke Back on the Path to Prosecutor General), *Sandē Mainichi,* May 23, 1993, pp. 170–71; "Yoshinaga Yūsuke," *Chūō kōron,* January 1994, pp. 118–19; and Mukaidani, *Chiken tokusōbu.*

26. Katō Hidenaka, "Nakamura Arrest Bares Extent of Influence Peddling," *Nikkei Weekly,* March 14, 1994. On Ozawa's liability to be arrested, see "Zenekon taiho 'senjō no rokunin' no X dē" (X-Day for the "Top Six" Construction Industry Arrests), *Shūkan Post* January 28, 1994, pp. 30–35. The top six include Ozawa Ichirō, Mitsuzuka Hiroshi, Kajiyama Seiroku, and Nakamura Kishirō, plus former prime ministers Takeshita and Nakasone.

27. Wakamiya Hirofumi, "Seikai saihengeki de saigō ni warau no wa dare ka" (Who Will Have the Last Laugh in the Restaged Political Drama?), *Gekkan Asahi,* October 1993, pp. 78–85; and "Mitchi to Ozawa ga nerau shin-shintō no michi" (The Path to the New "New Party" Toward which Mitchi [Watanabe Michio] and Ozawa Both Aim), *Aera,* October 11, 1993, pp. 22–23.

28. Glen S. Fukushima, "*Gaiatsu* Revisited," *Tokyo Business Today,* December 1993, p. 64; and " 'Okura-shō dokusai' bōkokuron" (The Ruin of the Country Under a "Ministry of Finance Dictatorship"), *Foresight,* December 1993, pp. 6–10.

29. Yamaguchi, *op. cit., Ekonomisuto,* p. 19.

30. Robert C. Angel, "Implications of Japan's July 1993 General Election: The People Have Mumbled," Unpublished paper, University of South Carolina, September 26, 1993.

31. Honzawa Jirō, *Seikai ōrai,* September 1993, pp. 10–15.

32. See, e.g., Uchida Michio, "Kanryō dokusai ni hangyaku suru nisei giin" (Second-generation Diet Members Who Are Rebelling Against the Bureaucratic Dictatorship), *Shūkan tōyō keizai* July 17, 1993, pp. 54–58.

33. *Nihon keizai shimbun,* November 5, 1993, morning edn., p. 1; Paul Eckert, "Hosokawa Moves to Cut Reliance on Bureaucrats," *Nikkei Weekly,* October 11, 1993; and "Coalition Throws Down Gauntlet to Bureaucracy's Policy-makers," *Nikkei Weekly,* January 10, 1994.

34. Oishi Nobuyuki, "Bureaucrats March to Their Own Beat," *Nikkei Weekly,* August 9, 1993.

35. Suzuki and Morozumi, *op. cit., Ekonomisuto,* p. 26.

36. See Chalmers Johnson, *MITI and the Japanese Miracle* (Stanford: Stanford University Press, 1982), pp. 254–55, 261–63.

37. See Kaga Kōei, "Naitō kyokuchō wa naze yametaka" (Why Did Bureau Chief Naitō Resign?), *Bungei shunjū,* March 1994, p. 172; and "Naitō kyokuchō ga buchi-makeru tsūsanshō no naibu antō" (MITI's Internal Feud and Bureau Chief Naitō's Anger), *Shūkan bunshun,* January 13, 1994, pp. 40–43.

38. Kaga Kōei, "Kumagai tsūsanshō yo, hinsei geretsu wa anata no kata da"

(MITI Minister Kumagai, You Are Mean-Spirited), *Shūkan bunshun,* February 24, 1994, pp. 182–85.

39. *Aera,* January 3–10, 1994, pp. 13–14.

40. Hayasaka Shigezō, "Saigō ni narikirenakatta otoko" (The Man Who Could Never Be a Real Saigō), *Bungei shunjū,* October 1993, pp. 128–41. Cf. M. Iwata, *Ōkubo Toshimichi: The Bismarck of Japan* (Berkeley: University of California Press, 1964).

41. See Yamaguchi Toshio, "Ozawa Ichirō no kenkyū" (Research on Ozawa Ichirō), *Bungei shunjū,* October 1993, pp. 142–49, particularly p. 149. Not all comparisons have been so favorable to Ozawa. One writer, Okamoto Kōji, compares him to the ultra-rightist theorist Kita Ikki. See "Ozawa Ichirō to Kita Ikki," *Shokun,* March 1994, pp. 210–22.

42. Yamaguchi, *op. cit., Ekonomisuto,* p. 19.

11 THE PATTERNS OF JAPANESE RELATIONS WITH CHINA, 1952–1982

1. Ogata Sadako, "Japanese Attitudes Toward China," *Asian Survey,* 5 (August 1965), p. 389.

2. Kōsaka, *Saishō Yoshida Shigeru ron (On Prime Minister Yoshida Shigeru)* (Tokyo: Chūō Kōron Sha, 1968), pp. 7–8, 61–62. For Yoshida's own explanation, see Yoshida Shigeru, *Kaisō jūnen (Recollections of Ten Years)* (Tokyo: Shinchō Sha, 1957), Vol. III, p. 72. For an analysis of the importance of these early decisions, see Nagano Nobutoshi, "Kyōdō-seimei to sensō sekinin no shori" (The [Sino-Japanese] Joint Communiqué and the Treatment of War Responsibility), *Chūō kōron,* October 1982, p. 152. The text of the Yoshida letter is printed in Ishikawa Tadao, Nakajima Mineo, and Ikei Yū, eds., *Sengo shiryō Nitchū kankei (Documents on Postwar Sino-Japanese Relations)* (Tokyo: Nihon Hyōron Sha, 1970), pp. 18–19. For Japanese views that Dulles actually wrote the letter, see Mainichi Shimbun, ed., *Nihon to Chūgoku: seijōka e no michi (Japan and China: The Road to Normalization)* (Tokyo: Mainichi Shimbun Sha, 1971), pp. 32–35.

3. Mainichi, *Nihon to Chūgoku,* p. 26. For the background and significance of Anglo-American differences over which Chinese government Japan should recognize, see Hosoya Chihiro, "Yoshida shokan to Bei-Ei-Chū no kōzu" (The Yoshida Letter and the American, British, and Chinese Designs), *Chūō kōron,* November 1982, pp. 72–88; and Roger Dingman, "The Anglo-American Origins of the Yoshida Letter, 1951–1962," in David J. Lu, ed., *Perspectives on Japan's External Relations: A Festschrift in Honor of Dr. Tsunoda Jun* (Lewisburg, Pa.: Bucknell University, Center for Japanese Studies, 1982), pp. 26–35.

4. On this point, see Mainichi, *Nihon to Chūgoku,* p. 30; and Ogata Sadako, "The Business Community and Japanese Foreign Policy: Normalization of Relations with the People's Republic of China," in Robert A. Scalapino, ed., *The Foreign Policy of Modern Japan* (Berkeley: University of California Press, 1977), pp. 196ff.

5. Ogata, "Japanese Attitudes," p. 394.

6. Gene T. Hsiao, "Prospects for a New Sino-Japanese Relationship," *The China Quarterly,* 60 (October–December 1974), pp. 727–28.

7. Among numerous sources, see in particular Ikeda Masanosuke, *Shina min-zokusei no kaimei (Explanation of Chinese Ethnic Characteristics)* (Tokyo: Naigai Jijō Kenkyū-jo, 1971); Tagawa Seiichi, *Matsumura Kenzō to Chūgoku (Matsumura Kenzō and China)* (Tokyo: Yomiuri Shimbun Sha, 1972); and Makiko Hamaguchi-Klenner, *The China Images of Japan's Conservatives* (Hamburg: Institut für Asienkunde, 1981). For an important review of the Hamaguchi-Klenner work, see Ijiri Hidenori, in *Rekishi to mirai*, 8 and 9 (September 1982), pp. 185–89.

8. Murakami Hyōe, "Gendai Nihon o toi-naosu" (Inquiring Again into Contemporary Japan), *Chūō kōron*, January 1983, pp. 168–71.

9. Ishikawa Tadao, *Watakushi no mita Nihon gaikō (My Views on Japanese Diplomacy)* (Tokyo: Keiō Tsūshin, 1976), pp. 20–32.

10. Etō Shinkichi, "Postwar Japanese-Chinese Relations," *Survey*, 18 (Autumn 1972), pp. 64–65.

11. The term *"fumie* diplomacy" is mine, but it was inspired by a remark in Hamaguchi-Klenner, *The China Images*, p. 64. For a picture of a *fumie*, see E. Papinot, *Historical and Geographical Dictionary of Japan* (Tokyo: Tuttle, 1972), p. 109. For an example of the humiliating statements the Japanese trade negotiators were forced to sign, see the Joint Communiqué on Sino-Japanese Memorandum Trade Discussions, April 19, 1970, in Ishikawa, et al., *Sengo shiryō*, pp. 462–63.

12. Nakajima Mineo, "Mao and His Career as Seen by Japanese Writers," Paper presented to the Association for Asian Studies Annual Meeting, Chicago, April 2, 1982, pp. 14–16. Uncritical writing about China was not, of course, confined to Japan. See Sheila K. Johnson, "To China with Love," *Commentary*, June 1973, pp. 37–45.

13. Ogata, "Japanese Attitudes," p. 392.

14. See Miyoshi Osamu, "How the Japanese Press Yielded to Peking," *Survey*, 18 (Autumn 1972), pp. 103–25.

15. Fukui Haruhiro, "Tanaka Goes to Peking: A Case Study in Foreign Policymaking," in T.J. Pempel, ed., *Policymaking in Contemporary Japan* (Ithaca: Cornell University Press, 1977), pp. 62–63. I do not mean to imply that Fukui's analysis is totally wrong, only that his standard version requires some revision in the light of information that was published in Japan on the tenth anniversary of normalization.

16. The primary sources for this discussion are Nakajima Mineo, " 'Hori shokan' wa watakushi ga kaita" (I Wrote the "Hori Letter"), *Bungei shunjū*, October 1982, pp. 144–53; and Nakajima Mineo, "Ikasarenai Nitchū kōshō no kyōkun" (Lessons of Sino-Japanese Negotiations That Have Not Been Heeded), *Chūō kōron*, October 1982, pp. 136–50. Also see Kishimoto Kōichi, *Issei no michi: Hori Shigeru to sengo seiji (Seeking Sincerity: Hori Shigeru and Postwar Politics)* (Tokyo: Mainichi Shimbun Sha, 1981); and Kusuda Minoru, *Shuseki hishokan: Satō sōri to no jūnenkan (Chief Secretary: Ten Years with Prime Minister Satō)* (Tokyo: Bungei Shunjū Sha, 1975). Ishikawa Tadao also critically analyzes the terms of normalization in *Watakushi no mita Nihon gaikō*, pp. 35–118.

17. Hamaguchi-Klenner, *The China Images*, p. 27.

18. Quoted in Gene T. Hsiao, "The Sino-Japanese Rapprochement: A Rela-

tionship of Ambivalence," in Gene T. Hsiao, ed., *Sino-American Detente and Its Policy Implications* (New York: Praeger, 1974), p. 165.

19. For the full text of the Zhou-Tanaka communiqué, see *The China Quarterly*, 52 (October–December 1972), pp. 782–83.

20. See the comments of Kuriyama Shōichi, a section chief in the Ministry of Foreign Affairs' Treaties Bureau, in Jiji Press, Political Department (Jiji Tsūshin Sha Seiji Bu), ed., *Dokyumento Nitchū fukkō (Documents: Sino-Japanese Restoration)* (Tokyo: Jiji Tsūshin Sha, 1972), p. 220. Kuriyama himself opposed inclusion of the anti-hegemony clause in the communiqué and was not unaware of its potential significance. The fullest treatment of the internal debate among Japanese officials on this and other issues of China policy during the 1970s is by Nakano Nobutoshi, *Tennō to Tō Shō-hei no akushu: jitsuroku Nitchū kōshō hishi (The Handshake Between the Emperor and Deng Xiaoping: Secret History of the Record of Sino-Japanese Negotiations)* (Tokyo: Gyōsei Mondai Kenkyūjo, 1983), pp. 69–74 and *passim*.

21. Yung H. Park, "The 'Anti-hegemony' Controversy in Sino-Japanese Relations," *Pacific Affairs*, 49 (Fall 1976), p. 477.

22. Joseph M. Ha, "Moscow's Policy Toward Japan," *Problems of Communism*, 26 (September–October 1977), pp. 61–72. See also Hong N. Kim, "The Fukuda Government and the Politics of the Sino-Japanese Peace Treaty," *Asian Survey*, 19 (March 1979), pp. 297–313; Avigdor Haselkorn, "Impact of Sino-Japanese Treaty on the Soviet Security Strategy," *Asian Survey*, 19 (June 1979), pp. 558–73; and Peggy L. Falkenheim, "The Impact of the Peace and Friendship Treaty on Soviet-Japanese Relations," *Asian Survey*, 19 (December 1979), pp. 1209–23.

23. Park, "The 'Anti-hegemony' Controversy," pp. 483–84.

24. See Daniel Tretiak, "The Sino-Japanese Treaty of 1978: The Senkaku Incident Prelude," *Asian Survey*, 18 (December 1978), pp. 1235–49.

25. See *The China Quarterly*, 74 (June 1978), pp. 437, 446–47.

26. Hirasawa Kazushige, "Japan's Emerging Foreign Policy," *Foreign Affairs*, 54 (October 1975), p. 161; and Keizai Koho Center, *Japan 1982: An International Comparison* (Tokyo: Keizai Koho Center, 1982), p. 52.

27. *The China Quarterly*, 76 (December 1978), p. 949.

28. Japan External Trade Organization, *China: A Business Guide* (Tokyo: JETRO, 1979), preface.

29. "Japan-China Economic Ties Become Seriously Strained," *Japan Economic Journal*, 19 (February 10, 1981), p. 1. The most complete treatment of the Baoshan case is by Chae-jin Lee, *China and Japan: New Economic Diplomacy* (Stanford: Hoover Institution Press, 1984), pp. 30–75.

30. JETRO, *China Newsletter*, 32 (May–June 1981), p. 1. See also "Another Look at the Baoshan Complex" (including "Baoshan Chronology") in the same issue, pp. 8–9, 12–13.

31. Aoki Akira, "Kyōkasho 'gohō' o hikiokoshita shimbun no taishitsu" (The Character of the Press That Gave Rise to the "False Reports" on Textbooks), *Seiron*, October 1982, pp. 30–43; and Okada Hidehiro, " 'Kyōkasho kentei' wa Chūgoku no naisei mondai da" ("Textbook Screening" Is Really a

Chinese Domestic Issue), *Chūō kōron,* October 1982, particularly pp. 85–87. *Shinryaku* (aggression) and *shinkō* (attack) have exact Chinese equivalents— namely, *qinlue* and *jingong.* For a photograph of a page from a Japanese textbook in which *shinshutsu* is used for the "invasion" of China, see *Japan Echo,* 9 (Winter 1982), front cover.

32. "Political Intentions Seen Behind Chinese Protest," *The Japan Times,* August 10, 1982.

33. The *Sankei* reports of September 7, 8, and 9 are reprinted in *Seiron,* October 1982, pp. 82–83; and in *Shokun,* November 1982, pp. 74–77 (including the attempted expulsion of *Sankei*). See also Kurume Keiji, "Kyōkasho kyanpēn no shikakenin 'Asahi' 'Mainichi' setsu o kenshō suru" (Verifying the Theory That Asahi and Mainichi Contrived the Textbook Campaign), *Seiron,* October 1982, pp. 78–81; Morinaga Kazuhiko, "Kyōkasho mondai ni kan suru shimbun hōdō hihan" (Critique of Newspaper Reports on the Textbook Problem), *Jiyū,* October 1982, pp. 69–74; Watanabe Shōichi, "Banken kyo ni hoeta kyōkasho mondai" (The Textbook Problem: Watchdogs Barking at Shadows), *Shokun,* October 1982, pp. 22–44; Watanabe Shōichi, "Kyōkasho mondai dai-shimbun no hanzai" (The Textbook Problem: Crimes of the Great Newspapers), *Shokun,* November 1982, pp. 24–47; and Kōyama Kenichi, "Shimbun kisha no rinri o tou" (Inquiring into the Ethics of Newspaper Reporters), *Bungei shunjū,* November 1982, pp. 94–114.

34. "Beijing Lauds Nakasone War Statement," *The Japan Times Weekly,* February 26, 1983; and *Liberal Star* (published by the LDP), 12 (March 10, 1983), p. 1.

35. Aoki, *Seiron,* October 1982, p. 32.

36. "Education Ministry Document Explains Textbook Revisions," *The Japan Times,* August 11, 1982.

37. See T.J. Pempel, *Patterns of Japanese Policymaking: Experiences from Higher Education* (Boulder, Col.: Westview, 1978).

38. See Lawrence W. Beer, "Education, Politics, and Freedom in Japan: The Ienaga Textbook Review Cases," *Law in Japan,* 8 (1975), pp. 67–90. For a sample in English of Ienaga's biases, see Ienaga Saburō, *The Pacific War, 1937–1945: A Critical Perspective on Japan's Role in World War II,* trans., Frank Baldwin (New York: Pantheon, 1978). For an interview with Ienaga on the textbook controversy of 1982, see *Asahi jyānaru,* September 10, 1982, pp. 6–9. See also "Textbook Screening System Legal," *The Japan Times Weekly,* April 5, 1986, p. 2.

39. Aoki, *Seiron,* October 1982, p. 32; Kurume, *ibid.,* October 1982, p. 81; and Kobori Keiichirō, "Kyōkasho mondai: watakushi no teigen" (The Textbook Problem: My Proposal), *Shokun,* October 1982, p. 53.

40. For these and other analyses of Chinese motivations in the controversy, see Okada, *Chūō kōron,* October 1982, pp. 82–96; Tobari Haruo, "Kyōkasho mondai de Nihon o mōretsu hihan" ([China's] Violent Criticism of Japan Over the Textbook Problem), *Tōa,* September 1982, pp. 52–61; and Nakajima Mineo, "Chūgoku hōdō de kangaeta koto" (My Thoughts on the Chinese News Reports), *Seiron,* October 1982, pp. 72–77.

41. See, in particular, Shibata Minoru, "Souru de mita kyōkasho mondai" (The Textbook Controversy Seen from Seoul), *Keizai ōrai,* October 1982, pp. 86–95.

42. See Murata Kiyoaki, in *The Japan Times,* August 20, 1982; and Tagawa Kenzō, in *ibid.,* September 5, 1982.

43. See, e.g., Shiota Yōhei, "Misshitsu no Asahi shimbun funsō hishi" (Secret History of the Asahi Newspaper's Inner Disputes), *Shokun,* January 1983, pp. 142–69; and Watanabe Shōichi and Kōyama Kenichi, "Asahi shimbun wa Nihon no purauda ka" (Is the *Asahi* Japan's *Pravda?*), *Shokun,* April 1983, pp. 24–44.

44. See John Boyle, "China and Japan: The Images and Realities of Asian Brotherhood," in Lu, ed., *Perspectives,* p. 4.

45. Cf. Chalmers Johnson, "How China and Japan See Each Other," *Foreign Affairs,* 50 (July 1972), pp. 711–21; and Miyazaki Tōten, *My Thirty-three Years' Dream,* trans. Etō Shinkichi and Marius B. Jansen (Princeton: Princeton University Press, 1982).

46. Cf. Hilary Conroy, "Comparing America's War in Vietnam and Japan's War in China," in Lu, ed., *Perspectives,* pp. 15–25.

12 Reflections on the Dilemma of Japanese Defense

1. "Bōei daigakkō sotsugyō-shiki ni okeru naikaku sōri daijin kunji-nado" (The Prime Minister's Address at the Defense Academy's Graduation Ceremony), March 17, 1985. *Bōei antena* (Defense Antenna), (Published by the Director General's Secretariat, Japanese Defense Agency), no. 307, April 1985, pp. 3–4.

2. See, for example, Nakasone's speech of October 7, 1985, at the Foreign Correspondents' Club of Japan. *Asahi shimbun,* October 8, 1985.

3. *Asahi shimbun,* evening edn., September 20, 1985. On the Official Secrets Bill, see *Japan Times Weekly,* November 9, 1985, p. 4.

4. On August 15, 1985, accompanied by the entire cabinet and in formal dress, Nakasone made the first *official* visit by a government official in the postwar era to Yasukuni Shrine. See *Los Angeles Times,* August 16, 1985. A month later, officially sanctioned student demonstrations erupted in Beijing protesting the visit. On October 17, Nakasone declined to make a return visit to Yasukuni to attend the autumn festival, which set off further protests from Hashimoto Ryūtarō (Okayama Second District, Tanaka faction), head of the "LDP Dietmen's Club to Visit Yasukuni Shrine." Hashimoto charged that Nakasone's decision not to visit Yasukuni Shrine during its annual autumn festival gave the impression that he had succumbed to strong pressure from China. Kyodo News Agency, October 21, 1985, as reported in Foreign Broadcast Information Service (FBIS), *Daily Report: Asia and Pacific,* October 21, 1985, p. C2.

5. Henry Scott Stokes, "Lost Samurai: The Withered Soul of Postwar Japan," *Harper's Magazine,* October 1985, p. 63.

6. See "China and Peace" and "40th Anniversary: Victory Over Japan," in *China Reconstructs,* 34:9, September 1985.

7. W. Theo Roy, "The Japanese Phoenix," *International Journal on World Peace,* 2:2, April–June 1985, pp. 38–39.

8. *Japan Times Weekly,* September 28, 1985, p. 3.

9. Edward A. Olsen, *U.S.-Japanese Strategic Reciprocity: A Neo-Internationalist View* (Stanford: Hoover Institution Press, 1984).

10. Japan Institute for Social and Economic Affairs, *Japan 1984: An International Comparison* (Tokyo: Keizai Kōhō Center, 1984), p. 82. (Figures for 1984 and 1985 are estimates.)

11. Kataoka Tetsuya, "Japan's Defense Nonbuildup: What Went Wrong?," *International Journal on World Peace,* 2:2, April–June 1985, pp. 10–29.

12. See, e.g., Zbigniew Brzezinski, "Japan Should End Free Ride by Devoting 4% of GNP to Aid and Defense," *Los Angeles Times,* August 13, 1985.

13. Masuzoe is a professor of international relations at Tokyo University. His comment on the 1 percent ceiling was made in a speech at Berkeley, California, September 9, 1985. Also see Masuzoe Yoichi, "Japan's Defense Posture: Toward Closer Cooperation with the United States," in Claude A. Buss, ed., *National Security Interests in the Pacific Basin* (Stanford: Hoover Institution Press, 1985), pp. 60–70.

14. Paul D. Wolfowitz, "Taking Stock of U.S.-Japan Relations" (Washington, D.C.: Department of State, Current Policy No. 593, June 12, 1984), p. 2.

15. Gerald L. Curtis, "Japanese Security Policies and the United States," *Foreign Affairs,* 59:4 (Spring 1981), pp. 853, 856.

16. See Chalmers Johnson, "Carter in Asia: McGovernism Without McGovern," *Commentary,* 65:1, January 1978, pp. 36–39.

17. For the count of 135 SS-20s in East Asia, see the Japanese Defense Agency's Tenth Annual White Paper, as reported in the *Los Angeles Times,* September 15, 1984. For the count of 13 bases, see Research Institute on Peace and Security, ed., *Asian Security 1984* (Tokyo: R.I.P.S., 1984), p. 41.

18. "Washington Does an About Face in Assessment of Nakasone," *Los Angeles Times,* December 6, 1984.

19. *Jiji Press,* November 1, 1985.

20. Hirano Minoru, "Nakasone's Tears," *Daily Yomiuri,* August 11, 1985.

21. *Japan Times Weekly,* October 19, 1985. Also see Kyodo News Agency, October 30, 1985, as reported in FBIS, *Daily Report: Asia and Pacific,* October 30, 1985, p. C1; and *Daily Yomiuri,* November 1, 1985.

22. See Larry A. Niksch, "Japanese Defense Policy: Issues for the United States" (Washington, D.C.: Library of Congress, Congressional Research Service, Foreign Affairs and National Defense Division, December 15, 1984).

23. The New York Times/CBS News/Tokyo Broadcasting System Poll, as reported in *New York Times,* August 6, 1985.

24. *Los Angeles Times,* August 8, 1985.

13 RETHINKING ASIA

1. Daniel S. Papp, "New Challenges for a New Administration in a New International Order," *The Global Review* (Winter 1993), pp. 2–4.

2. Alan Tonelson, "Clinton's World," *The Atlantic Monthly,* February 1993, p. 74.

3. Don Oberdorfer, *Clinton and Asia: Issues for the New Administration* (New York: Asia Society, 1993), p. 6.

4. Commonwealth of Australia, Senate, Standing Committee on Foreign Affairs, Defense, and Trade, *Japan's Defense Policy and Current Defense Development and Debates In Japan and the Region* (Canberra: Official Hansard Report, December 7, 1992), p. 18.

5. See, in particular, Nakanishi Akihiko and Ito Tatsumi, "Seijika to yakuza no kenkyū" (A Study of Politicians and Mobsters), *Bungei shunjū,* January 1993, pp. 118–31.

6. Okazaki Hisahiko and Okabe Tatsumi, "Subete wa Nichi-Bei dōmei atte koso" (Everything Depends on the Japan-U.S. Alliance), *Gaikō Forum,* October 1992, p. 7.

7. Frank Gibney, *Korea's Quiet Revolution: From Garrison State to Democracy* (New York: Walker, 1992), pp. 75–76.

8. These calculations are from Richard K. Betts (Columbia University), "Wealth, Power, and Instability: East Asia and the United States After the Cold War," *International Security* 18:3 (Winter 1993–94): 34–77, especially 53.

9. Andrew B. Brick, "The Yankee Traders' Message to Clinton: Trade Begets Democracy in China," *Heritage Foundation Executive Memorandum,* No. 346, December 2, 1992.

10. Instituto per gli Studi di Politica Internazionale, *1992: The Illusory Peace* (Milan: ISPI, 1992), pp. 13–14.

11. Donald C. Hellmann, "Japan and America: Through an International Looking Glass," Unpublished paper, c. 1992, p. 13.

12. Kenneth B. Pyle, *The Japanese Question: Power and Purpose in a New Era* (Washington, D.C.: AEI Press, 1992), pp. 81–83.

13. Richard J. Ellings and Edward A. Olsen, "A New Pacific Profile," *Foreign Policy,* no. 89 (Winter 1992–93), pp. 116–36.

14. D. M. Leipziger, et al., *The Distribution of Income and Wealth in Korea* (Washington, D.C.: World Bank, 1992), pp. xi–xii.

15. Edwin O. Reischauer, *Wanted: An Asian Policy* (New York: Knopf, 1955), p. 275.

14 HISTORY RESTARTED

1. Etō Jun and Nakanishi Terumasa, " 'Nichi-Bei dōmei' no yomei' " (The Last Days of the "Japanese-American Alliance"), *Voice,* July 1991, p. 113.

2. Francis Fukuyama, "The End of History?", *The National Interest,* vol. 16 (Summer 1989), pp. 3–18; and Alan Tonelson, "What Is the National Interest?", *The Atlantic Monthly,* July 1991, pp. 35–52.

3. Robert G. Gilpin, "The Global Context," in *The United States and Japan in the Postwar World,* eds. Iriye Akira and Warren I. Cohen (Lexington: University Press of Kentucky, 1989), pp. 3–5.

4. Cf. James Fallows, "Containing Japan," *The Atlantic Monthly,* May 1989, pp. 40–54.

5. Kissinger, as quoted by Walter LaFeber, in Iriye and Cohen, eds., *United*

States and Japan, p. 105; see also Thomas B. Ginsburg, "A Colder Peace? Issues in the U.S.-Japan Security Alliance," Asia Foundation, Center for Asia Pacific Affairs, *CAPA Report,* 1, April 1991, p. 20.

6. Tonelson, *op. cit.,* p. 46.

7. The reference is to Morita Akio and Ishihara Shintarō, *"No" to ieru Nihon (The Japan That Can Say "No")* (Tokyo: Kōbunsha, 1989); Ishihara Shintarō, Watanabe Shōichi, and Ogawa Kazuhisa, *Sore de mo "No" to ieru Nihon (The Japan That Can Still Say "No")* (Tokyo: Kōbunsha, 1990); and Ishihara Shintarō, *The Japan That Can Say No* (New York: Simon and Schuster, 1991). Cf. John E. Carbaugh, Jr., and Kase Hideaki, eds., *Teki to shite no Nihon: Amerika wa nani o ikatte iru no ka (Japan as the Enemy: What Makes America Angry?)* (Tokyo: Kōbunsha, 1991).

8. For use of the term "emotional friction," see Okamoto Yukio, "Ningen kankei to shite no Nichi-Bei kankei" (The Japanese-American Relationship as [a Problem of] Human Relations), *Chūō kōron,* July 1991, p. 155.

9. William Watts, "Initiatives for Improving Japan-U.S. Communication," *IHJ Bulletin,* vol. 11, no. 2 (Spring 1991), p. 4.

10. Ogura Kazuo, " 'Rinen no teikoku' to 'sōshitsu no min' to no kiretsu" (The Crevice Between "the Empire of Ideas" and the "Lost People"), *Gaikō Forum,* June 1991, pp. 4–11.

11. See Paul Kennedy, *The Rise and Fall of the Great Powers* (New York: Random House, 1987). See also Chalmers Johnson, "The Future of Japanese-American Relations: Seeking A New Balance," National Bureau of Asian and Soviet Research, *Analysis,* 2, 1990, pp. 21–27.

12. Nakasone Yasuhiro, from the *Yomiuri shimbun,* Asia Foundation, Translation Service Center, *Articles from the Japanese Press,* No. 1498, August 26, 1991.

13. Discussion between Kojima Akira, member of the Editorial Board of the *Nihon keizai shimbun;* Iida Tsuneo, member of the International Japanese Culture Research Center; Terasawa Yoshio, director general of the Multilateral Investment Guarantee Agency; Yakushiji Taizō, professor of Keiō University; Saitō Seiichirō, professor of Rikkyō University; and Yamamoto Takuma, chairman, Fujitsū, Inc., on "Zento tanan no Amerika keizai" (The Many Future Difficulties of the American Economy), *Voice,* May 1991, pp. 100–25.

14. *Ibid.,* p. 117.

15. Etō Jun and Homma Nagayo, "Nihonjin wa naze Amerika ga kirai ka" (Why Japanese Dislike the United States), *Bungei shunjū,* June 1991, p. 107. Only a few years ago Homma was arguing that "We should be free from cultural nationalism, pernicious symptoms of which are now found in Japan." See Iriye and Cohen, eds., *United States and Japan,* p. 219. It seems that Professor Homma has himself become a "pernicious symptom."

16. Asai Motofumi, "The World's Credit Card Policeman," Asia Foundation, Translation Service Center, No. 1458, May 6, 1991; Christopher Layne, "Why the Gulf War Was Not in the National Interest," *The Atlantic Monthly,* July 1991, p. 80.

17. *Asahi Evening News,* October 5, 1990; and Funabashi Yōichi, *Reisengo*

(After the Cold War) (Tokyo: Iwanami Shinsho, 1991), p. 220 (on smart bombs but dumb VCRs).

18. Funabashi, *Reisengo,* pp. 93, 96.

19. *Voice,* July 1991, pp. 115, 118.

20. David Arase, "Japan in Post-Cold War Northeast Asia," Paper presented to the Institute of Southeast Asian Studies' Workshop on Major Powers and the Security of Southeast Asia: The Post-Cold War International Order, Kuching, Sarawak, September 4–8, 1991, pp. 23, 29.

21. William J. Barnds, "The United States and Japan: A Time of Troubles," Asia Foundation, Center for Asia Pacific Affairs, *CAPA Report,* 2, June 1991 (4 pp.).

22. Quoted in "Kibishii shisen: kachikan toi-hajimeta Bei" (Strict Gaze: America Begins to Question Our Value System), *Asahi shimbun,* January 6, 1991, p. 1.

23. *Yomiuri shimbun,* October 24, 1990, p. 1.

24. Sasaki Takeshi, "Postwar Japanese Politics at a Turning Point," *Japan Foundation Newsletter,* vol. 18, nos. 5–6, May 1991, pp. 1–7.

25. *Ibid.,* p. 6.

26. Aurelia George, "Japan's America Problem: The Japanese Response to U.S. Pressure," *The Washington Quarterly* (Summer 1991), pp. 17, 18.

27. Ginsburg in Asia Foundation, *CAPA Report,* 1, pp. 17–22.

28. Joseph S. Nye, Jr., "Soft Power," *Foreign Policy,* 80 (Fall 1990), pp. 153–71.

29. Nakanishi Terumasa, "A New Regional Order," *Journal of Japanese Trade and Industry,* May–June 1991, p. 11.

30. See Inoguchi Kuniko, *Posuto-haken shisutemu to Nihon no sentaku (The Post-hegemonic System and Japan's Options)* (Tokyo: Chikuma Shobō, 1987).

31. Nakasone Yasuhiro, "Nihon wa samitto de dokuji senryaku o Soren mō ichidan no seiji kaikaku hitsuyō" (Japan Should Adopt Its Own Summit Strategy Requiring Much More Political Reform from the Soviet Union), *Nikkei Business,* July 8, 1991, p. 76.

32. Nakasone Yasuhiro, from the *Yomiuri shimbun,* Asia Foundation, Translation Service Center, *Articles from the Japanese Press,* No. 1498, August 26, 1991.

33. Satō Hideo, "Japan's Role in the Post-Cold War World," *Current History,* April 1991; reprinted in Dean Collinwood, *Japan and the Pacific Rim* (Guilford, Conn.: Dushkin, 1991), pp. 126–30.

34. Inoguchi Kuniko, "Wangango no sekai chitsujo" (World Order After the Gulf), *Nihon keizai shimbun,* March 19, 1991, p. 27; trans. in *Economic Eye,* vol. 12, no. 2 (Summer 1991), pp. 24–26.

35. For further details, see Robert Gilpin, *The Political Economy of International Relations* (Princeton: Princeton University Press, 1987).

36. See John Welfield, *An Empire in Eclipse: Japan in the Postwar American Alliance System* (London: Athlone Press, 1988), p. 2.

37. *The Future of U.S.-Japan Relations,* Foreign Policy Institute, School of Advanced International Studies, Johns Hopkins University, August 1991 (9 pp.).

38. William H. Gleysteen, Jr., "Comment," in *Yen for Development: Japa-*

nese Foreign Aid & the Politics of Burden-Sharing, ed. Shafiqul Islam (New York: Council on Foreign Relations Press, 1991), pp. 27–33.

39. Lawrence B. Krause, "Regionalism in World Trade: The Limits of Economic Interdependence," *Harvard International Review* (Summer 1991), p. 4. See also Clyde V. Prestowitz, Jr., Alan Tonelson, and Robert W. Jerome, "The Last Gasp of GATTism," *Harvard Business Review*, March–April 1991, pp. 130–38.

40. See Inwoo Chang, "HDTV: The Latest High-Tech, High-Stakes Battleground," *Harvard International Review* (Summer 1991), p. 51.

41. See *Aera*, April 16, 1991, pp. 6–9.

42. John Gerard Ruggie, "Unraveling Trade: Global Institutional Trade and the Pacific Economy," in R. Higgott, R. Leaver, and J. Ravenhill, eds., *Pacific Economic Relations in the 1990s: Cooperation or Conflict?* (Boulder, Col.: Lynne Rienner, 1993), p. 18.

43. U.S.-Japan Semiconductor Trade Agreement, signed June 11, 1991, Washington, D.C., by Ambassador Murata Ryōhei and U.S. Trade Representative Carla Hills (text from the Office of the United States Trade Representative). Also see Bruce Stokes, *The Inevitability of Managed Trade: The Future Strategic Trade Policy Debate* (New York: The Japan Society, 1990).

44. I. M. Destler, "The United States and Japan: What Is New?" Paper presented to the 32nd Annual Convention of the International Studies Association, Vancouver, B.C., March 21, 1991, pp. 24–25.

45. For discussions of these issues by both Japanese and Americans, see the series of books published by the Society for Japanese Studies: *The Trade Crisis: How Will Japan Respond*, ed. Kenneth B. Pyle (Seattle, 1987); *Japanese Investment in the United States: Should We Be Concerned?* ed. Kozo Yamamura (Seattle, 1989); and *Japan's Economic Structure: Should It Change?* ed. Kozo Yamamura (Seattle, 1990).

46. Peter Ennis, *Tokyo Business Today*, January 1990, p. 30.

47. Iida Tsuneo, International Japanese Culture Research Center, Kyoto, in *Nihon keizai shimbun*, May 6, 1991, p. 15.

48. Harry G. Gelber, "National Power, Security and Economic Uncertainty," Institute for the Study of Conflict, Ideology and Power, Boston University, April 1991, pp. 35–36.

49. Ōkita Saburō, "Japan: Better to Spend These Billions on Aid Than on Arms," *International Herald Tribune*, Tokyo, April 17, 1991. See also Ōkita Saburō, *Approaching the 21st Century: Japan's Role* (Tokyo: The Japan Times, 1990).

50. Sakakibara Eisuke, *Shihon-shugi koeta Nihon (The Japan That Has Gone Beyond Capitalism)* (Tokyo: Tōyō Keizai Shimpōsha, 1990).

51. Noda Masaaki, "Nihon kabushiki kaisha-kō 'samurai shihon-shugi' no mujun to genkai" (The Contradictions and Limits of Japan, Inc.'s "Samurai Capitalism"), *Shūkan daiyamondo*, August 31, 1991, pp. 72–77.

52. Terasawa Yoshio in *Voice*, May 1991, p. 110. See also Nakatani Iwao, "The Nature of 'Imbalance' Between the U.S. and Japan," Proceedings of the Seventh Biennial Conference of the Japanese Studies Association of Australia, *Japan and the World*, Australian National University, Canberra, July 1991, I, pp. 33–39. At the 1991 Annual Meeting of the Board of Governors of the World

Bank and the IMF, Mieno Yasushi, head of the Bank of Japan, said, "Experience in Asia has shown that although development strategies require a healthy respect for market mechanisms, the role of the government cannot be forgotten. I would like to see the World Bank and the IMF take the lead in a wide-ranging study that would define the theoretical underpinnings of this approach and clarify the areas in which it can be successfully applied to other parts of the globe." World Bank, Press Release No. 16, October 15, 1991, p. 6.

53. Aida Yūji, "Amerika no hōkai" (The Collapse of America), *Voice,* September 1990, pp. 116–34.

54. *Daily Japan Digest,* vol. 2, no. 160, September 11, 1991, p. 1.

55. *Nikkei Business,* July 8, 1991, p. 79.

56. See Chalmers Johnson, 'Where Does Mainland China Fit in a World Organized into Pacific, North American, and European Regions?' *Issues and Studies,* vol. 27, no. 8, August 1991, pp. 1–16.

57. Karel van Wolferen, "Japan: No Brakes, No Compass," *The National Interest,* (Fall 1991), p. 27.

58. "Blocking Out a Yen Block," *The Economist,* September 17, 1988, pp. 35–36.

59. Funabashi Yōichi, "Don't Circle the Wagons: East Asian Economic Bloc Wrong Answer to Western Regionalism," *Asahi Evening News,* March 15, 1991.

60. Hadi Soesastro, "Concepts of the Pacific Basin in the Western Pacific," Paper presented to the Seminar on the Pacific Basin, Mexico City, February 12–14, 1991, p. 14.

61. "Apprehension Over Trading Blocs," *Los Angeles Times,* July 30, 1991, p. B7.

62. William Watts, "The United States and Japan: Communications Disconnect," *Daily Japan Digest,* vol. 2, no. 169, September 24, 1991, pp. 4–5. See also "Yomigaeru 'kichiku Bei-Ei' to 'hai-Nichi' no shinshō" (The Resurrection of the Mental Images of "Brutal America and England" and "Anti-Japanese"), *Aera,* vol. 4, no. 23, June 4, 1991, pp. 9–39.

63. Murakami Kaoru, "Nichi-Bei kankei ga sengo saiaku" (Japan-U.S. Relationship Worst Since World War II), *Zaikai tembō,* July 1991, pp. 128–33.

64. Ogura Kazuo, *op. cit.* (note 10).

65. *Ibid.,* p. 9.

66. Izawa Motohiko, from *Rekishi kaido,* Asia Foundation, Translation Service Center, *Articles from the Japanese Press,* no. 1305, April 2, 1990.

67. Iriye and Cohen, eds., *United States and Japan,* p. 189.

68. Okamoto Yukio, *op. cit.,* p. 149.

69. Ishihara, *The Japan That Can Say "No,"* pp. 26–32.

70. *Asahi shimbun,* January 9, 1991, p. 1.

71. "Posuto Maruta ni okeru Nihon no chii" (Japan's Position After Malta), *Chuo kōron,* March 1991, pp. 50–52.

72. Ogura Kazuo, *op. cit.,* p. 8.

73. Printed text of speech to the Japan Society, New York City, December 4, 1990.

74. Barnds, Asia Foundation, *CAPA Report,* 2, June 1991.

75. "Loose Talk from Japan," *Los Angeles Times,* January 23, 1992; and

David E. Sanger, "A Top Japanese Politician Calls U.S. Work Force Lazy," *New York Times,* January 21, 1992.

76. "Former Japanese Foreign Minister Says U.S. Business System Is Not the Best," UPI, Tokyo, March 11, 1992.

77. George Friedman and Meredith LeBard, *The Coming War with Japan* (New York: St. Martin's Press, 1991), p. 401. Sales figures are given in *Los Angeles Times,* February 16, 1992.

Acknowledgments

Essay 1 was copyrighted in 1984 by the Institute of Middle Eastern Studies, University of Haifa, and first appeared in a special issue of *Asian and African Studies* (vol. 18, no. 1) entitled *Japan Thirty Years After the Occupation: Political, Economic and Cultural Trends*, edited by Ben-Ami Shillony.

Essay 2 has not been previously published in English but appeared in Spanish as "Valores Sociales y la Teoria del Desarrollo Economico Tardio en el Este de Asia," in Omar Martinez Legoretta, ed., *Industria, Comercio y Estado: Algunas Experiencias en la Cuenca del Pacifico* (Mexico: El Colegio de Mexico, 1991), pp. 11–26.

Essay 3 was copyrighted in 1993 by the Regents of the University of California, and is reprinted from the *California Management Review*, vol. 35, no. 4, by permission of the Regents.

Essays 4, 6, 8, and 9 were copyrighted by and are hereby reprinted with the permission of the Society for Japanese Studies. Essay 4 was included in the special volume edited by Kozo Yamamura, *Japan's Economic Structure: Should It Change?* (1990). Essay 6 was first published in *The Journal of Japanese Studies*, vol. 2, no. 1 (Autumn 1975); Essay 8 in vol. 6, no. 1 (Winter 1980); and Essay 9 in vol. 12, no. 1 (Winter 1986).

Essays 5 and 10 have not been previously published. Essay 5 was presented at a Workshop on "Japan as Techno-Economic Superpower: Implications for the United States," sponsored by the Center for National Security Studies of Los Alamos National Laboratory, in Santa Fe, New Mexico, November 18–19, 1993.

Essay 10 was presented at a panel of the Association for Asian Studies annual meeting, March 25, 1994.

Essays 7 and 12 were first copyrighted by the Regents of the University of California and are hereby reprinted with the permission of the Regents. Essay 7 first appeared in *Asian Survey* vol. 14, no. 11 (1974), and Essay 12 in vol. 26, no. 5 (1986).

Essay 11 was copyrighted in 1986 by the University of British Columbia and first appeared in *Pacific Affairs,* vol. 59, no. 3.

Essay 13 is hereby reprinted with the permission of *The National Interest,* where it first appeared in no. 32 (Summer 1993).

Essay 14 was first published in *Pacific Economic Relations in the 1990s: Cooperation or Conflict?*, edited by Richard Higgott, Richard Leaver, and John Ravenhill. Copyright © 1993 by the Australian Fulbright Commission. Used with permission of Lynne Rienner Publishers, Inc.

Index

382 · *Index*